MOVING IN THE SHADOWS

We dedicate this book to all the minority women who have lost their lives to men's violence and to the BME women's organisations which strive to create a safer and more just world

LIZ: *In memory of my partner Corinna Seith, who died in 2010, and to my daughter Ema, close friends and colleagues who enabled me to dare to live and think again*

HANANNA: *To my parents, Nazir and Farkhunda, with love. Also, thanks to Steve Woodhouse for his support and patience*

YASMIN: *To my mother – Shahida Rehman – for your love and dedication. In recognition of the high price you have paid and continue to pay for ensuring we had a better life and were able to have the choices you were denied. To Ranjit and Shirley for your invaluable friendship, continuous support and encouragement, but most of all for helping me to find my voice and to step out of the shadows*

Moving in the Shadows
Violence in the Lives of Minority Women and Children

Edited by

YASMIN REHMAN

LIZ KELLY
London Metropolitan University, UK

HANNANA SIDDIQUI
Southall Black Sisters, UK

ASHGATE

Published by
Ashgate Publishing Limited
Wey Court East
Union Road
Farnham
Surrey, GU9 7PT
England

Ashgate Publishing Company
101 Cherry Street
Suite 3-1
Burlington
VT 05401-3818
USA

www.ashgate.com

British Library Cataloguing in Publication Data
Moving in the shadows : violence in the lives of minority women and children.
1. Minority women–Violence against–Great Britain. 2. Children of minorities–Violence against–Great Britain. 3. Minority women–Violence against–Great Britain–Prevention. 4. Children of minorities–Violence against–Great Britain–Prevention. 5. Minority women– Services for–Great Britain. 6. Victims of family violence–Great Britain. 7. Victims of family violence–Services for–Great Britain. 8. Minority women–Legal status, laws, etc–Great Britain.
I. Kelly, Liz. II. Rehman, Yasmin. III. Siddiqui, Hannana.
362.8'292'089-dc23

Library of Congress Cataloging-in-Publication Data
Rehman, Yasmin.
Moving in the shadows : violence in the lives of minority women and children / by Yasmin Rehman, Liz Kelly, and Hannana Siddiqui.
    p. cm.
Includes bibliographical references and index.
ISBN 978-1-4094-3317-0 (hardback : alk. paper) — ISBN 978-1-4094-3318-7 (ebook) 1. Minority women—Violence against—Great Britain. 2. Minority women—Crimes against— Great Britain. 3. Children of minorities—Crimes against—Great Britain. 4. Children and violence—Great Britain. I. Kelly, Liz. II. Siddiqui, Hannana. III. Title.
HV6250.4.W65R447 2013
362.88082'0941—dc23

2012024261

ISBN 9781409433170 (hbk)
ISBN 9781409433187 (ebk – PDF)
ISBN 9781409472803 (ebk – ePUB)

Printed and bound in Great Britain by the MPG Books Group, UK.

Contents

List of Figures and Tables

Figures

Tables

Notes on Contributors

Mohamed A. Baleela graduated at the University of Khartoum. He has a Masters Degree in Social Sciences from the University of Wales, a Certificate in Counselling for Refugees, from the Tavistock Centre in London, and a post-graduate Diploma in International Human Rights Law from London School of Economics. Mohamed is Manager of Al-Aman Family Safety Project, part of Domestic Violence Intervention Project (DVIP) and is a trained violence prevention worker. He has worked with men from the Arabic speaking community for more than nine years. Prior to joining DVIP, Mohamed was Human Rights Advocate, and a researcher at the University of Wales.

Carlene Firmin was a Senior Policy Officer at Race on the Agenda (ROTA), an organisation she joined in 2005, where she co-ordinated ROTA's work on serious youth violence and led the Female Voice in Violence research programme. Carlene previously led ROTA's youth-led research into weapon carrying in London, *Building Bridges*, for which she received a London Peace Award in 2008.

She is also the founder of the GAG project: Gendered Action on Gangs/Girls Against Gangs/Girls Affected by Gangs. GAG empowers gang-affected young women to apply the gender duty in their local areas, and act as local advisors on gender and youth violence issues. This programme of work has been picked up in other European countries and global forums, including presenting at the United Nations 54th Convention on the Status of Women in New York.

Carlene has an MSc in Social Policy and Planning from the London School of Economics and a degree in Philosophy from Cambridge University, she is currently undertaking a Professional Doctorate at the University of Bedfordshire.

Ava Kanyeredzi is a doctoral candidate at the Child and Woman Abuse Studies Unit, London Metropolitan University. Her PhD research 'Knowing what I know now … Black women talk about violence inside and outside of the home' examines how black women seek help for violence and how experiences of violence impact on their relationship to their bodies.

Liz Kelly is Professor of Sexualised Violence at London Metropolitan University, where she holds the Roddick Chair on Violence Against Women and is Director of the Child and Woman Abuse Studies Unit (CWASU). She has been active in the field of violence against women and children for more than three decades – as a founding member of a refuge, rape crisis centre and women's centre and more recently as an engaged academic, including being co-chair of the End Violence Against Women coalition.

She is the author of *Surviving Sexual Violence* which established the concept of a 'continuum of violence', and over 150 research reports, book chapters and journal articles. CWASU is recognised as one of the world leading research centres on violence against women, and has completed over 100 research projects (go to www.cwasu.org for a complete list) and are known for their work on making connections between forms of gender based violence, and between violence against women and abuse of children.

CWASU also run the only MA on Woman and Child Abuse in Europe, with students from the UK, Europe, Africa, Asia and Latin America. The MA has been designed to provide 'thinking time' for practitioners, to deepen their understanding and reflect on practice from the global North and South.

Marai Larasi MBE is the Executive Director of Imkaan, a UK-based national second tier organisation dedicated to challenging violence against Black, Minority Ethnic and Refugee women and girls. She has worked in the Violence Against Women and Girls (VAWG) field for nearly two decades, at both operational and strategic levels, and has developed and led cutting edge services and programmes which address gender-based violence within marginalised groups.

Marai's activism, public policy work and overall practice are underpinned by a strong commitment to equality and social justice. She is described as a *'thought-provoking'* and *'inspirational'* public speaker and has addressed numerous and varied audiences in the UK and internationally, covering a range of themes including VAWG, women's homelessness, and equality.

Marai is the co-chair of EVAW (the End Violence Against Women Coalition) and the co-chair of Women's Aid, England. She also contributes to a number of working groups at regional, national and international level.

Dr Comfort Momoh, MBE is a FGM Consultant and Public Health Specialist with extensive experience of holistic women centred care, a researcher of women's health and a strong campaigner/supporter for the eradication of FGM. In 1997 she established, and still runs, the African Well Woman's Clinic at Guy's and St Thomas Foundation Trust.

Comfort acted as an expert witness for the All Party Parliamentary Hearing on Female Genital Mutilation for England and Wales in 2000 and for Scotland in 2005. She represented the World Health Organisation at the World Congress of Gynaecology and Obstetrics in October 2009 in South Africa.

She received award from the Queen of England as a Member of British Empire (MBE) in 2008 for services for women's Health and an Honorary Doctorate Degree from Middlesex University.

Comfort provides training and speaks at conferences at local, national and international levels. She is a visiting lecturer at King's College London.

Swati Pande is a PhD student at the Child and Woman Abuse Studies Unit, London Metropolitan University. Her area of research is the discourse of child sexual abuse in Hindi. For the last seven years she has worked as a social worker in voluntary and statutory organisations. She has also been a volunteer at the Rape and Sexual Abuse Support Centre in South London. Swati is a feminist practitioner and her chapter is based on research carried out in 2009 inspired by her experiences as a survivor, social worker, domestic violence advisor and support worker for survivors of rape and sexual abuse.

Pragna Patel is a founding member of the Southall Black Sisters and Women Against Fundamentalism. She worked as a co-ordinator and senior case worker for SBS from 1982 to 1993 when she left to train and practice as a solicitor. In 2009 she returned to SBS as its Director. She has been centrally involved in some of SBS' most important cases, campaigns, policy developments, research and legal reforms in respect of violence against women, forced marriage, immigration and religious fundamentalism. She has written extensively on race, gender and religion.

Phil Price is the Project Manager of perpetrator services for the Domestic Violence Intervention Project in London. He co-ordinates programme development and delivery across the Violence Prevention Programme at DVIP with responsibility for: assessments, individual work and group work with men around their use of violence and abusive behaviour to partners.

Phil also has substantial experience in the substance misuse sector, working in both tier two and tier three treatment settings. He completed a BACP Accredited Training in Integrative Psychotherapy, which included an 18 month clinical placement within a statutory mental health psychological service working psychotherapeutically with dual diagnoses/personality disordered clients. He undertakes both individual and group-work with men who have been violent to (ex) partners. He also delivers training in working with Domestic Violence Perpetrators on behalf of DVIP

Yasmin Rehman is a doctoral candidate at the School of Oriental and African Studies. Her area of research is polygyny and English law. Yasmin is a freelance consultant and trainer working on issues of gender, faith and equalities and diversity.

Yasmin has worked for more than 25 years on violence against women and social justice issues. As Director of Partnerships and Diversity with the Metropolitan Police Service, Yasmin had strategic lead for Domestic Violence; Violence against Women, Hate Crime and Honour Based Violence. She was the Deputy Association of Chief Police Officer (ACPO) lead for Honour based Violence from 2004–7. She has worked on a number of international projects with agencies in Sweden, USA, Canada, South Africa, India, Pakistan and the United Arab Emirates.

Yasmin is currently Chair of the Board of Trustees of Domestic Violence Intervention Project (DVIP), Chair of the Centre for Secular Space, (Interim), Chair of Henna Asian Women's Project and a member of Women against Fundamentalisms (WAF). She is an independent member of Kent County Council Adoption Panel and a Fellow of the Muslim Institute.

Dr Makeba Roach studied medicine at Kings College London, and did an intercalated BSc in International Health at University College London. She has recently completed an MSc in Public Health at the London School of Hygiene and Tropical Medicine. Makeba is currently training to be a General Practitioner in London. She has a longstanding research interest in female genital mutilation (FGM), with her current focus being on how UK specialist trainees in Obstetrics and Gynaecology understand and form opinions about FGM and female genital cosmetic surgery.

Dr Emilie Secker is the Advocacy Programme Officer for Stepping Stones Nigeria, a UK-based child rights charity which works with Nigerian partner organisations to provide food, education and healthcare to vulnerable and disadvantaged children in the Niger Delta region and to advocate for their rights at the local, national and international levels. She is a former Honorary Fellow of the Law School of Lancaster University and holds a PhD in International Human Rights Law. Dr Secker has previously researched and published on children's rights, the right to participation and the right to development.

Hannana Siddiqui has been involved in working on race and gender issues for nearly 30 years and has worked at Southall Black Sisters for 25 years where she has undertaken casework, policy development and campaigning on violence against black and minority women, immigration/asylum and no recourse to public fund issues. This has included work on battered women who kill, in particular the famous case of Kiranjit Ahuwalia, which reformed the law on provocation. She also campaigned to introduce legal reforms on domestic violence and immigration in 1999, and helped to create changes in 2012 that allow victims of domestic violence with no recourse to public funds to access benefits and housing. Her work on forced marriage contributed to the introduction of guidelines for professionals and to the Forced Marriage (Civil Protection) Act 2007. She was an original member of the Home Office Working Group on Forced Marriage, established in 1999. Other work includes researching suicide and self-harm among Asian women and policy interventions on so called 'honour killings' or honour based violence. She has also undertaken international work, lobbying on the Convention for the Elimination of All Forms of Discrimination Against Women (CEDAW). She was a founding member of Women Against Fundamentalism and is a Board Member of the End Violence against Women coalition.

Debora Singer is the Policy and Research Manager at Asylum Aid where she has worked since May 2004. Asylum Aid is a registered charity which provides free legal representation to asylum seekers which established the Women's Project in 2000. The project aims to enable women fleeing serious human rights violations to gain protection in the UK through its casework, research, lobbying and campaigning. Debora manages the Women's Project and lobbies and campaigns on issues affecting women asylum seekers as well as coordinating all Asylum Aid's policy and research work. As part of this, she launched the Charter of Rights of Women Seeking Asylum in 2008, to persuade the UK to adopt a gender sensitive asylum system.

Previously Debora worked as a Policy Manager at Victim Support focusing on issues of sexual violence, domestic violence and human rights as they affected victims of crime. In 2006 she obtained a distinction for her Masters degree in Refugee Studies and Asylum Aid published her research on women asylum seekers and international human rights mechanisms. Debora was awarded an MBE in the 2012 New Year Honours List for services to women.

Sharon Smee is Director of Gender Equality Consulting providing women's rights policy, research and technical support to non-governmental organisations worldwide. Formerly, she was Women's Rights Advisor at ActionAid UK and Chair of the Violence Against Women Working Group of the UK Gender and Development Network. Prior to joining Action Aid, Sharon was Justice Policy Officer at the Fawcett Society where she led Fawcett's Commission on Women and the Criminal Justice System. Sharon is a solicitor and has practiced law in both Australia and the UK. She has a Masters degree in International Relations and has authored numerous research and policy reports on women's rights issues.

Shaminder Takhar is Senior Lecturer in Sociology at London South Bank University. Her research interests and publications are centred on race, ethnicity, gender, sexualities, education and social justice. Her most recent research funded by the British Academy concerns the under representation of South Asian women in local politics. She has also researched South Asian women's political agency and her book, *Gender, Ethnicity and Political Agency: South Asian Women Organizing* is due to be published by Routledge in 2012. She is currently working on an edited book and has published in refereed journals.

Ravi K. Thiara is Principal Research Fellow, Centre for the Study of Safety and Well-being, University of Warwick, UK. She has conducted extensive research in the UK and elsewhere and written widely on violence against women. She has been actively involved in highlighting issues for black and minority ethnic women and children affected by violence and abuse for nearly 25 years.

Jackie Turner is a lawyer now working as an independent consultant. She is part of a research consortium, under the direction of Professor Liz Kelly of London Metropolitan University Child and Woman Abuse Studies Unit, with partners from Germany and the Netherlands. The consortium recently completed a study for European Commission to assess the possibilities, opportunities and needs to standardise European Union legislation on violence against women, violence against children and sexual orientation violence. She has worked with the European Women's Lobby as independent external evaluator of a 3-year Nordic-Baltic Pilot Project, established to develop a regional programme for the provision of support services to women trafficked for sexual exploitation, and to strengthen the gender-equality perspective in regional policies and anti-trafficking initiatives. She has lectured and spoken at a number of conferences, most recently on human trafficking for commercial exploitation at the International Institute of Higher Studies in Criminal Sciences, Siracusa, Italy in May 2010. Simultaneously, she is undertaking doctoral research at London Metropolitan University's Child and Woman Abuse Studies Unit. The focus of her research is an investigation of intersections between criminal groups involved in human trafficking and their respective diasporas in transit and destination countries.

Moving in the Shadows: Introduction

Liz Kelly

This book has been 18 months in the making, as we sought researchers and practitioners who had new and important things to say about violence and minority women. Whilst there has been an ongoing and specific focus on these issues in research and practice in the UK, the emphasis in published work has been on South Asian women and domestic violence (see also, Thiara and Gill, 2010). We celebrate and draw on this richness, while simultaneously seeking to extend our knowledge: both in terms of the minority communities addressed and the forms of violence covered. To an extent we have succeeded, but there remain substantial gaps which future research and volumes will need to fill. In particular, childhood and adult sexual violence and sexual exploitation in minority women's lives and the specificities of many communities remain in the shadows.

The focus of the book is minority women living in the UK, but not only do the issues explored traverse geographic borders, a number of authors make explicit links to the wider contexts and communities which form part of minority women's lives.

All of the editors have worked for nearly three decades or more across activism, specialised violence against women (VAW) organisations, research and policy development – indeed we know each other through these connections. Whilst not always agreeing in particular debates and being part of an argumentative feminist tradition, we share a philosophical approach which locates VAWG (violence against women and girls) within gendered power relations that intersect with other axes of power and inequality, alongside a passionate feminist commitment to protecting women and girls from violence in the present and preventing it in the future. These are also the ambitions of countless other women across the globe, now backed by policy in the UN and regional bodies including the Council of Europe. For us, such a future involves far more than policies and conventions, it requires nothing less than a profound transformation in 'relations of ruling' (Smith, 1993) at the personal, local, national and global levels. Whilst the achievements of women's movements, on every continent, in relation to violence against women and girls are impressive – including vastly increased recognition, innovative responses which place women at the centre, legal reform and policy development – levels of violence remain stubbornly high, seemingly impervious to interventions. We know more about how to end violence and deal with its legacies in individual lives than how to reduce its prevalence across social groups and populations. At the same time, feminist revolutions are more subversive than those rooted in the violent overthrow of existing regimes: with the transformations more evident in relationships, households, streets and cafes (see also Walby, 2011). Perhaps we need more subtle ways of measuring change.

Key Concepts

We have not set a policy on language use for authors, as there are ongoing debates and different positions on how to refer to racialised minorities. In this introduction both minority women (as in the title of the book) and Black and Minority Ethnic (BME) are used, but in other chapters different formulations appear. Each variation, however, is rooted in an understanding that race and/or ethnicity continues to be a key social division, reproducing power relations which disadvantage those who are minoritised whilst privileging the majority white British population. Some have the additional disadvantage of uncertain immigration status, including being an asylum seeker or victim of trafficking (Singer, Turner).

The concept of intersectionality has become so ubiquitous in social theory that its original links to VAWG has been overshadowed. In her second paper exploring the concept Kimberley Crenshaw (1991) discusses not only how the lives of women of colour in the US fall through the gaps between the women's and civil rights movements, but also how this plays out in responses to VAW. As several chapters in this book attest (Patel, Siddiqui) black feminists in the UK were developing similar analyses, demonstrating the important, but rarely acknowledged, conceptual and theoretical innovation which the VAW field has generated through the insights of engaged academics and reflexive practitioners.

Some contemporary uses of intersectionality deploy it as merely a bigger word for multiple discrimination, others reduce it to a descriptive term for a myriad of potential identities. We draw on a shared understanding that in Crenshaw's work the concept was an explicit assertion that layers of inequality are not simply additive: multiple discrimination is not adequately explained as gender + race + class. In stating that inequalities 'intersect' Crenshaw was arguing that this alters meanings and experience: one is not black and a woman, but a 'black woman' – race changes gender and gender changes race. If we introduce whiteness into the picture – the aspect of race which tends not be racialised, the taken for grantedness of majority positions – the intersection becomes one where positions of inequality and privilege converge, producing what Mieke Verloo (2011) has termed 'interference'. To date intersectional analysis had tended to focus on positions of marginalisation, but there is no in principle reason why the framework cannot accommodate more complex positionings – such as those of minority men who use violence against women and girls. The two chapters which address working with perpetrators of violence (Baleela, Price) both argue for such an approach, albeit without drawing directly on the concept of intersectionality. They document the tests in practice of adapting models and ways of working to encompass the lives of minority men whilst still holding them to account for their use of violence.

We failed to commission a chapter on 'brown masculinities',[1] perhaps because most writers here have paid attention to those men whose positioning challenges hegemonic masculinity and heteronormativity (Connell, 2008). Far less has explored minority masculinities and gendered violence. An illuminating exception is *Holding your Square* (Mullins, 2006), which focuses on street based masculinities among men of colour in the USA. Violence functions here as a form of 'gender capital' in which masculinity is a reputational performance: enactments and rituals of power over women and between men and boys. Whilst some work on gangs in the UK is beginning to explore the contradictions for men who occupy subordinated masculinities, as Carlene Firmin argues whilst minority men are racialised, they are less commonly gendered: we need intersectional analysis and practice here too.

Many of the chapters on minority women's experiences explicitly use intersectionality to illuminate the complex contexts which minority women inhabit. These entrap individuals in violence through: limiting the possibilities or potential costs of disclosure (Kanyeredzi, Pande, Patel, Singer); the failure of agencies to respond appropriately (Firmin, Larasi, Roach & Mommoh, Siddiqui); and/or limiting minority women's space for action (Rehman, Singer, Turner). Sharon Smee opens the book, outlining the many ways in which intersectional positions disadvantage minority women across the criminal justice system – as victims, offenders and employees. She notes that whilst there is increased recognition of the needs of minority women the focus tends to be on either race or gender, reflected in the absence of intersectional data which would allow for more complex analyses.

All of the contributors eschew hierarchies of oppression seeking to present more nuanced approaches which locate people in time and space – what is sometimes termed 'situated'. The situations in which individuals find themselves are the outcome of social, political, economic and cultural histories and conjunctions. This situatedness is a strong theme in a number of chapters: Carlene Firmin explores gang associated sexual violence; Jackie Turner the context of trafficking; Debora Singer the asylum process; Emelie Secker and Yasmin Rehman accusations of spirit possession or witchcraft. Whilst the forms of violence perpetrated are similar, the context in which they take place and/or the status of the woman/child affects what it is possible to say, when and to whom. Not to mention how, if at all, their words will be heard, believed and responded to. We are not arguing here that each woman's experience is unique, but rather that we need to be more curious and careful about the contexts which are not only conducive to VAW (Kelly, 2007), but also make it harder to name and reducing the likelihood of being believed/taken seriously, leaving women without protection or support. These themes are further developed by Ava Kanyeredzi in terms of delayed help-seeking amongst women

---

1   A term considered more inclusive than 'Black masculinities'.

with African Caribbean heritage, Swati Pande with respect to the absence of words in Hindi to name sexual violence, Ravi Thiara on the particulars for BME women of post-separation violence and Shaminder Takhar raises the rarely discussed violence which may result if Asian lesbians 'come out' to family and community. Hananna Siddiqui presents the case of Banaz Mahmood, which starkly illuminates the lethal consequences of agencies failing to understand or take seriously the particular situations of young minority women. All of these chapters alert us to the 'situatedness' of women in relation to a number of forms of violence, and the vital necessity of our understanding these coercive contexts. This needs to be distinguished from the current practice focus on 'needs', whilst critical in terms of responding to individuals, attention to 'situatedness' demands a more analytic focus on how women are positioned along intersecting axes of power.

The continuum of violence against women

The concept of the continuum of violence is over 25 years old (Kelly, 1987) and has been recently re-visited (Brown and Walklate, 2011). In its original formulation, reflecting the experiences of the 60 white women interviewed, it did not include harmful practices or sexual exploitation. Subsequent extensions have addressed trafficking (Kelly, 2007) and forced marriage (Anitha and Gill, 2009). The continuum was theorised in two ways: as 'a basic common character that underlies many different events' and 'a continuous series of elements or events that pass into one another and cannot be readily distinguished' (Kelly, 1987: 76). The former encapsulates the view that the many forms of intimate intrusion, coercion, abuse and assault are connected, the latter that the categories used to name and distinguish forms of violence – whether in research, law or policy – overlap. Both meanings are drawn on in chapters in this volume, including in the call by many to integrate forms of violence specific to minority women into the overarching concept of VAWG (Larasi, Roach & Mommoh) and one (Rehman) asks whether polygyny should be included within this framing. The moving accounts of women and children on the harms of polygny for them, coupled with its implications for gendered power in relationships, leads Yasmin Rehman to introduce the concept of harmful marriage practices, another dimension on the continuum of violence. Hannana Siddiqui uses the continuum to show how forced marriage, domestic and sexual violence are all part of honour based violence, raising the challenging question of whether this is a separate form of VAWG or is more accurately described as a conducive context/motive for it. Jackie Turner echoes this in outlining the overlaps between trafficking, forced marriage, child sexual abuse and sexual violence suggesting that traffickers are far more attuned to these connections than policy makers and practitioners. She argues that we should understand women's limited access to safe migration, occupying the bottom of a 'hierarchy of mobility', as a 'dangerous intersection', which creates a conducive context for VAWG. Shaminder Takhar suggests heteronormativity may be a form of 'symbolic violence' which prevents Asian lesbians from 'coming out', further stretching the continuum concept.

One assumption underpinning the continuum was that the vast majority of women experience some from of intimate intrusion in their lifetime, with sexual harassment more common than, but connected to, rape and sexual assault (Kelly, 2011). The only 'more or less' in the continuum concerned prevalence – which forms of violence were most common in women's lives – but this was not discussed in relation to race/ethnicity. The statement that VAW is no respecter of race or class is commonplace, suggesting that it is spread evenly across female populations. Recent dedicated VAW prevalence studies in France and Germany suggest that this may not be the case (Condon et al, 2011), with minority women experiencing both higher rates of violence and levels of male dominance and control (p64), especially within intimate partner violence. We have yet to have such dedicated studies in the UK, and the British Crime Survey data we do have is not detailed enough to undertake similar analysis. There is stronger evidence, for the UK and US, which shows that minority women take longer to seek help, and thus suffer ongoing abuse for longer (Kanyeredzi, Thiara) – a finding echoed for Turkish women in the German prevalence study (Condon et al, 2011: 65). Remaining for longer in abusive relationships can mean more frequent and possibly more serious violence, and for some minority women this involves abuse by multiple family members (Siddiqui, Thiara). James Ptacek's (1999) concept of 'social entrapment' may be useful here – suggesting that toxic conjunctions of sexism, racism, language access and immigration status narrow women's possibilities for naming violence and seeking support. Indeed some perpetrators use women's uncertain status or limited knowledge about their rights as a further form of coercive control (Rehman, Thiara).

Although the question of whether minority women experience higher levels of violence in the UK remains an open one, there are documented commonalities and differences in the aftermath of sexual violence where loss of agency and self-determination were shared whilst minority women had to negotiate variations in sexual norms and the issue of honour (Pederson, 2011). Interestingly, the minority young women using Danish support services viewed their situations as entirely different from those of majority young women (op cit). This self-culturisation both increased the constraints on them in terms of disclosure (see also Pande) and had negative impacts on their ability to regain agency (see also Takhar). Research that involves both minority and majority women enables such exploration of similarities and differences.

The thorny issue of culture

A number of chapters disavow culture as an explanation for violence, but argue that it is an important contextual factor in responding appropriately (Larasi, Patel, Rehman). The rejection of cultural explanations is in part due to the implicit presumption that only 'others' – minorities and not majorities – have culture. In the case of the UK this is invariably accompanied by viewing minority cultures as less modern/'civilised' and more patriarchal. One outcome of this 'way of seeing' is that the same form of violence is explained differently depending on whether the victims and/or perpetrators come from minority/majority cultures. A recent study of domestic violence homicides in Switzerland demonstrated precisely this (Gloor and Meier, 2011): the commonality of gendered power relations which underpinned the use of lethal violence was lost. Makeba Roach and Comfort Mommoh raise this question in relation to FGM, asking why genital surgery for non medical reasons is illegal and a harmful practice when undertaken for 'cultural' reasons, yet allowed – even advertised – when defined as 'cosmetic surgery' or 'labiaplasty'. Surely the latter is as much to do with cultural norms as the former. A similar anomaly is highlighted by Yasmin Rehman in relation to polygny and bigamy, although here the invocation of culture, and especially religion, functions to enable minority men to engage in practices which are illegal under civil law.

At the same time all anthropologists would argue that 'culture matters': it is used for something in violence – by perpetrators and their apologists to justify their behaviour, by those responding to it and in the meanings available to victim-survivors to make sense of it. But as Yakin Erturk (2012) illustrates powerfully, the reassertion of culture (and religion) as core aspects of identity runs the danger of essentialising and fixing the cultures of 'others', naturalising inequality and constructing minority women as lacking in agency. This leads some well-meaning practitioners to think that they must 'save' women and children, rather than using the empowerment approach supported by many contributors to this book. Moreover, some versions of multi-culturalism commended a non-interventionist stance in minority communities, meaning that minority women were afforded less protection (Patel, Siddiqui).

We argue that cultures and communities are always in process, being (re) created. Whilst cultures are normative, norms can and do change and are invariably contested from within, reflecting struggles about power, with gender, sexuality and generation amongst the most contentious arenas (Patel, Roach & Momoh, Siddiqui, Takhar). Some women within minority cultures experience high levels of surveillance, have restricted social networks and are subjected to local and transnational regimes of control. Others, belonging to the same groups, are among the most committed and creative activists on VAWG (Kelly, 2010). Every community could be inspired by the efforts of women across the globe to name, respond to and prevent violence.

Dangerous territory

These debates and tensions are increasingly played out through the issue of faith, as a number of chapters illustrate (Larasi, Patel, Rehman, Siddiqui). This is not just a matter of fundamentalists in religions of all shades seeking to roll back hard won rights of women, or even the entry of faith groups into the provision of funded public services and the decrease of secular spaces valued by women (Patel). There is increasing evidence of faith being used as a mechanism through which women and children are abused. The implication of Christian priests/ministers and nuns in the sexual and physical abuse of children is well documented. Emilie Secker and Yasmin Rehman challenge us to deepen our understanding of how witchcraft accusations serve to legitimise violence and abuse. They argue that this should be understood as a form of ritualised abuse, and it has been recognised and named as such by working groups in the police and social services. That this has been so easily accepted, compared to the contestation of this term when applied to the practices of white adults in the 1980s/1990s (Scott, 2001) raises the question of whether such actions are more 'believable' when attributed to 'others? Or is a critical difference that the intense and still unresolved earlier debate concerned Satanic practices, not a recognised religion, and the accusations concerned sexual abuse rather than the evidence of dead and mutilated bodies? That said recent legal cases have established that belief systems have been used to justify brutality and abuse and several chapters deepen our understanding of how religious beliefs, interpretations and practices are implicated in legitimising violence and abuse (Ballela, Rehman).

Human rights

Human rights has become an important framing for VAWG in the UK, recognised in successive government strategies and linking to international commitments under the UN Convention for the Elimination of all forms of Discrimination against Women (CEDAW). This international common language places obligations on states to protect women from violence and take actions to eliminate it. Jackie Turner explores the reach of human rights from the perspective of trafficked women arguing that the re-framing of the issue as one of security and immigration has resulted in a loss of even a rhetorical linkage to equality and discrimination – vividly demonstrated by the current Westminster government removing trafficking from its VAWG policies. Similarly, Debora Singer illuminates how the status of asylum seeker places this group of women outside those whose human rights are recognised and, at least in theory, protected.

Interventions

A number of chapters demonstrate the importance for minority (and all) women of spaces and places where VAWG is not normalised, in which women are empowered rather than diminished, where they can find their voice, renew their aspirations and be inspired by each other (Firmin, Larasi, Patel, Siddiqui). In the UK there is no right to such services and nor is their provision mandated by law, as in Germany and Spain. The financial crisis, and current austerity measures in response to it, has accentuated changes which are placing the future of the much envied specialised VAWG services in the UK in jeopardy (Coy et al, 2009). The impacts of commissioning and the localism agenda appear to have disproprtionately affected BME women's organisations (Larasi, Patel, Siddiqui) and there are growing concerns about the implications for specialist FGM clinics in the NHS (Roach & Mommoh). As service provision contracts, this will increase women's reliance on their informal networks, which are often either constraining or more limited (as in spread across the globe and thus not easily available) for minority women.

Simultaneously, feminist interventions on VAWG have focused on demanding that the state fulfil its obligations to protect women and provide access to justice: when women and girls invoke the countervailing power of the state, interventions should ensure that their right to lives free from violence is realised. A number of chapters graphically demonstrate that minority women are less likely to receive such responses; albeit for various reasons, including their immigration status (Singer, Turner) and/or mistrust of the criminal justice system and statutory services (Kanyeredzi, Siddiqui, Smee).

Sharon Smee shows that contrary to many predictions and assumptions minority women do report violence to the police, but they are less likely to see a successful prosecution in part due to an increased likelihood of withdrawing their complaint. Whether a stronger focus should be placed on protection, in both feminist thinking and public policy, is further illustrated by discussions (Patel, Siddiqui) on recent debates on the introduction of a new criminal offence of forced marriage. The conundrum of recognising the ambivalence of young women faced by the prospect of their parents being prosecuted if they seek protection alongside the importance of consistency in approaches to, and messages about, all forms of VAWG has taxed many contributors to this book. In one sense this reflects a tension between the preference for protection and support amongst victim-survivors and the demand from women's movements that perpetrators be held to account for their behaviour. The adoption by the UN and Council of Europe of formal requirements on states to ensure all forms of VAW are criminal offences places an emphasis on prosecution. As Hannana Siddiqui notes we need to create more spaces in which to debate the balance, overlaps and tensions between protection and prosecution.

This is but one example of the many dilemmas we now have to negotiate as both the knowledge and policy landscapes become more complex, and even in some senses contradictory – we have greater commitment to VAWG in terms of national and local policies at the same time as the community based women's organisations which have developed innovative responses for over three decades face the greatest threats to their continued existence. Jackie Turner's chapter explores policy shifts in relation to trafficking, with the coalition government abolishing the UK Human Trafficking Centre (UKHTC) and making the Border Agency (UKBA) responsible for identification and responses to victims. Yet the issue is invisible on UKBA's website. Currently, only a third of those referred within the National Referral Mechanism are formally recognised as victims of trafficking, thus two thirds are denied access to this crucial gateway into protection and rights. This move away from the original framing within gender equality and human rights to security and immigration has not been a positive one for victims of trafficking.

Carlene Firmin examines the policy and provision challenges to responding appropriately to young women affected by gang associated violence. Here it is not just victimisation which must be addressed but the implication in, and for some perpetration of, violence and the additional risks of retaliation if interventions fail to provide holistic protection. Situated at several intersections these young women fall through the gaps between ungendered responses to gang related violence and adult women's services ill-suited to this age group and the coercive contexts they inhabit and are part of. However, her chapter and Sharon Smee's intersectional analysis of women's involvement in drug smuggling offer new models of how to explore the inter-connections between women's victimisation and offending.

One loss in the increasing engagement of statutory services and policy makers with VAWG, which a number of chapters seek to correct, has been survivors' voices and perspectives. The concepts of silence and silencing have been ubiquitous in discussions of VAWG, with more attention paid to silence that is imposed than that which is chosen. We need to pay more attention to the potential benefits and costs of speaking and whose voices are heard. Pragna Patel illustrates this with the case of one young woman, influenced by her brother, whose desire to be veiled at school muted the voices of the majority of Muslim girls at the same school for whom the existing policy provided a space in which they were afforded a freedom from injunctions to piety. Sharminder Takhar reinforces this insight through her discussion of the growing numbers of young Asian women who quietly use going to university as a space to explore and exercise sexual agency. The importance of hearing directly from minority women on their experiences of key interventions – such as Specialist Domestic Violence Courts (SDVCs), Multi-Agency Risk Assessment Conferences (MARACs) and domestic and sexual violence advocacy services – is stressed by Sharon Smee.

When invited to contribute to policy debates, women are often insightful and clear. As Pragna Patel and Hannana Siddiqui illustrate, minority women want equal rather than 'special' treatment, actively seek and appreciate the spaces and options provided by secular community based women's organisations.

Out of or Back to the Shadows?

The challenge we set ourselves and our contributors was to explore both commonalities and differences in the lives of minority women – in the forms of violence they experience, their meanings and consequences. It remains the case that in seeking to end violence, access justice, protection and/or support minority women still have to negotiate stereotypes, the barriers for some of language and immigration status, community distrust and the potential of racism. As more and more minority women choose to no longer remain in the shadows we face a new policy context which threatens to roll back many of the gains made to date. A recent study by Towers & Walby (2012), for example, found a reduction of 31 per cent in local authority expenditure on VAW, and this is just the first year of austerity measures. At the 2012 British Sociological Association annual conference Sylvia Walby asked the telling question whether the period of incremental feminist social democracy, in which much was achieved with respect to violence, is over. An accompanying question for this volume is whether it will be BME women who lose most and earliest? Marai Larasi's chapter ends the book with a poignant query: in adapting to funding regimes and performance culture have BME women's organisation sold their soul?

The future for BME victim-survivors and the organisations established to support them is uncertain, and there is a not inconsiderable risk that rather than emerging from the shadows, the contraction in services and access to protection and justice will confine them to the margins, where entrapment in violence is more likely. Internal divisions and debates between BME women's organisations about the best ways to respond to VAW are also considered a challenge (Siddiqui). At the same time, Marai Larasi argues that feminist coalitions have been practising solidarity (Mohanty, 2003) and finding new ways of working politically with intersectionality. Pragna Patel concludes her chapter arguing that now, more than ever, we need coalitions of those willing to challenge power in all its guises, which includes a commitment to question our own orthodoxies. 'Moving out of the shadows' refers to movement - women moving, women on the move - movements of women which will continue to endeavour to shine the lights of recognition and knowledge on all forms of violence and abuse.

References

Anitha, S & Gill, A. 2009. Coercion, Consent and the Forced Marriage Debate in the UK. *Feminist Legal Studies*, 17 (2): 165–184.

Condon, S, Lisse, M, Schrottle, M. 2011. What do we know about gendered violence and ethnicity across Europe from surveys. In Thaira, R, Condon, S, & Schroettle, M. (Eds) *Violence Against Women and Ethnicity: Commonalities and differences across Europe*. Berlin, Barbara Buarich. pp. 59–76.

Connell, R W. 2008. *Gender* (2nd Edition). Cambridge, Polity Press.

Crenshaw, K. 1991. Mapping the margins: intersectionality, identity politics and violence against women of color. *Stanford Law Review*, 43, 1241.

Coy, M., Kelly, L., Foord, J. 2009. *Map of Gaps 2*, Equality and Human Rights Commission & End Violence Against Women (EVAW) campaign. Available at: http://www.endviolenceagainstwomen.org.uk/data/files/map_of_gaps2.pdf [Accessed: 12 May 2011].

Erturk, Y. 2012. Culture versus Rights Dualism: a myth or a reality? Available at http://www.opendemocracy.net/5050/yakin-erturk/culture-versus-rights-dualism-myth-or-reality [Accessed: 27 April 2012].

Gloor, D & Meier, H. 2011. Culture and ethnicity in re(constructing domestic homicides. In Thaira, R, Condon, S, & Schroettle, M. (Eds) Violence Against

Women and Ethnicity: Commonalities and differences across Europe. Berlin, Barbara Buarich. pp. 399–413.

Kelly, L. 1987. *Surviving Sexual Violence*. Cambridge, Polity Press.

Kelly, L. 2007. A conducive context: Trafficking of persons in Central Asia. In M. Lee (Ed), *Human Trafficking*. London, Willan Publishing.

Kelly, L. 2010. Introduction. In R.Thaira and A. Gill (eds) *Violence Against Women in South Asian Communities: Issues for Policy and Practice*. London, Jessica Kingsley. pp. 9–14.

Kelly, L. 2011. Preface. In J Brown and S. Walklate (Eds) *Handbook on Sexual Violence*. London, Routledge. pp. xvii–xxvi.

Mohanty, C. 2003. *Feminism without Borders: Decolonizing Theory, Practicing Solidarity*. Duke University Press.

Mullins, C, 2006. *Holding Your Square: Masculinities, Streetlife, and Violence. Cullumpton*, Willan.

Pease, B. and Rees, S. 2008. Theorising men's violence towards women in refugee families: towards in intersectional feminist framework. *Just policy: a journal of Australian social policy*, 47, pp. 39–45.

Pederson, B. 2011. Ethnicities in the aftermath of sexualised coercion – common issues and diverse personal meanings. In Thaira, R, Condon, S, & Schroettle, M. (eds) *Violence Against Women and Ethnicity: Commonalities and differences across Europe*. Berlin, Barbara Buarich, pp. 170–185.

Ptacek, J. 1999. *Battered Women in the Courtroom: The Power of Judicial Responses*. Northeastern University Press.

Thaira, R, Condon, S, & Schroettle, M (Eds). 2011. *Violence Against Women and Ethnicity: Commonalities and Differences across Europe*. Berlin, Barbara Buarich.

Thaira, R & Gill A (Eds). 2010. *Violence Against Women in South Asian Communities: Issues for Policy and Practice*. London, Jessica Kingsley.

Scott, S. 2001. *The Politics and Experience of Ritual Abuse: Beyond Disbelief.* Milton Keynes, Open University Press.

Smith, D. 1993. *Texts, Facts, and Femininity: Exploring the Relations of Ruling*. New York, Routledge.

Towers J & Walby, S. 2012. *Measuring the impact of cuts in public expenditure on theprovision of services to prevent violence against women and girls*. Trust for London. Available at http://www.trustforlondon.org.uk/VAWG%20Full%20 report.pdf [Accessed: 6 May 2012].

Verloo, M. 2011. 'Gender equality policies as interventions in a changing world'. Keynote *Gender and Politics ECPR Conference*, Budapest 13 January. Available at http://www.ecprnet.eu/sg/ecpg/documents/keyNotes/Gender_ equality_policies_as_interventions_in_a_changing_world.pdf [Accessed: 22 May 2012].

Walby, S. 2011. *The Future of Feminism*. Cambridge, Polity Press.

Walby, S. 2012. Gender, violence and the cuts. Paper at British Sociological Conference, Leeds 11 April.

PART I
Perspectives

Chapter 1

At the Intersection:
Black and Minority Ethnic Women and the
Criminal Justice System

Sharon Smee

Introduction

The sexism inherent in the British criminal justice system has been the subject of much feminist critique (Kennedy 1992, Wedderburn 2000, Fawcett Society 2009). There has also been acknowledgement of racial prejudice and disadvantage across criminal justice agencies, particularly following the Stephen Lawrence Inquiry which branded the Metropolitan police force 'institutionally racist'(MacPherson 1999). These developments have led to an increased mainstream policy focus on the discrimination faced by women and ethnic minorities who come into contact with the criminal justice system in the United Kingdom. This chapter seeks to tease out what we know about Black[1] and minority ethnic (BME)[2] women's encounters with the criminal justice system – as victims, offenders and practitioners – and their implications for policy and practice.

The public sector equality duty contained in the Equality Act 2010 requires all public authorities (including criminal justice agencies) to ensure that due regard is paid to the need to advance equality of opportunity for women who share a protected characteristic including race. In theory this should result in a criminal justice system which is more responsive to the distinct needs of ethnic minority women and a more integrated approach across equality strands. However, in practice criminal justice responses and policy related discourses continue to overlook the intersectional identities of BME women. As Crenshaw (1992) argues in her examination of the race and gender dimensions of violence against women of colour, the intersectional discrimination in BME women's lives cannot be 'captured wholly by looking at the

---

1   This Chapter uses the capitalised form of 'Black' and 'White' to recognise that such terms are as much socially created as any linguistic, tribal or religious ethnicity (see MacKinnon, 1993).

2   The term BME is not used to suggest that women falling within this category have identical experiences or needs when accessing justice. Rather, it is used in recognition of the shared barriers and marginalisation faced by BME women attempting to navigate the criminal justice system.

race or gender dimensions of those experiences separately' (p.1244). It is the location of ethnic minority women at the intersection of race and gender which distinguishes their experiences from BME men and from White women.

The argument that BME women's experiences of the justice system will be shaped by how race and gender disadvantage intersect and interact with each other is not a recent insight (Chigwada-Bailey 2003). There is also an increasing volume of research which speaks to the needs and experiences of BME women engaging with the criminal justice sector (Gelsthorpe 1996, 2007, Gill 2010, Gill and Anitha 2011, Gittens 2004, HM Inspectorate of Prisons 2009, Puwar 2003, Roy et al. 2011, Smee and Moosa 2010, Thiara and Gill 2009, Women's National Commission 2009). This chapter will argue that, despite this research and developments in the discrimination law framework, criminal justice agencies continue to focus on race *or* gender discrimination. There is also a propensity for these responses to differ according to the categorisation of BME women as survivors of violence, offenders or practitioners in the criminal justice sector. For example, BME female offenders are largely excluded from wider policy responses to racism within the prison system while violence against BME women is frequently defined in 'cultural' terms so that their experiences are segregated from wider responses to gender-based violence.

In interrogating the experiences of BME women across the criminal justice system this chapter will consider the intersecting patterns of racism and sexism, whilst noting the paucity of cross-tabulation of data by both ethnicity and gender throughout the criminal justice system. It will be contended that what is missing is a common understanding of the intersectional identity of BME women which identifies the specificities of BME women's experiences as survivors of violence, offenders and practitioners across criminal justice agencies while still locating these needs within wider strategies to address racism and sexism within the criminal justice system.

Criminal Justice Responses to Violence Against BME Women

Despite years of campaigning by women active within minority communities, it is only within the last decade that there has been a growing awareness by the Government and criminal justice agencies of violence against ethnic minority women, particularly in relation to domestic violence and harmful practices such as female genital mutilation, forced marriage and so-called 'honour'-based violence.

As Patel (2008) argues, with this focus there has been an increasing dilemma in the law's response to violence against BME women as the legal system struggles to reconcile the 'culture is no excuse' approach with the need for protection of multiculturalism and religious identity often to the detriment of women's rights.

This approach has frequently led to the experiences of BME women being framed in 'cultural' terms so that their needs and experiences are segregated from other women's experiences of violence (Siddiqui 2008). In turn, this can undermine a broader understanding of ethnic minority women's experiences of violence by statutory agencies and lead to responses which focus on 'culture' or 'ethnicity' (or even non-intervention due to cultural or religious sensitivity) rather than the race *and* gender dimensions of violence against women. In this way, criminal justice interventions may actually reinforce existing power imbalances. For example, BME women have described instances of the inappropriate promotion by the police of informal mediation within communities as a response to violence against women (Women's National Commission, 2009).

Campaigning by groups such as Southall Black Sisters and the End Violence Against Women (EVAW) Coalition has sought to draw attention to this racialised categorising of violence and has called for the inclusion of all forms of violence against BME women within an integrated cross-government strategy based on the principles of equality and human rights (Southall Black Sisters and EVAW, 2011). Strategic policies have been developing such as the UK Coalition Government's *Call to End Violence against Women and Girls: Action Plan* launched in March 2011 which includes a specific focus on BME women (Home Office, 2011a). Alongside this, there has also been a growing body of research on the experiences of BME women as survivors of gender-based violence in the United Kingdom, particularly in relation to South Asian women and the experiences of refugee women (see, for example, Thiara and Gill 2009). However, in practice, the criminal justice system has been slow to understand, let alone respond to, the intersectional discrimination faced by BME women experiencing violence.

Despite a requirement under the previous gender and race equality duties (and the new Public Sector Equality Duty), agencies have been inconsistent in their collection and publication of data on the ethnicity of women accessing the criminal justice system. While statistics are sometimes collected on the sex of victims of violence, and are also sometimes collected on the ethnicity of victims, it is quite rare for them to be analysed by both ethnicity and sex in the same sample. For example, in the Crown Prosecution Service Violence against Women Crime Report 2010–11, of those with a recorded gender (87%) 84 per cent were female. However, ethnicity was not recorded for over half of the victims, making it impossible to do intersectional analysis. To date, the most detailed study (a project of the BME organisation Imkaan), which collected data from ten BME violence against women services across the United Kingdom, revealed that out of 106 women, a formal report to the police was made in 37 per cent of cases and a fifth of women were supporting a prosecution (Thiara et al., 2010).

The lack of a complete picture of BME women's experiences is due not only to inadequate data recording by criminal justice agencies but also to a focus on specific communities by policymakers. For example, Roy et al. (2011) notes in relation to female genital mutilation that the predominant focus is on girls from the Horn of Africa which means the needs of affected women and girls from Northern Sudan, Eritrea, Ethiopia, Egypt, Sierra Leone, Gambia, Liberia and Kurdish communities are overlooked. There is also a gap in research in relation to forced marriage outside South Asian communities (Chantier et al. 2009, Hester et al.

2008, Refuge 2010, Roy et al. 2011). This is not to argue that a focus on particular groups is unhelpful; in fact, as Gill (2009) contends, it may be necessary to do so where a specificity needs to be understood in order to respond to particular forms of violence against women. However, it does mean that there is a need for a better understanding of the experiences and needs of communities which are less visible within research, policy and service provision (Roy et al. 2011).

Criminal justice interventions have also focussed on certain forms of violence associated with BME women – female genital mutilation, forced marriage and 'honour'-based violence are targeted within the Coalition Government's Action Plan on Violence against Women and have also been the focus of strategic planning within criminal justice agencies (ACPO 2008, Crown Prosecution Service 2011, Home Office 2011a). However, these policy responses often overlook the links between harmful practices and other forms of violence against women such as sexual violence (Roy et al. 2011). The challenge is to identify the specificities of the manifestations of violence affecting BME women without reinforcing cultural stereotypes and while still locating this violence within the wider context of gender-based violence. For example, as Dustin and Phillips (2008)[3] note, a focus on honour-based violence threatens to 'exaggerate the cultural component in what remains a form of domestic violence' but at the same time a failure to train the police on the specifics of this manifestation of violence against women may expose women to cultural stereotypes.

The national framework

Since 1985, female genital mutilation has been a criminal offence in the UK. The Female Genital Mutilation Act 2003, which came into force in England, Wales and Northern Ireland in March 2004, increased the penalty to a 14-year sentence. This new legislation also made it illegal for a UK national or permanent resident to perform, or to assist in performing, female genital mutilation outside of the UK. The Metropolitan Police investigated 46 allegations of female genital mutilation in 2008/09 and 58 in 2009/10 (Metropolitan Police Service 2010). However, there has, to date, been no prosecution for female genital mutilation in the UK. In comparison, in France, more than 37 cases have been tried, although this approach has been criticised as being overly intrusive (Comic Relief 2010). Multi-agency practice guidelines were launched in the UK in February 2011 and will be reviewed in 2012 (Home Office 2011c) and Crown Prosecution Service Guidance was published in November 2011 (Crown Prosecution Service, 2011). A national multi-agency forum has also been established. However, the Female Genital Mutilation Co-ordinator post within Government was abolished in 2011 prompting concerns about effective implementation of the multi-agency guidelines (Williams 2011). Notably, despite frustration about the lack of prosecution in the UK, research with focus groups of

---

3   Dustin M. and Phillips, A. 2008. 'Whose agenda is it?: abuses of women and abuses of `culture' in Britain'Ethnicities, 8, 3. 405–424.

BME women indicated some support for the legislation as an important tool for educating communities that female genital mutilation is unacceptable (Roy et al. 2011, Women's National Commission 2010).

There are no specific criminal offences on so-called honour-based violence or forced marriage. However, there are a number of relevant criminal offences in existing legislation including murder, kidnap, abduction, domestic or sexual violence, common assault and grievous bodily harm (Roy et al. 2011). During the period December 2008 to April 2010, the Metropolitan Police recorded 366 forced marriage incidents and 100 forced marriage offences, and 414 honour-based violence incidents and 228 offences in London (MacFarlane 2011). In comparison, the Forced Marriage Unit (FMU) provided 1735 instances of advice and support related to possible forced marriage in 2010 alone (FMU 2010).

As with any form of violence against women, the number of prosecutions is much lower than recorded offences. In 2010–11, there were 41 cases of forced marriage and 234 cases of 'honour'-based violence prosecuted across the UK, with a success rate of just under 50 per cent and 52 per cent respectively (Crown Prosecution Service 2011). The Crown Prosecution Service (CPS) initiated a pilot project in December 2007 (implemented in April 2010), using a flagging system to improve monitoring alongside specialist guidance and training for prosecutors, to increase prosecution rates in 'honour'-based violence and forced marriage cases. While, it is still too early to determine whether this will have an impact on prosecution rates, the requirement for local CPS areas to provide performance-related data will provide a useful monitoring framework going forward (Crown Prosecution Service 2011, Roy et al. 2011).

The criminalisation of forced marriage was proposed in 2005, recommended in 2011 by the Home Affairs Committee in addition to the current civil remedy under the Forced Marriage (Civil Protection) Act 2007 (House of Commons, Home Affairs Committee 2011) and, most recently, the Government announced an intention in June 2012 to make forced marriage a specific criminal offence. However, the risks associated with criminalising forced marriage – such as reinforcing racist stereotypes, deterring women from seeking help and fragmenting laws relating to violence against women (Gill 2009, Roy et al. 2011) – may outweigh any perceived advantages.

Accessing the criminal justice system

Intersecting patterns of racism and sexism will impact on BME women's choices as to whether and how they interact with the justice system. In fact, feminists have argued that the inability of the law to recognise the different ways in which women exercise agency may make it an inadequate route to justice for women (Kelly, Coy and Foord 2009). Research indicates that BME women experiencing violence are less likely to seek help from statutory services (Rai and Thiara 1997) and that BME women who suffer violence do not get help until they have had an average of 17 contacts (compared to 11 contacts for White women) with criminal justice agencies (Brittain 2005). Significantly, 100 per cent of the women surveyed by Imkaan stated that being supported by a BME service was a central factor in helping them feel safe to access the criminal justice system (Thiara et al. 2010) suggesting that specialist support which takes into account the race and gender dimensions of violence against women is crucial for engagement with the justice system.

BME women seeking to access justice must negotiate not only the attitudes and stereotypes surrounding violence against women but also additional barriers such as language, community structures and the potential for a racist response from criminal justice agencies and wider society. For example, Black people are at least six times more likely and Asian people are around twice as likely to be stopped and searched by the police as White people (EHRC 2010). While, the majority stopped are men, the disproportionate targeting of certain ethnic groups means that Black women and Asian women will be more likely to have witnessed or to have known someone who has been stopped and searched than White women, which, in turn, may increase distrust of the police. Similarly, how services respond to a range of equality issues not only to violence against women, affects levels of confidence in that service and whether women feel safe to report violence (Women's National Commission 2009).

Interestingly in a study of rape allegations reported to the Metropolitan Police (Stanko 2007, 2010) there was an over-representation of reporting by Black victims (23%) and an under-representation of White (59%) and Asian victims (7%). Whether this is due to the support of specialist services, a disproportionate incidence of rape among Black women in London or rape being seen as an issue which it is more 'acceptable' to report in certain communities is unknown. However, what it demonstrates is the necessity of data being routinely presented by ethnicity and gender so that patterns of reporting can be analysed and responses developed.

BME women may not report violence to the police because of fear of ramification for their communities as well as reprisals from family and community structures (Burman, 2003, Chakraborti and Garland, 2003).This will be shaped by each household/community context of power imbalances and gender norms and the ways individual women choose to exercise agency. However, frequently criminal justice responses are based on either protecting ethnic minority women as a 'vulnerable' group rather than identifying the needs of individual women (Gill 2010) or erring on the side of non-intervention because of cultural oversensitivity (Roy et al. 2011). Neither will garner the trust of BME women.

The CPS notes that one of the main problems in domestic violence cases relates to victim retraction due to the close and often intimate relationship between the defendant and victim. One in three of all failed domestic violence cases in 2010–11 failed because the victim either did not attend court or retracted their evidence; compared to approximately one in ten for all prosecutions (Crown Prosecution Service 2011). The current lack of disaggregation of data by ethnicity makes it very difficult to gauge the impact of ethnicity on these retraction rates. However, 'practice based' evidence suggests ethnic minority women may be more likely to retract their evidence (Fawcett Society 2009). A review which was conducted into rape allegations reported to the Metropolitan Police (Stanko 2007) also indicates attrition may vary between different ethnic groupings. In the study, a higher proportion of allegations by Asian victims were crimed: 73 per cent, compared to 66 per cent for White and 63 per cent for Black victims; charging rates did not follow this pattern, with 18 per cent of allegations by White and 17 per cent of allegations by Black victims resulted in a charge, compared with only 6 per cent of those by Asian victims. Therefore, two-thirds of allegations of rape by Asian victims were crimed but did not result in charges. This illustrates the importance of *targeted* services to support BME women from initial reporting through to court as well as the need for the strengthening of alternatives to the criminal justice system to ensure the safety of women who decide not to report or who may be susceptible to retraction.

Ethnic minority women with uncertain immigration status face additional barriers to reporting. While a consideration of immigration laws and the access to protection and support for women who have an insecure immigration status is outside the scope of this chapter, it should be noted that this acts as a barrier to accessing the criminal justice system. Women may fear being deported or losing custody of their children if they approach authorities and these fears are often manipulated by abusive spouses (Women's National Commission 2010). Lack of knowledge of the legal avenues available and a shortage of specialist legal advice and representation compound this problem (Rights of Women 2010b). Significantly, in applying for indefinite leave to remain under the domestic violence rule the most persuasive evidence of domestic violence is a court conviction, a police caution or evidence from the police (Rights of Women 2010a). Consequently, barriers to accessing the criminal justice system may also impact on immigration status creating a vicious cycle of insecurity.

Access to legal aid will also impact on BME women's engagement with the justice system. Research by Rights of Women (2010b) demonstrated that a significant proportion of BME respondents who were experiencing violence may not have taken steps to address this abuse because they were not eligible for legal aid. Further, time limited legal aid is often completely inadequate in complex domestic violence, trafficking and immigration cases, particularly if communication takes place through an interpreter (Fawcett Society 2009). Proposed changes to legal aid, which remove types of civil and family law cases from its scope, will exacerbate the current situation, particularly given the interlocking nature of problems such as debt, employment, housing and immigration issues with violence against women (Lady Brenda Hale 2011, Ministry of Justice 2011e).

Language barriers can impede access to justice and interpretation support can be far from adequate. Evidence submitted to Fawcett's Commission on Women and the Criminal Justice System (2009) revealed that in trafficking cases the fact that a female victim is communicating through an interpreter has been used to advance the defendant's case. These communication barriers may also be compounded by police and prosecution barristers who fail to understand the realities of ethnic minority women's experiences of violence. For example, Gill (2010) notes that police responses to recent cases of forced marriage and honour killings too often minimise the severity of the violence involved or implicitly blame the victim for not leaving the family. The introduction of specialist CPS lead prosecutors with expertise on forced marriage and 'honour' based violence may assist in alleviating these practices (Home Office 2011c).

Independent Domestic Violence Advisors (IDVAs) and Independent Sexual Violence Advisors (ISVAs) have been introduced to provide support for victims negotiating the criminal justice system. However, under-resourcing of the scheme, inconsistency in approaches between areas and the lack of specialist BME services to refer women for long term support means appropriate responses cannot be guaranteed (Fawcett Society 2009).The diversion of resources to these initiatives also means that there is less funding for specialist service provision and community-based approaches to addressing violence against women - both of which are avenues through which BME women are more likely to seek support and to access justice.

There has also been little examination of the responsiveness of other criminal justice initiatives such as specialist domestic violence courts (SDVCs) to the needs of ethnic minority women. An evaluation indicated a lower success rate in areas where there was a high proportion of ethnic minority defendants (Her Majesty's Court Service 2008). However, whether this indicates SDVCs are not meeting the needs of BME women or is in fact a reflection of the high levels of victim withdrawal or ambivalence towards the criminal justice system requires further research. Similarly, it is unclear how responsive Multi-Agency Risk Assessment Conferences (MARACs) are to the needs of different groups of women in the context of domestic violence. MARACs are meetings intended to share information about high risk cases in order to prevent serious harm, develop a safety plan and put all possible support in place. However, it is difficult to guarantee that MARAC members understand the different implications of total disclosure for minority women and take additional precautions (Izzidien 2008). In fact, concerns have been raised about this process breaching privacy rights (Coy and Kelly 2010, Fawcett Society 2009) and not being representative of the communities it serves such as through a lack of representation of BME agencies providing support for women who have experienced violence (Steel et al. 2011).

Within the criminal justice system there remains a gap in services to address the long term support needs of women. Roy et al. (2011) note this support is particularly crucial for BME women due to the likelihood of repercussions from family and the community when women report violence and during and after legal proceedings. However, mainstream policy measures aimed at reducing violence affecting ethnic minority women have disproportionately focused on enforcement and criminal justice outcomes rather than holistic responses which address prevention, early intervention and support services (Dustin and Phillips 2009, Roy et al. 2011).

BME Women Offenders – Minorities within a Minority

The relationship between female offending and histories of violence and abuse (Rumgay 2004) is now more widely acknowledged by criminal justice agencies. One in three women in prison report having experienced sexual abuse and over half have suffered domestic abuse (Prison Reform Trust 2011). Since the *Corston Report* (2007) into women offenders and women at risk of offending in England and Wales, there has been greater recognition of the specific needs of female prisoners as well as an increase in alternatives to custody for low-level women offenders (Home Office 2011c). To date, these initiatives have not led to a reduction in the number of women in prison. In December 2011 there were over 4,228 women in prison – an increase from a female prison population of 4,161 a year previously (National Offender Management Service 2011). However, they have led to the introduction of gender specific standards for women prisoners (2008), a national service framework (2008), changes to full search arrangements (2009) and specific targets to reduce the size of the women's prison estate (APPG on women in the penal system 2011).

Within this emerging policy framework there has been an acknowledgement that BME women, and particularly foreign national women, remain disproportionately represented within the female prison population. In 2010, Black women made up 15.1 per cent of the women's prison population, and in 2011, foreign national women comprised 15 per cent of female prisoners (Ministry of Justice 2011b). While there is a higher proportion of White men than White women in prison, there is a higher proportion of Black women than Black men in prison. There are also relatively more female prisoners in the category Chinese or Other (3.4% of the female prison population in 2008) than in the male prison population (1.5%). Combined, these numbers suggest that ethnic minority women are more likely to be found in the prison population than ethnic minority men (Walby, 2010).

The *Corston Report* (2007) recognised that BME women, as 'minorities within a minority,' may have additional needs and problems when negotiating the penal system. This review, together with campaigning by groups such as the Fawcett Society and Women in Prison and the work of the Women and Young People's Group within the National Offender Management Service, has led to acknowledgment that BME women can face additional discrimination based on race. Most notably, the Gender Specific Standards on Women Prisoners (2008) contains guidance on the needs of women from Black and minority ethnic groups, addressing practical issues such as access to canteen goods, sensitivity to clothing with cultural or religious significance and health and education needs.

This framework is an important step forward in beginning to identify the different challenges facing BME women in the prison system. However, the current approach falls short in two key ways. Firstly, there remains a lack of analysis as to how needs may differ within the women's prison population and how wider criminal justice responses to women offenders may impact on or disadvantage women from different ethnic backgrounds (HMIP 2009, Smee and Moosa 2010). Secondly, when the needs of BME women are acknowledged it continues to be as a sub-set of the female prison population rather than also as part of wider policy responses to racism within the prison system. For example, the National Offenders Management Service Race Review Report (2008), the culmination of a five year programme within the prison service to address race issues, does not even mention the specific needs of black and minority ethnic women (HMIP 2009).

Offending history and sentencing

Women from Black and minority ethnic groups are more likely to receive a prison sentence than White women for a first time offence. Inspectorate surveys between 2003 and 2006 revealed that for 67 per cent of BME women it was their first time in prison, compared to 41 per cent of White prisoners. This pattern is even more apparent for BME foreign national women with 73 per cent in prison for the first time compared to 43 per cent of British nationals (HMIP 2009). This may be partly explained by the sentencing decisions being affected by societal perceptions of women who do not conform to traditional stereotypes (Chigwada-Bailey 2003, Daly 1994). For example, research has shown that African-Caribbean women are less likely to receive probation (Gelsthorpe 2006). However, it could also reflect the different offences for which White and ethnic minority women are convicted – again, highlighting the importance of intersectional analysis of statistics.

Significantly, more BME women are convicted of the illegal import and export of drugs and given the deterrent model of harsh prison sentences for drug offences, receive long prison sentences (HMIP 2009). Many of these women (known as 'drug mules') are frequently first time offenders who are driven by poverty and desperation and typically do not own or use the drugs. They are often the victims of exploitative relationships and are rarely 'high up' in criminal gangs (Hibiscus 2011, Fawcett Society 2009). Research by the Sentencing Council with twelve drug mules found that a trusted person commonly made the arrangements for the trip (Sentencing Council 2011c). The concept of 'gender entrapment' (Ritchie, 1996) developed in relation to incarcerated African American women may have something to offer in extending understanding here.

New sentencing guidelines for drug offences by the Sentencing Council include standardised sentences for importation drug offences based on the weight of the drug and the level of involvement of the individual (Sentencing Council 2012). An acknowledged aim is to bring about a 'downward shift' in the sentences of drug mules on the basis that 'current sentencing levels are sometimes disproportionate to the levels of culpability and harm caused' (Sentencing Council 2011b). However, Fleetwood (2011) argues that the new guidelines may not result in the desired effect because drug mules tend to carry larger quantities of drugs usually without knowing the weight or being misled about the quantity. Fleetwood's research, involving international cocaine and heroin traffickers in prisons in Ecuador, revealed that mules typically carry from one to six kilos but professional traffickers (aware of current sentencing guidelines) only carry around one to two kilos. Previous findings from research looking at drug trafficking through Heathrow airport found similar disparities between men and women in terms of not only weight, but also that women were more likely to be carrying class A drugs (Harper et al. 2002). Careful teasing out of intersectionality includes the ways in which BME women are exploited within drug trafficking.

Almost half (46%) of foreign national women in prison are serving a custodial sentence for drug offences, compared to 21 per cent of women of British nationality (Ministry of Justice 2011c). These women are largely from Nigeria, Jamaica and South Africa (Prison Reform Trust 2011). However, data suggests there is much more at play than just issues of nationality. Firstly, there is a much lower proportion of foreign national men, 25 per cent, serving a custodial sentence for drug offences (Ministry of Justice 2011c). Further, Black and minority ethnic prisoners are more likely to be under immediate custodial sentence for import/export than their White counterparts (77% compared to 30%) (HMIP 2009). Lastly, while there is limited analysis of the proportion of women imprisoned for drug offences by offence type and ethnicity, data reveals that in June 2005, 65 per cent of women imprisoned for drug offences were British Nationals of whom 26 per cent were Black and minority ethnic. Significantly, more than two thirds (69%) of these British Black and minority ethnic women were imprisoned for unlawful import/export offences (HMIP 2009).

There has also been an increase in the number of foreign national women imprisoned for fraud and holding false documents, making up 16 per cent of foreign national women in prison in 2010 (Ministry of Justice 2011c). A submission made by the Poppy Project to Fawcett's Commission on Women and the Criminal Justice System (2009) stated that poor legal advice is resulting in trafficked women pleading guilty to charges (such as holding false documents) whilst evidence about their trafficking has not been raised in their defence. This could explain the increase in the number of female prisoners from Eastern European countries and from China and Vietnam serving sentences for deception (an average sentence of 12 months) and holding false documents (8½ months) (Prison Reform Trust, 2011).

Much of the focus of the *Corston Report* (2007) and subsequent calls for community alternatives to custody has been on the devastating impact of short sentences of less than six months, on non-violent women offenders (Fawcett Society, 2009). In 2010, 61 per cent of women were sentenced to custody for six months or less (Ministry of Justice 2011b). However, factors such as the lengthy sentences associated with import/export drug offences, mean ethnic minority women are more likely to be serving long sentences. At 30 June 2010, 81.5 per cent of women sentenced for 6 months or less were White while 82.7 per cent of Black/Black British and 86.7 per cent of Asian/Asian British female prisoners were serving sentences of 12 months or longer (Ministry of Justice, 2011c). Therefore policy responses which prioritise alternatives to custody for female offenders serving short sentences will disproportionately exclude women from ethnic minority backgrounds.

Differential experiences within the women's prison population

Aside from the focus on alternatives to custody for low-level women offenders, criminal justice responses to women offenders have identified specific needs such as self-harm and mental health problems, substance-related needs, histories of violence and abuse and resettlement needs. However, very little attention has been paid as to how these needs may differ among the female prison population. The thematic report by the HM Inspectorate of Prisons into adult women from BME backgrounds (2009) is a significant step forward. The findings illustrate that while BME women face similar barriers to White women prisoners, they are further disadvantaged by racial discrimination and may in fact have different needs altogether in some respects.

The needs of BME women must also be seen within the wider context of the institutional racism of the prison system. Recent research undertaken by the Prison Reform Trust found that 41 of 71 prisoners interviewed said that they had experienced racism in the previous six months and almost two-thirds did not submit a complaint about it (Edgar 2010). Both BME women and foreign national women said they had poorer access to complaint forms and were more likely to have felt threatened or intimidated by staff (HMIP 2010). In inspectorate surveys, 26 per cent of BME women report victimisation by staff compared to 16 per cent of White women (HMIP 2009). Asian women reported the highest levels of victimisation by other prisoners than any other male or female prisoner group (HMIP 2005).

The Gender Specific Standards on Women Prisoners note that women from ethnic minorities are susceptible to certain illnesses and that special attention should be paid to BME women with mental health problems. Nevertheless, there is very little analysis as to how the inter-play of race and gender inequalities may impact on access to appropriate healthcare. The largest project to date into the health of female prisoners (Plugge et al. 2007) did not distinguish the differential health needs of BME women. Further, HMIP thematic reports have revealed that prison healthcare departments are not systematically recording nationality and ethnicity in clinical records (HMIP 2006). This lack of information on diverse needs within the female prison population, together with limited health information in different languages and practices such as the use of prisoners to translate for others (HMIP 2009b), may act as barriers to health services meeting the needs of BME women.

Substance abuse interventions may also be failing to take into account the intersectional needs of BME women. Inspectorate surveys (HMIP 2009) revealed BME women are less likely to have had problems with alcohol or drugs on their arrival into prison (18%) than their White counterparts (41%) and are also less likely to be dependent on heroin (Shah et al. 2011). Yet research has revealed that drug services tend to concentrate on heroin abuse and there is a paucity of services directly targeting BME offenders together with a lack of BME staff in drug programmes (Fountain et al. 2007, HMIP 2009). Further, much of this research on the responsiveness of drug treatment programmes is focused on ethnic minority male prisoners. As a result, interventions such as drug importer programmes which may be relevant to a large proportion of BME women may be being overlooked.

Self-harm has been a focus of research and programmes in the female prison population. In 2010, women accounted for 47 per cent of all incidents of self-harm despite representing just 5 per cent of the total prison population (Ministry of Justice 2011). While the majority of self-harm incidents are carried out by White prisoners (HMIP 2009), there is little analysis of self-harm by race. A recent safety in custody statistics bulletin from the Ministry of Justice disaggregates self-harm by gender, age and time in prison but not ethnicity (Ministry of Justice 2011d). The limited research that has been conducted suggests self-harm among ethnic minority women may require a different response. For example, self-harm among BME women prisoners has been found to be associated with drug dependence but this is not the case for White women (Home Office 2003). Further, lower levels of self-harm among BME women does not necessarily equate to low levels of mental distress. In fact, in testing to measure psychological ill-health in prison, foreign national women prisoners scored higher than British women and men despite reporting fewer thoughts of self-harm (HMIP 2009).

In 2008, the CEDAW Committee expressed concern over the higher rates of mental illness and depression in ethnic minority women (CEDAW Committee 2008). BME women are more likely to be exposed to risk factors which may increase susceptibility such as debt, living in urban areas and feelings of marginalisation (HMIP 2009). Further, particular groups of women may respond to mental illness in different ways. Asian women, for instance, are up to three times more likely to commit suicide than other women (Husain 2006). BME women may also be subject to racial stereotyping within mental health services so that they are more likely to be diagnosed with certain illnesses than others (Mind 2010). Although based on analysis of BME women in the wider population, these risk factors are likely to be compounded for women offenders in the institutionally racist prison environment. Despite this, Lord Bradley's review of people with mental health problems in the criminal justice system (2009), which contains detailed analysis of the problems faced by particular groups (including ethnic minority groups and women), did not include any examination of the particular needs of ethnic minority women. Therefore while recommendations considered race and gender separately, the failure of the review to consider the ways in which race and gender intersect and interact, means that the specific mental health needs of BME women may be overlooked.

Communication and language barriers can make an intimidating environment such as police custody units, the court room or the prison estate even more confusing and isolating. This is often exacerbated for foreign national women who may have an increased fear of incarceration because of their perception or experience of the penal system in their home country (Fawcett Society 2009). Very few prison staff are bilingual, which is aggravated by the locality of female prison estates. In 2010, at Drake Hall Prison almost 50 per cent of prisoners were from a BME background compared with only 3 per cent of staff (HMIP 2009). Inspectorate research found that at most prisons there was insufficient translated material for women who did not speak English and very little use of phone interpretation services, even for confidential matters (HMIP 2010).This can lead to BME women being less able to seek help and can also lead to increased levels of depression.

Lack of family contact is a central issue for all women, particularly given the small number and locations of female prison estates. The average distance adult women in prison are held from home is 55 miles (Prison Reform Trust 2011). However, given the concentration of ethnic minority communities in cities, this distance is likely to be even greater for BME women meaning they are less likely to receive visits from their families and more likely to face difficulties when it comes to accessing resettlement support. For foreign national women, contact with family is even more difficult to sustain. Telephone calls may be prohibitively expensive and often difficult to arrange because of time differences (HMIP 2010). Difficulties ensuring adequate care for children from the time they are taken into police custody may also be compounded for certain ethnic minority groups. For example, more than half of Black African and Black Caribbean families in the UK are lone parent families compared to less than a quarter of White families and just over a tenth of Asian families (HMIP 2009).

Hamlyn and Lewis (2000) in their study into women's resettlement needs noted that BME women reported less choice in relation to the work they did in prison and were more likely to see prison work as a form of punishment. BME women are also more often employed in contract workshops while their White counterparts are more likely to be employed in jobs which offer skills training with vocational qualifications (Jacobson 2010). Both foreign national and BME women were less likely to know who to contact for help with resettlement issues than their White counterparts (HMIP 2010). Recent research commissioned by Clinks and the Prison Reform Trust found that some prison staff believed ethnicity to be irrelevant to the resettlement process, since no prisoner had ever brought their attention to the issue (Jacobson 2010).

Approximately one third of women prisoners lose their homes whilst in prison (Social Exclusion Unit 2002). For BME women this may be even more problematic, particularly given the acute housing shortages in urban areas where they are more likely to live and the problems BME women face accessing private sector and public housing (Chigwada-Bailey 2003, Gill and Banga 2008). This may also compound difficulties BME women encounter regaining custody of their children. For women from some ethnic minority groups, attitudes to offending within families and communities may result in additional stigma being attached to imprisonment which can also lead to difficulties accessing housing, support services and employment (Chigwada-Bailey 2003). Foreign national women may also endure additional challenges due to uncertain immigration status which will impact on the services they can access and can also result in women being held in custody beyond their release date. Organisations such as Women in Prison are working to build the capacity of local BME community groups to better meet the needs of women offenders upon their release back into the community.

Change from Within – the Need for a Representative Justice Sector

The responsiveness of the criminal justice system to the intersectional needs of BME women is also shaped by the composition of the system itself. The Gender Equality Duty and the Race Equality Duty (now replaced by the Public Sector Equality Duty) were seen as having the potential to improve the representativeness of the criminal justice system with employers required to undertake initiatives to encourage women, and in particular ethnic minority women, to move into areas of the sector where women are under-represented. However, while there have been some inroads at the lower levels of each of the criminal justice agencies, BME women remain under-represented, particularly at senior levels.

As of March 2010, there were no ethnic minorities in the Supreme Court, Court of Appeal or among Heads of Divisions. There was one ethnic minority female judge in the High Court and five ethnic minority women among 680 circuit court judges (Judiciary of England and Wales 2010). Within the police force, ethnic minority women make up just 0.26 per cent of Chief Inspectors, 0.1 per cent of superintendents and there is only one BME woman represented on ACPO (Home Office 2009). Women make up only 36 per cent of total prison service staff, with only seven per cent of these from an ethnic minority background (HM Prison Service 2009).

Notably, the probation service has a high proportion of female employees, including at senior levels. There are also no significant differences between male and female staff in terms of the representation of ethnic minority groups. This could suggest that workforces with a higher proportion of female staff are also likely to be more diverse in terms of the representation of other minority groups. According to the latest figures available at the time of writing, ethnic minority groups made up 12.9 per cent of total probation staff (Ministry of Justice 2007).

One of the significant problems in addressing under-representation is the lack of reliable statistics giving the full picture of the composition of criminal justice agencies. Frequently data is separately collated according to ethnicity and gender with no cross-tabulation of this information, so that BME women remain an invisible statistic. For example, research by the Judicial Diversity taskforce usefully demonstrates the current gender and ethnicity make-up of the legal professions and the Judiciary. However, there is no attempt to capture the intersection of race and gender so that efforts to increase judicial diversity are likely to overlook the distinct needs of these women (Ministry of Justice 2010). Compounding this data gap is the fact that information on ethnicity is often collected voluntarily which means the ethnicity of a large part of the sample may be unknown. In a Bar Council survey of practising barristers in 2009/10, 13.1 per cent of barristers did not disclose their ethnicity (Sauboorah 2011).

Experiences of discrimination are not uniform or homogenous but what is consistent is the lack of recognition of the intersectional discrimination on the grounds of sex and race which BME women are likely to face in criminal justice agencies. They will encounter the elements of institutional sexism which women face working in the male dominated culture which continues to exist across the criminal justice system (Fawcett Society 2009). However, they are also likely to face additional barriers to career development on the grounds of race. One female police officer stated:

> Through my service I have suffered racism as well as sexism, and have challenged the behaviour formally. This has taken a lot out of me. I do feel that as a Black officer and a female I have to work twice as hard as white officers in order to be accepted (Smee and Moosa, 2010, P31).

Research conducted on the views of staff from ethnic minority background working in the prison system found that covert and structural racism was the most widespread cause for concern (Prison Reform Trust 2006). Ethnic minority staff who feel isolated in workplaces where there are few ethnic minorities may be reluctant to report racial harassment, particularly when complaints are investigated by senior staff who are typically White. This is likely to be compounded for ethnic minority women who may have even less representation at senior levels, be even more marginalised and face both sexist and racist attitudes and practices in the 'boys club' network of the criminal justice sector (Smee and Moosa 2010).

While in-depth research on the experiences of BME women as practitioners in the criminal justice system is lacking, research that has been conducted with BME female police personnel revealed feelings of *invisibility* in terms of their capability and needs for career development while at the same time feeling highly *visible* in relation to scrutiny of their work and being treated through a lens of racialised sexual objectification (Puwar 2003).

While there have been attempts to improve diversity among entry level staff across criminal justice agencies, there has been a failure to address career progression and retention. Data suggests that there is a lower level of retention among ethnic minority staff. In 2007, 6.1 per cent of police officers who were dismissed or resigned in their first six months of service were ethnic minorities in comparison to a rate of 3.1 per cent among White officers (Bennetto 2009). The legal profession also reflects similar trends with the percentage of ethnic minorities and women who resigned from a sampling of law firms being higher than the percentage which was promoted (Black Solicitors Network 2008). There has been little analysis of how retention rates may differ between men and women from different ethnic minority groups but the scant data which has been collected suggests that the issue is even more significant for BME women. The National

Offender Management Service Diversity Review 2009/10 revealed that the highest leaving rate was among BAME females at approximately 5.5 per cent while the rate among BAME men was just over 3 per cent (HMIP 2011).

Experiences of racist practices and attitudes, such as over-policing towards family and community members may also deter women from seeking a career within the justice sector (Criminal Justice System Race Unit 2005). Community expectations may also affect the type of roles in which BME women seek employment. In the prison service, 30 per cent of Asian females were in administrative positions. In contrast, a quarter of Black females were in prison officer positions (HM Prison Service 2011).

Conclusion

This chapter has focused on the intersections of sexism and racism in BME women's lives, and how this illuminates the unique barriers they face as survivors of violence, offenders and as practitioners in the criminal justice system. Over the last decade, there have been some important policy developments to improve the responsiveness of the justice system. However, these have tended to build upon the experiences of ethnic minority men and White women, frequently rendering invisible the intersectional identities of BME women. Despite increased research and campaigning by BME women's organisations, mainstream policy responses have a propensity to focus on race *or* gender discrimination rather than considering how these forces interact and intersect with each other.

BME women's experiences of violence are frequently framed in 'cultural' terms by criminal justice agencies so that their needs and experiences are segregated from other women's experiences of violence. This leads to a focus on 'culture' or 'ethnicity' rather than the race *and* gender dimensions of violence against women. In contrast, BME women engaging with the justice system as offenders, often find their needs subsumed within general responses to women offenders and ignored in wider policy responses to racism within the prison system. Meanwhile, the experiences of BME women as practitioners in the criminal justice sector are frequently overlooked in attempts by policymakers to increase the diversity and responsiveness of the justice system.

The lack of policy focus on the experiences of BME women has resulted in a significant gap in the collection of disaggregated data to track and identify how different groups of women are affected by, and engage with, the criminal justice system. There is also evidence of reluctance to progress measures which would increase understanding of the intersectional discrimination faced by BME women. For example, Section 14 of the Equality Act 2010 prohibits direct discrimination on the basis of a combination of two protected characteristics. This combined discrimination law may have assisted criminal justice agencies (through an understanding and consideration of how discrimination can involve the unique combination of racism and sexism) to proactively prevent intersectional discrimination. However, the Coalition Government has decided not to take forward this provision.

The criminal justice system must change to recognise the ways in which differing forms of violence against women intersect (Thiara and Gill 2010). This necessitates a common understanding of the intersectional identity of BME women which informs policy-related discourse and responses across the criminal justice system. The challenge is to identify the specificities of BME women's experiences as survivors of violence, offenders and practitioners across the justice system, without reinforcing cultural stereotypes and while still locating these needs within wider strategies to address gender inequality and racism in the criminal justice system. Discrimination often operates most fiercely at the junction where different forms of prejudice intersect and it is in this context that the experiences and specific needs of BME women must be understood – not as an afterthought but as part of an integrated approach to gender justice.

References

All Party Parliamentary Group on Women in the Penal System. 2011. *Women in the penal system: Second report on women with particular vulnerabilities in the criminal justice system*, London: Howard League for Penal Reform.

Allen A. 2009. *Barriers to Application for Judicial Appointments Research*, prepared for the Judicial Appointments Commission, London: British Market Research Bureau.

Anitha, S. 2007. *DV Inquiry: Submission to Home Affairs Committee*, London: Imkaan.

Anitha, S. and Gill, A. 2009. Coercion, consent and the forced marriage debate in the UK. *Feminist Legal Studies* [Online] 17:165–184. Available at: http://www.ccrm.org.uk/images/docs/2.2acoercionandconsent.anithaandgill.2009.pdf [Accessed: 18 December 2011].

Association of Chief Police Officers. 2008. *Honour'-based violence strategy* [online]. Available at: http://www.acpo.police.uk/documents/crime/2008/200810CRIHBV01.pdf [Accessed: 20 December 2011].

Bennetto, J. 2009. Police and Racism: *What has been achieved 10 years after the Stephen Lawrence Inquiry Report*, London: Equality and Human Rights Commission.

Black Solicitor's Network. 2009. *Diversity League Table 2008, A Report from the Black Solicitors Network*. London: Black Solicitor's Network.

Brittain, E. 2005. *Black & minority ethnic women in the UK*. London: Fawcett Society.

Burman, E. 2003. 'Taking refuge? Domestic violence, "race" and asylum', *Asylum*, 13, 3.

Chakraborti, N. and Garland, J. 2003. 'Under-researched and overlooked: an exploration of the attitudes of rural minority ethnic communities towards crime, community safety and the criminal justice system', *Journal of Ethnic and Migration Studies,* 29, 3. 563–572.

Chantier C. Gangoli, G. and Hester M. 2009. Forced marriage in the UK: Religious, cultural, economic or state violence? *Critical Social Policy,* November 2009, Vol. 29 no. 4.587–612.

Chigwada-Bailey, R. 2003. *Black women's experiences of the criminal justice system. Race, gender and class: a discourse on disadvantage,* Second edition. Winchester: Waterside Press.

Committee on the Elimination of Discrimination against Women 2008. *Concluding Observations: United Kingdom of Britain and Ireland,* 41st session, CEDAW/C/GBR/CO/6, 18 July 2008.

Comic Relief 2010. *What are the key factors necessary to support government legislation to bring about abandonment of harmful traditional practices, with a focus on Female Genital Mutilation?* London: Comic Relief.

Corston, J. 2007. *The Corston Report: A report by Baroness Jean Corston of a review of women with particular vulnerabilities in the criminal justice system.* London: Home Office.

Coy, M., Kelly, L., Foord, J. 2009. *Map of Gaps 2,* Equality and Human Rights Commission & End Violence Against Women (EVAW) campaign, available at: http://www.endviolenceagainstwomen.org.uk/data/files/map_of_gaps2.pdf [Accessed: 15 May 2011].

Coy, M and Kelly L. (2010) *Islands in the stream: An evaluation of four London independent domestic violence advocacy schemes,* available at: www.cwasu. org [Accessed: 2 February 2012].

Crenshaw, K. 1992. Mapping the Margins, *Stanford Law Review,* Vol 43, 1241 – 1299.

Criminal Justice System Race Unit. 2005. *BME Communities' Expectations of Fair Treatment by the Criminal Justice System,* London: The Criminal Justice System Race Unit.

Crown Prosecution Service. 2011. *Violence against Women Crime Report 2010–11,* Management Information Branch, November 2011, available at: http://www.cps.gov.uk/publications/docs/CPS_VAW_report_2011.pdf [Accessed: 23 December 2011].

Department of Health. 2009. *The Bradley Report: Lord Bradley's report of people with mental health problems or learning disabilities in the criminal justice system,* London: Department of Health.

Edgar, K. 2010. *A Fair Response: developing responses to racist incidents that earn the confidence of black and minority ethnic prisoners,* London: Prison Reform Trust.

Equality and Human Rights Commission. 2010. *Stop and Think: A critical review of the use of stop and search powers in England and Wales.* Manchester: Equality and Human Rights Commission.

Fawcett Society Commission on Women and the Criminal Justice System 2009, *Engendering Justice – from Policy to Practice: Final report of the Commission on Women and the Criminal Justice System*, London: The Fawcett Society.

Fawcett Society Commission on Women and the Criminal Justice System. 2007. *Women and Justice*, London: The Fawcett Society.

Fawcett Society Commission on Women and the Criminal Justice System. 2006. *Justice and Equality*, London: The Fawcett Society.

Fawcett Society Commission on Women and the Criminal Justice System. 2004. *Commission on Women and the Criminal Justice System Report*, London: The Fawcett Society.

Female Prisoners Welfare Project (FPWP). 2011. Hibiscus Response to Breaking the Cycle: Effective Punishment, Rehabilitation and Sentencing of Offenders [online]. Available at: http://fpwphibiscus.org.uk/?p=758 [Accessed: 5 June 2011].

Fleetwood, J. 2011. 'Five Kilos – Penalties and Practice in the International Cocaine Trade' *British Journal of Criminology* Volume 51 Issue 2 March 2011.

Fountain J. Roy A, Anitha, S, Davies K Bashford, J and Patel, K. 2007. *Issues Surrounding the Delivery of Prison Drug Services in England and Wales with a focus on Black and Minority Ethnic Prisoners*, Centre for Ethnicity and Health, University of Central Lancashire: Centre for Ethnicity and Health.

Gelsthorpe, L. 2006. The experiences of female minority ethnic offenders: the 'other other', in *Race and Probation*, edited by S. Lewis, P. Raynor, D. Smith and A. Wardak, Devon: Willan Publishing.

Gelsthorpe, L. Sharpe, G and Roberts J. 2007. *Provision for Women Offenders in the Community*, London: Fawcett Society.

Gill A. and Banga, B. 2008. Black, minority and refugee women, domestic violence and access to housing, *Better Housing Briefing*. London: Race Equality Foundation. Available at: http://www.better-housing.org.uk/briefings/black-minority-ethnic-and-refugee-women-domestic-violence-and-access-housing [accessed: 5 June 2011].

Gill, A and Anitha, S, 2011. Forced Marriage: Introducing a social justice and human rights perspective, London: Zed Books.

Gill, A. 2010. Reconfiguring 'honour'-based violence as a form of gendered violence in *Honour, violence, women and Islam* edited by M. M. Idriss and T. Abbas. Abingdon: Routlege, 218–31.

Gittens, M. 2004. *What About Us: Black Women in Policing research paper,* Part 1, National Black Police Association Women's Group.

Hale, Lady B. 2011. *Equal Access to Justice in the Big Society*, Sir Henry Hodge Memorial Lecture. Available at: http://www.supremecourt.gov.uk/docs/speech_110627.pdf [Accessed: 3 July 2011].

Hamlyn, B. and Lewis, D. 2000. Women Prisoners: A Survey of Their Work and Training Experiences in Custody and on Release. *Home Office Research Study 208*. London: Home Office.

Harper, R. L., Harper, G. C. and Stockdale, J. E. 2002. The role and sentencing of women in drug trafficking crime. *Legal and Criminological Psychology*, 7: 101–114.

Her Majesty's Court Service, Home Office & Criminal Justice Service, 2008. *Specialist Domestic Violence Courts Review 2007-08: Justice with Safety.* [online]. Available at: http://www.crimereduction.homeoffice.gov.uk/dv/dv018a.pdf [Accessed: 20 May 2011].

Her Majesty's Prison Service. 2011. *Annual Staff Diversity Review 2009-10*, March 2011 Available at: http://www.hmprisonservice.gov.uk/assets/documents/10004C68diversity_review_09-10.pdf [Accessed: 20 May 2011].

Her Majesty's Inspectorate of Prisons (HMIP). 2005. *Parallel Worlds: A thematic review of race relations in prisons*, London: Home Office.

Her Majesty's Inspectorate of Prisons. 2006. *Foreign National Prisoners: A Thematic Review.* London: Home Office.

Her Majesty's Inspectorate of Prisons. 2009. *Race Relations in Prisons: Responding to Adult Women from Black and Minority Ethnic Backgrounds.* London:HMIP.

Her Majesty's Inspectorate of Prisons. 2009b. *Annual Report 2007-08*, London: The Stationery Office.

Her Majesty's Inspectorate of Prisons 2010. *Women in Prisons: A short thematic review*, London: HMIP.

Hester, M, Chantler, K. & Gangoli, G. 2008. *Forced marriage: the risk factors and the effect of raising the minimum age for a sponsor, and of leave to enter the UK as a spouse or fiancé(e)*, School for Policy Studies, University of Bristol, available at: http://www.bristol.ac.uk/sps/research/fpcw/vawrg/completed.shtml [Accessed: 30 December 2011].

Home Office. 2003. *The Substance Misuse Treatment Needs of Minority Prisoner Groups: Women, Young Offenders and Ethnic Minorities,* Home Office Development and Practice Report No. 8.

Home Office. 2008. *National Domestic Violence Delivery Plan: Annual Progress Report 2007/2008, October 2008*, London: Home Office.

Home Office. 2009. Police Service Strength England and Wales. [Online: 31 March 2009]. Available at: http://www.homeoffice.gov.uk/rds/pdfs09/hosb1309.pdf [Accessed: 20 May 2011].

Home Office 2011a. *Call to End Violence Against Women and Girls: Action Plan.* London: Home Office.

Home Office. 2011b. *Call to End Violence Against Women and Girls: Equality Impact Assessment*, London: Home Office.

Home Office 2011c. *Call to End Violence Against Women and Girls: Action Plan Progress Review.* London: Home Office, November 2011.

House of Commons, Home Affairs Committee 2011. Forced Marriage, HC 880, Eighth Report of session 2010–12 Report, Together with Formal Minutes, Oral and Written Evidence, London: TSO.

Husain, M. Waheed W. and Husain N. 2006. Self-harm in British South Asian women: psychosocial correlates and strategies for prevention. *Annals of General Psychiatry*, 5:7.

Izzidien, S. 2008. *I can't tell people what is happening at home: Domestic abuse within South Asian communities: the specific needs of women, children and young people*, London: NSPCC.

Jacobson, J. Phillips P and Edgar, K2010. *Double Trouble: Black, Asian and minority ethnic offenders' experiences of resettlement*, London: Clinks & Prison Reform Trust, November 2010.

Judiciary of England and Wales 2010, Annual Diversity Statistics, [Online: March 2010,]. Available at: http://www.judiciary.gov.uk/publications-and-reports/statistics/judges/annual-diversity-statistics/stats-annual-diversity-statistics-2010.htm?wbc_purpose=Basic&WBCMODE=PresentationUnpubli shed.

Kennedy, H. 1992. *Eve was Framed: Women and British Justice*. London: Vintage.

MacFarlane A. 2011. Statistical analysis of harmful practices against women in Roy, S. Ng, P. and Larasi, I. 2011. *The Missing Link: a joined up approach to addressing harmful practices in London*, London: Imkaan.

Macpherson, W. 1999. *The Stephen Lawrence Inquiry: Report of an Inquiry*, [online: February 1999] available at: *http://www.archive.officialdocuments. co.uk/document/cm42/4262/sli-00.htm* [Accessed: 17 May 2011].

MacKinnon, C.A. 1983. Feminism, Marxism, Method, and the State: Toward Feminist Jurisprudence, *Signs*, Vol. 8, No. 4, pp. 635–658.

Metropolitan Police Service 2010.*Female Genital Mutilation – MPS Project Azure*, Report: 8. 4 November 2010. Available at: http://www.mpa.gov.uk/committees/cep/2010/101104/08#h2005 [Accessed: 18 December 2011].

Mind. 2010. *Statistics 3: Race, culture and mental health* [online], available at: http://www.mind.org.uk/help/people_groups_and_communities/statistics_3_race_culture_and_mental_health [Accessed: 20 May 2011].

Ministry of Justice. 2007, *Human Resources Workforce Profile Report*, Issue 4 [online], available at: http://www.probation.homeoffice.gov.uk/files/pdf/Workforce%20Profile%20Report%202006%20Issue%204.pdf, [Accessed: 20 May 2011].

Ministry of Justice, 2008. *Race Review 2008, implementing race equality in prisons – five years on*, London: National Offender Management Service.

Ministry of Justice, 2009. *Statistics on Women and the Criminal Justice System*, London: Ministry of Justice.

Ministry of Justice. 2010. *Judicial Diversity Report [online]* available at: http://www.justice.gov.uk/downloads/publications/policy/moj/judicial-diversity-report-2010.pdf [Accessed: 20 May 2011].

Ministry of Justice. 2011a. *National Offender Management Service Population and Capacity Briefing for Friday 16/12/2011*, London: National Offender Management Service.

Ministry of Justice. 2011b. *Offender Management Statistics Quarterly Bulletin: April to June 2011*, London: Ministry of Justice.

Ministry of Justice. 2011c. *Offender Management Caseload Statistics 2010*, London: Ministry of Justice.

Ministry of Justice. 2011d. *Safety in Custody 2010 England and Wales*, London: Ministry of Justice.

Ministry of Justice. 2011e. *Legal Aid Reform: Scope Changes*, Equality Impact Assessment, Available at: http://www.justice.gov.uk/downloads/consultations/eia-scope-changes.pdf [Accessed: 18 May 2011].

National Offender Management Service. 2008. *Women Prisoners,* Prison Service Order 4800, 28 April 2008.

Norman, N. and Barron, J. 2011. *Supporting women offenders who have experienced domestic and sexual violence* [online Women's Aid Federation], available at: http://www.womensaid.org.uk/domestic_violence_topic.asp?section=0001000100220048&sectionTitle=Women+in+prison [Accessed: 20 December 2011].

Patel, P. 2008. Faith in the State? Asian Women's Struggles for Human Rights in the U.K., *Feminist Legal Studies [online]*, (2008) 16:9–36, Available at: http://www.ccrm.org.uk/images/docs/2.2acoercionandconsent.anithaandgill.2009.pdf [Accessed: 18 December 2011].

Prison Reform Trust. 2006. *Experiences of Minority Ethnic Employees in Prisons*, London: Prison Reform Trust.

Prison Reform Trust. 2011. *Bromley Briefings: Prison Factfile,* Available at: www.prisonreformtrust.co.uk , December 2011 [Accessed: 31 December 2011].

Puwar, N. 2003. *Pilot Research Project on the Barriers facing BME Female Police Personnel,* 21 September 2003.

Rai, D.K. & Thiara, R. 1997. *Redefining Spaces: The Needs of Black Women and Children in Refuge Support Service and Black Workers in Women's Aid,* Bristol: Women's Aid Federation of England.

Refuge, 2010. *Forced Marriage in the UK: A scoping study on the experience of women from Middle Eastern and North East African Communities*, London: Refuge.

Richie, B.1996. *Compelled to Crime: The Gender Entrapment of Black Battered Women*, New York: Routledge.

Rights of Women. 2010a. *Seeking Refuge? Domestic Violence, immigration law and 'no recourse to public funds,* London: Rights of Women.

Rights of Women. 2010b *Measuring Up? UK Compliance with international commitments on violence against women in England and Wales*, June 2010.

Roy, S. Ng, P. and Larasi, I. 2011. *The Missing Link: a joined up approach to addressing harmful practices in London*, London: Imkaan.

Rumgay, J. 2004. *When Victims Become Offenders: In Search of Coherence in Policy and Practice,* London School of Economics.

Sauboorah, J. 2011. *Bar Barometer: Trends in the Profile of the Bar, The General Council of the Bar of England and Wales,* Pilot statistical report, Bar Council,

March 2011. Available at: http://www.barcouncil.org.uk/assets/documents/ Bar%20Barometer,%20March%202011.pdf [Accessed: 18 May 2011].

Sentencing Council. 2012. *Drug Offences: Definitive Guideline,* Available at: http://sentencingcouncil.judiciary.gov.uk/docs/Drug_Offences_Definitive_ Guideline_final_(web).pdf [Accessed: 26 August 2012].

Sentencing Council. 2011a. *Drug Offences Guideline: Public Consultation,* [online: March 2011], Available at: http://sentencingcouncil.judiciary.gov. uk/docs/Drug_Offences_Guideline_Public_Consultation_.pdf [Accessed: 18 May 2011].

Sentencing Council. 2011b. *Annual Report and Financial Report 2010-2011,* [online]. Available at: http://sentencingcouncil.judiciary.gov.uk/docs/ Sentencing_Council_Annual_Report_2010-2011_web.pdf [Accessed: 19 December 2011].

Sentencing Council. 2011c. Drug 'mules': twelve case studies, *Analysis and Research Bulletins,* March 2011, [online], available at: http://sentencingcouncil. judiciary.gov.uk/docs/Drug_mules_bulletin.pdf [Accessed: 19 December 2011].

Shah S, Plugge EH, Douglas N. 2011. Ethnic differences in the health of women prisoners. *Public Health.* 2011 June; 125(6):349–56.

Siddiqui, H. 2008. "Making the Grade? Meeting the challenge of tackling violence against ethnic minority women", *Seeing Double – Race and Gender in Ethnic Minority Women's Lives,* London: Fawcett Society.

Smee, S. and Moosa, Z. 2010. *Realising Rights: Increasing Ethnic Minority Women's Access to Justice,* London: The Fawcett Society.

Social Exclusion Unit. 2002. *Reducing Reoffending by ex-prisoners,* London.

Southall Black Sisters and End Violence against Women Coalition. 2011. Ending Violence against Black and Minority Ethnic Women and Girls: What BME women want: 10 key actions for a safer world, [online campaign leaflet], available at: http://www.endviolenceagainstwomen.org.uk/data/files/take_action_on_ safety_for_bme_women_jan_2011.pdf [Accessed: 19 December 2011].

Stanko B. 2010. *Rape Review – Understanding attrition in rape allegations in London* [online presentation] Available at: http://www.unb.ca/fredericton/arts/ centres/mmfc/_resources/pdfs/12stanko.pdf [Accessed: 22 December 2011].

Stanko, B. 2007. *The attrition of rape cases in London: A Review,* London: Metropolitan Police Service.

Steel N., Blakeborough L. and Nicholas, S. 2011. *Supporting high-risk victims of domestic violence: a review of Multi-Agency Risk Assessment Conferences (MARACs)* Research Report 55 [Home Office: online], available at: http:// www.homeoffice.gov.uk/publications/science-research-statistics/research- statistics/crime-research/horr55/horr55-report?view=Binary [Accessed 20 December 2011].

Stephen-Smith, S. 2008. The POPPY Project, *Detained: Prisoners with no crime, Detention of trafficked women in the UK,* London: Eaves.

The joint Home Office and Foreign and Commonwealth Office Forced Marriage Unit www.fco.gov.uk/fmu

Thiara, R and Gill A. 2009. *Violence Against Women in South Asian Communities: Issues for Policy and Practice*, London: Jessica Kingsley Publishers.

Thiara, R.K, and Roy, S. 2010. *Vital Statistics: the experiences of BAMER women & children facing violence & abuse*, London: Imkaan.

Walby, S. Armstrong, J. and Strid, S. 2010. *Physical and Legal Security and the Criminal Justice System: A Review of Inequalities*, London: Equality and Human Rights Commission.

Wedderburn, D. 2000. *Justice for women: the need for reform ; the report of the Committee on Women's Imprisonment*, London : Prison Reform Trust.

Williams, R. 2011. Female circumcision prevention post abolished by government. *The Guardian* [online 30 March 2011] Available at: http://www.guardian.co.uk/society/2011/mar/30/female-circumcision-prevention-post-abolished [Accessed: 18 December 2011].

Women's National Commission. 2009. *Still we rise: report from WNC focus groups to inform the cross-government consultation "Together we can end violence against women and girls"*. London: Women's National Commission.

Chapter 2

Multi-faithism and the Gender Question: Implications of Government Policy on the Struggle for Equality and Rights for Minority Women in the UK

Pragna Patel

In the UK, historically, the struggle for the human rights of black and minority women, especially South Asian women also involved a robust challenge to the politics of multiculturalism which although useful in confronting racism, was problematic in respect of struggles for gender equality (Patel and Siddiqui 2009). However, in more recent times, this struggle has developed under the shadow of the politics of multi-faithism, a regressive development at the heart of which lies the use of religion as the main basis for social identity and mobilisation.

The revival of religion as the main marker of identity has led to a greater accommodation of religion within state institutions and in the wider public culture; reflecting a number of global and national economic, political and social trends. The result is a diminishing welfare state and an increase in the de-secularisation of public spaces, which has in turn led to a corresponding rise in the communalisation (community groups and civil society organising solely around religious identities) of minority communities.

This shift from 'multiculturalism' to 'multi-faithism' is a process which actually started in the aftermath of the Rushdie affair, but has accelerated under successive government agendas on 'Cohesion', 'Integration' and the 'Big Society'. In the process, a complex web of social, political and cultural processes have been reduced by both State and community leaderships into purely religious values. But the pressure to characterise communities primarily through the prism of religion has compounded a problematic assumption at the heart of multi-faithism: that minorities are both easily defined and homogeneous. Characterising minorities (and, indeed, the majority) according to 'faith', confines identity as well as communal institutions, within narrow, static categories that neither reflect nor serve their constituent members, especially vulnerable sub-groups such as women and sexual minorities.

Multi-faithism has led to the emergence of the most reactionary, patriarchal and conservative if not fundamentalist religious identity politics and has entrenched the power of so-called religious leaders, who seek to monopolise and control local resources and constituencies even though they do not represent the people on whose behalf they claim to act.[1] This political use of religion has involved the appropriation of progressive and secular language and spaces created through struggles for democracy and equality. For instance, religious fundamentalists and 'moderates' alike are engaged in substituting the demand for equality with the demand for 'religious literacy'. That is, the demand for the State to recognise the supposedly 'authentic' theological values and traditions of minorities, but not the recognition of the diverse, outward-looking, often conflicting, syncretic, liberal, cultural, political, religious and secular traditions, including feminist traditions, within a community. In doing so, many religionists subvert the concepts of human rights, equality and discrimination so that they are interpreted to be compatible with dogmatic or conservative interpretations of religious values. It is a demand which elements of the left are all too willing to accommodate. Needless to say, this development has very specific consequences for all progressive struggles but especially for those waged by minority women, whose bodies have become the battleground for the control of community representation.

This chapter examines the impact of de-secularisation in public institutions such as the welfare and legal system on South Asian women, especially on their struggles for exit options in the face of violence and abuse. I seek to show the complex ways in which both the State, the religious right and often even progressive left forces have (ab)used concepts of 'community' and 'autonomy' to silence internal dissent and to disconnect feminist struggles from legitimate claims about the universality of human rights.

Religion in the Cohesion and the Big Society Agendas

The notion of 'faith communities' was vigorously promoted by New Labour in the late 90s as it sought to move away from the multicultural project and instead embrace religion as an important component of its race and regeneration policies. Civil unrest in the north of England in 2001, 9/11 and the London bombings in particular, gave New Labour the impetus it needed to pursue an assimilationist approach that centred around the promotion of so called 'British values' but which paradoxically included promoting a multi-faith agenda. In other words, one product of the 'War on Terror' was the State's deliberate pursuit of contradictory domestic policies in the name of cohesion and integration: to create more 'moderate' versions of Islam and to promote this and other religious identities within public institutions.

---

1   The Women Against Fundamentalism (WAF) definition of religious fundamentalism is adopted here, meaning modern political movements which use religion to gain or consolidate power over communities and resources. I do not mean personal religious observance, which may be considered a matter of individual choice.

Ignoring criticisms about structural inequality and institutionalised racism which fuelled the unrest (see Bradford District Race Review Panel 2001), New Labour embarked on a regeneration programme that involved funding faith-based schools and City Academies, introduced laws against incitement to religious hatred[2] and generally promoted inter-faith forums and provided State funding for faith-based projects. Faith leaders were encouraged to get more involved in shaping public policies at all levels and in delivering local services on a range of issues. Often, this has amounted to direct State sponsorship of religious right and fundamentalist organisations, most visibly but not only Muslim religious right institutions, that often masqueraded as 'moderates'. Many so called moderates such as the Hindu Forum of Britain, the Hindu Council and the Muslim Council of Great Britain used the space opened up by New Labour's cohesion and faith agenda to impose highly politicised definitions of religious identity and to put themselves forward as the 'authentic' voice and guardians of that identity. Their aim is to assume communal authority and leadership, particularly where this involves control of female sexuality and family values. Many also are sympathetic to, or have links with and foster, religious fundamentalist movements abroad.[3]

SBS was the first black and minority women's organisation to critique New Labour's faith agenda. Historically our work has highlighted how social policy development on race discrimination has always excluded women and other powerless sub-groups from definitions of 'community'. SBS therefore has a long history of interrogating aspects of the multicultural approach for its effects in marginalising women, an important reminder of the long and hard struggles that have been waged to compel the State to support black and minority women's demands for protection from State institutions in the face of violence and abuse (see Sahgal 1990). For a short while, it appeared as if some progress had been made when in 1999, Mike O'Brien the then Home Minister who led the Forced Marriage Working Group, famously announced that "multiculturalism cannot be an excuse for moral blindness" (Siddiqui 2003). Since then however, a dual and contradictory approach to minority women has been evident.

On the one hand, there is greater recognition of specific forms of violence such as honour-based violence and forced marriage together with improved legal remedies and practices, although it has to be said that such recognition is not without its problems since the issues are increasingly tied to the 'clash of civilisations'

---

2   Racial and Religious Hatred Act 2006

3   See Awaaz (2006) document *'The Islamic Right – Key Tendencies'*, which traces the Muslim Council of Britain's roots to the long standing Islamic Right political party – the Jamaati-I-islami (JI) from the Indian Sub-Continent. Awaaz no longer exists but it was a UK based secular network of organisations and individuals set up to monitor religious hatred in South Asia and the UK. Amongst other things, it researched the links between so called 'moderate' Hindu organisations such as the Hindu Forum of Britain and the Hindu Council UK and Hindu Right organisations in India responsible for fomenting hatred, violence and genocide against Muslims.

discourse that pits secular human rights as 'western' values against the 'cultural backwardness' of Muslims and other minorities, and, to a growing right wing, anti-immigration agenda. On the other hand, the increasing de-secularisation of public spaces in tandem with the assault on the welfare state, not only threatens to erode the gains that have been made but it also actually threatens the very survival of secular feminist projects like that of SBS. The most famous example of this was the successful battle for survival waged by SBS in the face of local authority withdrawal of funds in the name of 'cohesion' and 'integration'.[4]

The promotion of the faith agenda has since accelerated under the Coalition government with implementation of the notion of the Big Society and the localism agenda. In fact Baroness Warsi, the then Minister without Portfolio and Co-Chairman of the Conservative Party has, without any sense of irony, pursued the matter with an evangelical zeal. She has made it clear that unlike the previous government, her party does do God.[5]

Baroness Warsi has campaigned against the secular nature of the UK's public culture by recasting religious groups as a besieged minority: she has made it clear that a Conservative government will need to "reverse the damage done by Labour's pursuit of a secular agenda since 1997". More recently, she has condemned what she and others have described as 'aggressive' or 'militant' forms of secularism and likened it to Nazism:

> For me one of the most worrying aspects about this militant secularisation is that at its core and in its instincts it is deeply intolerant. It demonstrates similar traits to totalitarian regimes – denying people the right to a religious identity because they were frightened of the concept of multiple identities.

Warsi argues further for the: "need to give faith a seat at the table in public life ... intolerant secularisation has to be held back by reaffirming the religious foundations on which our societies are built" (cited in Wintour 2012).

Through successive governments then, the British State has vigorously promoted a religious or faith-based agenda based on the assumption that secularism is incompatible with religious authenticity. Pursuit of the faith-based

---

4 In 2007, Ealing Council decided to cut funding to SBS on the grounds that specialist services for black and minority women worked against the interest of 'equality', 'diversity' and 'cohesion'. It argued that the very name Southall Black Sisters and the existence of the organisation was unlawful under the Race Relations Act 1976 because it excluded women in the majority community. SBS was therefore seen as discriminatory and divisive. SBS fought a political campaign against closure and on 18th July 2008 brought a successful legal challenge against Ealing Council at the High Court in London, where our right to exist as a secular specialist provider of domestic violence services to black and minority women was affirmed.

5 Speech given by Baroness Warsi at the Conservative Party conference in Manchester, 5th October 2009.

agenda is partly to do with a perceived need to appease conservative religious leaderships within those communities, and partly in the belief that the right to manifest religion signifies equal treatment of minorities – a belief shared by many equality and human rights institutions across Europe and amongst considerable sections of the so called progressive left movements. Demands for separate faith schools, personal dress codes, blasphemy laws and personal laws to cover marriage, divorce and child custody have all been taken to represent a strong counter hegemonic voice to 'western' secular cultural impositions, and to that extent minority rights are increasingly and almost exclusively linked to the right to manifest religion. Our concern at SBS is that, in the process, the State is unable to distinguish between valid or legitimate demands for equality and those that simply mask inequality, promote other forms of intolerance and uniformity of religious identity. The space to manifest religion has grown but the space to be free from religion, especially within social institutions from which the most vulnerable sub groups seek guarantees of liberty and equality, is shrinking daily.

Religion, Autonomy and Women's Rights

In recent feminist discussions on intersectionality[6] and violence against women, it has become fashionable to talk of the intersection of religion and gender and refer to the need to develop a feminist response that is sensitive to the growth of religious values especially in the light of anti-Muslim racism (see, for example, Braidotti 2008).[7] Yet questions of which social and political forces are at play in demands for greater accommodation of religious identity and who defines religious values and for what purpose, are rarely considered. Instead, notions of 'community' and 'autonomy' – the cornerstone of feminist analysis, embodied in campaigns for freedom, especially in the private sphere, are being used to shore up a regressive multi-faith framework. The negative interface of religion with gender power relations is the most overlooked category in such intersectional analysis and yet this precise failure contributes to and perpetuates experiences of marginalisation and powerlessness amongst vulnerable minority women.

---

6   Intersectionality as a theoretical concept was first introduced by Kimberly Crenshaw (1991). But the theoretical framework for understanding race provided by Nira Yuval Davis and Floya Anthias (see for example, Anthias & Yuval-Davis, 1992) also helped us to articulate the complex connections between race, nationality, class and gender: their analysis encouraged a simultaneous anti-racist and anti-sexist gaze at all forms of social relations that reproduce power and powerlessness. Above all, they argued for developing a politics of solidarity across feminist and anti-racist struggles.

7   Rosi Braidotti and other feminists, including Saba Mahamood and Sarah Bracke, call for an adjustment in feminist thinking so that it embraces the new wave of religious mobilisations. For a critique of this perspective see Dhaliwal (2012).

Recent responses to demands for the accommodation of religious female dress codes provide an insight into how the question of female 'autonomy' or 'agency', especially for Muslim women, has been addressed. In 2002, for instance, we witnessed the case of Shabina Begum, a 14 year old Muslim girl, who wanted to wear the *jilbab* (full ankle length dress) rather than a *salwar kameez* (long tunic and trousers) and head scarf, which conformed to her secondary school's uniform policy. The school refused her permission to wear the *jilbab* as a result of which she took legal action against the school for breaching her human right to manifest her religion and to an education as she was effectively barred from attending school unless she complied with its uniform policy.

In 2006, the House of Lords (now known as the Supreme Court) delivered a judgment stating that Shabina's rights to manifest her religion or belief and her right not to be denied an education had not been violated, and that any infringement was necessary and proportionate for the protection and well being of the wider school community. The judges argued that the school had a carefully considered uniform policy which took account of 'mainstream' Muslim opinion in that it had taken advice from Muslim parents, community leaders and other Islamic theological experts. The Court praised the school for showing respect for Muslim beliefs in a way that was 'inclusive, unthreatening and uncompetitive.'

However, the Court's decision was also based on an understanding of the political context in which Shabina came to exercise her so called 'agency'. In the course of the judgment, the Court alluded to the fact that Shabina's challenge had been motivated by those who sought to impose a political religious identity on women and young girls at the school. Specific mention was made of the fact that in all her dealings with the school, Shabina was represented by her older brother who appeared to be part of an extreme right Muslim political group. At one point, the group held demonstrations outside the school, protesting interestingly, not against the school uniform policy, but against the education of Muslim children in secular schools! The demonstrations had the effect of intimidating other Muslim girls who complained of harassment and interference from the group. The Court emphasised the fact that the other Muslim girls did not support Shabina's demand, fearing that if she was successful, they too would be pressurised into wearing a *jilbab*. They feared the deep divisions that would be created between those who are perceived to be pious and those who are perceived to have lost their religious way. They were afraid that if they did not conform they would be labelled 'bad' Muslim girls. The Court recognised that the school had in fact carefully balanced the need to respect its diverse population with the need to enable those who do not wish to conform to a religious identity, to do so without fear of repercussions.

Whilst there is much to commend the overall judgment and in particular its nuanced approach to religious identity and religious fundamentalism,[8] in my view, there is a case for arguing that the Court did not go far enough in disrupting

---

8   Baroness Hale's analysis was influenced by Nira Yuval Davis and Gita Sahgal, whose 1992 publication *Refusing Holy Orders* was quoted.

multicultural assumptions about how community values are represented, since what was also legitimised is the strategy adopted by the school in pursuit of multi-faithism and social cohesion. However, since the ruling, the judgment has been criticised from a so called 'feminist' perspective for not going far enough in the other direction. The Court has been accused of not taking account of or 'respecting' Muslim women's 'autonomy'. For example, in a recent book on feminist re-interpretations of classic legal judgments, Mahelia Malik (2010) has re-written the judgment from a perspective which argues that the Court's reasoning was not sufficiently context sensitive in that it failed to recognise that what Shabina was doing was exercising her autonomy and choice as a young Muslim female in an environment where Muslims as a minority are constantly demonised and discriminated against and that the Court should have shown sensitivity to the choices that she made by affording her flexibility in how she defined herself at that particular moment.

Whilst correct to locate the case in the context of heightened anti-Muslim racism, Malik fails to mention other equally pernicious political developments which also formed the context in which Shabina made her challenge. She conveniently skips the important fact that Shabina's choice of identity was no individual act of agency but was profoundly shaped by political processes that involve the privileging of a political religious (Islamist) identity over others. In her re-written judgment, there is only passing reference to the political demonstration and contestations that took place in and outside the school ('some elements of confrontation'), and she downplays Shabina's brother's 'involvement', when in fact, it was her brother who was determining what was necessary to comply with Muslim beliefs. Although in the commentary to the 'feminist' judgment, it is claimed that Shabina's brother was acting on behalf of their widowed mother who did not speak English, it is clear from the facts that Shabina's brother did not just confine his role to that of an interpreter relaying their mother's views and wishes but instead appeared to act as his sister's guardian. Most crucially, Malik fails to examine how the religious identity that Shabina adopted was perceived as threatening and detrimental by the Muslim girls themselves. Malik dismisses the fact that the majority of other Muslim girls of the same age as Shabina wanted no change in the dress codes, presumably because what they had achieved in respect of the school uniform policy had been developed through their own complex negotiations and battles with their parents and community for some degree of autonomy. In Malik's analysis, unlike that of Baroness Hale's judgment in the House of Lords, the voices of a group of Muslim young women are nowhere to be heard. In doing so, she sacrifices the demand for gender equality for the sake of the right to religious freedom. She asserts that the fears expressed by the Muslim girls should not lead to 'State coercion of those young women who wear religious dress out of free choice' (Malik 2010, 342). It is true that some women do veil out of choice, but the facts of this case do not support such a conclusion. Ultimately, Malik has nothing to say about the lack of choice or the fear and discrimination that would have been the lot of the many young and vulnerable Muslim girls for whom non-compliance would have been perceived as a transgression from their 'faith' which can carry real consequences. She merely suggests vague 'social policy measures' aimed at men in the community who coerce women but which make no sense in the absence of State accountability in respect of guaranteeing protection to the most vulnerable. Ultimately there is a failure to recognise that it was the many young Muslim girls who gave a negative meaning to the dress code that Shabina wanted to adopt and not the Court itself, as Malik (2010) misleadingly asserts.[9]

Malik's response is typical of the way in which all too often, discussions of Muslim female agency is removed from the increasingly transnational religious political and social movements that give rise to the kind of demands that Shabina was making. The critical point is that Shabina's agency was constrained and framed through the position of her brother who wished to make a wider statement about the secular nature of a State run school. His actions suggest the unfolding of a bigger power struggle for the control of female sexuality and women's freedoms and rights more generally, which is central to the religious right project. This is the point that the other Muslim girls so readily recognised.

In a context where religious identity is increasingly defining new social relations, demands for the right to exercise religious freedom are assumed to be legitimate and progressive and any ethical questioning of the nature and implications of such demands is frequently suspended. As has been observed by Sukhwant Dhaliwal (2012):

> ... it is religion and forms of piety rather than questions of women's rights and sexuality that constitutes subalternity and counter hegemony especially because minority religions are characterised as derided and contained. Pious women in particular are presented as out of (imperially imposed) time, posing a significant challenge to the feminist project and to the dominant narrative where rights are premised on a secular language and the notion of a secular public sphere.

Ultimately, such 'pious' forms of so called feminism seek to align themselves with, rather than challenge, religious right movements which in the UK have increasingly dominated the 'anti-racist' or 'anti-imperialist' counter voice: the goal being to bring secularism into disrepute as a 'western' concept and to restrict minority women's exit options from oppressive patriarchal family practices.

---

9   'It is not for this House or the school to impose an external, unilateral and pejorative meaning upon the religious dress she has chosen' (Malik 2010, 344).

The Southall Black Sisters Study: Cohesion Faith and Gender

In 2009/2010, SBS conducted an exploratory study to map the impact of these shifts in government policy (Patel and Sen 2010). We sought to shed light on whether or not the revival of religion constitutes the counter-voice of the many black and minority women who seek our assistance or helps them to secure their rights in contexts where they are vulnerable and marginalised.

The study came out of the concrete experiences of the withdrawal of funding for services for black and minority women provided by SBS. This funding crisis signified the start of the de-secularisation of public policy and of relations between the state and ethnic minorities in the UK. What began as a local issue unfolded into a struggle for the defence of progressive secular spaces and for the very meaning of equality itself.

In-depth interviews were conducted with 21 women from different religious backgrounds. The results showed that the vast majority were acutely critical of aspects of their tradition, culture and religion for perpetuating gender inequality, discrimination and violence. Although most were believers and often turned to religion for spiritual sustenance, none expressed any sense of belonging to a faith-based community. Their responses blasted a hole in the assumption that those who have limited access to or interaction with broader society identify with their particular faith communities.

All but one woman made a clear differentiation between believing and being part of a 'faith community'; they viewed religion as a matter of personal choice or belief, rather than the basis of a social identity. Most (n=19) also located themselves along a multiple axes of difference, according to age, gender, ethnicity and nationality. When asked what aspects of their identity that they felt most strongly about religion was not amongst the top three. The majority identified themselves according to their current geographical locality, or their country or region of origin, or primarily described themselves as a woman or as a mother. Indeed, the most significant aspect of how women chose to identify themselves was largely determined by their experiences of gender discrimination and oppression. Another significant finding is that for many, their common humanity was also their main source of identification. Perhaps this is not surprising in the context of their experiences of abuse, violence and marginalisation which left them feeling stripped of their humanity, but it is deeply significant in the current context.

> Islam does not force anything on anyone so why should those who live within it force others? I want my children to know what it says in Islam. The main principle is to live by humanity, They should not look at colour. The poet Iqbal – our greatest poet said, whether black or white, poor or rich, old or young, we should all obey Allah. If there is no difference for Allah, why do we bring about difference? I like his (Iqbal's) idea of unity for all human beings.

Far from inspiring confidence and trust, faith groups evoked a range of fears about religion and faith-based organisations. Every single woman was acutely aware of the gendered impact of religious dogma and expressed very strong negative sentiments of mistrust and alienation from faith-based leaders.

> Because of izzat (honour), I was not allowed to live in Pakistan. I was told to get married. Because of izzat. I was told to sacrifice myself for the sake of my family. What am I, a sacrificial goat? They told me it was my religious duty.

They strongly opposed religious prescriptions against women, and feared abuse of power by religious leaders, including sexual harassment and exploitation. Much of their rejection sprang from actual experiences of seeking protection and help from religious leaderships in the UK or in countries of origin. Women also talked about the potentially divisive impact of religion by recounting personal experiences or stories of war, divisions, hostility and problems caused by the politics of communalism when entrenched in social institutions.

> We came to educate our children but if we have our own separate schools then we will fight on the basis of faith. This is what happened in history. Our leaders have separated India from Pakistan. The poor have suffered. Look at the state of the countries – India, Pakistan and Iran – this is terrible! We will have segregated communities.

Although many women were practicing believers, none were involved in the management or decision making processes of the religious institutions that they often attended. Their lack of power also explained their scepticism about religious institutions which many saw as corrupt, exploitative and unaccountable places. They recognised religious institutions not simply as places of religious worship but as profoundly reactionary political and gendered spaces.

> Doesn't make a difference if there are men or women trustees – they feel superior to devotees… [I] don't know why they have to feel so superior. It is the public that gives them their status. The politics of these places is very dirty. Very corrupt – that's the word – corruption. If anyone rebels against their ideas they would be against that persons – they never encourage women to divorce until it happens to their own daughter.

Many talked of internal religious, class and caste divisions and discrimination, and of rifts and fights between rival factions of trustees of religious institutions seeking to assert their power and authority and/or financial gain. The lack of transparency and accountability of religious institutions only increased their general distrust of faith based organisations and their ability to address the needs of women.

I would like my views represented by women not by community and religious leaders. What would others know about women's issues? We are struggling to fit into this country and community. If religious leaders bring their laws where can we run to? There will be more suicides, depression, castaways, conversions. It would be the biggest disaster.

Perhaps the most striking feature of the lived reality of the women interviewed is that none saw their identity as fixed and unchanging. Their narratives demonstrated how they occupied spaces at the intersection of a number of cultural and religious and non-religious traditions. Their practices and traditions were syncretic and undogmatic and it was precisely such fluidity that created moments of happiness in otherwise relentlessly difficult and traumatic circumstances.

Tomorrow I go to celebrate Valentine's Day. Islam says we shouldn't dance. I used to get awards for dancing. I love celebrating Valentine's Day. I will wear red clothes and red lipstick and get a red rose from my husband. I wear lots of make up and perfume. I also love celebrating Christmas and Easter. These are small pieces of happiness.

Women in this study negotiated and contested their identities on a daily basis. This is precisely why they all cherished the secular space provided by SBS which they experienced as an empowering space that enabled them to gain access to other ideas, traditions and cultures and most importantly, a space that unlocked their access to secular State services, which many regarded as the final safety net in their struggle to assert their fundamental human rights and freedoms.

These findings show that whilst religion is relevant to the lives of vulnerable and marginalised minority women, they also want real autonomy and choice in how they seek to define themselves and live their lives. The women in the SBS research wanted to be free from inhuman and degrading treatment, valued their right to life, to choice in marriage, to privacy, to freedom of expression, to an education and to a fair trial. They were adamant that if religious leaders/institutions take control and become providers of services, this will close down the rich, creative, syncretic, fluid and dynamic expressions of identity that they have struggled to create: replacing it with conservative, illiberal and fundamentalist identities that will subjugate them to the gate-keepers of so called authentic religious traditions.

Religious Laws and the Family

In the domestic arena, the State has allowed the demand for freedom *of* religion to overshadow and undermine the demand for freedom *from* religion which comes mainly from marginalised and vulnerable groups within minority communities like the women who seek the support of SBS. This is nowhere more evident than in the attempts by religionists to forge a social contract with the State that recognises the right for minorities to govern their internal (mainly family) affairs in accordance with religious laws. Unsurprisingly, in an economic context where controlling time consuming litigation and slashing the legal aid budget is an overriding objective, the demand for religious personal laws to govern marriages or family matters for example, has gained support from prominent judicial and political figures.[10]

SBS has nevertheless urged the State, including the judiciary and the legal system, to exercise extreme caution in seeking to involve religious leaders and institutions in legal arbitration on family matters. We believe that it will signal a mixed message and greatly undermine the gains that have been made so far by minority women.

Without a shadow of a doubt, over the last three decades, secular black and minority women's projects across the UK have been the driving force behind successful campaigns and services for women who experience gender-based violence including specific cultural and religious forms of harm within black and minority communities. By establishing advice centres, counselling services and refuges, black and minority women have challenged community norms that reproduce a culture of denial and silence. In the process they have developed the analysis and the experience needed to challenge State and community practices that justify and excuse violence against women. Despite often operating in contexts of great hostility, these efforts have led to new laws, improved legal interventions and helped to create statutory guidelines on a range of issues such as domestic violence, honour related crimes, forced marriage and child abuse. It is this work, not the work of religious and community leaders or institutions that has led to increased awareness and to progress in respect of black and minority women's human rights.

Yet in spite of this history of achievement, support for and engagement with religious forums such as the Muslim Arbitration Forum (MAT) is gathering pace. On the face of it, formalised religious forums of arbitration such as the MAT present themselves as professional bodies that seek to adhere to formal legal rules of engagement and to non-discriminatory principles. But what they are, in fact, seeking to do is to create the conditions for the establishment of parallel legal systems based on divine law. Quite apart from the fact that in the UK, there is no substantive evidence that the majority of Muslims including minority women want religious arbitration in respect of personal and family matters, we know from women's experiences of formal and informal religious arbitration systems that they are gender biased and discriminatory (Bano 2007).

The respondents in the SBS study strongly opposed any religious arbitration in family matters as they believe that religion inherently discriminates against

---

10   See, for example, a speech given by the Lord Chief Justice of England and Wales, Lord Phillips, at the East London Muslim Centre on 3rd July 2008, endorsing the use of sharia laws in martial disputes. Available at http://www.matribunal.com/downloads/LCJ_speech.pdf. Accessed 5.4.2012

women and can never guarantee their equality or their well being. Most expressed considerable fear of religious authority which they regarded as a continuation of the community collusion that they experience when seeking to address problems of violence and oppression.

> I would never go to a temple or gurdwara for help. I wouldn't feel happy about talking about myself. I feel they would judge me ... I couldn't trust them to keep things confidential ... I come to SBS to share my innermost feelings. I have never been anywhere else. I couldn't go to a gurdwara or temple or masjid. I would rather die than go there.

> There is no need for religious laws. Because if you look at the Hindu religion, we had things like sati [immolation of widows]. Everyone has the right to live. Hindu religion will never treat women equally. Hinduism says that a husband is like a God and not to answer back ... Not right. Everyone should be treated equally in law.

Domestic Violence and the MAT

A look at how the MAT works suggests that their fears are not misplaced. The MAT is unequivocal in its overall aim which is to resolve civil disputes in accordance with 'Islamic Sacred Laws'.[11] In respect of family matters, this means reconciling conflicting parties for the sake of upholding family or religious values, even where there is evidence of abuse and violence. Current practices show that the MAT is dealing with family matters in ways which are at best profoundly discriminatory against women and children and, at worst, place their lives at risk. One particularly disturbing practice is the MAT's active involvement in criminal proceedings on domestic violence, despite stating that it is unable to deal with criminal offences: it has used its position of power to persuade the CPS to drop charges and to encourage women to reconcile with abusive partners.[12] There is also evidence to show that the MAT has undermined the legal rights of women in other ways. In one case involving inheritance of family property following the death of parents, a woman was given less than her brothers because religious law deemed that she should be dependent on her brothers for financial support (see One Law for All 2010, 19).

These cases suggest that the sole purpose of the MAT is to keep the family intact at any cost without reference to critical questions of protection and the safeguarding of human rights. This is of course the reality of most women's experiences of religious forums. More often than not, women are prevented from obtaining a divorce; their experiences of abuse are denied or minimised and they

---

11   See http://www.matribunal.com. Accessed 2.5.2012
12   See http://www.matribunal.com/cases_family.html. Accessed 1.5.2012

are blamed or told to try harder to make their marriage work. In other cases, where separation is granted, they are pressurised into giving up their children in order to safeguard the religious identity of their children. Both fly in the face of established good practice in cases of domestic violence and as such could amount to the violation of women's human rights in which the State by its acquiescence is implicated.

Forced Marriage

Similar problems abound in respect of approaches to forced marriage. In the MAT report *Liberation from Forced Marriages* (MAT, undated) the practice of forced marriage is defined as a 'cultural' practice that needs to be distinguished from 'Islamic' values. However, the problem with this approach is that it fails to acknowledge the perception and reality of those who are forced into a marriage, often through a combination of interchangeable cultural and religious norms and practices. The report distinguishes between 'appropriate free will marriage' and 'inappropriate free will marriage', which clearly gives a license to 'judges' and 'scholars' of Islam to determine the 'Islamic' values that in their view should underpin a marriage, which may nevertheless be oppressive and abusive for women and sexual minorities.

SBS is of the view that the aim of the MAT is to present itself as a legitimate mediator on this issue, it is an attempt to oust the position of feminist organisations that have historically campaigned on forced marriage, demanding accountability from the very people who now seek to preside over such cases. It is highly revealing that the report makes no mention of the need to refer to women's organisations with an established track record in assisting the victims of forced marriage to assert their right to choice in marriage, and no account is taken of the prohibition on reconciliation, the need to do risk assessments or other guidelines on good practice that are now accepted across a range of statutory institutions.

There is nothing in the operation of the MAT to suggest that it is progressive on women's rights, irrespective of what it publicly states and of the views of some individuals associated with it. The sole aim of religious arbitration tribunals such as the MAT is to mediate and adjudicate according to sacred religious laws which by their very nature would be unchallengeable and to exclude what is considered to be 'western' secular law in respect of personal and family matters. By doing so, the MAT seeks to create separate tiers of justice. This is the real cause for concern – decisions on matters relating to minority women, family, property and children's cases may be unlawful, yet will not be scrutinised by the courts. There is no impartial judicial oversight of such bodies to ensure compatibility with relevant discrimination and human rights legislation, unless a complaint is made – which will be rare. This leads to uncertainty, confusion and more injustice in a sphere where rights violations already arise due to the lack of legal aid, support services, information and ignorance. Backing religious forums such as the MAT, will therefore in effect, mean State backing for the most discriminatory and often abhorrent practices to be endorsed and will actually *enforce* a lack of choice on the most vulnerable within minority communities, especially women and children.

The assumption that women who access such religious arbitration forums are doing so voluntarily and are therefore exercising their autonomy is a false premise, since few women, irrespective of their backgrounds, have the legal knowledge or the resources to withstand pressure to conform to custom or invoke a broader set of citizenship and human rights. It is precisely because of the lack of any internal democratic means of accountability and other difficulties in securing their safety from within their communities that many minority women, as the SBS study shows, prefer to seek protection through a range of secular state agencies. There is also concern that the very existence of parallel legal systems will encourage relevant legal and public bodies to defer decision-making in respect of family matters to the religious tribunals for the sake of expediency and out of fear of being labelled 'racist' or 'Islamaphobic'.

Another concern is that the MAT, like other religious forums, are presiding over a system of profoundly arbitrary decision making since in such tribunals one of many interpretations of Islamic law will be invoked. Even if some minority communities are homogeneous in terms of their religious affiliation, they are nevertheless heterogeneous in their beliefs and practices. There are countless traditions, including liberal traditions within all religions but not all are reflected in official understandings of minority religions. For example, there are numerous interpretations and applications of Sharia law, which vary across ethnic, national and cultural differences. Yet it is only the dominant, conservative if not fundamentalist voices within communities that decide who is and is not a member of the religious or faith community.

By recognising and endorsing the work of the MAT and other religious tribunals, the State will in effect be privileging and sponsoring the most dominant interpretations of religion which are patriarchal, rigid and homophobic and fostered by those religious leaders who shout the loudest and hold the most institutional power. The political context and issues of power from which flow demands for separate legal systems cannot, therefore, be overlooked. They are made by those who have specific political agendas and who are themselves unrepresentative of and unaccountable to the communities that they claim to represent.

Human Rights and Religious Laws

By engaging with the MAT, the State will also in effect be legitimising the application of different standards of rights to different communities. This will inevitably result in State collusion with religious bodies in coercing minority women to waive their rights under domestic and international human rights law. This despite the fact that a government can be held accountable under international law (as well as the domestic non-discrimination law) for the support of any mechanism such as a tribunal or a court which does not treat women as full persons before the law, subjects them to degrading questions and investigative procedures and impedes them from leaving violent relationships in which they may be suffering torture or ill-treatment and are at risk of losing their lives.[13] The main problem is that such religious laws are based on the creation of specific religio-political identities which strengthen rather than undermine hegemonic, patriarchal structures of power within minority communities.

The MAT and other similar religious forums in the UK are not open to State regulation to make them compatible with human rights as some have naively recommended (Shariatmadari 2012). Quite apart from the fact that practically and financially it will be difficult for a cash-strapped State legal system to regulate a multitude of local religious institutions, politically it will not be considered timely to do so. Evidence from around the world confirms that religious personal laws are extremely difficult to reform or regulate, mainly because of the overwhelming political interests involved in the promotion of specific religious identities and values (International Council on Human Rights Policy 2009).

The duty to exercise due diligence, in order to prevent, investigate and punish acts of violence against women including those carried out by non-State actors is a necessary function of a democratic State. In our view, this duty is clearly being subverted by the State's accommodation of demands for personal religious laws to govern family affairs. In the final analysis the question that remains unanswered is why despite evidence of discrimination and denial of rights especially for women, there is such widespread acceptance that family law can be culturally specific rather than subject to universal human rights norms.

Conclusion

Since the late 90s, religion has become the main basis of social identity and mobilisation against racial inequality and discrimination in the UK. The current discourses on 'Cohesion' and the 'Big Society' and the paradoxical shift to multi-faithism has effectively redrawn minority communities as 'faith communities' and placed power firmly in the hands of minority religious institutions that are authoritarian and patriarchal, if not fundamentalist. These institutions and their leaderships seek to promote narrow, homogenised and specific political identities that bear little or no resemblance to the rich, syncretic and undogmatic religious

---

13   See for example European Council Resolution 1464 on women and religion in Europe which clearly states that all members states of the Council of Europe (including the UK) must protect all women against all violations of their rights based on or attributed to religion by, amongst other things, refusing to recognise family and personal codes based on religious principles or to apply them. The decision in Opuz v Turkey [2009] ECHR 33401/02 (9 June 2009) may also have direct implications for cases where there is State failure to afford adequate state protection because of the operation of personal religious laws.

and secular traditions that exist in all communities. In the process, the multiplicity and intersectionality of identities and oppression is denied.

Religion is implicated in violence along a range of dimensions, including violence against women but this is often masked by the demand for 'respect' and 'tolerance' for cultural and religious practices especially in relation to the law and the family. This, in turn, is adversely affecting the exit routes that minority women have struggled to create to protect themselves from violence and abuse. Notions of 'community' and female 'autonomy' have been utilised by religionists and the State and even so called progressives and feminists in ways that pose a fundamental threat to the universality of human rights and to the secular fabric of legal and other public institutions that are so central in gaining access to justice and protection.

Questions of intersectionality in debates on violence against women in minority communities will therefore have to be alert to ways in which religious discrimination can be used to both claim access to, and control over, resources whilst at the same time perpetuating misogyny and discrimination against women and other sub groups and deterring positive State intervention in family matters. The connection between gender, equality and religio-political movements needs to be urgently examined since it has human rights ramifications for the UK. The current promotion of faith based projects in all areas of civil society is in danger of compromising the gender equality agenda, especially for black and minority women and for sexual minorities. Ultimately, there needs to be constant vigilance against the instrumentalisation of women's issues by both the State and religionists in pursuit of other agendas.

References

Anthias, F. and Yuval-Davis, N. 1992. *Racialised Boundaries: Race, Nation, Gender, Colour and Class and the Anti-racist Struggle.* London: Routledge.

Awaaz. 2006. *The Islamic Right- Key Tendencies.* London: Awaaz. Available at: http://www.centreforsecularspace.org/sites/default/files/AWAAZ,%20 Islamic%20Right%20Key%20Tendencies(1).pdf. Accessed 30.2.2012

Bano, S. 2007. Muslim Family Justice and Human Rights: The Experience of British Muslim Women, *Journal of Comparative Law* 2(2) 38–67.

Bradford District Race Review Panel. 2001. *Community pride not prejudice – making diversity work in Bradford – The Ouseley Report* Bradford: Bradford Vision.

Braidotti, R. 2008. In Spite of Times: the Post-secular Turn in Feminism. *Theory, Culture and Society* 25 (6) 1–24.

Crenshaw, K. 1991. Mapping the margins: intersectionality, identity politics, and violence against women of colour. *Stanford Law Review* 43(6) 1241–1299.

Dhaliwal, S. (2012) *Religion, Moral Hegemony and Local Cartographies of Power: Feminist Reflections on Religion and Local Politics*. PhD thesis submitted to Goldsmiths, University of London.

International Council on Human Rights Policy. 2009. *When Legal Worlds Overlap: Human Rights, State and Non-State Law*. Versoix, Switzerland: International Council on Human Rights Policy. Available at: http://www.ichrp.org/files/reports/50/135_report_en.pdf. Accessed 2.5.2012.

Malik, M. (2010) Regina (SB) v Governors of Denbigh High School in R. Hunter, C. McGlynn, and E. Rackley (eds) *Feminist Judgments: From Theory to Practice*. Oxford: Hart Publishing.

Muslim Arbitration Tribunal (undated) *Liberation from Forced Marriages*. Nuneaton: MAT. Available at: http://www.matribunal.com/downloads/MAT%20Forced%20Marriage%20Report.pdf. Accessed 2.5.2012.

One Law for All. 2010. *Sharia Law in Britain: A Threat to One Law for All and Equal Rights*. Available at: http://www.onelawforall.org.uk/wp-content/uploads/New-Report-Sharia-Law-in-Britain.pdf. Accessed 2.5.2012.

Patel, P and Sen, U. 2010. *Cohesion, Faith and Gender*. London: Southall Black Sisters.

Patel, P. and Siddiqui, H. 2009. Shrinking Secular Spaces: Asian Women at the Intersect of Race, Religion and Gender, in R.K. Thiara and A.K. Gill (eds) *Violence Against Women in South Asian Communities: Policy and Practice*. London: Jessica Kingsley.

Sahgal, G. 1990. Fundamentalism and the Multi-Culturalist Fallacy' in Southall Black Sisters (eds) *Against the Grain: A celebration of survival and struggle – Southall Black Sisters 1979 – 1989*. London: SBS.

Shariatmadari, D. 2012. Sharia law compatible with human rights, argues leading barrister'. The Guardian 16 January 2012. Available at: http://www.guardian.co.uk/world/2012/jan/16/sharia-law-compatible-human-rights. Accessed 2.5.2012.

Siddiqui, H. 2003. 'It was written in her kismet': forced marriage in R. Gupta (ed) *From Homebreakers to Jailbreakers: Southall Black Sisters*. London: Zed Books.

Wintour, P. 2012. 'Militant secularisation' taking hold of British society, says Lady Warsi *The Guardian* 13 February 2012. Available at: http://www.guardian.co.uk/world/2012/feb/13/militant-secularisation-christianity-lady-warsi. Accessed 2.5.2012.

Yuval Davis, N, & Sahgal, G. 1992. *Refusing Holy Orders*. London: Virago Press.

Chapter 3
Violent Intersections:
Re-visiting the Traffic in Women and Girls

Jackie Turner

Introduction

Human trafficking is a complex phenomenon, not least because there is no common understanding of what it actually is. Despite recent international consensus on the definition of the *crime* of trafficking in persons,[1] approaches to the *problem* of human trafficking have become diverse and, on occasion, oppositional. Where early efforts to combat trafficking were triggered by a 'racialized social panic about the "White Slave Trade"', perceived 'gendered migration patterns' (Kempadoo 2005: 10) and concerns about the soliciting of white women into prostitution against their will (Saunders and Soderlund 2003: 16), current concerns about trafficking centre on migratory patterns associated with globalization, and the growth of transnational organized crime. This has resulted, firstly, in law enforcement being placed at the centre of counter-trafficking strategies, which can operate to the detriment of victims of cross-border trafficking (Lee 2011, Segrave et al. 2009) and, secondly, in a failure to recognize trafficking as violence against women to the detriment of all trafficked women, including victims of domestic trafficking (Turner 2012).

---

1   This is to be found at Article 3a of the United Nations Optional Protocol to Prevent Suppress and Punish Trafficking in Persons, Especially Women and Children, which provides that: "Trafficking in persons" shall mean the recruitment, transportation, transfer, harbouring or receipt of persons, by means of the threat or use of force or other forms of coercion, of abduction, of fraud, of deception, of the abuse of power or of a position of vulnerability or the giving or receiving of payments or benefits to achieve the consent of a person having control over another person, for the purpose of exploitation. Exploitation shall, at a minimum, mean the exploitation of the prostitution of others or other forms of sexual exploitation, forced labour or services, slavery or practices similar to slavery, servitude or the removal of organs.' The Protocol – sometimes referred to as the Palermo Protocol, which will be the term adopted here – supplements the United Nations Convention Against Transnational Organized Crime which entered into force in September 2003, followed by the Palermo Protocol in December 2003.

Approaches to Trafficking

During the latter part of the last century, and in the European context, the re-emergence of the traffic in women and girls for the purposes of sexual exploitation is particularly associated with the presence of large numbers of United Nations (UN) personnel in parts of South Eastern Europe. International peacekeepers and law enforcement officers stationed in Bosnia and elsewhere following international intervention in wars and conflicts in the region, contributed to the burgeoning trade, both as consumers and traffickers (Bolkovac and Lynn 2011, Human Rights Watch 2002). Local women's non-governmental organizations (NGOs) for victims of domestic violence found their already scarce resources stretched even further as they struggled to cope with the needs of victims of trafficking (Limanowska, B. 2002). The UN, initially resistant to local and internal pressure to combat the trade, eventually adopted a zero tolerance policy and established an Ad Hoc Committee responsible for consulting on and drafting what has become the main international instrument against trafficking, the Protocol to Prevent, Suppress and Combat Trafficking in Persons, Especially Women and Children (Palermo Protocol).

In appending the Palermo Protocol to the UN Convention Against Transnational Organized Crime, however, the focus has shifted from trafficking as violence against women to trafficking as cross-border crime dominated by international organized criminals. This has set the scene for Western governments in particular, including the United Kingdom (UK), to approach the crime of trafficking as a threat to the sovereignty and security of the nation state, a process which has seen its transformation from a 'poorly funded, NGO women's issue in the early 1980s' [into] 'the global agenda of high politics' (Wong 2005: 69). And it is during the course of this transformation that much has been lost in our understanding of the problem. Whilst debate on human trafficking has evolved alongside a developing human rights discourse, rarely is trafficking now expressly conceived in the literature as violence against women. Instead, as Maggie Lee (2011: 10–11) elaborates '[t]here are six major conceptual approaches commonly used to make sense of the problem of human trafficking – as a modern form of slavery; as an exemplar of the globalization of crime; as synonymous with prostitution; as a problem of transnational organised crime; as a migration problem; and as a human rights challenge'. From this it is clear just how far approaches to (the re-emergence of) trafficking have digressed from its origins as an 'NGO women's issue' in the 1980s. There is no mention of trafficking as violence against women. This may, to some extent, remain implicit – although problematically so – in conceiving of trafficking as synonymous with prostitution,[2] as it may also in the framing of trafficking as a human rights challenge. However, human rights have something of a chequered history when it comes to the human rights of women, especially in the arena of violence against women (see, for example, MacKinnon 2005) where they have been 'long on rhetoric but short

---

2   It is problematic in that debate quickly becomes mired in contested issues around women's consent and agency (see, e.g. Lee 2007, 2011).

on decisive action' (Turner 2012: 33) in tackling the causes and consequences of trafficking and other forms of gender-based violence and discrimination. Moreover, the human rights approach is not, in any event, the favoured approach of most Western governments including, as indicated, the UK government, with the consequence that the protection of women and children is a corollary only of the protection of state sovereignty rather than an end in itself.

Whilst the subordination of the rights of women – and children – to the interests of the state is neither new nor surprising, the absence of the express framing of trafficking as violence against women in much of the literature and discourse on trafficking allows government off the hook and leaves much ground to be recovered. This is not to say that re-defining the problem as violence against women would get government on the hook, but it might shed more light on how, what is a violation of women's human rights becomes recast as a violation of state sovereignty. Further, when trafficking is expressly conceived as violence against women and consequently as gender-based discrimination[3], the task of recovering lost ground becomes a little easier since what (re-)emerges is that it shares much in common with other forms of violence against women, and hence has its roots in deep-seated gender ideologies the world over.

Intersecting Vulnerabilities

Under the terms of the Palermo Protocol, trafficking can be broken down into its constituent parts of action, means, and motive and understood as a process involving recruitment, movement and exploitation – especially of women and children. In turning a critical – and gendered – gaze on each of those constituent parts, the ways in which gender ideologies operate locally and, more particularly, how they intersect with other forms of discrimination, can be observed throughout all stages of the process of trafficking, as layers of vulnerability are uncovered. Women and girls are vulnerable to exploitation, not just because of their gender, but because gender ideologies intersect with poverty, xenophobia, racism and homophobia to render some women and girls more vulnerable again on grounds of ethnicity, caste, class, sexuality or disability. In foregrounding trafficking as violence against women, these commonalities and intersections become clearer. For example, whilst sexual exploitation is commonly taken to mean the trafficking of women and girls into international sex industries, it is now increasingly understood to

---

3   The Convention on the Elimination of All forms of Discrimination Against Women (CEDAW) is the main international instrument addressing discrimination against women. CEDAW Committee, General Recommendation 19, 11th Session, 1992, provides that the definition of discrimination at Article 1 of CEDAW includes gender-based violence, that is, violence that is directed against a woman because she is a woman or that affects women disproportionately. Available at: http://www.un.org/womenwatch/daw/cedaw/recommendations/recomm.htm; accessed 8 June 2011.

encompass forced marriage, so-called 'mail order' brides, 'temporary wives', 'marriages of convenience' and/or domestic work (Erez et al. 2009).

This broader and, indeed, deeper understanding of trafficking and sexual exploitation sheds light on the many inter-connections between and within forms of violence against women in different contexts, relationships and life courses along a continuum of sexual violence as originally conceived (Kelly 1988). Simultaneously, when viewed through the lens of intersectionality – or intersectional discrimination – factors such as race or ethnicity can be seen to intersect with gender-based discrimination to further entrench race- and gender regimes and reproduce stereotypes which traffickers will readily exploit. Research on the sex industry in the UK, for instance, indicates that men who buy sex and who express a preference for women of a specific ethnic background fall into one of two categories: those who prefer women of the same ethnic background and those seeking the 'exotic other' (Coy et al. 2007: 17). Elsewhere, while there is no evidence of demand for the labour of *trafficked* persons, the evidence does indicate that the purchasers of cheap labour tend to seek out 'members of groups that not only lack social protection but that are also socially stereotyped as "naturally" servile or otherwise "naturally" suited to working in poor conditions for little recompense' (Anderson and O'Connell Davidson 2002: 25). Traffickers need to know their markets but, unlike government, they are also keenly attuned to the further divisions of class, caste and other factors, as well as how these manifest themselves in communities and given localities, at home and abroad, to structure power relations and to create and remove layers of vulnerability and protection. It is within these layers that the most vulnerable can be targeted for both recruitment and exploitation. As Liz Kelly suggests, reflections such as these 'illustrate the necessity of deeper explorations of the many ways in which gender and ethnicity play a part in the complex structuring and diverse consequences of trafficking in persons' (Kelly 2007: 85).

While such deeper explorations of intersectional discrimination are yet to be found in much of the literature on trafficking, intersectionality itself has been explained through the metaphor of a traffic intersection:

> ... [t]hese roads are seen as separate and unconnected but in fact they meet, cross over and overlap, forming complex intersections. Women who are marginalized by their sex, race, ethnicity, or other factors are located at these intersections. The intersections are dangerous places for women who must negotiate the constant "traffic" through them "to avoid injury and to obtain the resources for the normal activities of life" (Crenshaw 1991: 1241)

Of course, when it comes to the trade in persons, women are themselves part of the constant traffic, but these overlapping and intersecting vulnerabilities are rarely taken into account, as the problem of human trafficking is lost to the crime of trafficking in persons.

Trafficking, Migration and Border Control

The UK locates trafficking within both organized crime and cross-border movement, that is, migration frameworks so that trafficking is primarily regarded as 'an organized immigration crime problem' (Serious Organised Crime Agency 2009). Among the consequences of this combined approach is the attempt to combat trafficking through tighter border controls. This is explicit in the UK government's Action Plan on Tackling Human Trafficking:

> As human trafficking often involves crossing international borders, it is essential that measures to address it are mainstreamed into the UK's immigration system. Dealing effectively with human trafficking will be an integral part of the new Border and Immigration Agency's business, delivering the Agency's objectives to strengthen our borders and ensure and enforce compliance with immigration laws (Home Office and Scottish Executive 2007).

In subsuming anti-trafficking measures within an overall framework of migration control, the rationale is that a tighter border regime will not only catch would-be illegal immigrants, it will also 'catch' trafficked victims (O'Connell Davidson 2006: 10). This approach finds favour with a number of writers (see, for example, Rijkin 2003, Stoecker and Shelley 2005) but is disputed by others who suggest that restrictive immigration regimes actually drive migratory processes (see, for example, Beare 1999, Jordan 2002, Ould 2004) which, in turn, may drive women in particular – as more vulnerable to exploitation – into situations of trafficking (Kelly 2005).

The particular vulnerability of women, whilst notionally acknowledged at national level, is specifically acknowledged in international law and human rights discourse. It derives from their subordinate status within gender orders worldwide (Connell 2009). Wars, economic crises, failing states and economies, and the disparate effects of globalization all disproportionately and adversely affect women. Globalization in particular has created deep divisions and inequalities, and contributed to what has come to be called the 'feminization of poverty'.[4] These events and conditions operate as push or expulsion factors, driving countless individuals to leave their homes and communities and, for those with the means, their countries. On the other hand, pull factors in destination countries create attractive options for would-be migrants and traffickers alike.

Increasingly, demand for women in the global service economy, including the sex industry, has fuelled the migration of women. Here, recent evidence suggests that, whilst women retain primary responsibility for care in the family, they are increasingly not only migrating, but migrating alone, in search of work, and their remittances are more frequently coming to represent the family's main source of income (International Labour Organisation 2004). Women's independent

4   See Badden (1999) for a presentation of the data and an analysis of this concept.

migration, however, has largely been 'hidden from history' as previous studies have tended to focus on women as a 'residual category' of those left behind, or as 'dependent family members' (Vertovec and Cohen 1999). Migration, however, exacerbates gender-linked vulnerabilities. Women's agency is vitiated, on the one hand, by increased dependence on sponsors, employers, husbands and their own ethnic or racial communities; on the other hand, state controls and ambiguous laws in source and destination countries operate to force women into irregular channels of migration and into informal or unregulated employment sectors. This is the case not only with respect to migratory flows from the Global South to the Global North, but also with respect to migration regimes in the Global South (Bindhulakshmi 2010).

The divisions and inequities associated with globalization, poverty, violence and restrictions on access to the means of safe migration, created by structural and systemic discrimination against women, are the 'dangerous intersections' which women must traverse and through which they have to negotiate a route to survival. Some authors consider this 'feminization' of (ir)regular migration to be among the most significant social phenomena of the last few decades (Castles and Miller 1998, Kofman et al. 2000, Sassen 2002). And in an age characterized by a 'world in motion' (Inda and Rosaldo 2002), global human mobility is big business. As governments and large corporations compete for the 'brightest and the best' (Kapur and McHale 2005), those with enough money and/or sought-after skills and talents enjoy a freedom of movement denied to those in more dire straits. Here, the 'feminization' of both poverty and (ir)regular migration combine amid layers of multiple discriminations to consign considerable numbers of women migrants to the bottom of a 'hierarchy of mobility' (Bauman 1998: 87–88), where increased reliance on intermediaries, facilitators, loan sharks, and smugglers drive them into 'survival circuits' (Sassen 2002: 225), and render them more vulnerable to falling into the hands of traffickers along what has been described as 'the murky continuum of migration, smuggling and trafficking' (Turner and Kelly 2009: 193).[5]

Concealed within these dynamics, however, is widespread violence against women. Such violence is perpetrated because wars, failing states and other crises bring with them a breakdown in law and order and allow men to violate women with impunity; or it is perpetrated as a targeted strategy of ethnic conflict and genocide, much of it rooted in patriarchal and colonial histories, or the re-configuration of nation states; or it is violence perpetrated as a matter of course because even in times of peace and relative prosperity, gender-based violence is prevalent in all societies. This violence – rape, child sexual abuse, domestic- and other violence against women at home and in the community – is also 'hidden from

---

5   The concept of a continuum is not new to discourse on trafficking and various scholars have considered, for example, the 'migration-trafficking nexus' (Piper 2005) and the operation of a 'continuum of facilitation' (Skeldon 2000) in relation to both regular and irregular flow of migrant labour. Kelly (2005) argues that trafficking itself should be regarded as a continuum.

history' and rarely recognized as among the expulsion or push factors, not only in women's decisions to migrate, but also in their further vulnerability to trafficking and exploitation (ibid). Here, the findings of several studies highlight histories of violence experienced by significant numbers of women prior to being trafficked (see, for example, International Organization of Migration 2001, Poppy Project 2004, Zimmerman et al. 2006). These continuities are obscured, however, by a narrow focus on the forms of violence to which women are subjected within and as part of the trafficking process, rather than understanding trafficking itself as part of a continuum of violence against women. In taking such a narrow view, critical connections are lost, not just between international and domestic trafficking, but also between intersecting structural and systemic discriminations which render some women more vulnerable to trafficking than others – in all countries. It removes violence from among the push factors and conceals its role in how, within the trafficking process, push and pull factors graft onto one another to create 'the fertile field' (Kelly 2005), or conducive contexts in which some women are driven, and others exercise what choice they have, to leave their homes, by whatever means, and to seek survival and sustainable livelihoods elsewhere.

Hence, the framing of trafficking as a migration issue is essential to a deeper understanding of the problem of trafficking, but problematic in the context of the crime of trafficking in persons. Whilst conditions in source and transit countries operate in discriminatory fashion to both disproportionately and adversely impact women's mobility and safe migration, tighter border controls in destination countries similarly discriminate in their impact to disproportionately deny women access to the means of making a living and re-paying debts. At the end of what may have been a hazardous journey, border controls operate as a sorting system, separating the 'wanted' from the 'unwanted', and consequently serve as a form of 'institutional distribution of survival and death' (Balibar 2001: 16). And women, more impacted by the 'counter-geographies of globalization' (Sassen 2002), more hampered by restrictions in access to legal migratory processes – especially from South to North – and hence, more vulnerable to traffickers, are also more likely to become victims of what Maggie Lee calls 'the violent logic of global trafficking control' (Lee 2011: 153). In foregrounding law enforcement and state security within counter-trafficking measures, human trafficking has not so much been 'mainstreamed into the UK's immigration system', as it has consolidated its framing as a subset of illegal migration. The effect of this is to mainstream racial- and gender inequality into a selection process designed less to distinguish trafficking victim from illegal migrant and more to distnguish the 'tourist' from the 'vagabond' (Bauman 1998).[6]

---

6   In terms of Bauman's 'hierarchy of mobility', the 'tourists' are those whose wealth and/or skills afford them near total freedom of movement, whilst the 'vagabonds', forced to move by dangerous and life-threatening circumstances, face the greatest barriers to freedom of movement.

Victim Identification in Cross-border and Domestic Trafficking

Although the scale of trafficking – into, within and out of the UK – is unknown, it is more than likely that women and, indeed, girls are falling through an immigration net the primary purpose of which is to 'catch' illegal migrants, this despite the UK Border Agency (UKBA) being one of two competent authorities in the UK for the identification of trafficking victims under the National Referral Mechanism (NRM).[7] This, however, would not be apparent from a visit to the UKBA website.[8] There, a search for 'human trafficking' will produce a number of 'hits', many of which simply provide links to means of reporting immigration crime, while a search for 'national referral mechanism' produces 'no search results'. Indeed, one searches in vain in the most recent annual report for any reference at all to human trafficking or obligations under national, international and human rights law to identify and protect trafficking victims. Instead, the objectives of the agency are asserted to be threefold, namely: to protect our borders and our national interests; to tackle border tax fraud, smuggling and immigration crime; and to implement fast and fair decisions (UKBA Annual Report and Accounts 2009–2010: 4). Nor do any statistics appear to be readily and publically available through UKBA on the numbers suspected and/or confirmed to be victims of trafficking. By contrast, the second competent authority, the United Kingdom Human Trafficking Centre (UKHTC), does publish such information on the operation of the NRM. Whilst this is welcome, the statistics themselves are far from reassuring and, again, give rise to fears that women – and, indeed, children – are falling through the net. The figures are not gender disaggregated but they do show that the majority of referrals for both adults and minors are for suspected sexual exploitation, followed by labour exploitation and domestic servitude. Further, that while children are more likely to be confirmed as victims of trafficking, many are not and, for adults, many of whom will be women, the overwhelming majority – some two thirds – of those initially referred are not subsequently confirmed as victims of trafficking.[9] A significant proportion of these women and children come from non-European Union countries including, for example, Nigeria, China, Vietnam and Sierra Leone.

---

7   The NRM was introduced in the UK in April 2009 following ratification of the Council of Europe Convention on Action against Trafficking in Human Beings in December 2008. It serves as a framework for the identification of victims of trafficking and as a gateway to support services, providing suspected trafficking victims a 45 day minimum period of reflection and recovery. UKBA is designated as the competent authority to deal with referrals identified as part of the immigration process. The UK Human Trafficking Centre (UKHTC) - now subsumed within the Serious Organised Crime Agency (SOCA) – deals with referrals from the police, local authorities and some non-governmental organisations (NGOs).

8   http://www.ukba.homeoffice.gov.uk/ - last accessed 27 June 2011

9   Full details of the breakdown of categories and associated statistics can be found at http://www.soca.gov.uk/about-soca/about-the-ukhtc/statistical-data; accessed 28 June 2011

Children may have come to join family – or purported family members, and some women may have entered the UK on spousal, student or tourist visas. Certainly none were 'caught' in the immigration net, whether as illegal immigrants or as trafficking victims, but all subsequently came to the attention of the authorities – local social care services, NGOs or the police – who referred them under the terms of NRM, based on 'reasonable grounds' that they were suspected victims of trafficking for sexual or other labour exploitation. Moreover, in the case of women, their written consent to the referral will have been required, indicating they identified themselves as victims of trafficking and exploitation.

There will undoubtedly have been many factors which arose during the course of investigations into the status of the women and children in question, and which account for the failure to translate 'reasonable grounds' into 'confirmed grounds', but details of those investigations and decision-making processes are not themselves publically available. Where research has accessed such processes, however, the evidence suggests that they are highly gendered and racialized with decision-making processes influenced by dominant stereotypes about how a victim should 'look' and 'behave'. These, in turn, derive from 'the 'ideal' image of innocent and passive victim, subject to extremely exploitative conditions' (Segrave et al. 2009: 51). In the UK, despite having toolkits, guidelines and checklists for the identification of trafficking victims, these more recent findings reflect those of other researchers in relation to the decisions of immigration officers' on asylum seekers (see Weber and Gelsthorpe 2000, Weber 2003), as well as research on perceptions of victimhood in the context of domestic violence and rape; this, more specifically, also identifies distinctions between 'innocent' and 'blameworthy' victims (Christie 1986), and addresses how such 'victim blaming' impacts on particular social groups (Edwards 1989, Lees 1996). In the context of international trafficking, migrant women face the double jeopardy arising, firstly, from the conflation of counter-trafficking measures with border control, which has contributed to the 'criminalisation of migrants' (Welch 2003, Melossi 2003, 2005) and, secondly, from "[t]he construction and utilisation of the 'real' victim paradigm [...] compounded by prejudices held by officers making these decisions, particularly in relation to gender, race and ethnicity and in relation to sex workers" (Segrave et al. 2009: 53). Hence, women exploited in the UK's sex industries, or trafficked into and within the UK for domestic servitude or other exploitative labour purposes, may find that their avenues of escape from conditions of exploitation are policed through preconceived notions of race- and gender-appropriate behaviours, with the risk that access to support, protection and justice may be available only to those able to perform paradigmatic victimhood.

The UK has been given a clean bill of health in the most recent United States (US) Department of State Trafficking in Persons Report[10] and retains its position

---

10   The US State Department oversees the compilation of annual country reports assessing government efforts to comply with minimum standards for the elimination of trafficking as defined by s108 of the (US) Trafficking Victims Protection Act 2000.

as a Tier 1 country (Trafficking in Persons Report 2010: 333–338). It is said that the government fully complies with the minimum standards for the elimination of trafficking. In its recently published Action Plan – *Call to End Violence Against Women and Girls* (Home Office 2011) – however, the government has removed trafficking and has, therefore, disassociated it from other forms of violence against women; this despite the assurance that among its aims is to continue to 'promote the domestic implementation of CEDAW' (Convention on the Elimination of All Forms of Discrimination Against Women) – which specifically calls for *integrated* national action plans on violence against women.

Simultaneously, the coalition government moved swiftly, during its first year in office, to displace UKHTC, originally located in Sheffield and with a wide remit, not just in terms of the coordination of law enforcement efforts, but also including research, training and work with civil society. UKHTC was ostensibly reconstituted within the Serious Organised Crime Agency (SOCA) in London but the skills, knowledge and expertise accumulated during its few years of operation have arguably been irretrievably dispersed. More recently, government has taken this one step further with the announcement, by the Home Secretary, that SOCA will now be subsumed within a National Crime Agency which will also take over the work of the Child Exploitation and Online Protection Centre (CEOP).[11] The new agency's work will include border policing and is intended as a 'powerful crime fighting body', focusing on organised crime such as 'drugs, people trafficking and prostitution – nationally, regionally and internationally'.[12] These changes are set to further consolidate and conflate trafficking control with crime and migration control, whilst doing little to address the 'differential freedom of movement' (Lee 2011: 6) which has such profound implications for all migrants, but especially for women. In this way, UK immigration policy increasingly reflects and reinforces the 'hierarchy of mobility' which distinguishes desirable and undesirable immigrants – from 'high value migrants', through 'skilled workers', 'temporary workers', to 'other categories'[13] – with increasingly hard-to-meet entry/settlement requirements as one descends the hierarchy. Moreover, even more recent government proposals

---

Countries are placed in one of three tiers, with tier one being the highest ranking tier, indicating sufficient compliance. Countries assessed as making insufficient efforts or failing to comply with the minimum standards may face sanctions, including the withdrawal of US non-humanitarian aid and assistance.

11   Details of an extensive re-organisation of the police, including the creation of the new National Crime Agency, were unveiled were unveiled by the Home Secretary in 2010 in a Home Office Consultation Paper – Policing in the 21st Century. http://www.homeoffice.gov.uk/publications/consultations/policing-21st-century/; accessed 8 June 2011

12   As reported in News UK, 8 June 2011: http:/www.bbc.co.uk/news/uk-13678653; accessed 8 June 2011

13   Although the system is not yet fully operational, it is a 'tier-cum-points' system which plainly favours those at the 'top' of the hierarchy. The 'other category' includes domestic worker. For details, see: http://www.ukba.homeoffice.gov.uk/workingintheuk/tier1/. Accessed 11 June 2011

set out plans to 'break the link between temporary and permanent migration' so that in future only '[a] small number of exceptional migrants will be able to stay permanently but for the majority, coming here to work will not lead automatically to settlement in the UK' (Immigration Minister Damien Green: 9 June 2011).[14]

These measures will inevitably lead to a further criminalization of irregular migration in which the human rights of trafficked victims are subsumed within 'a logic of security', and 'migrants, boat people, asylum-seekers or trafficked women are integrated in a continuum of danger' (Aradau 2004: 252) to the State – rather than located along a continuum of violence against women. This, in turn, renders even more invisible the underlying structural, systemic and intersecting discriminations which make women and girls particularly vulnerable, and obscures the continuities and overlaps between international and domestic trafficking. Here, the UK, like many Western European countries, has been slow to recognize internal trafficking, a fact which has been attributed to different recording systems.

> It has to be stressed that, because nationals are not 'expected' to be victims of human trafficking, many criminal justice systems may tend to identify their own citizens not as victims of trafficking but as victims of other crimes, such as sexual exploitation, kidnapping or forced labour. The difference in how the data is categorized may thus be masking similarities between countries' domestic trafficking situations (United Nations Global Initiative to Fight Human Trafficking 2009: 10).

Arguably, however, 'expectations' as to who may be a victim of trafficking are themselves rooted in deep-seated preconceived notions pertaining to race and gender. The focus in UK media reports for several months during the course of 2011[15] highlighting the ethnicity of a number of men arrested in connection with internal trafficking and trafficking-related offences, as well as that of their victims, has done little to contribute constructively to a debate which requires careful exploration of the interplay between gender and ethnicity in different contexts and, instead, harks back to the racialized social panic about a white slave trade referred to above. It also studiously avoids any exploration of the interplay between other factors – how ethnicity intersects with constructions of masculinity and femininity within a framework of heteronormativity, and the ways in which these factors impact on power relations, as well as on risk-taking behaviours and perceptions of the 'exotic', or the simply 'available', 'other'.

---

14   See: http://www.ukba.homeoffice.gov.uk/sitecontent/newsarticles/2011/june/12government-migration-proposals; accessed 11 June 2011

15   A number of articles have appeared in both the tabloids and the broadsheets, some feature length, as for example in the Times in January 2011. See, e.g. STOP THE TRAFFIK for further detail at: http://stopthetraffik.wordpress.com/2011/01/11/uk-sex-gangs-its-about-cash-not-culture/ Accessed 8 June 2011

Lost Connections

It is the failure to recognize trafficking as located along a continuum of violence against women – intersecting with a multiplicity of other factors – which obscures how vulnerabilities to trafficking internationally resonate in vulnerabilities to trafficking at home. This failure is not only a function of government's conflation of counter-trafficking strategies with migration control. It is also a function of government policy with respect to black, ethnic and minority communities. Here, the voices of immigrant and minority women, already marginalized by their sex and ethnicity, are further silenced by policies of multiculturalism which 'construct minority communities as homogenous, with static or fixed cultures and without internal divisions along gender, caste or class lines' (Patel 2000: 95). This has led to what has been termed the 'paradox of multicultural vulnerability' (Schacher 2001: 3), whereby government attempts to address some of the disadvantages affecting minority communities create other vulnerabilities, particularly for minority women. In doing so, government is trading the realities of internal division for a notion of social cohesion rooted in the fiction that those who claim to represent the 'community' in fact do so. Again, in the words of Pragna Patel (2005:95):

> ... [t]he consequent power relations and internal contestations of power that flow from such division are not recognized. Also, the model is undemocratic since relations between the state and minority communities are mediated through unelected self appointed community leaders, who are men, usually from socially conservative backgrounds with little or no interest in women's rights or social justice. Most are from religious backgrounds and their interests lie in preserving the family and religious and cultural values. The expectation that women will conform to religious and cultural dictates in order to transmit cultural values from one generation to the next is therefore considered crucial by such leaders.

Hence, the precise manner in which power relations manifest themselves in degrees of privilege and inequalities becomes obscured; this not only precludes more nuanced analyses of intersecting and insidious discriminations, but also operates to legitimate a relativist approach to women's rights which permits the invocation of culture/faith to justify and/or differentiate violence against women.

These important debates remain largely hidden in the shadows in much of the discourse on (the re-emergence of) trafficking as we move further and further from its roots in a 'poorly funded NGO women's issue'. The 'global agenda of high politics' has not served women well as the counter-trafficking strategies of the West become ever more conflated with migration control, the policing of state borders and the violent exclusion of unwanted migrants. Here, human trafficking, in particular the trafficking of women and girls and state responses to the problem, are embedded in deep-seated discriminatory regimes which govern women's mobility and labour, as well as reproducing and reflecting the gendered and racialized notions of victimhood which restrict women's 'space for action'

(Kelly 2007: 89) to forge sustainable livelihoods and/or to escape conditions of exploitation. While women bear the brunt of economic, social and political crises at home and throughout the world, they are forced to negotiate a path to survival through layers of discrimination which intersect with an 'increasingly sophisticated culture of control' (Segrave et al. 2009: 31). These various factors operate to render women both more vulnerable to trafficking and to impede their exit from exploitative conditions.

Conclusion

In her thought-provoking and persuasively-argued publication, Maggie Lee (2011) pleads for 'a sociological re-imagining of trafficking' as a social problem, and for a foregrounding of a human rights agenda. In her view, '[h]uman rights may not be enough, but they are the best we have' (ibid: 156). This may be the case but, as the above illustrates, if we accept a human rights agenda which fails to foreground violence against women, the rights of women to be free of the violence of trafficking will remain aspirational, and the rights of black, ethnic and minority women will be further marginalized under the guise of respect and cultural tolerance. Nor should we forget the lessons of the early 1990s, reflected in the words of Kelly (2001):

> ... [i]t was not the goodwill or political acumen of the UN that resulted in the Declaration on Violence Against Women and Human Rights in 1993, but a global coalition of women from every continent who created a new understanding of human rights and lobbied at each and every opportunity.

In re-visiting the re-emergence of human trafficking as the NGO women's issue it once was, it is likely to take a new global coalition of women from every continent to create a 'new' understanding of human trafficking – a re-imagining of the problem which locates it on a continuum of violence against women and which acknowledges the particular vulnerabilities of migrant and minority women in a globally stratified world.

References

Anderson, B. and O'Connell Davidson, J. 2002. *Trafficking: a demand led problem? A multi-country pilot study*. Save the Children, Sweden. [Online] Available at: http://gaatw.org/publications/The%20Demand%20Side%20 part1.pdf. Accessed 8 June 2011.

Aradau, C. 2004. 'The perverse politics of four-letter words: risk and pity in the securitisation of human trafficking', *Millennium – Journal of International Studies*, 33(2): 251–78.

Baden, S. 1999. 'Gender, Governance and the Feminization of Poverty', Background Paper No. 2, *Women and Political Participation: 21st Century Challenges.* Meeting organised by the United Nations Development Programme, New Delhi, 24–26 March.

Balibar, E. 2001. 'Outlines of a topography of cruelty: citzenship and civility in the era of global violence', *Constellations,* 8: 15–29.

Bauman, Z. 1998. *Globalization: The Human Consequences.* Cambridge: Polity Press.

Beare, M. 1999. 'Illegal migration: Personal tradegies, social problems, or national security threats?', in P.J.Williams (ed.) *Illegal Immigration and Commercial Sex – The New Slave Trade.* London, Portland: Frank Cass, pp. 11–41.

Bindhulakshmi, P. 2010. "Gender Mobility and State Response: Indian Domestic Workers in the United Arab Emirates" in Rajan, S. Irudaya, (ed.) *Governance and Labour Migration: India Migration Report 2010 (16381).* New Delhi: Routledge.

Bolkovac, K. and Lynn, C. 2011. *The Whistleblower, Sex Trafficking, Military Contractors and One Woman's Fight for Justice.* New York: Palgrave MacMillan.

Castles, S. and Miller, M. 1998. *The Age of Migration.* London: Macmillan.

Christie, N. 1986. 'The Ideal Victim' in E.A.Fattah (ed) *From Crime Policy to Victim Policy.* Basingstoke: MacMillan.

Connell, R. W. (2009) *Gender.* Cambridge: Polity Press.

Coy, M., Horvath, M. and Kelly, L. 2007. *'It's just like going to the supermarket': Men buying sex in East London.* Child and Woman Abuse Studies Unit: London Metropolitan University.

Crenshaw, K. 1991. 'Mapping the margins: intersectionality, identity politics and violence against women of color', *Stanford Law Review* 43, 1241.

Edwards, S. 1989. *Policing Domestic Violence.* London: Sage

Erez, E., Adelman, M. and Gregory, C. 2009. Intersections of Immigration and Domestic Violence: Voices of Battered Immigrant Women." *Feminist Criminology,* 4(1): 32–56. DOI 10.1177/1557085108325413.

Home Office and Scottish Executive 2007. *UK Action Plan on Tackling Human Trafficking.* London: Home Office.

Home Office 2011. *Call to End Violence Against Women and Girls,* London: Home Office. [Online]. Available at: http://www.conservativewomen.org.uk/docs/CallToEndViolenceAgainstWomenAndGirls.pdf. Accessed 8 June 2011.

Human Rights Watch 2002. *Hopes Betrayed: Trafficking of Women and girls to Post-Conflict Bosnia and Herzogovina for Forced Prostitution.* [Online] Available at: http://www.unhcr.org/refworld/topic,459d17822,45b61f642,3e3 1416f0,0.html

International Labour Organisation (ILO) 2001. *Labour Migration and Trafficking within the Greater Mekong Subregion.* Bangkok: ILO.

Inda, J.X. and Rosalda, R 2002. 'Introduction: a world in motion', in J.X. Inda and R. Rosalda (eds) *The Anthology of Globalization: A Reader.* Oxford: Blackwell, pp. 1–34

International Labour Organisation (ILO) 2004. *Towards a Fair Deal for Migrant Workers in the Global Economy.* Geneva: ILO.

Jordan, A. 2002. 'Human Rights or Wrongs? The struggle for a rights-based response to trafficking in human beings', in R. Masika (ed.) *Gender, Trafficking and Slavery.* Oxford: Oxfam, pp. 28–37.

Kapur, D. and McHale, J. 2005. *Give Us your Best and Brightest,* Brookings Institution Press.

Kelly, L. 1988. *Surviving Sexual Violence* Polity Press.

Kelly, L. 2001. *From Marginal to Global Issue: Three Decades of Research and Activism on Violence Against Women.* Inaugural Professorial Lecture, University of North London. [Online]. Available at: http://www.cwasu.org/publication_display.asp?type=8&pageid=PAPERS&pagekey=51. Accessed 8 June 2011.

Kelly, L. 2005. *Fertile Fields: Trafficking in Persons in Central Asia.* Vienna: IOM (International Organization for Migration).

Kelly, L. 2007. 'A conducive context: Trafficking in persons in Central Asia', in M. Lee (ed), *Human Trafficking.* Willan Publishing: Uffcolme, Collumpton.

Kempadoo, K. 2005. 'From moral panic to global justice: Changing perspectives on trafficking', in K. Kempadoo, J. Sanghera and B. Pattanaik (eds) *Trafficking and Prostitution Reconsidered – New Perspectives on Migration, Sex Work and Human Rights.* Boulder, CO: Paradigm Publishers.

Kofman, E., Phizacklea, et al. 2000. *Gender and International Migration in Europe: Employment, welfare and politics.* London, UK: Routledge.

Limanowska, B. 2002. *Trafficking in Human Beings in South Eastern Europe,* UNICEF. [Online] Available at: http://www.childtrafficking.com/Docs/unicef_unohchr_osce_2002_trafficking_in_south_eastern_europe.pdf. Accessed 8 June 2011.

Lee, M. 2007. *Human Trafficking.* Willan Publishing: Uffcolme, Collumpton.

Lee, M. 2011. *Trafficking and Global Crime Control.* Sage Publications Limited: London.

Lees, S. 1996. *Carnal Knowledge: Rape on Trial.* London: Penguin.

Melossi, D. 2003. '"In a peaceful life": migration and the crime of modernity in Europe/Italy', *Punishment and Society,* 5(4): 371–97.

Melossi, D. 2005. 'Security, social control, democracy and migration within the "Constitution" of the EU', *European Law Journal,* (11)1: 5–21.

O'Connell Davidson, J. 2006. 'Will the real sex slave please stand up?' *Feminist Review,* 83: 4–22.

Ould, D. 2004. 'Trafficking and international law', in C. van den Anker (ed.) *The Political Economy of New Slavery.* New York: Palgrave Macmillan.

Patel, P. 2000. The Intersection of Gender and Racial Discrimination: Considerations in the Light of the UK Experience. *Interrights Bulletin* Volume 13 No 3, 2000.

Piper, N. (2005) 'A Problem by a Different Name? A Review of Research on Trafficking in South-East Asia and Oceania', *International Migration,* 43: 203–233.

Poppy Project 2004 *When Women are Trafficked: Quantifying the Gendered Experience of Trafficking in the UK.* London: Poppy Project. [Online] Available at: http://www.eaves4women.co.uk/POPPY_Project/ Documents/ Recent_Reports/Detained.pdf. Accessed 8 June 2011.

Rijken, C. 2003. *Trafficking in Persons – Prosecution from a European Perspective.* The Hague: Asser Press.

Sassen, S. 2002. 'Women's burden: counter-geographies of globalization and the feminization of survival', *Nordic Journal of International Law,* 71: 255–74.

Saunders, P. and Soderland, G. 2003. 'Threat or opportunity? Sexuality, gender and the ebb and flow of trafficking as discourse', *Canadian Woman Studies,* 22(3–4): 16–24.

Schachar, A. 2001. Multicultural Jurisdictions: Cultural Differences and Women's Rights. Cambridge.

Segrave, M., Milivojevic, S. and Pickering, S. 2009. *Sex Trafficking: International Context and Responses.* Collumpton: Willan.

Shelley, L. 2005. 'Human trafficking as a form of transnational crime' in M. Lee (ed), *Human Trafficking.* Willan Publishing: Uffcolme, Collumpton.

Skeldon, R. (2000) 'Trafficking: A Perspective from Asia', *International Migration,* 38: 7–29.

Stoecker, S. and L. Shelley 2005. (eds) *Human traffic and transnational crime: Eurasian and American perspectives.* New York: Rowman and Littlefield Publishers.

Trafficking in Persons Report (2010). Washington, DC: Department of State.

Turner, J. and Kelly, L. 2009. Trade Secrets: Intersections between diasporas and crime networks in the constitution of the human trafficking chain. *British Journal of Criminology,* March 2009; 49(2) 184–201).

Turner, J. 2012. Means of delivery: the trafficking of women into prostitution, harms and human rights discourse in M. Coy (ed) *Prostitution, Harm and Gender Equality,* Farnham, Surrey: Ashgate Publishing Limited.

UK Border Agency 2009–2010 *Annual Report and Accounts,* Home Office: HMSO.

United Nations Global Initiative to Fight Trafficking in Persons 2009. *Trafficking in Persons, Analysis on Europe.* Vienna: United Nations Office on Drugs and Crime.

Vertovec, S. and Cohen, R. eds.,1999. *Migration, Diasporas and Transnationalism,* The International Library of Studies on Migration.

Weber, L. and Gelsthorpe, L. 2000. *Deciding to Detain: How Decisions to Detain Asylum Seekers are Made at Ports of Entry.* Institute of Criminology, University of Cambridge, June.

Weber, L. 2003. 'Down that Wrong Road: Discretion in decisions to detain asylum seekers arriving at UK ports', *The Howard Journal of Criminal Justice,* 42(3), 248–62.

Welsh, M. 2003. 'Ironies of social control and the criminalization of immigrants', *Crime, Law and Social Change,* 39: 319–37.

Wong, D. 2005. 'The rumor of trafficking', in Van Schendel, W. and Abraham, I. (eds) *Illicit Flows and Criminal Things: States, Borders and the Other Side of Globalization.* Bloomington, IN: Indiana University Press, pp. 69–100.

Zimmerman, C., Yun, K., Shvab, I., Watts, C., Trappolin, L., Treppete, M., Bimbi, F., Adams, B., Jiraporn, S., Beci, L., Albrecht, M., Bindel, J., and Regan, L. 2003. *The health risks and consequences of trafficking in women and adolescents: Findings from a European study.* London: London School of Hygiene & Tropical Medicine.

Chapter 4
Sexuality and South Asian Women: a Taboo?

Shaminder Takhar

> South Asian women talk freely about sex? You're kidding, right? This would
> never happen in a million years. Though outsiders perceive India to be the land
> of the 'Kama Sutra', those of us who grew up in South Asia and the diasporic
> communities know better. Actual conversations about sexuality – especially
> female sexuality – are minimal and take place most often in the form of rumours
> or whispers, and in discreet corners (Makker, 2010)[1]

Despite the difficulties associated with speaking about sexuality as outlined in
the statement above (which probably resonates with many), there have been
developments within the South Asian diaspora and India which have attempted to
normalize sexuality *and* to move beyond viewing the linked terms 'Asian' and 'gay'
as problematic. The subjugation of sexual identities such as 'gay' and 'lesbian' has
been met by resistance from a variety of organizations and individuals. Whilst this
'road to freedom' regarding the expression of sexuality has been bumpy *and* is an
unfinished project, there is also a great deal to celebrate. This chapter therefore
traces what we mean by sexuality and the contradictory ways in which (hetero)
sexuality is perceived and understood in South Asian communities. It then moves
on to looking in more detail at lesbianism and the developments in recognition
of alternative sexualities. It will be shown that living in the closet is preferable to
'coming out' for some women due to the violence of internalized oppression and
reprisals within the community.

Expressing Sex and (Hetero)Sexuality

One understanding of sexuality is that it involves sex and human desire therefore
it "would appear to embrace ideas about pleasure *and* physiology, fantasy *and*
anatomy [involving] the realm of the psyche and the material world" (Bristow,
1997: 1). The pleasure principle in sex relates to individual choice yet its
expression also invokes high levels of anxiety. Jeffrey Weeks writing in the mid
1980s stated that: "it [sexuality] has become a moral and political battlefield
[and] there is a struggle for the future of sexuality" (Weeks, 1985: 4–5). Sexuality

---

1   http://www.boloji.com/index.cfm?md=Content&sd=Articles&ArticleID=7417.
Accessed 12 March 2012.

therefore is not just a matter of individual choice. It involves negotiating moral, cultural, religious and political terrains, something which has featured in the struggle by South Asian women.

Historically, sex and sexuality feature in all societies but when it concerns South Asian women it is a taboo subject (Ratti, 1993). Rani Kawale (2003) notes that discussions about sexuality are unacceptable in South Asian communities, its respectable form being limited to the confines of marriage and religious rules (op cit) with pre-marital engagement in sexual relations prompting considerable anxiety (Puri, 1999). This moralistic stance is seen to be contradicted because India continues to be seen as the land where the *Kama Sutra* originates. This famous book appears to feature Indians as erotic beings – a kind of exoticised sexuality that acknowledges the sensuality involved in: "learning how to be a happy heterosexual [and how] heterosexual identity is learned as a phobic marking of what you are not i.e. homosexual" (Bhattacharyya, 2002: 24). Similarly, racialised discourses have presented South Asian women simultaneously as exotic, licentious and repellent rendering "lesbian sexuality largely invisible" (Brah, 1996: 79). It would appear therefore, that happiness and sensuality are usually associated with being male and heterosexual whilst women's roles are seen as contradictory and ambiguous yet *necessary* (Holland et al., 1998) – after all it is the body of the female that is required for men to achieve normative heterosexuality.

The aim of this chapter is not to present South Asian women as a homogeneous group but as members of communities that hold different attitudes towards honour and shame. Women's bodies are usually thought of as carriers of tradition, culture and the honour of the family, therefore it should not come as a surprise that community surveillance operates as a deterrent to 'illicit' heterosexual activity amongst young women. Women are often seen as complying with this moral code or 'rules' for acceptable expressions of femininity because the penalty involves loss of reputation, being unmarriageable, ostracism from familial structures and in some instances violence. Young women are for these reasons "faced with an apparent choice between personal liberation and cultural loyalty" (Das Gupta and Das Gupta, 2002: 113).

Communities and families are therefore central to how we can understand the presumed 'compliant' behaviour of and adherence to gendered sexual norms by South Asian women. However, there are many opportunities for South Asian women to engage in pre-marital sex and this is evident when young women take full advantage of their parents' wishes to attain a high level of education by studying at a university away from their home town. It is a strategy employed by many to win freedom (albeit for a short time) and to escape the restrictions imposed on them (Wilson, 1978, 2006; Brah, 1996; Rait, 2005; Bhopal, 2010), although recent commentary notes an increase in those who remain living with their parents (Bhopal, 2010:101). South Asian communities have also recognised how educated women are able to negotiate for an educated marriage partner and simultaneously improve the social status of their parents (Ahmad, 2001; Ramji, 2003; Tyrer and Ahmad, 2006). Sexual involvement at university, therefore, poses a small risk compared to gains made in the marriage prospects of daughters. Despite the moral code surrounding sex and sexuality South Asian women in the diaspora and in India have and continue to circumvent control over their bodies by engaging in pre-marital sex (Wilson, 2006; Puri, 1997; Das Gupta and Das Gupta, 2002). At the same time, there have also been developments in many cultural forms which have brought the issue of sex and sexuality to light.

Sexualities and Cultural Forms

In the last decade developments concerning the celebration of South Asian women's sexuality, has included Meera Syal and other South Asian actors featuring in the production of *The Vagina Monologues* in Britain. The show seeks to celebrate female sexuality and challenge a number of taboo subjects. An equivalent called *Yoni Ki Baat* was produced in the United States by South Asian Sisters in 2003 following a daring move by the Kimaaya Theatre Company (Bangalore) to produce *The Vagina Monologues* in India which resulted in protests by lawyers against it. *Yoni Ki Baat* is still being performed and it has proved to be a resounding success, covering subjects such as "domestic violence, abuse, menstruation, masturbation, orgasms, marriage, religious faith, and political protest" (Makker, 2010). Such performances simultaneously raise awareness of the control exerted by the community and family whilst empowering actors, contributors and audiences. Their agency is brought to the fore and can be contrasted to representations of female sexuality in Indian popular cinema whereby a woman is presented as either 'good' (upholding traditions and morals) or 'bad' (deviant and sexualized). The narratives of these films support the 'good' woman based on the *devi* (female goddess) who does not transgress boundaries i.e. who lacks sexual agency. The 'bad woman' is constructed as the 'whore': "the immoral temptress who lures men to their destruction with her abundant sexuality [because] she challenges the status quo and may have the power to overturn it completely" (Das Gupta and Das Gupta, 2002: 116). Another representation of women involves the revenge narrative and usually concerns women as victims of rape or gang rape seeking revenge on men (Gopalan, 2008).

Although cultural forms do not necessarily herald greater freedom for women, the creation of these spaces is important because they challenge powerful discourses of female sexuality, particularly when there is female transgression. Transgression is shown in Monica Ali's fictional work, *Brick Lane* (2003) which represents a (seemingly) passive diasporic woman who goes through a 'sexual awakening'. The Bangladeshi community, in its attempt to regain control over women's sexuality under the guise of racism, threatened to hold protests against filming an adaptation of the novel in London's East End in 2006 – such is the fury of patriarchy when it is challenged. Patriarchal control in South Asian communities expects women to conform and uphold respectability through self-sacrifice and the denial of self-expression. Although disempowerment in South

Asian communities is variable, where such disempowering discourses exist for heterosexual women, how can women who are considered 'other' i.e. lesbian become empowered and claim their agency? The empowerment of South Asian lesbians is related to structural issues of power. Located at the intersection of race, gender and sexuality, we can see that prevailing patriarchal discourses privilege men over women *and* heterosexuality over homosexuality. Indeed "empowerment can be seen to be a dynamic which has to be constantly and continually negotiated and this is particularly the case in individual sexual relations" (Carabine, 1996: 27). However, if the personal or the individual is emphasised, there is a risk of losing the collective nature of political mobilization, including challenges to current constructions of heterosexuality, and its connections with violence against women, by the gay and lesbian movement (Rich, 1980).

To return to cultural forms, we have witnessed a significant representation of homosexuality in films, television drama and literature alongside a growing visibility of people with 'other' sexualities. So has the battle been won? It would appear not when we give some consideration to subjugated identities within alternative identities: a South Asian lesbian identity has been long in the making.

> South Asian culture is rampant with homophobia – but a homophobia so silent that people literally don't know the language for homosexuality […]. It is viewed as a Western phenomenon even though images of gays and lesbians have been part of the history of the subcontinent for thousands of years […] There are also references to homosexuality in the Kama Sutra (Khan, 2002: 65).

The most noticeable works here include Deepa Mehta's film *Fire* (1996) in which two married women become involved in a 'forbidden' relationship and the provocative and questioning collection of photographs by Parminder Sekhon and Poloumi Desai (2003) in *Red Threads,* which shows the existence of a vibrant British Asian 'queer scene'. Although *Red Threads* has not generated a negative response, the film *Fire* which was shown in Indian cinemas in 1998 attracted a violent response from the right wing Hindutva party Shiv Sena. Interestingly the negative appraisal of the film was not only made by right wing Hindu nationalists but also left leaning feminists, commentators and journalists (Gopinath, 2005). This was not the first time that a cultural form depicting 'other' sexualities had come to the attention of the public and the moral brigade in India. In 1942, Ismat Chughtai's *Lihaf (The Quilt)* written in Urdu was published and created controversy for presenting a tale of the relationship between an upper class Muslim woman and her female servant. The relationship is viewed through the eyes of a girl who witnesses noises made by the two women from underneath the quilt. Predictably, Chughtai was charged with obscenity in 1944. The controversial nature of the book was in its representation of the desiring female body which was deemed to be a bigger threat than the desiring homosexual male. Thus we return to the body of the female which is a battleground upon which the integrity of the nation rests, therefore, *The Quilt* and *Fire* were seen by many as stains on the impeccable character of the Indian nation and a contamination of Indian culture (Derne, 2000; Gopinath 2005; Kapur, 2000; Thadani, 1996; Vanita, 2009). Sexuality as a site of agency depicted in *Fire* and *The Quilt* poses a threat and a challenge to *expected* heteronormativity of South Asian women. Cultural representations are therefore important creative spaces where alternative or 'other' sexualities can be presented, although the link to real lived experiences may not be so straightforward. This is evidenced in the problems associated with 'coming out' as opposed to living in relative safety within the closet.

Sexuality, Agency and 'Coming Out'

The coupling of the words 'Asian' and 'gay/lesbian' appear to be problematic i.e. a contradiction with each regarding the other as 'the other'. Yet men and women have shown that they can be both in history. Homosexuality is not a recent phenomenon brought on by exposure to western, liberal values that has resulted in the corruption of South Asian youth morality. Homosexuality has existed in ancient India yet there appears to be selective amnesia regarding this fact as demonstrated in *Sakhiyani* (Thadani, 1996). Thadani researched lesbianism in India which dates as far back as 4000 BC and in her introduction to the history of same sex relationships she comments on 'othering'.

> My aim is to excavate layers of erotic memories and thus recreate historical continuums from the location of the present context of lesbian invisibility [...] [It is claimed that] in one form or another that homosexuality came from the other, be it Western, Greek or Arabic. This technique of "othering" functions as a form of exiling, rendering invisible and excommunicating anything which may be seen as representative of homosexual and homoerotic traditions (Thadani, 1996: 6).

Far from 'rendering invisible' the work of Ruth Vanita (2002) demonstrates the impact of homosexuality (existing in a variety of cultural forms) on the Indian subcontinent. This includes attempts to marry by lesbian couples in India revealing how women who have had no exposure to western ideas of sexuality have expressed their desire to be with a same sex partner (Vanita, 2009). The marriage of a same sex couple is based on the love marriage Hindu ceremony between an ancient heterosexual couple (Shakuntala and King Dushyanta). Indeed when there is opposition to this union by family members there are also reports of joint suicides. The invisibility of lesbianism, the lack of a word for this sexuality (see also Pande, this volume) and the isolation experienced by women, some who were married and identified themselves as 'married lesbians' is also evident in India in the early 1990s (Thadani, 1996). Whilst the situation in India has changed, some women prefer to live in the west where they are 'free' to express their sexuality.

This is implicit in the constructions of the lesbian as western and exiled from India. For those who have the choice of living in the 'West', the question is posed in terms of the choice between a physical cultural exile, a rupture with one's past, or a sexual exile. The consciousness of one's lesbian identity makes it even more painful to live out a semi-closet existence (Thadani, 1996:119).

However, within the South Asian diaspora, "the 'lesbian' is [often] seen as 'foreign', as a product of being too long in the West, and therefore is annexed to the 'host' nation where she may be further elided – particularly if undocumented – as a nonwhite immigrant within both a mainstream (white) lesbian and gay movement and the larger body of the nation-state" (Gopinath, 2005:18–19). It would appear therefore that moving to the West does not resolve these tensions: the South Asian lesbian 'exile' is faced simultaneously with exclusion from the diasporic identity (for not being heterosexual) and the gay (male) and feminist identities (for being lesbian/Asian/black). This is not necessarily an easier path for living as a lesbian or coming out (Ratti, 1993; Suriyaprakasam, 1995; Siraj, 2011) which is reflected in the views of the women I interviewed in a recent research project.[2]

I think women find it hard to disclose their sexuality. (Meena, Director of Asian Women's Project)

This is the twenty first century, but I still think it is hard for women to be able to even conceive, as a South Asian woman, of being a lesbian. And then having got to that space to realize it, and then to talk to families about it, it's huge [especially if] there was no support and there was no network in terms of really being able to equip women to be able to do that [...] I think one of the hardest things for South Asian women is the fact that there is no space to be an out proud South Asian woman, who is a lesbian (Zoe, Consultant LGBT issues)

I couldn't do that to my dad and mum. I don't know what would happen if I told them ... personally I have a few friends that are gay and they're actually considering not telling the family and just going ahead and getting married because they just don't feel they have ... they're just not empowered enough to make the choice. (Sofia, Refuge Worker)

These narratives provide insight into the reluctance of women living in the UK to reveal their sexuality, intensified through fear of ostracism, isolation and violence. This is despite the progress made in cultural representations and the existence of

---

2   I interviewed women working in South Asian women's organizations about grassroots political activism and political agency. The sample was 29, with diverse religious backgrounds (1 Christian, 5 Hindu, 13 Muslim, 10 Sikh). The in-depth semi-structured interviews lasted 45–120 minutes.

Asian LGBT support organizations. One interviewee also referred explicitly to the reluctance of heterosexual women living in a refuge to accept that lesbian women fleeing violence due to disclosure of their sexuality were also suffering violence against women.

> It's a difficult one because I think there's still a lot of uneasiness and people are uncomfortable talking about it [sexuality]. We ask the question about their sexuality at the point of referral but some women will just be uncomfortable in answering that or they might just give you the answer that they think that you probably want to hear. But there are women who will tell us what their sexuality is. We've had women in the refuges who have been lesbian and we've had to deal with the issues in terms of living in a refuge with other women who have been showing ... like prejudice around that [issue] (Meena, Director of Asian Women's Project)

Thus, even within the confines of a safe space for women fleeing violence South Asian lesbians experience rejection, judgement, and disapproval (Thadani, 1996). Such contexts mean it is unsurprising that women attempt to hide their sexuality, including entering a heterosexual marriage. This denial of one's sexuality can be understood as a form of internalized oppression to avoid stigmatization and loss of honour for the family. Although one would assume that preservation of honour would result in self-preservation, it is not necessarily the case. This is evidenced in the rising numbers of South Asian women who experience mental health issues such as depression, self-harm and suicide (Fenton and Sadiq-Sangster, 1996; Chantler et al., 2001). Various writers have also commented on this with oppression and the threat of violence cited as taking a heavy toll on South Asian women's health and bodies (Burman et a.l, 2002; Burman and Chantler, 2003; Anand and Cochrane, 2005; Barn, 2008; Raleigh, 2009). Indeed being a lesbian (of any race) in the west has been shown to be a risky business – research suggests that the more closeted a woman is about her sexuality (passing as heterosexual) the more likely she is to suffer from mental health problems (Mooney-Somers and Ussher, 2000), a theme echoed by one of the research participants.

> Coming out is also a critical transition period and in terms of coming out, it's a bit like disclosing HIV status. You don't necessarily do it once, you have to do it over and over and over. And that can be quite difficult and challenging but over the years we have seen a difference [...] Lesbian and bisexual women may come in to contact [with the Project] because of mental health problems or self harm or something like that [...] For BME women, the issues are further compounded because of stigma and fear of disclosure. So they're less likely to disclose their sexual orientation (Avtar, Sexual Health Project Director).

Silence around sexuality is still found amongst South Asian women involved in same sex relationships in urban landscapes. Whilst the city affords them some anonymity, they continue to live their lives in the closet because they choose not to reveal their sexuality to families, friends, colleagues, community and even to themselves. The most subjugated identity is that of the Muslim lesbian which is taken up by Asifa Siraj (2011) in her study of one lesbian woman, not in a relationship, who remains in the closet for fear of reprisal from the community.

> They are silent, silent, absolutely. Not just women but other vulnerable sub-groups. You know, those who are homosexual, lesbians, and gays (Dipika, Director Asian Women's Project).

There are of course South Asian lesbian women who refuse to remain in the closet but the coming out process can result in a range of responses.

> I told my mum when I got my job at the Lesbian and Gay [Organization], because wherever I work my mum rings, you know, there is always something to ring for and being a lawyer there was a sense of, a problem [comes up] you sort it out. So, I had to give her my number and if I gave her my number it would say Lesbian and Gay [Organization] yea? So I gave it to her and I thought ok, I have to tell her. When I told her, she said: "I have just bought some new curtains upstairs, come, come to have a look at the new curtains upstairs." I am thinking I have just made the biggest disclosure ever, and I just was not sure I got too upset myself, but what was fabulous was for her to take in that information [and] to be able to respond to me immediately (Zoe, Consultant for LGBT issues).

Coming out for this participant was within the boundary of the mother-daughter relationship and she had not told her father. Although her sexuality was 'accepted' it was never referred to again. Similarly, another participant talked of how she had come out to her mother and the community yet the attitude of the community baffled her.

> My mother thinks what right do they have to say to me and her when I go to [home town], "it's still not too late to get married!" It's not too late to get married! And you know [pause] I have to say [pause] I think the hypocrisy in the community is just appalling (Anneka, Consultant for Women's Issues).

The lesbian sexuality of this participant was regarded as something temporary that could be 'cured' by marriage. The hypocrisy of the South Asian community is also evidenced by the numbers of girls and women who are victims of sexual abuse and sexual violence (Kelly, 2010; Thiara, 2010). Two participants revealed how they had been sexually abused by extended 'family' members which had resulted in self-harm. Managing one's emotions in a community that on the one hand abuses and on the other holds itself as guardian of morality through surveillance of women's sexuality has struck a chord with activists. The existence of women's projects such as Southall Black Sisters and the Newham Asian Women's Project, that challenge oppression and violence, occupy a position that is central to empowerment and women's agency (Thiara and Gill, 2010; Wilson, 2010).

South Asian women's involvement on issues of sexuality and sexual violence represents a movement towards social change; by no means an easy task for those with a lesbian identity which is further complicated by religion. Organizations such as the Naz Project, the KISS Group and the Saffra Group provide support for members and challenge stereotypical views such as the incompatibility of a lesbian identity with South Asian women, *and* of Islam with homosexuality (Kawale, 2003; SafraProject, 2003). The possibility that new spaces are opening up, especially amongst younger people who have the support of their parents, was also noted.

> We have seen younger and younger people coming out, younger and younger women coming out and making contact with the [...] Project, wanting to come to the [support] group. We've also had parents of young lesbians who have made contact with us who want to support their daughters. Equally, with some young men as well. They want to support their children but don't know how to go about it because they don't know who to talk to within their own community. They want to know about strategies on how to support their child. We have had situations where parents accompany their children to counselling sessions – they will drop them off and wait for them because they want to see their children move on to a much happier place where they're more accepting of their own sexuality. So we have very much seen a shift, but that's not to say that it's still not a very critical time for most people coming out, BME and non-BME (Avtar, Sexual Health Project Director).

One interviewee pointed to the need for a holistic approach, where sexuality and violence, alongside women's material needs, were all dealt with simultaneously.

> I would like to see an organization that supported South Asian women on a range of different issues from violence to sexuality to child care to education to a whole plethora [...] so that they can go to a place where they can get the support of other South Asian women and they could be part of a process of bringing about change (Zoe, Consultant LGBT issues).

Conclusion

This chapter has highlighted how and why sexuality is a complex and silenced subject when it concerns South Asian women. It also highlights gender relations within the 'South Asian community' by examining the role of patriarchal structures that seek to minimize transgression from the moral order and inhibit the expression of alternative sexualities such as lesbianism. This flies in the face of a growing movement which spans different continents – India, United

States, Canada and Britain – that seeks full recognition and equality. The dynamic nature of cultural processes and the increasing role of religion means that women remain under surveillance which in turn means challenging sexist and homophobic practices and discourses is to take significant risks. Yet there is a growing amount of academic and creative literature and cultural forms that deal with alternative South Asian sexualities. What we have witnessed is gradual change regarding female (hetero)sexuality, with young women claiming more freedom. Whether this translates into greater freedom for lesbian sexuality, and for all women to speak about sexual violence, remains an open question. The narratives of women working in organizations that challenge violence alongside the silencing of female sexual agency are testimony to the importance of women continuing to voice resistance to oppressive practices and violence and imagining a more optimistic future.

References

Ahmad, F. 2001. Modern Traditions? British Muslim Women and Academic Achievement. *Gender and Education,* 13 (2), 137–152.

Anand, S.A and Cochrane, R. 2005. The Mental Health Status of South Asian Women in Britain: a review of the UK literature. *Psychology and Developing Societies,* 17(2), 195–214.

Barn, R. 2008. Ethnicity, Gender and Mental Health: social worker perspectives. *International Journal of Social Psychiatry,* 54(1), 69–82.

Bhattacharyya, G. 2002. *Sexuality and Society: An Introduction.* London and New York: Routledge.

Bhopal, K. 2010. *Asian Women in Higher Education.* Stoke-on-Trent: Trentham Books.

Brah, A.1996. *Cartographies of Diaspora: Contesting Identities.* London: Routledge.

Bristow, J. 1997. *Sexuality.* London: Routledge.

Burman, E; Chantler, K; Batsleer, J. 2002. Service Responses to South Asian Women who Attempt Suicide or Self-harm: challenges for service commissioning and delivery. *Critical Social Policy,* 22(4), 641–668.

Burman, E. and Chantler, K. 2003. Across and Between: reflections on researching 'race', gender and mental health. *Feminism and Psychology,* 13(3), 302–309.

Carabine, J. 1996. Empowering Sexualities. In *Perspectives on Empowerment,* B. Humphries (Ed). Birmingham: Venture Press, 17–34.

Chantler, K; Burman, E; Batsleer, J. 2001. *Attempted Suicide and Self Harm – South Asian Women: A Report of a HAZ-funded Research Project,* Manchester: Women's Studies Research Centre, Manchester Metropolitan University.

Das Gupta, S. and Das Gupta, S. 2002. Sex, Lies and Women's Lives: an intergenerational dialogue. In *A Patchwork Shawl: Chronicles of South Asian*

Women in America, S. Das Gupta (Ed), London: Rutgers University Press, 111–128.

Derne, S. 2000. Men's Sexuality and Women's Subordination in Indian Nationalisms. In *Gender Ironies of Nationalism: Sexing the Nation,* T. Meyer (Ed), London and New York: Routledge, 237–258.

Fenton, S. and Sadiq-Sangster, A. 1996. Culture, Relativism and the Expression of Mental Distress: South Asian women in Britain. *Sociology of Health and Illness,* 18(1), 66–85.

Gopalan, L. 2008. Avenging Women in Indian Cinema. In *The Bollywood Reader.* R. Dudrah and J. Desai (Eds). Maidenhead: Open University Press, 97–108.

Gopinath, G. 2005. *Impossible Desires: queer diasporas and South Asian public culture.* Durham and London; Duke University Press.

Holland, J; Ramazanoglu, C; Sharpe, S; Thomson, R. 1998. *The Male in the Head: Young People, Heterosexuality and Power,* London: The Tufnell Press.

Kawale, R. 2003. Construction of Spaces by South Asian Lesbian/Bisexual Women. In *South Asian Women in the Diaspora.* N. Puwar and P. Raghuram, P (Eds). Oxford and New York: Berg, 181–199.

Kapur, R. 2000. Too Hot to Handle: the cultural politics of *Fire. Feminist Review,* 64, 53–64.

Kellly, L. 2010. Foreward. In *Violence Against Women in South Asian Communities.* R.K. Thiara, and A.K. Gill (Eds). London: Jessica Kingsley Publishers, 9–13.

Khan, S. 2002 Sexual Exiles. In *A Patchwork Shawl: Chronicles of South Asian Women in America.* S. Das Gupta (Ed).Rutgers University Press: New Brunswick, New Jersey, London, 62–71.

Khan, S. 1991. *Khush: A SHAKTI Report.* Camden: Camden Council.

Makker, V. 2010. South Asian Women in America Talk Sex, Break Myths. Available at: http://www.boloji.com/index.cfm?md=Content&sd=Articles&ArticleID=7417. [Accessed March 15, 2012]

Mason-John, V. 1995. (Ed) *Talking Black: Lesbians of African and Asian descent speak out.* London and New York: Cassell.

Mooney-Somers, J. and Ussher, J. 2000. Young Lesbians and Mental Health: the closet is a depressing place to be. In *Women's Health: Contemporary International Perspectives.* J. Ussher (Ed). London, UK: Wiley-Blackwell, 83–92.

Puri, J. 1999. *Woman, Body, Desire in Post-Colonial India: narratives of gender and sexuality.* New York and London: Routledge.

Raleigh, V. 2009. Suicide Rates in People of South Asian Origin in England and Wales. *The British Journal of Psychiatry,* 194, 561–571.

Ramji, H. 2003. Engendering Diasporic Identities. In *South Asian Women in the Diaspora* N. Puwar and P. Raghuram (Eds). Oxford and New York: Berg, 227–241.

Ratti, R. (Ed) 1993. *A Lotus of Another Color: an unfolding of the South Asian gay and lesbian experience.* Boston; Alyson Publications Inc.

Rich, A.1980. Compulsory Heterosexuality and the Lesbian Existence. *Signs: Journal of Women in Culture and Society,* 5(4), 631–60.

Safra Project. 2003. *Initial Findings: Identifying the difficulties experienced by Muslim lesbian, bisexual and transgender women in accessing social and legal services.*

Sekhon, P. and Desai, P. 2003. *Red Threads: the South Asian queer connection in photographs.* London: Diva Books.

Siraj, A. 2011. Isolated, Invisible, and In the Closet: the life story of a Scottish Muslim lesbian. *Journal of Lesbian Studies,* 15, 99–121.

Sukthankhar, A. 1999. *Facing the Mirror: Lesbian Writing from India.* London, Penguin Books.

Suriyaprakasam, S. 1995. Some of Us are Younger. In *Talking Black: Lesbians of African and Asian descent speak out.* V. Mason-John (Ed). London and New York: Cassell, 94–107.

Thadani, G. (1996) *Sakhiyani.* London and New York: Cassell.

Thiara, R. 2010. Continuing Control: child contact and post-separation violence. *Violence Against Women in South Asian Communities.* R.K. Thiara, and A.K. Gill (Eds). London: Jessica Kingsley Publishers, 156–181.

Thiara, R. and Gill, A. 2010. Understanding Violence Against South Asian Women: what it means for practice. In *Violence Against Women in South Asian Communities.* R.K. Thiara, and A.K. Gill (Eds). London: Jessica Kingsley Publishers, 29–54.

Tyrer, D. and Ahmad, F. 2006. *Muslim Women and Higher Education: identities,experiences and prospects.* Liverpool, John Moores University

Weeks, J. 1985. *Sexuality and Its Discontents: meanings, myths and modern sexualities.* London and New York: Routledge.

Wilson, A. 1978. *Finding a Voice: Asian Women in Britain.* London: Virago Press.

Wilson, A. 2006. *Dreams, Questions and Struggle: South Asian Women in Britain.* London and Ann Arbor, MI: Pluto Press.

Wilson, A. 2010. Charting South Asian Women's Struggles against Gender-Based Violence. In *Violence Against Women in South Asian Communities.*R.K. Thiara, and A.K. Gill (Eds). London: Jessica Kingsley Publishers, 55–79.

Vanita, R. 2002. Introduction. In *Queering India: same sex love and eroticism in Indian culture and society.* R. Vanita (Ed). New York and London; Routledge, 1–11.

Vanita, R. 2009. Same-Sex Weddings, Hindu Traditions and Modernity. *Feminist Review,* 91, 47–60.

PART II
Forms and Contexts of Violence

Chapter 5

Two Steps Forward, One Step Back: The Fight against Female Genital Mutilation in the UK

Dr. Makeba Roach and Dr. Comfort Momoh

Introduction

A surface glance at recent literature will reveal that female genital mutilation (FGM) is now widely accepted as a form of violence against women in international political, health and human rights spheres. However, the collection of practices we now label as FGM has a long and complex history in the UK. Clitoridectomy was routinely prescribed by some Victorian surgeons as a cure for alleged female 'deviances' such as nymphomania, masturbation and hysteria (Black 1997). Whilst British colonial authorities were vaguely aware of FGM, it was either regarded as a cultural oddity worthy of anthropological study, or used to justify the 'civilising' mission of the colonisers, rather than being seen as a threat to health or a targeted act of gender violence. In the 1970s, aided by the growing influence of Western media, white American feminists branded FGM as a brutal act of African male domination against seemingly defenceless African women. This theme has continued as a dominant but implicit thread in the development of the international discourse surrounding FGM, and may have hindered rather than helped the fight against it in some of the countries and communities still struggling to deal with post-colonial legacies. FGM's most recent return to the limelight has resulted from increased migration into the UK from certain countries across Africa, Asia and the Middle East, where removal of the clitoris and/or other external female genitalia is still routinely practiced.

The World Health Organisation (2010) estimates that between 100 and 140 million women and girls are living with the effects of FGM worldwide, and 3 million are at risk annually in Africa. There are several countries with particularly high FGM prevalences of over 80 per cent, mainly on the West Coast of Africa (Guinea, Mali) and the Horn of Africa (Egypt, Sudan, Eritrea, Ethiopia, Somalia) (UNICEF 2005, Feldman-Jacobs and Clifton 2010). In many of these countries, the act of FGM occurs against a wider backdrop of 'structural violence', a term popularised by medical anthropologist and physician Paul Farmer, referring to how women and other marginalised groups are rendered vulnerable by institutionalised political, economic, legal and religious inequalities (Farmer et al. 2006). More simply, it is "one way of describing social arrangements that put individuals and populations in harm's way" (Farmer et al. 2006: 1686). Whilst we may instinctually associate the idea of structural violence with developing countries, evidence suggests that poverty, exploitation and discrimination severe enough to constrain people's options are also present in the UK, particularly for recent migrants (Doctors of the World UK 2010). In the UK the most recent prevalence estimates available suggest that almost 66,000 women with FGM were resident in the UK in 2001, with over 21,000 girls aged eight or younger at high risk (FORWARD 2007). These figures are likely to have increased over the last decade: estimated net long-term migration to the UK in 2010 was 252,000 – the highest on record, with the majority of migrants coming from non-EU countries (Office for National Statistics 2011).

Weighty issues including gender, race, class, culture, power, health and human rights have informed global academic debate about FGM, and shaped national and international FGM policy and legislation. Yet as the prevalence of cosmetic genital surgery increases across Europe and North America, UK authorities are now facing accusations of hypocrisy, for condemning the medicalisation of FGM in black and minority ethnic (BME) women and girls, while ignoring non-therapeutic cosmetic alteration to the genitals of (largely white) women performed in unregulated private operating theatres, NHS hospitals and piercing shops (Essen and Johnsdotter 2004, Sheldon and Wilkinson 1998, Johnsdotter and Essen 2010).

This chapter draws on diverse subject areas including social constructivist theory and anthropology, to examine the main factors that have contributed to the current position of FGM as it relates to BME communities in contemporary UK society. It has two broad objectives: firstly, that readers who are new to the field may engage with the core issues in a meaningful way, and secondly, that readers who are already familiar with these issues can be updated with current developments and debates, set against today's background of economic upheaval, widespread Islamophobia, and a government-led backlash against immigration and multiculturalism.

What's in a Name?

Worthy of brief mention at the outset is the issue of terminology used to describe FGM (see Table 5.1). Readers may be familiar with other terms such as female genital cutting, female genital surgeries and female circumcision. These terms are often used instead of FGM, as some people think the term 'mutilation' carries implicit connotations of deliberate harm which may cause offence and alienate communities. Many activists argue that more neutral terms do not accurately convey the extent of the physical and psychological harms that can result from the practice. Regardless of the term used, Walley (2002: 45) rightly points out that: "[t]o lump together the diverse forms of the practice into a single term ... obscures the diverse geographic locations, meanings and politics in which such practices are embedded and rhetorically constructs a generic 'they' who such practices and a generic 'we' who do not." Walley blames this 'othe for the polarised responses that many people have towards FGM; either moral and politically-informed outrage, or deference to cultural relativism.

Semantics aside, when working with affected women and their families, it is important to be as sensitive as possible; in practice this may mean reflecting back the terminology they use in conversation, regardless of one's own personal preferences. While acknowledging the highly charged nature of this debate, this chapter uses the term 'female genital mutilation', because it is the preferred terminology of the authors, and it is used in current UK policy and legislation. To aid anatomical and geographical accuracy, the various WHO types of FGM (see Table 5.1) will be referred to specifically where relevant.

Table 5.1   WHO Definition and Classification of Female Genital Mutilation (adapted from WHO 2008)

WHO Definition of FGM	All procedures involving partial or total removal of the external female genitalia or other injury to the female genital organs for non-medical reasons.
WHO Type 1 (Clitoridectomy)	Partial or total removal of the clitoris and/or the prepuce.
WHO Type 2 (Excision)	Partial or total removal of the clitoris and the labia minora, with or without excision of the labia majora.
WHO Type 3 (Infibulation)	Narrowing of the vaginal orifice with creation of a covering seal by cutting and appositioning the labia minora and/or the labia majora, with or without excision of the clitoris.
WHO Type 4	All other harmful procedures to the female genitalia for non-medical purposes, for example: pricking, piercing, incising, scraping and cauterization.

Why do People Do It?

Although the WHO definition of FGM is clinical and precise, in reality most FGM procedures are done by local, older women who are highly respected in the community but not medically trained. The instruments used range from razor blades to pieces of corrugated iron sheets; these are seldom sterile, and it is not uncommon for the same instrument to be used on several girls at a time. There are exceptions: in Egypt for example, demographic health surveys reveal that between 30 and 75 percent of procedures are done by medical personnel in hospitals (WHO et al. 2009, Feldman-Jacobs and Clifton 2010). We will return to the issue of medicalisation later.

The range of reasons cited for practicing FGM is diverse, with significant variation both between and within countries where it is still performed. Reasons are often divided into four groups: psychosexual, religious, social and aesthetic

(Momoh 2005). Of course, in reality there may be elements from more than one of these categories behind each individual case, but this loose framework serves as a useful tool to aid understanding.

Psychosexual reasons given by practising communities include beliefs that FGM increases male sexual pleasure during intercourse, that the presence of a clitoris endangers a baby during delivery, or that FGM is necessary to curb a woman's sexual desire and prevent sexual infidelity. These are not dissimilar to the justifications for removal of the clitoris in 19th century England by gynaecologist Isaac Baker-Brown; he believed the procedure could cure women's hysteria and insanity which, he deduced, were caused by masturbation (Black 1997). Equally demonstrative of how surgery can be used to direct female sexual behaviour towards what is deemed culturally appropriate, is the operation to remove the clitoral hood used by various North American surgeons from the late 19th century until the early 1970s, to 'cure' women who were not able to experience orgasms while having missionary-position heterosexual sex with their husbands (Webber and Schonfeld 2003).

Many people staunchly defend FGM in the erroneous belief that it is a religious requirement in a similar way to male circumcision. Amongst practising groups where religion is the main motivation, FGM is most commonly performed in the name of Islam, yet it is not done by the majority of the world's Muslims. Some Orthodox Christians in Egypt and Falasha Jews in Ethiopia also perform FGM, but the practice pre-dates Islam, Christianity and Judaism. Another word used to describe type 3 FGM is *infibulation*, derived from the Latin word fibula (meaning 'clasp'), hinting at its use in ancient Rome to prevent female slaves from becoming pregnant (Momoh 2005).

Social reasons for FGM help explain why the practice is often held in such high esteem. FGM may be part of a celebratory ceremony or secret ritual that marks the transition from one significant life stage to another, be it from girl to woman, from woman to wife or mother, or even from wife to widow. In some groups, FGM is said to uphold family honour by making young girls eligible for marriage; indeed for many uneducated girls marriage provides the only means of accessing economic resources. Similarly, in poorer families the bride-price to be gained from marrying off a girl child may be vital for their survival, or used to send her male siblings to school.

Some practising groups such as the Kenuz Nubians of Egypt, find normal female genitalia ugly or unsightly, and think that the appearance of type 3 FGM is much more aesthetically pleasing. Anthropologist Fadwa El Guindi (2006: 27) was taken aback when asked by an Egyptian woman, with reference to female genitalia, "had *this* been your face, would you leave it as is?" Janice Boddy (1998, 2008) lived for two years in the northern Sudanese village of Hofriyat, where type 3 FGM sat comfortably in a wider local narrative which saw enclosure as essential for protecting precious items: impervious containers protected the staple bread, courtyard walls protected family homes, and infibulated genitals protected the pregnant womb. Boddy (1998: 100) insists that "[a]esthetics, of course, are never neutral; they are judgements of value, form, and conduct, suggesting suitable-natural, normal- dispositions toward the world."

Health Consequences

The potential complications of FGM are manifold (see Table 5.2), and may have immediate, short-term or long-term effects on both physical and psychological health. Much of the available literature documenting FGM complications is comprised of case reports of one or a few women, meaning it has been difficult to make accurate estimates of prevalence. A landmark multi-centre trial carried out by the WHO Study Group on FGM and Obstetric Outcome (2006) was the first to break this trend, looking at 28,000 women in six African countries. The trial showed that type 3 FGM was associated with increased risk of several adverse obstetric outcomes such as post-partum haemorrhage, extended maternal hospital stay and stillbirth or early neonatal death. Whilst this key data was most welcome, epidemiologist Ronan Conroy (2006) points out that the relative risk levels found in this study place FGM well behind maternal smoking as a risk factor in pregnancy.

Table 5.2   Health complications following FGM (adapted from WHO 2000)

Immediate	Haemorrhage, shock, anaemia, fractures/dislocations from being restrained
Obstetric	Urinary retention in labour, caesarean section, prolonged/ obstructed labour, foetal distress, perineal tears, post partum haemorrhage, need for anterior episiotomy, maternal death, neonatal death, stillbirth, ante-natal and post-natal wound infection
Gynaecological	Painful vulval scar, keloid scarring, abscess formation, rectovaginal or vesicovaginal fistula formation, vaginal atresia, dysmenorrhoea, oligomenorrhoea, pelvic infection, inclusion cysts, partial or complete labial fusion, haematocolpos, infertility, prolapse
Psychosexual	Fear and anxiety around sexual intercourse, vaginismus, anorgasmia, penetration difficulties, dyspareunia, post-coital bleeding, marital breakdown and divorce
Urinary	Urethral meatus injuries, urethral stricture, urinary retention, prolonged length of micturition, recurrent urinary tract infections, dysuria
Psychological	Fear of labour & delivery, post-traumatic stress disorder, depression

The 2007 CEMACH report investigated the 295 maternal deaths that occurred in the UK between 2003 and 2005, and was the first to directly mention FGM as a possible contributory factor in the death of an African woman. Poor understanding of her delivery needs meant that she was not referred to specialist FGM services, and was subjected to an unnecessary elective caesarean section. She experienced ongoing internal bleeding which was not explored surgically until two days later, when she suffered a cardiac arrest and died on the operating table (Lewis 2007: 81).

Some of the health complications of Type 3 FGM can be eased by a procedure called deinfibulation, in which an incision is made to open up the scar tissue covering the vagina and urethra. Deinfibulation cannot replace excised tissue, but it enables women to pass urine and menstrual products normally, have less painful intercourse and safely deliver their babies vaginally. While deinfibulation can be performed under local anaesthetic, it must be done with great care and sensitivity, as it can cause emotional upset and flashbacks. It is ideally performed before pregnancy, but can also be done after 20 weeks gestation (to allow adequate time for healing before birth), or alternatively during labour (Royal College of Nursing 2006). It is not advisable before 20 weeks gestation in case women suffer a miscarriage and retrospectively associate it with the procedure, causing further psychological trauma. It is illegal in England and Wales for healthcare workers to re-infibulate a deinfibulated woman after childbirth, which may be requested by the woman's relatives or the woman herself. There are currently 15 specialist FGM clinics across the UK. They are usually jointly run by midwives and gynaecologists, and take referrals from primary and secondary healthcare. They provide emotional support and medical advice for women who have undergone all types of FGM, undertake examinations where there are child protection concerns for girls at risk of FGM, and can provide evidence for asylum cases where women are fleeing FGM, either for themselves or their daughters.

Pleasure

When it comes to sexual pleasure, the language used in some FGM literature tends to be sweeping and inflammatory, and not rooted in research evidence. Of course, sexual sensation can be adversely affected due to damage to the clitoris and other parts of the genitalia, but the clitoris is a three-dimensional and largely internal organ, with a more substantial neurovascular supply than is documented in most anatomy textbooks. Recent research has demonstrated that the clitoris along with the distal portions of the urethra and vagina form a cluster, which is the locus of female function and orgasm (O'Connell et al. 2005). As we will discuss later in the chapter, cosmetic procedures that remove the same amount of genital tissue as some types of FGM, are carried out daily in the name of *increasing* sexual pleasure.

There is relatively little research into the sexual pleasure of women a
by FGM. In a systematic review of the available evidence, Obermeyer
found that the majority of studies measuring sexual activity and pleasure showed
no significant difference in self-reported sexual pleasure between women who had
undergone FGM and those who had not. At an international conference dedicated
to looking at the evidence surrounding psychosexual effects of FGM in 2004,
Amel Fahmy highlighted a problem that infiltrates much of the current research:
the presumed universality of the Western concept of 'sexuality' (Bur 2004). In
addition to clinical and anatomical aspects emphasised in the West, sexuality and
sexual pleasure are multi-dimensional concepts shaped by social processes and
cultural context, and as such, are open to constant shifts in definition and meaning
for women themselves. The factors women feel to be important with regards to
their sexual pleasure are not fixed, and can change in different environments. Thus
we must be cautious about making sweeping statements about the effects of 'FGM'
(thereby disregarding its many forms) on the sexual lives of *all* women. This said,
some small but relevant research studies that can be used for local and national
health advocacy are now emerging from the UK and other migrant-receiving
countries. A study of 18 East African women in Germany used questionnaires to
measure *female sexual function index* prior to and six months post-deinfibulation.
Sexual function improved in the areas of desire, arousal, satisfaction and pain, but
lubrication and orgasm remained unchanged (Krause et al. 2011).

Power and Patriarchy

While FGM is most often performed forcibly on young girls under the age of 10,
in some communities it is performed on adolescents and adult women – sometimes
with consent, other times by force. It is not necessarily a one-off event; a young
girl's first experience of type 3 FGM in Somalia may be followed by a series of
'openings' and 'closures', dictated by the claims of other people on her genitals.
This may begin with her husband cutting open her childhood scar with a knife
on their wedding night in order to consummate the marriage, an old woman re-
sewing her to ensure fidelity while her husband travels for long periods, a midwife
opening her up to allow the safe passage of a baby, and then closing her again
afterwards. This continuum exemplifies the interplay between embodiment and
power, described by Chambers (2008: 26) as occurring when "social norms are
transferred onto our bodies, and our bodies in their new forms act out these social
norms, perpetuating them by example."

FGM often occurs in communities where group social norms override
individual decision-making. The physical marks of FGM transform the genitals
and the whole body of a girl or woman into a family asset that can be traded and
subsequently altered, to constrain her behaviour within limits deemed appropriate
for her pre-determined role in the community. The complicating factor seen in
FGM that sets it apart from many other forms of gender-based violence is the

strongly held belief by parents and relatives that they are acting out of love in the best interests of the girl/woman. Close adult relatives, even a girl's mother, may be the ones who express its importance, who overtly or covertly arrange the procedure, or who actively hold her down while FGM is performed. The occasion may be marked with a big family or community celebration; making it even more difficult for the girl or woman to reconcile such a painful betrayal with the love she feels for her family, and her sense of belonging in the community.

Since FGM is often carried out forcibly without consent, the power that drives it is often assumed to be solely repressive, with the explicit aim of subjugating women, especially when increasing male sexual pleasure is offered as a reason for the procedure. While this repressive aspect of power is dominant in many cases, it cannot explain the less common scenarios where FGM is carried out solely to increase female pleasure, as proclaimed by young Sara Kaba girls in Chad who independently sought out traditional cutters to perform FGM against the wishes of their parents (Leonard 2000). Explaining their rationale to anthropologist Leonard, the women emphasised that they were not forced into it by their families. Their reasons included wanting to be like their friends, or sometimes sheer curiosity. Recent UK research revealed the story of a young Somali girl who asked her mother repeatedly to arrange for her to be sent back to Somalia and circumcised, because all her friends had had it done (Hemmings 2011). Leonard's ethnographic work was not initially well-received by international opinion leaders; it did not fit with the 'standard tale' of how and why FGM is performed, and as such, the stories of these girls and women were ignored.

Michel Foucault insists that we must additionally consider the more *creative* elements of power, which come to the fore in the social construction of choices and preferences. Foucault used the concept of the Panopticon, a prison designed by Jeremy Bentham to illustrate how creative power can come from *within* an individual to influence behaviour, and the importance of both body *and* mind in compliance with social norms. Chambers (2008: 23) describes the concept as follows:

> The Panopticon consists of cells arranged in a circle around a central watchtower. Each cell has a barred door covering the whole of the internal wall, and a window to the outside that illuminates the cell. As a result, surveillance is very efficient: each cell can be seen from the central watchtower ... [T]he central watchtower has blinds at the windows (an updated version would be a one-way mirror), ensuring that the prisoners never know whether or not the guard is looking at them.

Foucault theorised that over time prisoners would internalise the fear of being seen misbehaving by the guards, and become self-policing and habitually obedient in both mind and body. Chambers (2008: 23–24) continues:

As in the Panopticon, social norms do not need to be enforced by the explicit attention of others. Instead, enforcement and the corresponding surveillance is internalized by each individual, and is reinforced whenever the individual acts in compliance with the norm, or interacts with others in accordance to social expectations.

Buried underneath diverse claims of meeting religious obligations, coming of age, preventing sexual infidelity, upholding family honour, or even exercising independent choice, it is socially constructed patriarchal norms that perpetuate the practice of FGM. Chambers (2008: 39) writes regarding breast implants in the West:

> Choosing to have breast implants regardless of the desires of actual men is not the same as choosing to have them immune from patriarchal norms. It would be impossible to say that a woman's desire for breast implants were independent of patriarchal norms unless she lived in a non-patriarchal society. Her motivations, the meaning of the practice, and its effect on other people could not possibly be immune from patriarchal influence otherwise.

Migration and FGM

For both men and women, migration forces relatively fixed gender norms to enter a "process of negotiation and renegotiation where people find themselves located in shifting contexts of meaning and power relations" (Talle 2008: 64). This tension is experienced by refugees in particular.

> The refugee condition is paradoxical in the sense that people who, in great distress, flee from conflict and violence are forced to find security in places that in their sheer otherness or difference are often experienced as 'insecure'. The lack of familiarity with language, religion, modes of conduct as well as landscape intensifies the feeling of loss and vulnerability inherent in displacement/emplacement processes (Talle 2008: 67).

After interviewing Somali women who had migrated to the UK and Norway, Talle (2008) explored how the presence of FGM re-forged their cultural, religious and gender identities, within the local Somali community and wider Western society. The women moved from an environment where FGM is a feminising act of purification, to one where it is a de-feminising act of violence. What was once a physical mark of dignity, pride and belonging became a mark of disgust, shame and foreignness. A body with increased value that was thought to confer protection from rape and thus allowed freedom of movement, was instantly transformed into an inadequate body of less worth.

Morison et al. (2004) looked at attitudes towards FGM in young single Somalis living in London. While most of those who had lived in Britain from a young age showed less favourable attitudes towards FGM, 43 per cent of male participants and 18 per cent of females said they would definitely or probably circumcise their daughters in the future. In-depth interviews with some participants shed further light on the complexity of their negotiations between *here* and *there*: "I am against it, but then again it is tradition. I think people have it because our great grandmums had it and so on. But I am against it. I would not do it to my own kids" (Female participant, Morison et al. 2004: 93). Others were keen to maintain traditional beliefs and practices:

> I think circumcision (infibulation) is good for women because it makes them as they are supposed to be … no-one marries a girl who is not circumcised and I wouldn't want that for my children (Male participant, Morison et al. 2004: 93).

FGM and Islam

Qualitative peer research from community projects across the UK showed that tradition, culture and religion are often used interchangeably as justification for FGM by those who support the practice (Hemmings 2011). There is no mention of FGM in the Qur'an, and FGM has been openly condemned by leading Islamic clerics (TARGET 2006) but there remains much confusion in some practising communities about FGM and Islam. Some of this stems from the use of the term 'Sunna'. This word is often used by some communities to describe type 1 or 4 FGM, in contrast to the more severe type 3, but other communities use it as a term to refer to FGM in general. 'Sunna' is also the word used to refer to the collected sayings and habits (hadiths) of the Prophet Mohammed (peace be upon him) that are considered optional, but credit-worthy. One particular hadith in the Sunan of Abu Dawud (book 41, number 5251) says: "A woman used to perform circumcision in Medina. The Prophet (peace be upon him) said to her 'do not cut severely as that is better for a woman and more desirable for a husband'". Leading Islamic scholars have argued that this hadith lacks authenticity and therefore of little value (Muslim Women's League 1999), but it nonetheless offers a source for those who believe that FGM is religiously sanctioned.

One might infer that a wider national drive to promote the integration of migrants and British Muslims may have beneficial outcomes for young girls at risk of FGM. Yet now, more than ever, this possibility seems out of reach. Less than a year after winning a general election with bold promises to put a cap on immigration, Prime Minister David Cameron (2011) spoke in Munich about the failure of state multiculturalism in Britain, blaming "the passive tolerance of recent years". A tabloid-led drive to make immigration synonymous with terrorism, and to equate asylum-seekers with benefit fraud and health tourism, has encouraged a new wave of right-wing nationalism, most visible in groups such as the English Defence League. Intense Islamophobia in the UK and across Western Europe together with a government-led rejection of multiculturalism, has left many Muslim migrants

feeling isolated and unwanted; in such conditions families may cling to tr
like FGM in order to maintain a psychological, physical or even spiritual li
their countries of origin.

The cloak of secrecy that already surrounds FGM may be drawn tighter as communities seek the safety of being *insiders* in contrast to their *outsider* status in all other spheres of life in the UK. Recent evidence from certain migrant communities demonstrates a spectrum of responses and attitudes to FGM, but also hints at a collective knowledge of how to arrange FGM, both in the UK and abroad (Hemmings 2011). The alienation and disempowerment experienced after arrival in the UK prevents young girls and older women from accessing help and specialist services at precisely the time they may be most at risk.

Policy and Action

Thanks to tireless campaigning from grassroots community organisations, small non-governmental organisations (NGOs) and interested healthcare workers, the last decade has seen considerable progress in tackling FGM in the UK. The Female Genital Mutilation Act (Great Britain 2003) came into effect in 2004, and closed a loophole in the previous 1985 Female Circumcision Act by making it illegal to take a girl overseas to perform FGM, or even to be indirectly involved in making the arrangements for such a trip. Additionally, the new legislation increased the potential prison term for involvement in FGM from five to 14 years. To the frustration of many however, there have been no prosecutions yet in the UK. A recent qualitative peer research study aimed to discover the factors contributing to the continuation of FGM (Hemmings 2011). Undertaken as part of a three-year UK-wide Special Initiative to tackle FGM, the study trained community members to conduct in-depth interviews with 130 men and women of various ages and ethnic backgrounds, and identified several potential barriers to FGM law enforcement. These included: varied levels of awareness and perception of UK FGM law, relative powerlessness of young people *and* adults to resist pressure from respected family elders, and a lack of open and frank discussion about FGM between sexes and generations. The study's authors suggest that a false dichotomy present in much of today's FGM literature divides community members into those 'for' and 'against' FGM; in reality a spectrum of opinions exists, with people locating themselves in different positions over time.

The same study produced some useful recommendations that have real potential for changing attitudes towards FGM in practising communities. It proposes some strategies for rejecting FGM such as educating young girls about how to respond to threats of FGM, working on assertiveness and confidence, increasing religious knowledge, and educating community members about the next steps to take if they suspect a girl/woman is at risk. Other recommendations include creating opportunities and safe spaces in which FGM can be discussed openly without fear of shame or stigmatisation, and developing culturally compelling arguments against FGM other than just adverse effects on health, as many feel these are not relevant if they practice type 1 or type 4 FGM.

Organisational barriers to effective FGM law enforcement identified by Roach (2007) were: gender bias in the asylum process; insensitive treatment of women by health services; and failures in inter-agency cooperation in child protection. Deliberate efforts have been made to address the latter two points; with tangible results at local and national levels. Following a thorough and wide-ranging consultation period, the London Safeguarding Children Board (2007) released comprehensive safeguarding guidelines with an accompanying resource pack for use by professionals in health, education and social care. This has been echoed across the country with many Local Safeguarding Children Boards developing their own guidelines and offering practical training. FGM guidelines have been produced or revised by the Royal College of Nursing (2006), the Royal College of Obstetricians and Gynaecologists (2009), and the British Medical Association (2011). NGOs such as FORWARD and the FGM National Clinical Group are working tirelessly to raise the profile of FGM and advocate on behalf of women and girls affected by or at risk of FGM.

A cross-government FGM coordinator was appointed in September 2009 as part of the previous Labour government's strategy to end violence against women and girls, with a broad mandate that included encouraging greater inter-sectoral cooperation (HM Government 2009). In addition to coordinating the launch of a national awareness-raising campaign, the two successive holders of this post acted as a central point of contact for the many stakeholders working to fight FGM, and ensured FGM did not slip down the list of government priorities. The current Conservative-led coalition government promised to develop multi-agency guidelines on FGM in their own violence against women strategy document (HM Government 2010), and these were published in February 2011 to the delight of those organisations and individuals working in the field (HM Government 2011). It came as a shock to many then, when one month later the cross-government advisor post was axed. The responsibility for tackling FGM will now be shared between several government departments, which many activists fear will greatly hinder the implementation of the new guidelines, and halt the progress that has been made in recent years (Williams 2011). Economic factors are also affecting FGM work in other ways; a pioneering accredited course in the management of FGM for nurses and midwives was offered at Kings College London in 2008. The course ran for three successive years and some of its graduates have gone on to start FGM clinics in various locations. But government cuts in higher education funding prevented the course from running in its fourth year, and its future is now uncertain. With the looming prospect of radical reforms to the National Health Service, the effects on specialist FGM clinics nationwide are yet to be seen.

Much less headway has been made in tackling the third, and perhaps more indirect organisational barrier to the effective enforcement of FGM legislation: gender bias in the asylum process (Roach 2007). The Refugee Convention (United Nations 1951) defines a refugee as:

A person who owing to a well-founded fear of being persecuted for reasons of race, religion, nationality, membership of a particular social group or political opinion, is outside the country of his nationality and is unable or, owing to such fear, is unwilling to avail himself of the protection of that country; or who, not having a nationality and being outside the country of his former habitual residence as a result of such events, is unable or, owing to such fear, is unwilling to return to it.

It took almost 50 years for the UNHCR to issue specific guidelines on gender-related persecution within the context of the Refugee Convention, and acknowledge that "the refugee definition has been interpreted through a framework of male experiences, which has meant that many claims of women and of homosexuals, have gone unrecognised" (UNHCR 2002: 2).

The gender guidelines state that in certain cases, 'women' may qualify as a particular social group, and acknowledge that the failure of state protection required by the original refugee definition to qualify a 'well-founded fear' may not be relevant for women fleeing persecution from non-state actors such as their husbands or families. Acknowledgement that state authorities may be unwilling, or unable, to protect women and girls from FGM specifically can be found in separate guidance on refugee claims relating to FGM (UNHCR 2009). The guidance asserts that FGM-related asylum claims may be assessed within the Refugee Convention grounds of a particular social group (Article 23), political opinion (Article 25) and religion (Article 27). It identifies FGM as a form of persecution that disproportionately affects the girl-child, and recognises that situations may occur where families seek asylum based on fear of FGM being performed on their daughter(s). In such cases parents can be granted asylum based on their child's refugee status. The guidance also acknowledges that FGM is not necessarily a one-off event but can be a continuing form of harm, and can cause intolerable ongoing traumatic psychological effects, 'rendering a return to the country of origin intolerable' (UNHCR 2009: 9).

The Home Office responded to the UNHCR gender guidelines with an Asylum Policy Instruction (API) which provided guidance on how the United Kingdom Border Agency (UKBA) should process asylum claims with regard to gender (Home Office 2006). The API was subsequently revised and renamed as an Asylum Instruction (Home Office 2010) in response to widespread criticism of insensitive policies such as forcing women to take their children into the asylum interview if they could not arrange their own childcare. The revised Asylum Instruction specifically names FGM as a form of gender-specific persecution, and mentions the case of *Fornah v SSHD [2006] UKHL 46,* wherein 'uninitiated' or 'intact' women in Sierra Leone was found to constitute a particular social group (House of Lords [UKHL] 2006).

In addition to the above-mentioned materials available for decision makers in the asylum process, since 2004 there has been an annual audit of first-instance asylum decisions by the UNHCR representation to the UK (called the Quality

Initiative Project). Yet research published by NGO Asylum Aid (2011) highlights a persistently poor quality of initial decision making by case owners in women's asylum claims. The research examined the files of 45 women in three different UKBA regions (London, Cardiff and Leeds), and conducted in-depth interviews with nine of the women. The findings show that UKBA consistently makes the wrong decisions for female asylum seekers; 87 per cent of cases were initially refused by the UKBA, but 50 per cent of these decisions were reversed after appeal to immigration judges.

Several of the UKBA's own recommendations have yet to be implemented – when the research was published the two regional offices based in London still had no childcare facilities, and in the majority of cases examined, case owners changed several times during the processing of the asylum claim. Additionally, UKBA frequently failed to recognise women as a particular social group in cases of gender-related persecution, and were ignorant of the types of persecution that affect women specifically, causing case owners to wrongly doubt the credibility of applicants' accounts. A striking example of this can be seen in the following exchange:

> One woman described fearing that her daughter would be subjected to forced circumcision if returned to Sudan. Her case owner replied:
> Q: Can you clarify what you mean by circumcision?
> A: Circumcision
> Q: I have not heard of female circumcision. (Asylum Aid 2011: 39)

Ignorance about the practice of FGM and its status as a human rights abuse, combined with the culture of disbelief deeply ingrained in the UK asylum system, has potential to undermine the efforts of other government departments to combat FGM at home and abroad. Placing women and girls in harm's way by sending them back into situations where they are at high risk of FGM exposes inconsistencies in domestic and international policy, and may breed resentment towards UK authorities in communities that traditionally practice FGM. Ironically it is within these very communities that the success or failure of UK FGM legislation lies: they contain information that could lead to successful prosecutions, and the human resources needed to develop community-based prevention work.

Nip, Tuck

Further conflicts between government domestic and foreign policy are visible when considering medicalisation, which occurs when "[p]roblems that are often socio-culturally and interpersonally produced, and psychologically located, are treated through medicine" (Braun 2009: 242). Recent rapid and unregulated growth of female genital cosmetic surgery (FGCS) in the UK (Deans et al. 2011) has been fuelled by a long history of problematising female genitalia (Black 1997), and contrasts sharply with the unequivocal condemnation of the medicalisation of FGM (i.e. cases where healthcare providers perform FGM or re-infibulation) presented at an international level.

As awareness of the health complications of FGM grows, practising communities worldwide are turning to health professionals to perform FGM, hoping to reduce the associated risks. Demographic health surveys suggest that between 30 and 75 per cent of FGM procedures in Egypt are performed by health professionals (WHO et al. 2009, Feldman-Jacobs and Clifton 2010). In early 2010, the American Academy of Pediatrics (2010: 1092) controversially suggested that paediatricians could "reach out to families by offering a ritual nick as a possible compromise to avoid greater harm", but soon retracted this statement following international condemnation. A joint UN agency statement argues that medicalisation falsely bestows a degree of legitimacy on FGM while obscuring the human rights implications (WHO et al. 2009). Far from encouraging the abandonment of FGM, the statement argues, medicalisation is more likely to institutionalise it.

Healthcare staff in the UK who participate in FGM or re-infibulation may be removed from their respective professional registers (Royal College of Nursing 2006), but a simple internet search will quickly retrieve the websites of numerous private Harley Street clinics offering FGCS, naming procedures such as 'labial reduction', 'vaginal beautification' or 'G-spot rejuvenation'. A Department of Health (2006) information booklet available online for British patients considering cosmetic surgery describes 'female genital reshaping/ labial reduction/ labiaplasty' in the same terms used by UK legislation to define FGM. Epidemiologist Ronan Conroy (2006: 107) suggests that: "[i]t is Western medicine which, by a process of disease mongering, is driving the advance of female genital mutilation by promoting the fear in women that what is natural biological variation is a defect, a problem requiring the knife".

In a comprehensive review of labial surgery for well women, Liao et al. (2010) identified almost one thousand published cases of cosmetic labial surgery on females between the ages of 18 months and 68 years, the majority of patients being between 16 and 35 years. The review exposed a worrying lack of methodological rigour in the studies, with very short or non-existent post-operative follow-up. Surgery was provided on demand, with no investigation into the psychological background of dissatisfaction with appearance, no assessment of sexual function, and no attempt to compare patients' labia with published studies documenting the wide variations of 'normal' female genital measurements. The review's authors note how: "in one paper the authors created their own classification for abnormality without an explanation of its derivation, and patients who were normal by their own classification had also been operated on" (Liao et al. 2010: 22)

Bramwell et al. (2007) explored six British women's expectations and experience of labial reduction performed within the NHS, and found a key emergent theme was the process of accessing surgery. One woman deliberately overemphasised physical discomfort to her GP for what she knew was essentially a cosmetic procedure; other women described how their GPs described their genitals as "normal", but nonetheless referred them for surgery. This contradictory response may cause confusion for women, and is not necessarily acting in their best interests. Two out of the six women interviewed were dissatisfied with the results of the surgery and had a second operation.

Although the amount of healthy tissue removed during FGCS is often equivalent to that seen in Types 1 and 2 FGM, these procedures are marketed with a dominant rhetoric of female empowerment, freedom from the psychosexual distress associated with having 'ugly' genitals, and a woman's right to choose the fate of her own body. Johnsdotter and Essen (2010: 31) contrast this with the prevalent view of African women as victims, wherein: "[r]ather than being seen as reflexive actors and decision-makers, they are mirrored as passive 'bearers of tradition'". In neoliberal capitalist Western society, aggressive marketisation of sexuality and a lifestyle that demands constant self-improvement serve to separate culturally oppressed victims of FGM from empowered consumers of FGCS, who are implicitly deemed to be free of any cultural influence (Braun 2009). This can be seen in the UK FGM Act, which states that "cultural reasons" are not enough to justify FGM. In the eyes of the law, healthcare, and much of the general population, the word 'cultural' carries connotations of *otherness*, the foreign, and often, brown skin. Yet surely in our current patriarchal and hyper-sexualised society, aspiring to attain a genital appearance like that seen in digitally-altered pornographic photographs in the belief that it will bestow beauty and inspire sexual confidence can be argued to be as much a 'cultural' reason as any other. Tiefer (2008: 471) posits that through the increased availability of surgical enhancement technologies and market-led construction of sexual dysfunction, "[t]he cultural ideal becomes the cultural norm and the request for intervention becomes the request to be normal." Chambers (2008: 39) argues that in and of itself, "[c]hoice does not ... *suffice* to render an outcome just: there are circumstances in which a chosen practice remains unjust, and this is because practices are inherently social and thus do not depend on individuals' choices" (emphasis in original).

The way UK law is currently enforced, an adult Sudanese woman asking for her labia minora to be trimmed is likely to be questioned and informed that non-therapeutic alteration to her genitals constitutes FGM, which is illegal and punishable by up to 14 years in prison. In contrast, the effects of Western cultural norms on societal views of sex, gender and genitals, allow English and Welsh women to undergo illegal and non-therapeutic trimming, piercing and tightening of their genitalia in unregulated clinics without any hindrance. Johnsdotter and Essen (2010: 33) rightly assert that:

> ... problems emerge if we are expected to discriminate between European and African female genitals.

This constitutes a clear double standard, and the lack of regulation of cosmetic surgery undermines national and international efforts to eradicate FGM. In traditional migrant families who support FGM but are aware of UK legislation, there is currently nothing to stop them pressuring their daughter to see a private surgeon and paying for a legal labiaplasty. According to Johnsdotter and Essen (2010: 33):

> ... European laws need to include a paragraph stating that a woman above a specific age may choose to have her genitals modified, irrespective of ethnic background. That would protect children while placing adult women, of Western and non-Western origin alike, in the same category – that is, that they have the right to make decisions about their own bodies.

Conclusion

FGM is a deep rooted harmful traditional practice with huge significance for millions of people worldwide. However, there is increasing concern at all levels as to its relevance and purpose. FGM is closely linked with manipulating women's sexuality, and serves to maintain socially constructed patriarchal norms, although women are often the ones who arrange and perform the practice.

FGM and its perceived implications can provide a sense of identity and belonging in migrant communities, particularly when they feel marginalised or discriminated against. Promoting universal rights and accurate religious understanding are important steps towards empowerment for migrant women and their British-born daughters, which is in turn a key ingredient for real change at a grassroots level. Changing attitudes is a long-term process, so practising communities should be assisted in developing sustainable projects to prevent FGM that are easily accessible and locally controlled. To be truly successful, community and religious leaders must be involved in such projects from conceptualisation to implementation, and existing platforms like mosques used to speak out against FGM.

Professionals who have the potential to encounter women or girls at risk of FGM must stay up-to-date with current FGM policy at local and national levels, as well as the problems facing communities in dealing with this issue. FGM is a complex and challenging matter, and cooperation between governments, NGOs, professionals and communities is vital to enforce FGM legislation and end the practice.

Women and girls affected by FGM should have access to accurate information, and good quality safe healthcare. In practical terms this means funding must be maintained or even increased for FGM specialist clinics, and the importance of training for health care professionals must not be overlooked. Women whose care is adversely affected by limited knowledge, poor communication or lack of sensitivity are at risk of poor outcomes.

All human beings, regardless of age, gender, religion, colour or ethnicity have the right to physical and psychological integrity. Inconsistencies between government foreign and domestic policy with regards to FGM must therefore be highlighted and addressed. The fears of women seeking asylum in the UK from the threat of FGM must be recognised as valid rather than dismissed. The continuation of non-therapeutic and unregulated genital cosmetic surgery in

British women must be examined and questioned, as it is a major threat to the global fight against FGM.

References

Abu Dawud. *Sunan of Abu Dawud*.

American Academy of Pediatrics 2010. Ritual Genital Cutting in Female Minors. *Pediatrics*, 125, 1088–1093.

Asylum Aid 2011. *Unsustainable: the quality of initial decision-making in women's asylum claims*. London: Asylum Aid.

Black, J. 1997. Female genital mutilation: a contemporary issue, and a Victorian obsession. *Journal of the Royal Society of Medicine*, 90, 402–405.

Boddy, J. 1998. Violence Embodied? Circumcision, Gender Politics and Cultural Aesthetics. In: Dobash, R. E. & Dobash, R. P. (eds.) *Rethinking Violence Against Women*. Thousand Oaks: Sage Publications.

Boddy, J. 2008. Clash of Selves: Gender, Personhood, and Human Rights Discourse in Colonial Sudan. *Finnish Journal of Ethnicity and Migration*, 3, 4–13.

Bramwell, R., Morland, C. & Garden, A. 2007. Expectations and experience of labial reduction: a qualitative study. *BJOG*, 114, 1493–1499.

Braun, V. 2009. "The Women Are Doing It For Themselves". The Rhetoric of Choice and Agency around Female Genital "Cosmetic Surgery". *Australian Feminist Studies*, 24, 233–249.

British Medical Association 2011. Female Genital Mutilation: Caring for patients and safeguarding children. *Guidance from the British Medical Association*. London: British Medical Association.

Bur, M. 2004. *Advancing Knowledge of Psycho-sexual Effects of Female Genital Cutting- Assessing the Evidence. A Seminar Report*. Cairo: International Network to Analyse, Communicate and Transform the Campaign Against FGC/FGM/FC (Intact).

Cameron, D. 2011. Prime Minister's speech at Munich Security Conference [Online]. Munich, Germany. Available: http://www.number10.gov.uk/news/pms-speech-at-munich-security-conference/ [Accessed 23.09.2011.]

Chambers, C. 2008. Creativity, Cultural Practice, and the Body: Foucault and Three Problems with the Liberal Focus on Choice. In: Chambers, C. (ed.) *Sex, Culture and Justice: The Limits of Choice*. Pennsylvania: Pennsylvania State University Press.

Conroy, R. M. 2006. Female genital mutilation: whose problem, whose solution? *BMJ*, 333, 106–7.

Deans, R., Liao, L.-M., Crouch, N. S. & Creighton, S. M. 2011. Why are women referred for female genital cosmetic surgery? *Medical Journal of Australia*, 195, 99.

Department of Health 2006. Advice for patients on cosmetic surgery and non-surgical cosmetic treatments. In: Department of Health (ed.). http://www.

dh.gov.uk/prod_consum_dh/groups/dh_digitalassets/@dh/@en/documents/digitalasset/dh_4138410.pdf

Doctors of The World UK 2010. Impact Report 2009–2010. London.

El Guindi, F. 2006. "Had This Been Your Face, Would You Leave It as Is?" Female Circumcision Among the Nubians of Egypt. In: Abusharaf, R. M. (ed.) *Female Circumcision*. Philadelphia: University of Pennsylvania Press.

Essen, B. & Johnsdotter, S. 2004. Female genital mutilation in the West: traditional circumcision versus genital cosmetic surgery. *Acta Obstetricia Gynecologica Scandinavica*, 83, 611–613.

Farmer, P. E., Nizeye, B., Stulac, S. & Keshavjee, S. 2006. Structural violence and clinical medicine. *PLoS Medicine*, 3, 1686–1691.

Feldman-Jacobs, C. & Clifton, D. 2010. *Female Genital Mutilation/Cutting: Data and Trends. Update 2010*. Washington DC: Population Reference Bureau.

Forward 2007. *A Statistical Study to Estimate the Prevalence of Female Genital Mutilation in England and Wales- Summary Report*. London: Forward.

Great Britain 2003. *Female Genital Mutilation Act 2003: Elizabeth II*. Chapter 31. London: The Stationary Office.

Hemmings, J. 2011. *Tackling FGM Special Initiative. Full Report*. London: Trust for London, Esmee Fairbairn Foundation, Rosa, Options UK.

HM Government 2009. *Together We Can End Violence Against Women and Girls: A Strategy*. London: The Home Office.

HM Government 2010. *Call to End Violence against Women and Girls*. London: The Home Office.

HM Government 2011. *Multi-Agency Practice Guidelines: Female Genital Mutilation*. In: OFFICE, T. H. (ed.). London: The Home Office.

Home Office 2006. *Gender Issues in the Asylum Claim (Asylum Policy Instruction)*. In: United Kingdom Border Agency (ed.). London: Home Office.

Home Office 2010. *Gender Issues in the Asylum Claim (Asylum Instruction)*. London: UKBA.

House of Lords [UKHL] 2006. Opinions of the Lords of Appeal for judgement in the case Fornah (FC) (Apellant) v, Secretary of State for the Home Department (Respondent). UKHL 46. In: House of Lords (ed.).

Johnsdotter, S. & Essen, B. 2010. Genitals and ethnicity: the politics of genital modification. *Reproductive Health Matters*, 18, 29–37.

Krause, E., Brandner, S., Mueller, M. & Kuhn, A. 2011. Out of Eastern Africa: Defibulation and Sexual Function in Women with Female Genital Mutilation. *Journal of Sexual Medicine*, 8, 1420–1425.

Leonard, L. 2000. "We Did It for Pleasure Only": Hearing Alternative Tales of Female Circumcision. *Qualitative Enquiry*, 6, 212–228.

Lewis (Ed), G. 2007. The Confidential Enquiry into Maternal and Child Health (CEMACH). Saving mother's lives: reviewing maternal deaths to make motherhood safer – 2003–2005. *The Seventh Report on Confidential Enquiries into Maternity Deaths in the United Kingdom*. London: CEMACH.

Liao, L.-M., Michala, L. & Creighton, S. M. 2010. Labial surgery for well women: a review of the literature. *BJOG*, 117, 20–25.

London Safeguarding Children Board 2007. *Safeguarding children at risk of abuse through Female Genital Mutilation*. London: London Safeguarding Children Board.

Momoh, C. 2005. Female Genital Mutilation. In: Momoh, C. (ed.) *Female Genital Mutilation*. Oxford: Radcliffe.

Morison, L. A., Dirir, A., Elmi, S., Warsame, J. & Dirir, S. 2004. How experiences and attitudes relating to female circumcision vary according to age on arrival in Britain: a study among young Somalis living in London. *Ethnicity and Health*, 9, 75–100.

Muslim Women's League. 1999. *Position paper on Female Genital Mutilation* [Online]. Available: http://www.mwlusa.org/topics/violence&harrassment/fgm.html [Accessed 23.10.2011].

O'connell, H., Sanjeevan, K. & Hutson, J. 2005. Anatomy of the clitoris. *The Journal of Urology*, 174, 1189–1195.

Obermeyer, C. M. 2005. The consequences of female circumcision for health and sexuality: An update on the evidence. *Culture, Health and Sexuality*, 7, 443–461.

Office for National Statistics 2011. *Migration Statistics Quarterly Report November 2011 - Statistical Bulletin*.

Roach, M. 2007. *An Investigation into the Barriers to the Effective Enforcement of UK Legislation against Female Genital Mutilation*. BSc Dissertation, University College London.

Royal College of Nursing 2006. *Female Genital Mutilation - an RCN educational resource for nursing and midwifery staff*. London: Royal College of Nursing.

Royal College of Obstetricians and Gynaecologists 2009. *Green-top Guideline No. 53: Female Genital Mutilation and its Management*. London: Royal College of Obstetricians and Gynaecologists.

Sheldon, S. & Wilkinson, S. 1998. Female Genital Mutilation and Cosmetic Surgery: Regulating Non-therapeutic Body Modification. *Bioethics*, 12, 263–285.

Talle, A. 2008. Precarious Identities: Somali Women in Exile. *Finnish Journal of Ethnicity and Migration*, 3, 64–73.

Target. 2006. *Islam Outlaws Female Mutilation! Recommendations of the conference of scholars in Cairo, November 2006*. [Online]. Available: http://www.target-human-rights.com/HP-08_fatwa/index.php?lang=en& [Accessed 20.6.11].

Tiefer, L. 2008. Female Genital Cosmetic Surgery: Freakish or Inevitable? Analysis from Medical Marketing, Bioethics, and Feminist Theory. *Feminism and Psychology*, 18, 466–479.

UNHCR 2002. *Guidelines on International Protection: Gender-related persecution within the context of Article 1A(2) of the 1951 Convention and/or its 1967 Protocol relating to the Status of Refugees*. Geneva: United Nations.

UNHCR 2009. *Guidance Note on Refugee Claims Relating to Female Genital Mutilation*. Geneva: United Nations.

UNICEF 2005. *Female Genital Mutilation: A statistical exploration*. New York: UNICEF.

United Nations 1951. *Convention Relating to the Status of Refugees*. Geneva: United Nations.

Walley, C. J. 2002. Searching for "Voices": Feminism, Anthropology and the Global Debate over Female Genital Operations. In: James, S. M. & Robertson, C. C. (eds.) *Genital Cutting and Transnational Sisterhood: Disputing U.S. Polemics*. Chicago: University of Illinois Press.

Webber, S. & Schonfeld, T. 2003. Cutting History, Cutting Culture: Female Circumcision in the United States. *American Journal of Bioethics*, 3, 65–66.

WHO 2000. *A Systematic Review of the Health Consequences of Female Genital Mutilation Including Sequelae in Childbirth*. Geneva.

WHO 2008. *Eliminating Female genital mutilation. An interagency Statement UNAIDS, UNDP, UNECA, UNESCO, UNFPA, UNHCHR, UNHCR, UNICEF, UNIFEM, WHO*. Geneva: WHO.

WHO 2010. *Female Genital Mutilation. Fact sheet no 241*. Geneva: WHO.

WHO, UNFPA & UNICEF 2009. *Technical Consultation on Medicalization of Female Genital Mutilation*. Report from technical consultation held 20th–22nd July 2009.

WHO Study Group on Female Genital Mutilation and Obstetric Outcome 2006. *Female Genital Mutilation and obstetric outcome: WHO collaborative prospective study in six African Countries*. Lancet, 367, 1835–41.

Williams, R. 2011. *Female circumcision prevention post abolished by government*. The Guardian, Wednesday 30th March 2011.

Chapter 6

'It's all about stopping you from getting on with your life':
Post-separation Violence in the Lives of Asian and African-Caribbean Women

Ravi K. Thiara

Post-separation violence has increasingly been recognised as a significant issue for large numbers of women and children seeking to move on from abuse to safety. Women encounter numerous obstacles in ending abuse in their lives, including the legal and protection frameworks that exist to protect women from violence but which in fact often serve to reinforce it instead. Child contact, in particular, has been shown to be central to women's experiences of post-separation violence (Eriksson and Hester 2001; Humphreys and Thiara 2002; Jaffe et al. 2003). Poor professional understandings of post-separation violence, where domestic violence is typically perceived as a pre-separation experience, shape responses to women and frequently leave them without protection.

While there are many commonalities in women's experiences of post-separation violence, the experiences of black and minority ethnic women (BME), located as they are at the intersection of multiple systems of oppression/discrimination, can be particularly pronounced. This is not only because of the sometimes greater determination on the part of their partners and other family members to continue control over women and children after separation but also because professional responses frequently betray a lack of insight into the complexity of their lives. This not only amplifies violence and abuse in women's lives but also creates additional issues if professionals, with a poor understanding of post-separation violence anyway, fail to respond effectively to their issues. By drawing on existing knowledge as well as data from three research studies,[1] this chapter focuses on

---

1   This chapter draws on three qualitative studies undertaken by the author between 2005 and 2011. The first study conducted in 2005–6 included interviews with 15 African-Caribbean women – Thiara, R.K. 2006. African-Caribbean Women and Children affected by Domestic Violence in Wolverhampton. Wolverhampton: The Haven. The second interviewed 12 Asian women in 2007 as part of research exploring issues of child contact and post-separation violence in relation to women and children – see Thiara, R.K. 2010. Continuing Control: Child Contact and Post-separation Violence, in Violence Against

the ways in which the abuse contexts of BME women overlap with issues of post-separation violence in the context of child contact and form a continuum of violence and control, exacerbated by the inadequate responses of professionals. In recognition of findings which suggest that women who experience high levels of abuse are more likely to face post-separation violence, the first part of the chapter presents BME women's experiences of abuse before separation, moving on to a discussion of post-separation violence.

Abuse Before Separation

A proportion of men who are most abusive when living with women and children continue this pattern, both physically and psychologically, following separation (Burgess et al. 1997; Morrison 2001; Davis and Andra 2000; Mechanic et al. 2000). It follows, therefore, that women who are most vulnerable to post-separation violence are those who experience more serious physical and sexual abuse and/or coercive control before separation (Morrison 2001; Coleman 1997; Mechanic et al. 2000). Those women who experience abuse at the hands of multiple perpetrators, such as Asian women, are also likely to experience abuse, control and pressure from a wider range of people in the pre- and post-separation periods.

Research on BME women suggests that they tend to experience a wider range of serious abuse at the hands of men as well as other family members and that they stay in abuse for longer periods (Anitha 2011; Thiara 2005; Thiara and Gill 2012; for similar issues raised in the US see Nash 2005; Richie 2003). If women remain in abuse for longer the possibility for that abuse to increase in frequency and severity is a likely scenario. This was a finding of the child contact study in which all 45 women interviewed spoke about daily abuse, increasing in severity and frequency, at the time of separation (Thiara and Gill 2012). A study of 124 BME women, the biggest sample to date in the UK, found that over 40 per cent of women had lived with abuse for five years or more, with around a quarter of these being in abuse for five to nine years and 16.3 per cent for ten years or more (Thiara and Roy 2010). The reasons for this have been variously attributed to: women being placed under pressure to remain within families and accept abuse; women not knowing how things operate because they are new to the country or subjected to extreme isolation; and women's own sense of shame and failure at ending relationships. Moreover, the vast majority (91%) of women in this study were subjected to weekly abuse, for 46 per cent abuse occurred on a daily basis and

---

Women in South Asian Communities: Issues for Policy and Practice, edited by R.K. Thiara and A.K. Gill. London: Jessica Kingsley Publishers. The third study (referred to as the 'child contact study') conducted between 2008–2011 included interviews with 30 Asian and 15 African-Caribbean women – Thiara, R.K. and Gill, A. 2012. Domestic Violence, Child Contact, Post-Separation Violence: Issues for South Asian and African-Caribbean Women and Children, London: NSPCC.

attempted, or threats to, murder was reported by a quarter. While the perpetrator was a spouse or partner in two-thirds of cases, women had experienced abuse from other family members in over half of cases (op cit: 4).

Across all three studies, the majority of women reported a wide range of daily abuse, where, despite high levels of physical violence, many had been unable to access medical attention. The long term impact of this undermined their sense of self.

> He would swear at me, he would throw things at me. He would smash plates. He would throw me on the floor and he says 'bitch' that I am a 'little piece of shit' that I deserve to be treated like this.

Alongside the chronic abuse, isolation – often extreme – is frequently reported by many BME women along with high levels of control by men and their families. Being isolated from family and friends, whilst having their routines completely controlled by men, is exacerbated for those women who have no family or support networks. In such contexts, women often find themselves at the total whim of their partners and families, who frequently threw women out or made threats to 'send them back' to the country of origin.

> He physically threw me out with the two girls and took the key away from me. The girls were so scared … I didn't know where to go and I didn't have no money in my pocket and I am just new to the area … and then he calls me and says 'come back home or I will catch you and kill you'.

Financial dependence on men/families further limited women's options and took two main forms: being required to live in total financial dependence/poverty (more common among Asian women); men taking women's money if they worked or were on benefits (more common among African-Caribbean women). Abuse during pregnancy was also experienced by a significant number of the women in the three studies, with over half of both African-Caribbean and Asian women reporting this in the child contact research. Sometimes women were punished for becoming pregnant despite men's refusal to allow them to use contraception.

> I had two abortions but kept on getting pregnant. Then he would beat me for getting pregnant. He would pull a knife on me. Instead of contraception he wanted me to have abortions.

Sexual jealousy and allegations of promiscuity were also common experiences. For Asian women, this was frequently articulated by both men and their families to taint women's character and to justify abuse as well as to explain women's absence from the family. In the child contact study, sexual violence was reported by a significant number of the women, ranging from coerced sex to repeated rape (Thiara and Gill 2012).

While the issue of women's mothering and the undermining of the mother-child relationship have been explored by other research (Lapierre 2010; Morris, 2010; Radford and Hester 2006; Thiara et al. 2006), findings from the two studies involving Asian women show that for half of them abuse included the systematic denial of a relationship with their children, who were seen as the property of the fathers and their families. This has implications for post-separation violence, where children are often used as a vehicle for men to continue abusing women. Moreover, men have been reported to disregard the presence of children when being abusive towards their partners and often show a lack of concern about the effects of their violence on children (Harne 2003, 2011; Thiara 2010). Children living in situations of frequent abuse perpetrated over a long time are more likely to become victims themselves. Asian children in the child contact study were found to be more exposed to abuse because of the greater vulnerability and isolation of their mothers (Thiara and Gill 2012).

The regulation of women's behaviour in many Asian families and communities marked by collectivist values, where notions of *izzat* and *honour* shape responses, secures women's silence, since those who transgress risk being ostracised (Mullender et al. 2002; Gill 2004). For women in such families, involving others is viewed negatively because family matters are regarded as private. On the other hand, involving outsiders or authorities is considered by African-Caribbean women to reinforce stereotypes of family structures and let down the 'race'. Moreover, the widespread stereotyping and discrimination among statutory and voluntary services leads many African-Caribbean women to not trust agencies or professionals (Mama 1989; Rai and Thiara 1996; Sen 1997; Minhas et al. 2002; Thiara and Gill 2012). Thus, whilst the pressures on Asian and African-Caribbean women may differ they have the same outcomes – women delay seeking help and remain in abusive relationships for many years. They are entrapped not only by community shame and stigma but their own fears – of being thrown out of the country, having their children taken away from them or being regarded as a 'traitor to the race'.

Separation, which may take many years to effect, can be a difficult time, not least because it can lead to greater abuse. Children are often the deciding factor in when women separate (Mullender et al. 2002) and this is no different for BME women, who repeatedly mention their anxieties about the impact on children as motivating the final decision. Asian women have been found to resort to third party (professionals, friends or family) interventions in a crisis while African-Caribbean women, in the main, appear to deal with it themselves or enlist the support of friends or family members (Thiara 2006, 2011; Thiara and Gill 2012). Both feared reprisal from partners, with Asian women also having to contend with other family and community members.

Post-separation Violence

It is widely recognised that the decision to leave and separation itself constitutes a time of heightened risk, including for homicide and the murder of children (Saunders 2007). Hardesty and Chung (2006) in the US, argue that harassment, stalking and physical abuse either continues, or begins and escalates, for around a quarter to a third of women and that children may witness violence more frequently after separation (cited in Saunders 2007:4). The heightened risk of post-separation violence has increasingly been highlighted through a body of international research, mainly from the US, which has usefully been brought together by Brownridge (2006) in a review of the prevalence and risk markers, with contention about terminology and definitions also explored (op cit). This is further complicated for BME women, especially Asian women, for whom there are often greater numbers of people involved, suggesting that definitions may have to further accommodate these factors.

This body of research, dating back to the 1970s, though mainly published in the late 1990s, finds rates of post-separation violence ranging between 19 and 40 per cent, leading Brownridge to conclude that: "it appears that separated women have as much as thirty times the likelihood, and divorced women have as much as nine times the likelihood, of reporting non-lethal violence compared to married women" (2006: 516–517). The killing of women and children are extreme forms of post-separation violence (Saunders, 2004).

In the UK, the British Crime Survey showed that while separation was the best avenue of escape from domestic violence, for more than third (37%) of women violence either increased, took a different form, remained the same or commenced following separation (Walby and Allen 2004). A study of 161 separated women found that over three-quarters (76%) experienced further abuse and harassment: while this ceased after 6–12 months for the majority, more than a third (36%) continued to be abused more than a year after separation, with child contact a critical factor in on-going violence and abuse (Humphreys and Thiara 2003). An earlier study by Wilcox (2000) also found that a third of separated women experienced persistent violence, with research conducted in the early 1990s showing that separated women had five times the risk of intimate femicide compared to other women (Crawford and Gartner 1992). Research on domestic violence homicides in the UK further indicates that a large number of these involved separated women (Richards 2003; Saunders 2001).

Despite research recognition, little attention has been given to post-separation violence by the courts, the police and other professionals. In highlighting the failures of past family court judgements to take adequate account of post-separation violence, Humphreys considered judges to over-emphasise the presumption of contact and to ignore the continuing threat posed by abusive men to their former partners, though developments over the last decade appear to have led to some positive developments (1998:314). A study in the late 1990s showed that a third of domestic violence calls to the police came from women who had separated but were being harassed by ex-partners (Kelly 1998) but more recent research shows that when child contact issues are involved the police do not always respond positively (Thiara and Gill 2012). Indeed, the lack of effective intervention means women and children are unprotected when they do what policy, professionals and the public expect them to do – leave violent men. Separation does not necessarily create safety.

Child contact provides the greatest opportunity to abusive men for the continuation of post-separation violence. Disputes over children are closely connected by a number of researchers to on-going or worsening abuse of women (Hester and Radford 1996; Humphreys 1998). Within this, children may also be more likely to witness violence than before separation (Hardesty and Chung 2006). Moreover, where men may not have direct access to women and children, they have been reported to use the formal child contact process to harass their ex-partners through lengthy contact disputes or continuous litigation (Jaffe et al. 2003; Saunders 2007) alongside violence and harassment before, during and after child contact visits (Harrison 2008). The use of legal processes by men to gain continued access to women and children in order to continue abuse has been highlighted by past and recent research (Hester and Radford 1996; Humphreys and Thiara 2003; Thiara and Gill 2012). The difficulties experienced by those women who find themselves in such situations have led some researchers to suggest that child contact often replaces the intimate relationship as the avenue for men to control women (Eriksson and Hester 2001), thus making acrimonious child contact where there has been domestic violence itself a form of post-separation violence.

BME Women's Experiences of Post-separation Violence

> After I left he continued to harass me, threatened me. He was absolutely violent.
> He beat me up on the street. He's done a lot … It's so much.

Reflecting previous findings which indicate that large numbers of BME women are likely to face ongoing violence after separation, recent research found that the majority of BME women who were not living in a refuge reported post-separation issues. Over a third (35%) of these women experienced on-going abuse from a partner (including stalking, threats, violence), over a quarter (27%) experienced harassment and/or violence from extended family members, and just under a third (31%) experienced pressure from the wider community (Roy and Thiara 2012). Thus, not only is there a high likelihood of post-separation violence in BME women's lives but Asian women are very likely to be subjected to this by a range of other people as well as their ex-partners.

Previous research shows that of the 76 per cent of women who reported continuing abuse and harassment from their ex-partners, post-separation violence appeared to be less of a problem proportionally for BME women in the first six months (possibly explained by this group moving to a place of safety such as a refuge). However, it is noteworthy that those BME women who experienced it in the short-term experienced it for longer than their white counterparts (Humphreys and Thiara 2003). Together, these findings indicate that it is likely to take BME women longer to establish safety for themselves and their children, something that has clear implications for policy and practice.

The child contact study showed that post-separation violence was a reality for 78 per cent of separated Asian and African-Caribbean women with children who were involved in contact disputes with ex-partners. In most of these cases, this was severe and chronic (Thiara and Gill 2012). Child contact for such women can serve as a route through which abusive men and their families/friends gain access to women and children and continue to exert control and abuse in their lives. Since BME women can experience great isolation after leaving families and communities, this can result in greater vulnerability, making them more susceptible to post-separation violence as well as pressure to return.

Being subjected to threats to kill and physical violence, often, though not always, connected to demands to see children was a common experience for many women in the three studies. What is evident in many of the women's accounts is that children often provided the 'door' that men needed to have continuous access to women even though their presence did not deter men from using violence, as reflected in the words of one African-Caribbean woman.

> I'd split up with him and he would just come into the house to see his son and then the next day he just came in the day time and it's like coincidence that I was actually in. And because I wouldn't let him in he just broke into the house and beat me up, I had to go to hospital and that's when the contact broke down.

Given the increased options afforded by the development of communication technologies, abusive men are also reported to be more able to perpetrate post-separation harassment.

Much of the initial post-separation violence, often in the form of threats and intense emotional pressure, tended to be aimed at securing women's return to the relationship. When men realise this is unlikely, issues of contact and access to children come to the fore. Given the protracted nature of contact disputes, this can create a context for on-going abuse over many years, frustrating women's ability to reestablish lives and rebuild their sense of safety and self. Post-separation violence can be especially severe for those women whose partners are involved in other forms of criminality, such as drugs, or are a part of criminal networks. In such situations, the fear of reprisal from partners who made threats to women against involving the police can result in a lack of protection for women against their on-going violence. Often the pressure of dealing with severe and prolonged post-separation violence as well as living in fear compromised women's emotional and mental wellbeing.

He kept phoning me and using different names. Finally he got me on the phone and he said 'I'm going to rape you outside your work. You better watch your back at work. I'm going to wait for you outside your house'. That sent me into a spiral of despair … I had a breakdown. I cried my eyes out.

When the Legal Process Becomes a Vehicle for Abuse

The centrality of the legal process in the perpetration of post-separation violence has been highlighted by recent research (Radford and Hester 2006; Thiara 2010; Thiara and Gill 2012). For some men, a protracted process involving multiple court dates offers an avenue of continued access to women. It can also be used as a way of 'publicly' humiliating women and tainting their character in order to reclaim the 'honour' of the family or male honour/reputation.

BME women are often pressured to withdraw from the legal process, either in the family courts or if pursuing a criminal prosecution, through invocations of family honour to maintain the respect of the family and/or 'race'.

> I've known this man for twelve years and every single time a court case is approaching he does something to me. Whether it's by phone call or whether it's physical … It's almost witness intimidation. That's the only way I can describe it.

A tactic reported in the child contact study was men's use of the legal process to obtain information about women. There is often a lack of awareness on the part of legal professionals and the judiciary about these issues, as well as a lack of insight about the ways in which some men use the legal process to continue their abuse.

> It's pressure on the woman to withdraw the allegations from family members or even just give in to contact and not to go through the whole judicial process. Just a lot of bullying involved … And I suppose to what extent the judicial system should be alert enough to pick up on that kind of pressure. You see the problem is if a woman withdraws those allegations … the court would say why did you make them in the first place?

Use of child contact

As already noted, child contact and children are often used by abusive men to control, intimidate and undermine women (Radford and Hester 2006; Thiara 2010). As a result of poor understanding of post-separation violence among professionals, women are frequently left unprotected. Where men's attempts to control women fail, some resort to recruiting state agencies to collude with their abuse. This includes men reporting women to social services for the abuse and neglect of children, which results in greater scrutiny of women's parenting rather than men's violence. Some Asian men also argue in court that women are poorly placed to meet children's cultural and religious needs, as they have 'chosen' to live outside their communities: an argument that can find a sympathetic, though ill-informed, ear amongst some judges. Such undermining is also effected through the children who are frequently manipulated in men's bids to construct women as either 'mad' or 'bad' to professionals (Morris 2009).

BME women's isolation after separation in a societal context of racism can accentuate their desire that children have regular contact with fathers and families. This combines, for some, with pressure from families, or within themselves, not to let down their family, community or 'race'. However, although many women attempt to set up informal contact, this can be short-lived if it becomes a means for ongoing abuse (Radford and Hester 2006). Despite women's attempts to remain civil for the sake of their children, when their own safety and that of their children is compromised they may request that contact take place in supervised settings (Thiara and Gill 2012).

Skilled abusers are adept at using every avenue to perpetrate post-separation violence. Thus, not only are contact centres sites where women are abused, often through the use of their own languages which is not picked up by centre staff, but telephone contact with children can often become a vehicle for men to monitor and control women through the children: *'he will ask her so many questions about what I am doing, where I am, who I'm with'*. Children may also be taught words and behaviours, as ciphers for their father.

> When he used to drop off my daughter he would swear at me and behind my back he would teach my daughter bad things. He told her to swear at me, and when she used to come back to me, she would kick me and show me her finger. When I asked her who taught her that, she would name her father and his sister.

Such tactics by men, including the (ab)use of children to 'get back' at women are reported not to be taken seriously by CAFCASS[2] and other professionals, leaving women to deal with such destructive undermining and manipulation of children unsupported.

Threats of separation from children and abduction

In the rare instances where men are denied contact because of their abusive behaviour, or more commonly when they refuse to engage with the formal process but demand to see their children anyway, women report frequent threats of abduction. For BME men and families, the threat of separation from and/or abduction of children can be particularly coercive, forcing women to comply with their demands. The higher likelihood of victims of parental abduction being from minority ethnic groups was raised by a study in 2004 (Newiss and Fairbrother

---

2   The Children and Family Court Advisory and Support Service represents the interest of children involved in family proceedings.

2004). Again, women report that such threats were rarely taken seriously by professionals as they were seen to fall below the threshold of actual attempted abduction. Indeed, recent research suggests that allegations of abduction[3] are a particular feature of post-separation violence and are a significant issue for high numbers of BME women (see Thiara 2010). However, in most cases where abduction is alleged in the context of child contact, it is an act which falls short of the legal definition of abduction and may instead be more accurately seen as a form of violence/abuse which becomes more common as women become less accessible to direct forms of abuse after separation.[4]

Preventing women from moving on

Clearly, safety is an important factor in women's ability to move on with their lives and something that is completely undermined by post-separation violence, resulting either in constant moves or living in a state of fear. While domestic violence support services play a crucial role in assisting many women and children to live safe lives, even this can be inadequate for those women who are subjected to persistent post-separation violence. The following account from an African-Caribbean woman shows the determination on the part of her partner, even when she was living in a refuge.

> I see an erratic driver behind me. I get scared even more when I see its him through my rear view mirror. Even an ambulance with it's lights on couldn't stop him. I pulled over for the ambulance, he didn't. He pulled alongside me, wound down his window and was shouting at me. And the ambulance is behind bipping trying to get through ... and he's diagonally across the road and blocked my path so I can't go anywhere. And he's got out of his car and he's approaching my car. I managed to find my phone and dial 999 at this point. I felt sick. I feel sick talking about it.

Post-separation violence linked to child contact clearly frustrates women's attempts to establish independent and safe lives. However, despite the increasing

---

3   In this context abduction refers to situations where a parent (usually a father) is alleged to have kept children after contact; taken them from school; from the street; has taken them abroad or has threatened to take the children to another country.

4   The Child Abduction Act 1984 allows for only two types of abduction, parent abduction and stranger abduction. In the former 'a person connected with the child under the age of sixteen .... Takes or sends the child out of the United Kingdom without the appropriate consent'. 'Person connected with the child' includes a parent, the father, a guardian or a person with either a residence order or custody over the child and an offence is committed only if the child is taken out of the UK for a period exceeding one month. It is argued that at least one third of parental child abductions should not have been recorded by the police or should have been recorded as 'no crime' at a later stage according to the legal definition.

evidence of post-separation violence, there appears to be limited understanding of the issues among professionals. In the child contact research, even when women called the police after being subjected to serious assaults, officers regarded men's behavior as understandably related to wanting to see their children or as a 'tiff' over children rather than as repeat victimisation. As already noted, legal professionals, the judiciary and CAFCASS practitioners were also considered to be lacking insight into post-separation violence issues, especially for BME women, leading to many of these women remaining without protection and support.

Conclusion

Post-separation violence, where men and their families/community members/ friends attempt to continue to control the lives and choices of women and children after they have left the situation of violence, constitutes as a continuum (Kelly, 1988) of abuse in BME women's lives and disrupts their attempts to 'get free' from violence. While post-separation violence is an issue for many women, especially if they have children, for BME women this takes on greater significance as they often have to leave their community and/or may have to endure greater pressure to return to the family.

Since greater numbers of potential perpetrators are involved in the post-separation period, especially in the case of Asian women, this can create greater risk and continue for lengthy periods. Child contact and disputes over children are used by some men and families to continue abuse and can be seen to constitute a form of post-separation violence. For many women, this continuum of abuse serves to entrap them for many years and frustrates their attempts to rebuild their lives. Positive responses from agencies and professionals are key to women finding protection. Women's accounts reveal that their experiences are frequently not understood by professionals and they are left, unsupported, to deal with men's abuse alone. Clearly, when post-separation violence is neglected by professionals, risk and safety issues for women and children are also inadequately assessed, thus endangering women and children. The research discussed in this chapter provides compelling evidence for greater consideration to be given to issues of post-separation violence, as they affect BME women and children, within the service commissioning and planning processes, service delivery, and the training of professionals.

References

Anitha, S. 2011. Legislating gender inequalities: the nature and patterns of domestic violence experienced by South Asian women with insecure immigration status in the United Kingdon. *Violence Against Women,* 17 (10): 1260–1285.

Brownridge, D.A. 2006. Violence against women post-separation. *Aggression and Violence Behaviour, 11:* 514–530.

Burgess, A., Baker, T., Greening, D., Hartman, C., Douglas, J. and Halloran, R. 1997. Stalking behaviours within domestic violence. *Journal of Family Violence,* 12: 389–403.

Coleman, F. 1997. Stalking behaviour and the cycle of domestic violence. *Journal of Interpersonal Violence*, 12: 420–32.

Crawford, M. and Gartner, R. 1992. *Woman killing: Intimate femicide in Ontario 1974-1990.* Toronto: Women We Honour Action Committee.

Davis, K. and Andra, M. 2000. Stalking perpetrators and psychological maltreatment of partners: anger-jealousy, attachment insecurity, need of control and break-up context. *Violence and Victims*, 15: 407–25.

Eriksson, M. and Hester, M. 2001. Violent men as good enough fathers? A look at England and Sweden. *Violence Against Women, 7*: 779–798.

Gill, A. 2004. Voicing the silent fear: South Asian women's experience of domestic violence. *Howard Journal of Criminal Justice,* 43 (5): 465–83.

Hardesty, J.L. and Chung, G.H. 2006. Intimate partner violence, parental divorce, and child custody: directions for intervention and future research. *Family Relations, 55*: 200–210.

Harne, L 2004. Childcare, violence and fathering – are violent fathers who look after their children likely to be less abusive? in *Gender, Conflict and Violence,* edited by R. Klein and B. Wallner. Vienna: Studien-Verlag.

Harne, L. 2011. *Violent Fathering and the Risks to Children: The Need for Change.* Bristol: The Policy Press.

Harrison, C. 2008. Implacably hostile or appropriately protective? Women managing child contact in the context of domestic violence. *Violence Against Women,* 14(4): 381–405.

Hester, M., and Radford, L. 1996. *Domestic violence and child contact arrangements in England and Denmark.* Bristol: Policy Press.

Humphreys, C. 1998. Judicial alienation syndrome – failures to respond to post-separation violence. *Fam Law,* May: 313–316.

Humphreys, C. and Thiara, R. 2003. Post-separation violence: a public failure to protect. *Journal of Social Welfare and Family Law*, 25 (3): 195–214.

Jaffe, P.G., Lemon, N.K.D., and Poisson, S.E. 2003. *Child custody and domestic violence: A call for safety and accountability.* Thousand Oaks, CA: Sage.

Kelly, L. 1988. *Surviving Sexual Violence.* Cambridge: Polity Press.

Kelly, L. 1998. *Domestic Violence Matters.* London: Home Office.

Lapierre, S. 2010. More responsibilities, less control: understanding the challenges and difficulties involved in mothering in the context of domestic violence. *British Journal of Social Work,* 40: 1434–1451.

Mama, A. 1989. *The Hidden Struggle.* London: London Race and Housing Research Unit.

Mechanic, M., Weaver, T. and Resick, P. 2000. Intimate partner violence and stalking behaviour: exploration of patterns and correlates in a sample of acutely battered women. *Violence and Victims,* 15: 55–72.

Minhas, N., Hollows, A., Kerr, Y.S. and Ibbotson, R. 2002. *South Asian Women's Experiences of Domestic Violence: Pillar of Support.* Sheffield: Survey and Statistical Research Centre.

Morris, A. 2009. Gendered dynamics of abuse and violence in families: considering the abusive household gender regime. *Child Abuse Review,* 18: 414–427.

Morrison, K. 2001. Predicting violent behaviour in stalkers: a preliminary investigation of Canadian cases in criminal harassment. *Journal of Forensic Science,* 46: 1403–10.

Mullender, A., Hague, G., Imam, G., Kelly, L., Malos, E., and Regan, L. 2002. *Children's Perspective on Domestic Violence.* London: Sage.

Nash, S.T. 2005. Through black eyes: African American women's constructions of their experiences with intimate male partner violence. *Violence Against Women,* 11 (11), 1420–1440.

Newiss, G., and Fairbrother, L. (2004).*Child abduction. Understanding police recorded crime statistics: Findings 225.* Home Office Research, Development and Statistics Directorate: London.

Radford, L. and Hester, M. 2006. *Mothering Through Domestic Violence.* London: Jessica Kingsley Publishers.

Rai, D. and Thiara, R. 1996. *Redefining Spaces: The Needs of Black Women and Children and Black Workers in Women's Aid.* Bristol: Women's Aid Federation England.

Richards, L. 2003. *Findings from the multi-agency domestic violence murder reviews in London.* London: Metropolitan Police.

Richie, B.E. 2003. Gender entrapment and African American women: An analysis of race, ethnicity, gender and intimate violence in *Violent crime: Assessing race and ethnic differences,* edited by D.F. Hawkins. Cambridge: Cambridge University Press.

Roy, S. and Thiara, R.K. 2012. *Vital Statistics.* London: Imkaan.

Saunders, D.G. 2007. *Child Custody and Visitation Decisions in Domestic Violence Cases: Legal Trends, Risk Factors, and Safety Concerns.* Harrisburg, PA: VAWnet, a project of the National Resource Center on Domestic Violence/ Pennsylvania Coalition Against Domestic Violence.

Saunders, H. 2001. *Making contact worse.* Bristol: Women's Aid Federation of England.

Saunders, H. 2004. *Twenty-nine child homicides: Lessons still to be learnt on domestic violence and child protection.* Bristol: Women's Aid Federation of England.

Sen, P. 1997. *Searching for Routes to Safety.* London: London Borough of Camden Equalities Unit.

Thiara, R.K. 2005. The need for specialist domestic violence services for Asian women and children. London: Imkaan.

Thiara, R.K., Humphreys, C., Skamballis, A. and Mullender, A. 2006. *Talking to My Mum: Developing Communication between Mothers and their Children in the Aftermath of Domestic Violence. Report of Key Findings*. University of Warwick: Centre for the Study of Safety and Well-being.

Thiara, R.K. 2006. African-Caribbean women and children affected by domestic violence in Wolverhampton. Wolverhampton: The Haven.

Thiara, R.K. 2010. Continuing control: child contact and post-separation violence, in *Violence Against Women in South Asian Communities: Issues for Policy and Practice*, edited by R.K. Thiara and A.K. Gill. London: Jessica Kingsley Publishers.

Thiara, R.K. and Roy, S. 2010. *Vital Statistics*, London: Imkaan.

Thiara, R.K. 2011. 'Hard feisty women' – 'coping on your own': African-Caribbean women and domestic violence, in *Violence Against Women and Ethnicity: Commonalities and Differences across Europe,* edited by R.K. Thiara, S. Condon and M. Schroettle. Opladen, Germany: Barbara Budrich Publishers.

Thiara, R.K. and Gill, A. 2012. Domestic violence, child contact, post-separation violence: issues for South Asian and African-Caribbean women and children. London: NSPCC.

Walby, S. and Allen, J. 2004. *Domestic Violence, sexual assault and stalking: Findings from the British Crime Survey*. Home Office Research Study 276. London: Home Office. 2004

Wilcox, P. 2000. Me mother's bank and me nanna's, you know, support! Women who left domestic violence in England and issues of informal support. *Women's Studies International Forum*, 23: 35–47.

Chapter 7

Criminal Gangs, Male-Dominated Services and the Women and Girls Who Fall Through the Gaps

Carlene Firmin

Introduction

The experience that women and girls have of gang-related violence across the UK is rarely understood and often sensationalised. This chapter was produced in June 2011 and reflects where policy, practice and research had developed to that date.

Over the past five years there has been an increasing public debate, through newspapers, television documentaries and political statements on the 'phenomenon' of the 'girl gang' or 'gang-rape' but these debates often conflate, oversimplify and misrepresent traumatic, serious and complex forms of violence that affect women and girls across the country.

If we are to ask the question – does gang-related violence affect women and girls? – the answer would most definitely be 'yes'. If we were to wonder whether women play an active role and display agency in some forms of this violence, once again the answer would be 'yes'. Are women and girls victimised by criminal gangs? – 'yes' again.

All of this violence takes place within a male-dominated context, both ideologically and practically. As a result the female experience of violence within this context is very much gendered in a multi-faceted manner; a manner which is rarely appreciated by commentators or explored by policymakers and service providers.

Drawing upon the evidence base generated during ROTA's Female Voice in Violence Research Programme (FVV) and considering wider debates about violence against women and girls, race and ethnicity, violence, gangs and youth justice, this chapter will unpick the gendered experience that women and girls have of gang-related violence, considering the implications of this for policymakers and practitioners who want to turn the tide.

Context – England's Criminal Gangs

From the outset it is crucial to outline what I mean by 'criminal gang'. Over recent decades UK academics have sought to define what we mean by 'gang' in the UK context and have debated whether such a thing even exists. Of the many definitions, that offered by John Pitts is the most applicable for capturing the UK context that I am concerned with.

> A relatively, predominantly street-based group of young people who (1) see themselves (and are seen by others) as a discernible group, (2) engage in a range of criminal activity and violence, (3) identify with or lay claim over territory, (4) have some form of identifying structural feature, and (5) are in conflict with other, similar, gangs. (Centre for Social Justice 2009: 3)

It is important to outline, from the outset, how I understand the word 'gang'. From a public and media perspective the term 'gang' is used to capture many group-related offences, particular those that involve sexual violence. This chapter is only considering offences committed by street gangs as they have been defined above. Gang-related violence does not require multiple perpetrators to be present at any given time but the violence always takes place within the context of a street gang. This is distinct from multiple perpetrator offences that are routinely referred to as being committed by 'gangs' in a way that I would consider to be inaccurate (see also Horvath and Kelly, 2009).

This UK understanding is distinct from women gangs in the US: the history, structure and cultural context of criminal gangs are fundamentally different. It does not follow, from this difference that criminal gangs do not exist in the UK. From the research that I have conducted over the past five years I conclude that criminal gangs *do* exist in the UK. The academic debates on definitions, from Thrasher (1927) onwards in the US and by Hallsworth and Young (2004) and John Pitts (2008) in the UK, capture the complexity of understanding the term 'criminal gang'. Gangs, for example, that operate in Glasgow will be very different to those that operate in Liverpool, with further variations in Manchester, Birmingham, London, Nottingham, and Bristol. The distinctions offered by academics enable us to draw together differences and commonalities and set the scene within which gang-related violence takes place.

Girls and Gangs – An Academic Perspective

Academic consideration of girls and criminal gangs in the UK is scarce. Most notably, Susan Batchelor and Michelle Burman (2001) have investigated girls' use of violence inside and out of gang context. While their research is primarily concerned with girls in Scotland, they do identify some transferable concerns, particularly in relation to girls who are in the justice system or involved in violence.

They argue that developing effective practice to respond to girls and violence means gearing interventions to the *specific* needs and experience of the young women involved, rather than relying on programmes that have developed primarily for working with men. Additionally, professionals should pay "greater attention to the gendered context in which girls experience violence, both as perpetrators and victims" (Batchelor, Burman and Brown 2001:132). The hyper-masculine nature of criminal gangs means that the context that gang-associated women and girls navigate is specifically gendered, and the argument Batchelor et al. make for gendered interventions is therefore applicable beyond Scotland. While there may be historical, structural and behavioural differences between street gangs in Scotland and England, (for example Scottish gangs rarely use firearms and are often inter-generational), the hyper-masculine nature of gangs, and gang-related violence, is evident throughout the UK and internationally.

In their assessment of evidence on girls, gangs and violence, Burman and Batchelor (2009) critique research on gang-associated females that focuses purely on their victimisation, without considering their agency and propensity to be violent. Once again, these arguments are applicable across the UK and are significant for professionals who seek to work with gang-associated women and girls. However, trying to address their victimisation or their violence, exclusive of each other, will be insufficient.

The majority of academic literature on girls and gang violence is based on the US context. Anne Campbell's book *The Girls in the Gang* (1984) is one of the most comprehensive accounts of female agency and victimisation within criminal gangs. The complex relationship between the free and constrained choices made by the females who associated, or were directly involved, with criminal gangs is also discussed by Jody Miller (2001). Miller is keen to understand and assert the agency of female gang members. While Miller's arguments are important, the structure of American gangs, specifically those in which girls operate as 'gang members' or within all girl gangs, means that their agency is more explicit. In contrast, Batchelor and Burman argue that girl's agency often operates in a much more subtle fashion, and violence that they 'do' often occurs in private.

UK understanding has further limitations in relation to girls in England, given that the evidence base is strongly drawn from the experiences of white females, specifically in Scotland, while the US gang literature predominantly explores the experiences of 'gang members', rather than gang associates, who are African-American and Hispanic women and girls.

It is not possible to consider the impact of gang violence on females without paying consideration to the wives, girlfriends, sexual partners, mothers, sisters and friends of male gang members. It is the violence experienced by all of these females, in addition to those who identify as members of mixed gender gangs, which is the focus of this chapter. Service and policy responses to this group of vulnerable women and girls needs to be developed for their own protection and that of the wider public. One of the greatest challenges faced by those who wish to intervene is to reconcile the idea that many of these women and girls will have both victimised others and have been victimised themselves, and those that work with them will be seeking to reduce both the risk that they face and the risk that they pose.

Race and Ethnicity

Given the limited intelligence and research on gang membership in the UK, it is not possible to draw firm conclusions on the ethnic profile of gang members. However, a disproportionate number of men and boys from ethnic minority groups have been victims of gang-related murder and attempted murder. In addition criminal gangs operate, in the main, in and around urban parts of England and Wales where communities are more ethnically diverse. While Glasgow may present a different picture, it is commonly accepted that gang activity in Glasgow is very different to that in other parts of the UK due to its historic routes. Therefore, while there is no evidence to suggest that gang membership is disproportionately Black British, African, Caribbean, Turkish, Greek, Pakistani, Bangladeshi, Indian or White, the disproportionality in murder rates, and the racial tensions in some parts of the country, mean that gang-associated violence must be considered for women and girls from ethnic minority communities.

The fact that men and boys from ethnic minority groups, particularly those from African, Caribbean, and more recently Turkish communities, are disproportionately represented in murder and attempted murder statistics, has as significant impact on the women and girls they associate with, especially family members. Mothers, sisters and daughters interviewed over the course of FVV expressed continuous fear that their male relatives would be killed. This fear showed itself in all manner of ways including sleep deprivation, anxiety, panic attacks, paranoia, trauma and, for some, bereavement.

> Massive risks – and other people don't really appreciate that. People coming to your house and looking for your son; breaking down your door (Firmin 2010:45).

> Wherever I go I feel guilty cos of what me son did, everywhere I go my guilt will be with me (Firmin 2011:34).

The impact of gang-association on the mental health and emotional wellbeing of family members was exacerbated by concern for the loyalty they had for the family and an unwillingness to be seen to be cooperating with the police or social services.

> No one in my family would ever do that. If I done that to A (my sister) then I would be called a snitch for the rest of my life (Firmin 2011:36).

Interviews with males endorsed this position.

> You cannot snitch on family that is it (Firmin 2011:53).

The risks and harms faced by gang-associated female family members is stark, as is the lack of culturally specific service provision available to offer support and advice: also evident for women and girls in romantic or peer relationships with men and boys involved in criminal gangs. During FVV two significant issues emerged.

Firstly, in areas or cities where tensions existed between ethnic groups, criminal gangs also grew along racially segregated lines. This rarely occurred in London but in places like Birmingham tensions were more apparent. As a result girls explained their inability to date outside of their ethnic group as the outcome of their male siblings' involvement in criminal gangs.

Conflation of gang and racial loyalties creates difficulties for practitioners in ascertaining where risks lie: what may seem like a case of so-called 'honour'-based violence linked to racial tensions may actually be one that is driven by gang rivalries. It is important for professionals to be able to recognise these risks, and consult with those organisations who specialise in race equality and/or so-called 'honour-based' violence.

Consultation with wider organisations is also necessary for the second tension that the research identified. Professionals, in some local areas, inform families if they suspect a child is associating with criminal gangs as a form of early intervention. Unfortunately, on more than one occasion practitioners described how, having informed families, girls from ethnic minority communities were sent to other countries or withdrawn from school and severely punished. These reactions were not a response to the knowledge that a girl is gang-associated, rather their concern was that she is associating with males who are often older and perhaps from a different ethnic group. It is crucial for professionals to identify whether there is the potential for such a reaction before intervening with a family visit, whilst at the same time guarding against stereotyping ethnic minority families. Local community groups, those who specialise in race equality and culturally-specific violence against women services, need to be consulted in order to find the best way for families to engage in protecting or supporting their child.

Violence

As noted previously, violence is integral to the operation of a criminal gang. The life of those in, or associated with, criminal gangs, is one in which the navigation, avoidance, and deliverance of a range of forms of violence, is a matter of protection, intimidation, revenge and business. Dependent upon their gang-association women and girls will also engage in and/or experience gang-related violence.

Street Violence

While there may have been increased public and media driven anxiety about the rise in 'girl gangs' and girls being violent, in reality there is little evidence to justify this. There is evidence that the criminal justice system is processing more girls who are involved in violence, but it could be that girl's violence is being identified more rather than girls committing more violence.

In a criminal gang context women and girls have reported instigating, endorsing, experiencing and committing physical violence. When they were being interviewed for FVV girls discussed inflicting violence upon other girls, and on occasion upon other boys. Their motivations for such violence were multi-faceted and very often interlinked.

> I'm only violent with other girls if they have said something about one of my boys, then I might come in as the girl to deal with her first; they wouldn't jump in straight away unless she didn't learn her lesson (Firmin 2010:58).

> I had heard what she had been saying about me and couldn't let it continue ... Ok so maybe I went a bit too far but I was so vexed as well that I didn't care (Firmin 2010:58).

> They might do it to help their boyfriend or whatever, or to impress other gang members, to show their worth (Firmin 2010:56).

> 'Cos that is what you do; some people are your enemy and you see them that is just what you do. It's fun too: well not fun, fun, but when you have rushed someone and you are back with your boys you all catch joke about it and stuff (Firmin 2010:27).

> And you've got all of them going, you fucking will do that, and then what are you meant to do? Get battered until you give in? You just do it (Firmin 2011:37).

When boys were asked about this behaviour it was often belittled as women trying to 'be brave' or 'act like men' even though they obviously were not.

> If you cheat on them or if you say to them, they're gonna try and slap you or some crap like that (Firmin 2011:68).

> She thinks she's big in the game and no one can touch her (Firmin 2011:67).

While the boys' comments may oversimplify the motivations that women and girls described, and in many cases misrepresent the experience of females, there is an element of cross-over between the answers given by boys and girls. Some of the girls interviewed who participated in extreme violence, and inflicted this violence on men and boys as well as girls, did describe themselves as 'one of the boys'. For this small group of girls, who were concerned with 'doing business' with the boys or being seen as the same as them, 'manning-up' guarded against sexual violence: their hyper-masculine approach to conflict was one way of achieving self-protection.

Such motivations require further exploration. Why are some women violent? When women and girls are violent in different scenarios are there similarities in their motivations for engaging in violence? Are the explanations of power and control, often attributed to explain male violence, applicable to women and girls? In the scenarios outlined by participants in the FVV motivations were complex yet invariably linked to a relationship that women and girls had with men engaged in criminality.

Relationship Based Violence

Girls who are associated with gang violence, and those who are not, reported violence within intimate relationships. Such violence exists regardless of the fact that the Home Office does not define or recognise domestic violence where the victim is under-18. The current definition is:

> Any incident of threatening behaviour, violence or abuse [psychological, physical, sexual, financial or emotional] between adults who are or have been intimate partners or family members, regardless of gender or sexuality.

This recognises abuse within adult relationships regardless of gender and sexuality, but not regardless of age. This consistent lack of regard for the gender-based violence that girls experience in their relationships needs addressing as a matter of urgency, and a Home Office consultation on this is in process.[1]

In a gang context there are specific considerations that need to be taken account of. Firstly, occasions when a gang-member is violent and those when a gang-member engages in gang-related violence must be distinguished: gang members may be violent towards partners, friends, family, because they are violent, but the motive of the violence is not 'gang-motivated' or 'gang-related'. Gang members may also engage in violence that is motivated by inter- and intra-gang rivalry: this is gang-related violence. It is the latter that is of primary concern here. During FVV women and girls explained that their fear of violence was directly linked their partner's gang-association.

> I've been gun-butted by him as he was on his way out, and felt lucky that he didn't turn it round (Firmin 2011:42).

Women and girls also recalled violence at the hands of multiple gang members, even when they were in a relationship with only one of them.

> One time him and 10 of his mates turned up, kicked my door in and all battered me for something I'd said to him (Firmin 2011:42).

---

1 In summer 2012 the government announced its intention to change the definition to include young people.

> On a good few occasions I'd be sat there on the couch eating me tea or whatever
> and one of his mates would walk in and if I didn't say hi to him he'd punch me
> ... and he'd say 'yea well don't be rude' (Firmin 2011:45).

In addition, gang-affected, and non-gang-affected, women and girls discussed violence in their relationships. For girls under the age of eighteen this was often as brutal, traumatic and systemic as for adult women, even though few identified it as 'domestic violence'.

> My boyfriend broke my nose when I was 15 and no-one helped, no-one has even
> helped and I don't know what they would have done anyway, he watched me all
> the time, especially in school (Firmin 2011:44).

Physical injury included broken noses, broken collar-bones, broken legs, stabbing with glass and knives, forced miscarriage, bleeds on the brain, broken fingers and severe burns. The question remains: what is the impact of all of this violence on the mental health and emotional wellbeing of girls across the country?

Sexual Violence

> Things what X has done to me, pinned me to the couch and had sex with me
> and his friends have filmed it ... and they've all had copies of it and you learn to
> feel numb, when they're hitting ya and doing things to ya you learn to feel numb
> (Firmin 2011:45).

The form of violence which has received most public attention, in relation to girls and gang-related violence, is sexual violence. The statement that rape was being used as a 'weapon of choice' caught headlines[2] but the debate surrounding the statement failed to capture the real issues. Before we can begin to discuss sexual violence in this context it is important to make some clarifications and dispel some myths.

Myth 1: 'Gang-Rape'
The phrase gang-rape is often used to capture a range of sexual offences which are all actually distinct. It can be used to describe a rape involving multiple perpetrators who are not involved with a criminal gang.

a. Football hooliganism (football fans who engage in violence between rival groups of gangs)
b. A group of friends

---

2   http://news.bbc.co.uk/today/hi/today/newsid_8530000/8530932.stm

c. A fraternity[3]

These contexts are all very different to a rape involving multiple perpetrators who are involved in a criminal gang. The key difficulty with the phrase 'gang-rape' is that it conflates the number of perpetrators and whether they are part of a 'gang'. In addition, gang-associated sexual violence does not require multiple perpetrators, although this may sometimes be the case, it can describe exploitative, ongoing situations in addition to one-off sexual assaults.

The term 'gang' should be used to capture the motive of the assault, the specific relationship between the perpetrator and the victim and the level of risk associated with the incident/s given the broader criminal context within which it takes place. The number of perpetrators directly involved in the assault is irrelevant to the definition, the fact that a woman or girl considers an assault to be motivated by gang-association is central.

It is important to identify whether or not incidents of sexual violence are gang-associated given the level of risk involved with disclosure. There is also the added reluctance to come forward, when women and girls consider themselves to be criminally associated and therefore outside the protection of the state. These additional barriers to reporting gang-associated sexual violence need to be proactively challenged to disrupt the current status-quo.

Myth 2: Initiation
Much has been made in the media and political discourse about the use of gang-associated sexual violence as a means of formally initiating girls into criminal gangs. Over the course of FVV we found little evidence that this was the case and could not support this perception. When initiation was discussed it referred to male experiences for which the female victim was a commodity that enabled this to happen: in short, boys were initiated into criminal gangs by raping female associates or rivals, rather than the females themselves being formally initiated in this way.

The Truth about Gang-Associated Sexual Violence

Gang-associated sexual violence exists and is a pre-meditated weapon used between and within criminal gangs. It is used to punish, retaliate and threaten women and girls who are associated with, or engaged in, criminal gangs, and their male associates. It is a form of gang-related violence that is under-researched, rarely reported and where there is little chance of conviction due to the criminal associations, perceived or real, of the victims. Gang-associated sexual violence is based on motive, it may be used to initiate males, and can involve single, dual or multiple perpetrators. At present that is the evidence that can be drawn from the

---

3   University based social groups for male students. Research on the link with sexual violence has been done by Reeves Sanday (2007).

FVV project; nothing else can be ruled in or out at this point, and there is far more work to be done to establish prevalence, scale and appropriate responses.

Service Response

A range of services will respond to the risk faced by gang-affected women and girls; some will proactively work to address gang-specific risk and others will encounter it as a by-product of engagement for other issues such as sexual health, mental health and housing services. As the risk to gang-affected women and girls straddles a range of service areas, there are numerous complexities, gaps and barriers that face practitioners. In truth it is a challenge to develop an intervention which will meet the specific vulnerabilities and risks of this particular group, and as such services can at best have restricted impact, and at worst escalate the danger faced by gang-affected women and girls.

Male Dominated Service Spaces

Many of the girls who are affected by gang violence may be in contact with the youth justice system. They can be crudely segregated into those whose contact is explicitly the result of a gang-associated offence and those whose gang-association is not identified. For both, the system that they navigate is one that is 'male-dominated'.

- There are literally more boys accessing the service than girls: in 2008 girls made up a quarter of youth offending team caseloads (Nacro 2008).
- The justice system has been traditionally developed to respond to offending with men as the norm (Corston 2007).

This is echoed for girls who are in the justice system for an explicitly gang-related offence: youth violence programmes, in particular, have been developed to respond to male offending. Such behavioural programmes, operating within such a system, place girls at an increased level of vulnerability. The questions remain as to why, since it was conducted four years ago, the implications of the Corston report have not been sufficiently considered within the youth justice system.

Adult Women Service Spaces

The violence against women sector has provided an opportunity for girls to access gender-specific support and interventions. However, these interventions have been traditionally designed to work with adult women. While some services have been extended to work with young women and girls, the way they work with them is different and constrained by the fact that they are operating in a children services policy environment.

The Home Office definition of domestic violence fails to include victims under the age of 18, presenting a barrier to funding specialist interventions for this group. However, for women who specifically are seeking to exit a criminal gang, or who are fleeing gang members, domestic violence services may still not be fit for purpose. Fleeing a criminal gang is not the same as fleeing a violent relationship, although there are similarities. For women aged 18 or over, and in some local areas 16 and over, while they can access refuge accommodation when fleeing a violent relationship, a refuge is not required to support them if they are fleeing a criminal gang: this limitation is a justified one. It is not reasonable to assume that a refuge can simply accommodate women in these high risk situations. Provisions such as bullet-proof glass, being linked into relevant police forces that specialise in the local gang context, and training for staff to understand a criminal gang context, may all be essential to protect gang-affected women. There is the additional concern that such women could present a risk to other women who would access refuge provision, given the criminal associations or past behaviours that such women may have engaged in. Managing this risk is crucial to providing any form of refuge for women and girls who are at risk of criminal gangs.

In order for progress to be made when offering support for gang-associated women a gendered and risk specific safety plan is required. Without such a development, specialised VAW service providers will be compromised, service users placed at risk, and gang-associated women's needs will be neglected.

New Projects and Strategic Landscape

Sitting in between the violence against women sector and the youth justice system are projects that have been specially developed to work with gang-affected women and girls. While these programmes are scarce, and often struggle with funding, they do offer group and one-to-one work specifically designed to tackle the risks and vulnerabilities faced by gang-affected women and girls.

The difficulty is that such programmes rarely sit within local or regional strategic and operational plans for tackling gang-related violence. Instead, they operate in isolation from statutory processes, hindering their ability to make long-term impact. Strategic commitment and operational plans need to be in place, which engage all local services such as schools, housing, health, youth justice in order that:

- those women and girls who need the service most will be identified and referred into the programmes;
- information about risk and vulnerability will be shared appropriately amongst services while women and girls are taking part in such programmes;
- there will be an exit strategy to assist women and girls to leave their gang-association once the programme has finished.

Isolated commissioning of specialist interventions leaves local areas with the prospect that they are setting women and girls up to fail. Once girls access such interventions their vulnerability also increases, and if we cannot help them to exit then some would argue that we shouldn't be interfering with their lives. Without planned approaches to identify and refer those women and girls who are most in need of an intervention, local areas could be wasting scarce resources. If the right women and girls are not accessing specialist services then it is difficult to measure their success and the contribution that they make to tackling youth violence at a local level. If this approach is not embedded in the strategic approach of the local authority all of these gaps will continue to exist.

National vs Local Policy Responses

Given that a gendered approach to youth violence is not embedded in central government policy or strategy, it is difficult to insist that this approach is taken in local communities. Some attempts have been made by the Home Office and Department for Education to make reference to women and girls in strategies and guidance produced for tackling gangs but at present these attempts have been insufficient.

The most recent example of this was the inclusion of a chapter on women and girls in the Home Office guidance for the use of Gang Injunctions. Gang Injunctions are civil orders, introduced in 2010, which local authorities or local police forces can use in efforts to prevent gang-related violence. Injunctions can be used against anyone who is deemed to be engaging in, or encouraging, gang-related violence. Injunction conditions include sanctions that prevent people from entering certain areas, socialising with named individuals in public, wearing certain colours, owning a dangerous dog or using the internet to incite violence. In addition, courts are able to attach a positive requirement to an injunction which would require an individual to take part in activities with the view that this would enable them to exit criminal gangs. While there are multiple fundamental concerns with gang injunctions, including the fact that they only require a civil burden of proof but if breached can result in up to two years detention, most local areas would struggle to safely apply them to girls. Gender-specific interventions for girls are so scarce that appropriate positive requirements for girls would not exist in most local areas. Many girls who are gang involved are either related to and/or in a relationship with men involved in gang violence: how are they to be supported to exit those relationships while on their injunction? These two hurdles alone are significant and could mean that women and girls placed on injunctions could be at increased risk of harm and vulnerability due to insufficient support.

Until a gendered approach to tackling gang violence is embedded in local provisions and strategies, any gendered approach to national policy will be a challenge to implement. Risks posed, and faced, by gang-associated women and girls need to be considered consistently in local and national policy if they are to be truly addressed.

Conclusions

In order to prevent the risks faced, and posed, by women and girls who are associated with criminal gangs, professionals in the voluntary and statutory sectors need to be able to work consistently across their silos, and take a gendered approach to tackling gang-related violence. Each silo will face their own challenges due to the unique risks and vulnerabilities of this group of women and girls.

A specialist local response requires a strategic approach to tackling criminal gangs that acknowledges the experiences of girls. At an operational level, professionals need to operate across age, gender and race specialisms, and involve those who are experts in tackling local gangs. In my opinion, the greatest stumbling block is being able to respond to women and girls who are both victims and perpetrators/facilitators of serious violence. Both risks faced and risks posed need to be addressed, and this will be a challenge if agencies continue to work in the relative comfort of their silos.

However, even if a local authority were to adopt a specialist approach to tackling criminal gangs, two national policy areas are in need of review. The fact that the youth justice system has developed to respond to the deviance and criminality of boys, and the response to violence against women has traditionally identified victims of domestic violence to be adult women, means that responses to gang-associated girls will always be constrained. Until these two policy arenas fully acknowledge the age- and gender-specific risks and vulnerabilities of girls, both those who are gang-associated and those who are not, a gendered response to gang-related violence will always fall short.

References

Batchelor, S. 2001. The myth of girl gangs. *Criminal Justice Matters*, 43(1), 26–27.

Batchelor, S. 2009. Girls, gangs and violence: Assessing the evidence. *Probation Journal*, 56(4), 399–414.

Batchelor, S., Burman, M. and Brown, J. 2001. Discussing violence: Let's hear it for the girls. *Probation Journal*, 48(2), 125–134.

Campbell, A. 1990. Female participation in gangs, in Gangs in America, edited by C.R. Huff. Newbury Park, Ca: Sage.

Campbell, A. 1984. *The Girls in the Gang*. Oxford: Basil Blackwell.

Centre for Social Justice. 2009. *Dying to Belong: An In-depth Review of Street Gangs in Britain*. London: Centre for Social Justice.

Corston, J. 2007. The Corston Report. London: Home Office.

Department for Children, Schools and Families. 2010. *Safeguarding Children and Young People who may be Affected by Gang Activity*. Nottingham: DCSF Publications.

Firmin, C. 2010. *Female Voice in Violence Project: A Study into the Impact of Serious Youth and Gang Violence on Women and Girls*. London: ROTA.

Firmin, C. 2011. *This is It, This is my Life*. London: ROTA.

Hallsworth S. and Young T. 2004. Getting real about gangs. *Criminal Justice Matters*, 55, 12–13.

Home Office. 2010. *Statutory Guidance: Injunctions to Prevent Gang-Related Violence*. London: Home Office.

Horvath, M.A.H. and Kelly, L. 2009. Gang/group/multiple perpetrator rape: Naming an offence and initial research findings. *Journal of Sexual Aggression*, 15(1), 83–97.

McRobbie, A. and Garber, J. 1976. *Girls and subcultures: An exploration, in Resistance Through Rituals*, edited by S. Hall and T. Jefferson. London: Hutchison.

Miller, J. 2001. *One of the Guys: Girls, Gangs and Gender*. New York: Oxford University Press.

Nacro. 2008. *Responding to Girls in the Youth Justice System: Youth Crime Briefing*. London: Nacro.

Pitts, J. 2008. *Reluctant Gangsters: The Changing Shape of Youth Crime*. Cullompton: Willan Publishing.

Reeves Sanday, P. 2007. *Fraternity Gang Rape: Sex Brotherhood and Privilege on Campus* (2nd Edition). New York: New York University Press.

Thrasher, F.M. 1927. *The Gang: A Study of 1313 gangs*. Chicago, IL: University of Chicago Press.

Chapter 8

Possession or Oppression: Witchcraft and Spirit Possession Accusations as a Form of Ritual Abuse of Children and Women

Emilie Secker and Yasmin Rehman

Introduction

Witchcraft accusations against children and the physical and psychological abuse which results from them are increasingly recognised as a major issue when analysing and responding to violations of children's rights (Jahangir, 2009, Alston, 2009, Schnoebelen, 2009, Cimpric, 2010), with much of the most up-to-date research and commentary focusing on Africa and African diasporas. Numerous reports contain the oft-repeated statement that child abuse/violence against women and/or vulnerable adults is not condoned by any religion, that these are not faith based problems but problems for society as a whole. However, when that abuse is perpetrated in the name of faith, by religious officials such as priests, pastors, nuns, imams or takes place in a religious institution it becomes a faith-based problem. There is consequently a need for further analysis of how faith-based frameworks legitimise such ritualised abuse. Unfortunately, questioning or raising concerns about specific religious beliefs or practices can result in accusations of aggressive secularism or, for those within the faith group, being labelled as a heretic, blasphemer or non-believer. Such accusations are not without consequences and only serve to limit debate at best and at worst to silence survivors and protect the perpetrators. Fortunately, thanks to the immense courage of survivors and of those from within faith communities in naming the abuses, veils of silence are being lifted.

Whilst attention has focused primarily on witchcraft accusations against children in African countries, including the Democratic Republic of Congo, Angola, Sierra Leone and Nigeria, there is a developing consensus that this is also a growing issue for other states, including the UK. Following a number of high profile murders of children in the United Kingdom, linked to belief in spirit possession and witchcraft, there has been increasing discussion as to how best to address such forms of ritualised abuse. It remains the case that much of what we know concerns practices in Africa, or in the cases in the United Kingdom, about children of African origin. In this chapter we examine ritualised abuse resulting from a belief in spirits, black magic and witchcraft drawing in the second half of the chapter upon the work of Stepping Stones and other NGOs working in the Niger Delta and the emerging knowledge base. We begin, however, by outlining the current situation in the UK, where there has been relatively little research but a number of high profile cases have resulted in policy development, alongside widening the lens to encompass other minority communities in which belief in spirit possession has also been associated with abuse of children and adult women.

Emerging Awareness and Responses

Perspectives on ritualised abuse in the last decade in the United Kingdom have been fragmented and limited to children of Congolese, Angolan and Nigerian heritage within minority communities (Stobart, 2006). This emphasis reflects the high profile cases discussed below.

Although there have been a number of deaths[1] resulting from ritualised abuse in the 1990s, it was the tragic case of Victoria Climbié, in 2000, which brought the issue to national attention. During the public enquiry into her death, it emerged that professionals had missed several opportunities to intervene and protect Victoria from further harm. The review confirmed that prior to her death Victoria had been taken to a deliverance service – set up to 'cast out' demons and evil spirits – at a church in London.

In 2001, the torso of a boy aged between four and eight years old was found in the River Thames. Forensic examination confirmed that he was of Nigerian origin. The child was posthumously named 'Adam'. Despite extensive investigations the case remains unsolved although police believe that he was a victim of ritualised abuse. In 2005, two women and a man were convicted of child cruelty for torturing and threatening to kill an 8-year old girl known as child B who they believed was a witch.

The combination of these cases led the Metropolitan Police Service Child Abuse Investigation Command (SCD5) to establish a working group, Project Violet, in 2005. The project's aim was to raise awareness of ritualised abuse of children, to coordinate and manage the progress and quality of investigations and to work in partnership with child protection agencies, statutory, voluntary, community and faith groups. The initial focus was on the Congolese and Angolan communities but this has now been expanded to address practices in other African and some Asian communities. Project Violet has led to a wider recognition of ritualised abuse taking place in the United Kingdom and the production of guidance and training for professionals working in child protection.

---

1   Fareda Patel (1993), Cheung Ho (1993), Mary Odegbami (1994), Sylvester Orieso (1997) are some of those identified.

In 2006, the then Department for Education and Skills commissioned Eleanor Stobart to study the extent, nature and geographical reach of ritualised abuse of children resulting from a belief in spirit possession and witchcraft. The report (Stobart, 2006) analysed 38 cases involving 47 children. A perception of some form of difference by a Church elder or member of the community could lead to accusations of possession or witchcraft against the child. A number of markers of difference were identified among the children: disability; a learning difficulty; being identified as a particularly bright child; challenging behaviour including bed wetting, tantrums or nightmares. Various forms of abuse were also identified and included starving, beating, cutting, isolation, neglect and burning. One of the most disturbing findings is that ten of the children are known to have been taken overseas and what has become of them is not known. Eighteen children who had been abused following an accusation of witchcraft were placed in long-term foster care with two being placed in secure accommodation. A further 23 of their siblings were also placed in foster care even though they had not been accused of witchcraft or possession. The Stobart report made a number of recommendations including the need for central recording of cases to provide a clear national picture, the need for agencies such as police, social care, schools, immigration and DfES to work together to produce practice guidance, the need for better information regarding movement of children in and out of the United Kingdom and for places of worship to have child protection procedures in place. These recommendations were all accepted by the then Children's Minister Beverley Hughes but without allocation of resources to secure their implementation.

In 2011, the Department of Education established a working group to tackle 'faith based child abuse' and has recently published a National Action Plan. The focus of this group remains limited to African communities and specifically Christian churches. This emphasis on a specific minority and faith community is not in line with the findings of the Stobart Report which recorded ritualised abuse amongst Africans, South Asians and Europeans and across a number of faith communities. The narrow focus of the working group is not helpful. Nor is the limitation to children, as there are recorded cases involving the deaths of adults.

As the cases of Victoria Climbié, Adam and Child B show there can be connections between ritualised abuse and immigration: all three children had been brought into the UK by family members or carers. In 2009, ECPAT UK[2] and the Victoria Climbié Foundation (VCF) undertook a study which resulted in the publication of information and practice guidance for professionals working with child victims of trafficking.[3] In 2011, Anthony Harrison was convicted of using juju (ritual) oaths to control young girls he had trafficked into the United Kingdom. This was the first prosecution of its kind in Europe, confirming the long recognised use of rituals and threats to ensure the compliance and silence of

---

2   End Child Prostitution, Child Pornography and Trafficking of Children
3   http://vcf-uk.org/wp-content/uploads/2009/10/understanding_witchcraft.pdf

trafficked women and young girls trafficked from Africa to a life of prostitution or domestic servitude in Europe (Falola and Afolabi 2007; Kelly and Regan, 2000).

The disturbing case of Kristy Bamu and subsequent conviction of his sister and her boyfriend for his murder earlier this year has resulted in supplementary practice guidance and a training toolkit being issued, by the London Safeguarding Board in February 2012,[4] for professionals working with minority children and families.

Jinn, Kaala Jaddoo (black magic) and Nazar (evil eye)

Beliefs in evil spirits and faith-based practices to remove them extend beyond Christianity. The Qur'an contains references to *jinn*, supernatural beings that are created from smokeless fire unlike human beings who were created from clay. Both humans and *jinn*, according to the Qur'an, were created to worship Allah and shall be rewarded or punished for their deeds just like humans. Belief in *jinn* is commonplace amongst Muslims who are warned of their presence from an early age, especially the risks of being 'possessed' by *jinn* which can result in all manner of ill fate.

Kaala Jaddoo (black magic) and casting of *nazar* (evil eye) are also widely held beliefs across faith groups including Muslims, Hindus and Sikhs. Black magic or *jinn* possession and the evil eye are all presented as explanations for a host of difficulties that may have beset an individual – separation, family disunity, infertility, failure to produce a male child, illness and disability. From within a faith-based belief system resolution is to be found by seeking the correct religious guidance and adherence to the 'true faith'. Newspapers, television and word of mouth are all used to promote the services of religious officials who may be able to offer a solution in return for a donation should the afflicted individual so wish. We have heard many accounts from women of South Asian origin about holy men (Sikhs, Hindus and Muslims) operating in East London who will, for a fee, break black magic spells and cast out *jinns*. The Victoria Climbie Foundation is also aware of cases of belief in spirit possession amongst South Asians in Britain and across other minority communities.

There have been a number of known cases of death resulting from attempts to exorcise *jinn*. In 1993, Fareda Patel was beaten to death by family members and a religious preacher. Fareda had been suffering from depression following her marriage the previous year and this was identified, by the preacher, as a sign of *jinn* possession. In 2005, three month old Samira Ullah was murdered by her father Sitab Ullah, an educational development officer. He believed Samira was possessed by *jinn*. Samira's mother was convicted of child cruelty: Sitab had refused to allow his wife to feed Samira as he believed feeding the child was tantamount to feeding the *jinn* inside her. In 2011, Shayma Ali was convicted

---

4   Practice guidance for safeguarding children in minority ethnic culture and faith (often socially excluded) communities, groups and families

of murdering her four year old daughter whom she believed to be possessed by *jinn*. Although the convictions of Sitab Ullah and Shayma Ali were widely reported this did not result in the same level of attention being focused on the Muslim and South Asian communities as was being placed on the African community around the same time. This could be because the Muslim community were already the focus of intense debates surrounding other forms of abuse and violence, including terrorism.

At the Other End of the Spectrum

There are disturbing trends outside of minority faith communities which connect to the themes of spirit possession. On 1 November 2011, *The Times* published an article[5] stating that the NHS were using exorcism as an alternative form of treatment for patients with mental health problems. The article quotes Dr Rob Walker, a consultant psychiatrist and lecturer at Edinburgh University and Professor Robin Murray, Head of Psychiatric Research at Kings College Institute of Psychiatry, confirming that NHS professionals are working with pastors, priests and imams as part of a range of treatment interventions in cases where individuals believe they may be possessed. It would appear that accessing religious officials to assist in such treatment and minister deliverance is relatively easy as hospital chaplains would be expected to provide such a service. It is important to note that it is not only religious officials within minority communities that carry out deliverance and exorcisms. The Church of England currently employs 44 exorcists, one for every diocese in the country, appointed by the Archbishop of Canterbury. The Catholic Church too, has a number of exorcists or officials qualified to minister deliverance in the event of a paranormal incident or disturbance.

The Royal College of Psychiatrists issued a position statement and guidance to its members in August 2011 affirming recognition of spirituality and religion as part of good clinical practice. The guidance aims to set clear boundaries for clinicians in their dealings with religious officials pointing to: "… the benefits of considering spirituality and religion within an overall clinical assessment of a patient's condition, and also the potential benefits of considering spiritual and religious factors within treatment planning" (p5). This raises interesting questions. For example, what is the position of the government and health services on exorcisms within state agencies? Where are the connections between respect for an individual's faith, guidance on spirituality and endorsing religious practices for which there is no supporting scientific evidence and which have been linked to lethal violence? There is a tension between these policies and that of the Department of Education Working Group to address ritualised abuse of children in

---

5   http://www.hsj.co.uk/opinion/blogs/the-people-manager/dancing-with-the-devil-exorcism-in-the-nhs/5038132.blog

African Christian communities. Is this yet another case of one rule for the 'others' and another for the majority community?

Clergy Leading the Way

The Archbishop of York, John Sentamu, has openly talked about his own experience of helping a young girl to be free of 'something in her spirit' after she had been left traumatised having witnessed a goat being sacrificed.[6] Conventional medical interventions, he argued, had failed to help. Although he did not describe his actions as exorcism, his description is in line with commonly held understandings of such practices. The Archbishop discussed his work with the young girl during a debate in April 2012 about an amendment to the Health and Social Care Bill, tabled by psychiatrist and crossbench peer Baroness Hollins. The Archbishop of York called for the words 'spiritual health' to be inserted into a clause about the duty of the Secretary of State for Health, the NHS Commissioning Board and Clinical Commissioning Groups to improve the quality of services.

The Archbishop's comments are deeply worrying. He is the man tipped to replace Dr Rowan Williams as the next Archbishop of Canterbury. If this were to be the case John Sentamu would be the principal leader of the Church of England, the symbolic head of the worldwide Anglican Church, the third largest group of Christians in the world. The work described later in this chapter which seeks to question beliefs in spirit possession and witchcraft amongst African Christians would be problematic at best when the leader of the Church is a man who claims to have freed a young girl of 'something in her spirit' and employs exorcists.

The Cleric in the Corner

Ensuring training of religious officials in child protection laws and violence against women, and developing guidelines for professionals are all positive moves forward. But they are simply not enough when one considers the power of the messages of reinforcement in such beliefs being beamed into peoples' homes across the country from satellite television channels and the internet. There are an increasing number of channels broadcasting programmes offering spiritual guidance and religious resolution for matters ranging from marriage, divorce, finances, health and employment. One cannot underestimate the power of the clerics in the corner of our living rooms. The content and timing of programming on Religious TV channels deserves further scrutiny. Exorcisms, ministering of deliverance, casting out of *jinns* and overturning black magic spells can all be seen on television – American Evangelical, Black Christian, Muslim and other

---

6   http://www.telegraph.co.uk/news/religion/8867728/Archbishop-of-York-NHS-should-cater-for-spiritual-needs.html.

religious denominations have dedicated channels and broadcast such content. It would appear that women are targeted with this content broadcast mid-morning and mid-afternoon between school runs and in the early evening. Callers to these programmes are overwhelmingly women seeking advice and resolution to marital and family difficulties. Many of these broadcasts offer a direct studio phone link with a pastor, imam, or priest who is available to deal directly with an audience member's difficulty or problem. Through the medium of television these faith groups are reinforcing and promoting notions of spirit possession. Faith programming and broadcasting has, to date, not been a focus of research or policy. This must change if effective strategies are to be developed.

Witchcraft Accusations Against Children in Nigeria: History and Causes

The second part of this chapter draws upon lessons learnt from the experiences of NGOs in the Niger Delta region of Nigeria, which work seeks to address the issue of witchcraft accusations against children. The specific themes explored include: the history of witchcraft accusations and how they might be explained; the forms of violence and abuse which result; and how and why this should be understood as a form of ritual abuse. Recommendations for policy makers in those countries where witchcraft accusations against children are an increasing problem are presented.

Witchcraft accusations against children in Nigeria, and West Africa more generally, are a fairly new phenomenon. Although the belief in witches has a long and diverse history, and is found in a great many cultures around the world, elderly women (and sometimes men) have traditionally been the focus of the idea (Cimpric, 2010). However, in the late 1990s and early 2000s, a belief in child witchcraft began to be reported from several African countries including the Democratic Republic of Congo, Ghana and Nigeria (Nwadinobi, 2008, Foxcroft, 2009). In the most common manifestations the child is considered to have become possessed by an evil spirit, usually through ingesting food which contains the witchcraft spirit, which will force them to harm other family and community members (Foxcroft, 2009, Molina, 2005). In consequence it is believed to be essential that the witchcraft spirit is then removed from the child. The means for doing so are usually ceremonial and often violent (Akhilomen, 2006).

Religious convictions and practices clearly play a central role in understanding both the nature of the belief that children can be witches and in legitimising resultant abuse. The belief that all misfortune has a spiritual explanation is shared by many cultures around the world (Falola, 2001, Smith, 2001) and is commonly found across much of Africa. Thus problems such as poverty, disease and death are often considered the result of malevolent spirits. In the Niger Delta traditional belief systems have combined with certain forms of New Wave Pentecostal Christianity which specifically identify such malevolent spirits as 'witches' (Oha, 2000), and cements concepts of possession and deliverance (Onyinah, 2002). Such syncretic (blending of two or more belief systems) religions are prevalent in many African countries and are also increasingly found in western states, including the UK and USA, in part due to migration and the resultant establishment of branches of large African-based churches serving diasporic communities.

Furthermore, levels of hardship are particularly high in the Niger Delta, a region described by the UN Development Programme (2006) as: "suffering from administrative neglect, crumbling social infrastructure and services, high unemployment, social deprivation, abject poverty, filth and squalor, and endemic conflict" (p9). More recently, the UK Department for International Development reported in 2011 that: "Nigeria has a quarter of Africa's extreme poor, with 100 million of a population of 158 million living on less than £1 a day. In addition, Nigeria has 10% of the world's children out of school, and accounts for 10% of child and maternal deaths and 25% of global malaria cases" (p1).

The centrality of religious belief within Nigerian society means that, should misfortune occur, people will usually turn to the church for an explanation. In consequence, pastors are responsible for many of the accusations of witchcraft against children (Cahn, 2006), with case data demonstrating that around 30 per cent of children are first accused of witchcraft during the course of a church service and that in other cases a child is brought to a pastor in order to confirm an existing accusation of witchcraft (Foxcroft and Secker, 2010).

There is also a financial element to the role of churches in witchcraft accusations (Cimpric, 2010). Pastors commonly charge parents large sums of money in order to deliver children from possession by evil spirits. Many of Nigeria's richest pastors specifically promote an anti-witch agenda, leading large scale services known as 'crusades' in which they also purport to heal the lame, the blind and those with HIV/AIDS. The wealth and social status of such pastors serves to increase parents' and communities' trust in their diagnosis that a problem has been caused by a child who is a witch, in accordance with the 'prosperity gospel', which teaches that material wealth results from being favoured by God and thus serves to further reinforce the authority of the pastor. Additionally, the Niger Delta, in common with much of West Africa, is characterised by the proliferation of unregulated, unaffiliated churches, led by charismatic preachers, who have little or no official theological training. The authority of such men and women, combined with high levels of illiteracy, mean that their teachings and pronunciations are rarely challenged.

Whilst the particular nature of religious beliefs in the Niger Delta is a major contributing factor to children being accused of witchcraft, there are also a number of other characteristics which make certain children particularly vulnerable to such accusations. Case data indicates that children from single-parent families are particularly vulnerable, with around 70 per cent of accused children having parents who have divorced, or one or both parents dead (Foxcroft and Secker, 2010). Many accusations of witchcraft come from a step parent, who may not wish to support the child of a former relationship and uses an accusation of witchcraft as a means to legitimise the removal of child from a household. This is also reflected in cases of disputed inheritance, where a child may be accused by another family member in order to promote the accuser's claim to money or property.

Finally, there are clearly identifiable links between accusations of witchcraft and children who are perceived as 'different' in some way, as also noted in the UK through the Stobart report. This may be due to a physical or mental disability, with autism, hunchbacks and epilepsy being commonly considered evidence of witchcraft possession (Molina, 2005, Ogunjuyigbe, 2004). Paradoxically, a child who is particularly clever or outspoken may also be particularly vulnerable to a witchcraft accusation. Whilst children who already suffer some form of discrimination are particularly vulnerable, unlike other forms of ritual abuse there does not appear to be a gender dimension to witchcraft accusations in Nigeria, although Cimpric (2010) notes a significant bias towards boys being accused of witchcraft in the Democratic Republic of Congo.

Forms of Violence Resulting from Witchcraft Accusations

There are a number of ways in which witchcraft accusations against children can result in abuse. An accusation that a child is a witch usually means either action being taken by their family or community to address the perceived problem, or the advice of a church leader being sought. In most cases, this will then result in the child being subjected to violent activities designed to force a confession of witchcraft and/or drive out the spirit (Battarbee et al., 2009, Akhilomen, 2006).

The work of both international and Nigerian NGOs has identified and categorised a wide range of forms of abuse of children believed to be witches. Data from cases recorded in Akwa Ibom State in the Niger Delta indicates that around 80 per cent of children are abandoned or forced out of their home following an accusation (Foxcroft and Secker, 2010). This action is taken in order to remove the bad luck and negative actions that the children are believed to have caused/ perpetrated. In such cases children usually have no choice other than to live on the street, and become increasingly vulnerable to other rights violations, including lack of access to food, water, shelter and education.

A significant number of children also suffer extreme forms of violence including severe beatings, burning with acid, hot water or fire, poisoning, having nails or machetes driven into their heads and/or being sexually assaulted (Battarbee et al., 2009). Children may be imprisoned and starved in order to drive out the evil spirit. In some cases an explicit attempt is made to kill the child, with recorded cases of children being buried alive or drowned, or killed through beheading, acid burning and beating (Foxcroft and Secker, 2010; Battarbee et al., 2009).

Children who have been accused of witchcraft also face significant and long-lasting discrimination. Cimpric (2010) considers that: "once accused of witchcraft, children are stigmatized and discriminated for life" (p1), caught in a 'cycle of accusation' where their vulnerability to further accusations of witchcraft is hugely increased. Children who are believed to be witches, even if not abandoned, are usually excluded from school, refused medical treatment and ostracised by their family and community. The long-term material and psychological consequences for a child following an accusation of witchcraft are therefore likely to be severe, although no longitudinal studies exploring this have yet been conducted.

The forms and extent of violence against, and abuse of, children who are believed to be witches must, however, be understood in the wider context of understandings of child rights and child protection principles in Nigeria. There is a widespread lack of understanding of child rights laws and principles among both adults and children. Children are at the bottom of the social hierarchy, which means that the views, interests and experiences of the child are accorded little relevance and that the interests of the family and wider community are given prominence. If a child is stigmatised as a witch abuse is considered justified in the interests of perceived wider community protection. It is also relevant that all forms of violence towards children are generally more socially acceptable within Nigeria than many countries, particularly those in the West. Akhilomen (2006) comments that: "in Nigeria, like most parts of Africa, children are daily harassed, assaulted, beaten, bruised or maimed for the least trivial of reasons" (p240). Thus the familiarity and normalisation of violence and the dehumanising label 'witch' combine to provide justification for the abuse of children stigmatised as witches.

Witchcraft Accusations as a Form of Ritual Abuse

Witchcraft accusations against children, and their resultant abuse, clearly display significant similarities to other forms of ritual abuse (Scott, 2001). The abuse that results from witchcraft accusations against children has an inherent link to faith and belief and such abuse is primarily justified and legitimised via reference to that belief system. Furthermore, the violent and abusive treatment of children believed to be witches commonly takes place in a ritualised setting, designed to control and intimidate the victim. Children are aggressively persuaded that they are possessed by an evil spirit, as evidenced by forced confessions. Power structures also play a significant role, as indicated by the targeting of children, one of the most vulnerable and lower status groups in society.

Identifying witchcraft accusations against children as a form of ritual abuse would, therefore, most importantly lead to greater investigation and understanding of a relatively new and extremely hidden form of abuse of children. Techniques which have been developed for addressing other forms of ritual abuse may well prove to be of value, and lessons learnt in providing support to the victims of such abuse, and developing policy responses, can be applied.

Policy Implications

Policy development should draw upon the experiences of NGOs in Nigeria, which have identified a number of potential interventions which are of value in addressing the problematic issue of witchcraft accusations against children:

Firstly, it is essential to ensure communities, and in particular parents and children, are aware of the legal protections for children and vitally, that it is understood that these protections extend to children who are believed to be witches. Abuse of such children is socially and morally legitimised through the perception that they are no longer human and thus current protection mechanisms and standards of treatment do not apply to them. Emphasising the universality of both legal standards and child protection principles within key target communities helps to promote the concept that all children have the right to lives free from violence and abuse. Such interventions have, in the Niger Delta, led to the establishment of community advocates for child rights and referral systems for children accused of witchcraft from churches, schools and community leaders to NGOs and government agencies.

Secondly, the value of NGOs' relationships and knowledge of local communities cannot be underestimated. Communities often have legitimate reasons to mistrust government, both in Nigeria, where corruption, arbitrary arrest and police brutality are common, and within diasporas where they may encounter discrimination and intimidation. NGOs, particularly grassroots, community-based organisations, are viewed with less suspicion and can consequently undertake interventions on child witch accusations more effectively.

Thirdly, NGO experiences in the Niger Delta and elsewhere indicate that building relationships with church leaders and faith communities is crucial. Activities such as roundtable meetings with church leaders, which seek to promote improved child rights/child protection in a non-confrontational and supportive manner, are received much more positively than those which directly challenge belief systems. The latter is often dismissed as the imposition of 'Western' values and a form of neo-colonialism. This cooperative approach recognises that many communities have a deeply-held and sincere belief in the existence of witchcraft, and therefore seeks to sensitise them about whether children can be witches, and the most appropriate Christian response. Such interventions should focus on ensuring that church leaders have a sound theological understanding of the belief in witchcraft and are willing and able to support their constituents to address accusations of witchcraft in a manner consistent with child rights principles; for example, through praying for the child in private rather than public and abusive accusations and exorcism ceremonies.

Finally, it is evident that whilst understandings of this issue are developing and improving, analysis and policy responses remain fragmented. There is consequently a need for greater international cooperation between governments, international agencies, civil society and communities, in order to fully understand and address the various facets of this form of abuse. In particular, attention should be directed to understanding how the ritual abuse of children resulting from witchcraft accusations both stems from, and can exacerbate, other forms of violence and discrimination against children. The perspectives of the children involved and their priorities for developing policy responses should also form a key part of this analysis. There is a need for critical reflections on existing interventions in order to develop a coordinated response, both within and between states, in order to effectively address witchcraft accusations against children both in Nigeria and in the many other states where this phenomenon is a growing concern.

A Way Forward

Whilst understandings of, and responses to, ritualised abuse of children is developing, much needs to be done. First and foremost there needs to be clarity about the UK government's position on this issue. Is the government's concern only about rogue pastors in the African churches abusing children? If so, what is the justification of this in light of the evidence that the belief in sprit possession is more widespread and that it is taking place in a number of communities and affects adults as well as children? The state has a duty to protect its citizens – adults and children. This narrow focus on a specific minority and faith community will leave others vulnerable to violence and abuse.

Further research into ritualised abuse against children, women and vulnerable members of society is needed if an effective and holistic response is to be developed that makes the links between this and other forms of violence and abuse. Policy development should draw upon the experiences of NGOs such as Stepping Stones Nigeria and incorporate the interventions put forward above. It is important to continue to work with faith and community groups and child protection agencies, but it is crucial to expand such partnerships to include a wider range of social care agencies, specialist support services working with women, the disabled, mental health services and academics if a truly integrated response to protecting children and adults is to be developed. This issue cannot and will not be resolved by leaving it in the hands of faith leaders and faith communities.

The United Kingdom is not dealing with such issues in isolation. Next month will see the start of new court proceedings in Belgium, following years of campaigning by Fouad Hachmi, in the case of his sister Latifa who died during an exorcism carried out, it is alleged, to resolve her infertility. Learning from this and other cases and from the work of NGOs across the world is crucial in the development of a coordinated response to ritualised abuse.

Community groups such as Afruca are calling for legislation to outlaw the branding of children as witches and the prosecution of pastors carrying out exorcisms in Britain. Such acts are not covered by existing legislation and would be limited to specific forms of ritualised abuse. Would this be an effective way forward? Would it provide a deterrent to ritualised abuse of children?

We have the cases of those who have lost their lives, we have the voices of survivors and we have community activists and NGOs working on the ground. Are the government and faith institutions ready to step up?

References

Akhilomen, D. 2006. Addressing Child Abuse in Southern Nigeria. *Studies in World Christianity*, 12 (3), 235–248.

Alston, P. 2009. *Report of the Special Rapporteur on extrajudicial, summary or arbitrary executions, Philip Alston.* A/HRC/11/2, 27/05/2009.

Battarbee, L, Foxcroft, G and Secker, E. 2009. *Witchcraft Stigmatization and Children's Rights in Nigeria.* Shadow Report to the UN Committee on the Rights of the Child. [Available at: http://www.steppingstonesnigeria.org/images/pdf/Shadow_Report_Low_Res.pdf] Accessed 1 April 2012.

Cahn, N. 2006. Poor Children: Child 'Witches' and Child Soldiers in Sub-Saharan Africa. *Ohio State Journal of Criminal Law* 3, 413–456.

Cimpric, A. 2010. *Children Accused of Witchcraft: An Anthropological Study of Contemporary Practices in Africa.* UNICEF WCARO, Dakar.

Commission of the European Communities DG Justice and Home Affairs. 2001. *Research based on Case Studies of Victims of Trafficking in Human Beings in 3 EU Member States: Belgium, Italy and The Netherlands* JAI/2001/HIP/023. Available at [http://www.childtrafficking.com/Docs/payoke_on_the_road_de_rode_.pdf]. Accessed 13 April 2012.

Department for Education and Skills 2006. *Child Abuse Linked to Accusations of 'Possession' and Witchcraft. Research Report 750.*

Department for International Development. 2011. *Summary of DFID's Work in Nigeria 2011–2015.* Department for International Development, London.

Falola, T. 2001. *Culture and Customs of Nigeria.* Greenwood Press, Westport CT.

Falola, T. & Afolabi, N. 2007. *The Human Costs of African Migration.* New York Psychology Press.

Foxcroft, G. 2009. *Witchcraft Accusations: A Protection Concern for UNHCR and the Wider Humanitarian Community.* [Available at: http://www.steppingstonesnigeria.org/images/pdf/witchcraft_accusations.pdf] Accessed 1 April, 2012.

Foxcroft, G and Secker, E. 2010. *Report on Accusations of Witchcraft Against Children in Akwa Ibom State, Nigeria.* [Available at: http://www.steppingstonesnigeria.org/images/pdf/ssn_report_to_commission.pdf] Accessed 1 April 2012.

Jahangir, A. 2008. *Report of the Special Rapporteur on freedom of religion or belief, Asma Jahangir: Mission to Angola.* A/HRC/7/10/Add.4, 06/03/2008.

Kelly, L & Regan, L. 2000 *Stopping Traffic: Exploring the Extent of, and Responses to, Trafficking in Women for Sexual Exploitation in the UK.* London Home Office.

La Fontaine, J.S. 2009. *The Devil's Children:From Spirit Possession to Witchcraft: New allegations that Affect Children*. Farnham, Ashgate.

Lebling, R. 2010. *Legends of the Fire Spirits: Jinns and Genies from Arabia to Zanzibar*. New York, I.B. Tauris and Co. Ltd.

London Safeguarding Board, *2011. Practice guidance for safeguarding children in minority ethnic culture and faith (often socially excluded) communities, groups and families*. Available at http://www.londonscb.gov.uk/culture_and_faith/community_partnership_project. Accessed 20 April 2012.

Molina, J. 2005. *The Invention of Child Witches in the Democratic Republic of Congo*. Save the Children, London.

Muslim Parliament of Great Britain. 2006. *Child Protection in a Faith-Based Environment*. Available at [http://www.muslimparliament.org.uk/Documentlation/ChildProtectionReport.pdf] Accessed 14 April 2012.

Nwadinobi, E. 2008. *The Causes and Prevalence of Accusation of Witchcraft among Children in Akwa Ibom State*. UNICEF, Unpublished Research paper.

Ogunjuyigbe, P. 2004. Under-Five Mortality in Nigeria: Perception and Attitudes of the Yorubas Towards the Existence of "Abiku". *Demographic Research,* 11(2), 43–56.

Oha, O. 2000. The Rhetoric of Nigeria Christian Videos: The War Paradigm of The Great Mistake, in *Nigerian Video Films* edited by J. Haynes. Ohio University Centre for International Studies: Ohio, 192–199.

Onyinah, O. 2002. Deliverance as a way of confronting witchcraft in modern Africa: Ghana as a case history, *Asian Journal of Pentecostal Studies* 5 (1), 107–134.

Royal Society of Psychiatrists. 2011. *Recommendation for psychiatrists on spirituality and religion. Position statement.* Available at [http://www.rcpsych.ac.uk/pdf/PS03_2011.pdf] Accessed 23 April 2012.

Schnoebelen, J. 2009. *Witchcraft allegations, refugee protection and human rights: a review of the evidence*. UNHCR Research Paper No. 169.

Scott, S. 2001. *The Politics and Experience of Ritual Abuse: Beyond Disbelief.* Milton Keynes, Open University Press.

Smith, D. 2001. Ritual Killing, 419 and Fast Wealth: Inequality and the Popular Imagination in Southeastern Nigeria. *American Ethnologist,* 28(4), 803–826.

United Nations Development Programme. 2006. *Niger Delta Human Development Report*, United Nations Development Programme: Abuja.

Chapter 9

Lost for Words: Difficulties Naming and Disclosing Sexual Violence in Hindi

Swati Pande

Feminist activism and research have made significant contributions to the understanding of sexual violence and influenced policy, legislation and practice. One of the key themes has been recognising the role played by language and discourse in silencing or voicing women's experiences (Cameron 1992; Clark 1998; Kelly 1988; McConnell-Ginet 1989). Western feminist engagement with language took place in the context of a wider feminist movement (Cameron 1992). Given this background, 'breaking the silence' is not just a powerful metaphor but also a tangible act. Amongst other things, breaking the silence has meant talking about sexual violence, creating words and meanings to name this violence from women's perspectives and challenging the discourse that does not allow or represent women's realities and serves to excuse the abusers.

It is in this context that I look at the process of naming and disclosing sexual violence by Hindi-speaking women who live in an English-speaking mainstream society in the UK. Based on the research findings of an exploratory research study conducted in 2009, I suggest that whilst there is an acknowledgement of a 'language barrier' that has an impact on Asian women's access to services (Chand 2005), this barrier has not been subject to a nuanced feminist linguistic enquiry within a larger feminist analysis of sexual violence against Asian women.

I explore this language barrier by subjecting Hindi sexual vocabulary to a feminist linguistic analysis, drawing from the responses of Hindi-speaking members of the public and from professionals' experiences of working with survivors in statutory and voluntary sector organisations.

The findings show that the Hindi sexual vocabulary that emerged from the participants was very intricate. This has significant implications for how women's experiences are translated, named, recorded, validated and supported. It emerged that there was a lack of accessible words and commonly shared meanings. The dominant terms for naming rape and child sexual abuse are framed through concepts of 'honour' and shame. Thus sexual violence, rape and child sexual abuse is scaffolded by obscure terms open to multiple interpretations. The available words for male and female anatomy were swear words. The act of sex and sexuality were spoken through circumlocutions. There was also a lack

of shared meanings within the same speech community. In conclusion I suggest
that the Hindi sexual vocabulary and the discourse of sexual violence in Hindi is
restricted and is fraught with difficulties which cannot be remedied within a linear
translation process. This analysis demonstrates the necessity of discussion about
the additional and perhaps invisible dimensions to breaking the silence for Asian
Hindi speaking survivors.

Breaking the Silence in English

A significant shift in the available literature on sexual violence is evident from the
point where feminism started influencing how and what was being researched.
Feminists have also engaged with the relationship between language and sexual
violence, and understood it as part of the process of silencing women's experiences.
Kelly (1988) discusses the availability of a social definition of sexual violence as
being crucial in both highlighting the collective nature of the experience, as well
as making possible a social explanation. In her study, access to names came up as
an important theme in discussions of the experiences of incest survivors and their
inability to tell adults about what was happening to them.

Cameron (1998c) talks about feminist engagement with language both in
terms of language as feminist practice and feminist linguistic theory. Feminist
reconstruction of language changed the meaning of words that did exist, for
example rape and pornography, from the perspective of how it was experienced
by women. Kelly and Radford (1990) explored what women meant when they
said 'nothing really happened'. They suggest that despite the violation, women's
experiences were not defined as violence in the mainstream, where it is normalised
and minimised. Women classify these experiences as 'nothing happened' when
the likelihood of their experiences being validated is very low. Dworkin (1989)
challenged the etymology of words and the impact it has on framing women's
sexuality. Feminist linguistics have engaged with androcentricism in English
(Spender 1980) and also analysed the discourse that allows certain meanings to be
dominant. However, all of the above discussions have been in English, about the
English language.

Breaking the Silence in Hindi

The process of naming sexual violence acquires a complex character in the Asian
community. It has been suggested that the rate of disclosing sexual violence in
this community is much lower than in others (Gilligan and Akhtar 2006). This
has been explained through the concepts of shame and honour. Sen (2005) notes
that honour operates not just in the lives of Asian women but in a wider context.
According to her, it has been a feature in both western and eastern societies. In her
discussion on crimes of honour, she explores the schema of honour and dishonor

dynamics whereby honour is vested in an individual or collectively. It is through their being and behaviour that this honour is preserved or violated. The violation of the honour carries with itself penalties, which vary in severity depending on the level of breach. Codes of honour also define what it means to be a man and what it means to be a woman, with strict norms about public and private spaces and what can or cannot be discussed in them (Gill 2009). Wilson (2006) suggests that honour positions women in a way that means that they are responsible not only for their own acts but also for what is done to them by others. This has particular resonance for experiences of sexual violence.

Gill (2004) in her study in relation to codes of honour, on survivors of domestic violence, discusses the problems with naming. Telling would dishonour the family by making public that which, it is felt, ought to remain private. Her work resonates with Kelly's (1988) findings about women's naming of violence being heavily influenced by dominant masculinist discourse. Women in her study had difficulty naming their experiences based on existing limited social definitions.

Gill (2009) in her study of Asian rape survivors, refers to the socio-cultural context in which the violence takes place. For Asian women, linguistically, rape is framed in the language of 'honour being taken away' thus holding the survivor responsible for not being able to protect her honour. Here, honour emerges as an important consideration for disclosure. For those willing to tell, the honour framing sexual violence defines it by blurring the actual act of rape and by calling it honour being taken away.

Wilson (2006) comments that the concept of shame requires a woman to be watchful of her actions, her body and how she is perceived by others. She suggests that the concept of shame has a striking similarity with the male gaze. Shame and honour is thus essential in understanding the socio-cultural dynamics that frame sexual violence. In the above discussions, the role of language is noted as creating a barrier to women disclosing (Gilligan and Akhtar 2006) and as adding complexity (Gill 2009). However, language has not been analysed in depth for its implications in naming sexual violence in Hindi.

Being a Hindi Speaker, Asian, Woman and Survivor

Both the USA and the UK are linguistically diverse countries. The literature reviewed above has not sufficiently addressed this diversity: meaning the available discourse on sexuality, in languages other than English has not received the same level of scrutiny.

It has been acknowledged that 'women' are not a homogenous group with identical experiences of sexual violence (Wyatt 1985) and studying diversity does not just mean acknowledging differences, but a deeper understanding of how these differences impact people's experiences (Hill Collins 1991). The identities of Asian women in the UK exist at the intersection of race, class, ethnicity and gender. The influence of these intersections is formative in understanding how women talk about sexual violence in Hindi. The concept of intersectionality was introduced by Crenshaw (1994) to address the experience of violence for women of colour in the USA. Crenshaw proposes that in order to understand violence against women of colour it is important to take into account all the layers of their identities, as they interact with each other and the larger societal context, to place women in specific positions. Elaborating further Crenshaw talks about 'political intersectionality' with respect to anti-racist and feminist discourses. She suggests, if anti-racism is based on black men's experience of racism and feminism on white women's experiences of sexism, then women who are not white and who experience racism as well as violence and inequality within their own race are not present in either of the two discourses.

The concept of structural and political intersectionality is formative in understanding Asian women's experiences of sexual violence and disclosure. Not knowing English in an English-speaking country forms a barrier in a very complex way. A Hindi-speaking woman willing to disclose sexual violence at the first level needs a vocabulary through which to verbalise her experience, she then needs access to interpreters to engage with external agencies. If this access is not forthcoming her experiences will be silenced at this level. Once she does have access to an interpreter there needs to be agreed, shared meaning and a similar frame of reference in order to communicate. The absence of shared meanings has the potential of placing the multilingual professional in a position of power as they have access to two languages and can silence or highlight certain utterances. There is also the risk of a woman's experience being silenced if there is a different frame of reference for the interpreter or any other multilingual professional.

To illuminate the many pitfalls, this chapter explores the availability of sexual vocabulary in Hindi, the usage, as well as the accessibility, of words and shared meanings and most notably of the language in itself being a context conducive (Kelly 2005) to silencing or disclosure.

The Research Process and Findings

This section is based on research conducted at the Child and Woman Studies Unit, London Metropolitan University. I set out to explore the availability of Hindi sexual vocabulary and the impact it has on the process of disclosure. For the purpose of the study 'Asian women' has been used to represent women from the Indian subcontinent living in the UK. The word 'multilingual' was used for people who are able to speak Hindi and English. Some of the participants were able to speak more than these two languages but these two were a minimum requirement. Hindi is an Asian language; it shares its vocabulary with Urdu and Persian. It is primarily spoken in northern India and is one of the official languages of the country. The 2001 census data on ethnicity and religion found Indians to be the largest minority community in the UK. Indians are a culturally and linguistically diverse group. Unfortunately, the Office of National Statistics does not collect data on language to give a specific estimate of the number of people who speak Hindi in the UK. In a study focusing on London, Baker et al. (2000) found that over 300 different languages are spoken by London school children. Hindi is among the top 40.

The exploration of Hindi sexual vocabulary was carried out by locating words from the Sexual Offences Act 2003 in sentences which multi-lingual participants were asked to translate into Hindi (see Appendix and Table 9.1). In the absence of an exact translation, they were asked to list a word or expression that they felt captured the meaning. A back-translation methodology was then used to explore the words and the meanings that were presented and left out.

Table 9.1   Translations for Sex, Sexual Gratification, Sexual Feeling and Sexual Act

Word in English	Word in Hindi	Back Translation	Number of participants
Sex	Pyar	Love	3
	Miya Beewee ka rishta	Relationship between husband and wife	1
	Admi aurat Ka rishta	Relationship between man and woman	1
Sexual gratification	Anand	Pleasure	2
	Sharirik Sookh	Bodily Pleasure	2
	Maza	Fun	1
Sexual Feelings	Akarshan	Attraction	3
	Chah nahi hai	Does not want	2
	Pyar nahi karti	Does not love	1
	Letne ka jee nahi karta	Does not want to lie down	1
	Yaun sambandh nahi chahti	Does not want sexual relationship	1
Sexual Act	Gande Kaam	Bad/dirty Act	1
	Blue Film	Blue film	1
	Ashleel Sambhog	Obscene sex	1
	Sambhog karte hue dikhaya	To show someone having sex	1
	Bacche ko nanga film dikhaya	Show naked film to a child	1
	Sambhog dikhaya	To show sex	1

The study also sought to explore the relationship between Hindi sexual vocabulary and the disclosure of sexual violence. To address this, responses were sought from multilingual professionals who have contact with survivors of sexual violence in three different settings: law enforcement; specialist therapeutic services and outreach work.

In the sections that follow the main research findings are presented under a set of thematic headings which identify the ways in which this restrictive discourse is constructed.

Euphemisms and Circumlocutions

The Oxford English dictionary defines circumlocution as talking in a round about manner. Cameron (1998a) cites Showlater:

> The problem is not that language is insufficient to express women's consciousness but that women have been denied the full resources of language and have been forced into silence, euphemism and circumlocution (p193).

The words sex and sexual provide an interesting example for understanding how euphemisms and circumlocutions appear in Hindi sexual vocabulary (see Table 9.1). For the word 'sex', there was an accurate translation given by eight participants. When 'sex' was placed in 'child sexual abuse' (see Table 9.2) the number of accurate translations went down to just four and there were five circumlocutions that identified harm being done to children but not the sexual nature. When the same word 'sexual' was placed in the context of sexual gratification, there were two accurate translations and five circumlocutions. For 'sexual feelings', there was just one accurate translation and eight responses that had no sexual connotation at all. In 'sexual act', there was just one accurate translation and six circumlocutions.

The meaning as well as the translation for the words sex and sexual changed with the context. There was a clear, one-word translation for sex whilst the results for sexual were inaccurate. For sexual act, the focus shifted to bad acts or obscenity. For sexual feelings, the focus shifted to feelings and for sexual gratification, the focus shifted to gratification. In each of the inaccurate translations, the meaning of 'sexual' is lost. The terms 'orgasm' and 'digital penetration' (see Table 9.3) had the least number of responses and most of these were circumlocutions. Orgasm was translated in general terms with no sexual connotation and for digital penetration there was no reference to parts of the body.

The methodology did not enable exploration of the reason why participants were unable to provide specific translations, although Gill (2009) states that interpretations become vastly more difficult when socio-cultural norms render situations ambiguous.

Table 9.2   Translations for Child Sexual Abuse

Word in English	Word in Hindi	Back Translation	Number of Respondents
Child Sexual Abuse	Bal Durvyavahar	Child maltreatment	1
	Bal Atyachar	Child cruelty	1
	Baccho ke saath dur vyavahar	Child maltreatment	1
	Baccho ke saath galat kaam karna	To do something wrong to children	1
	Baccho ke saath bura kaam karna	To do bad things to children	1
	Baccho ke saath harkate karna	To do activities with children	1
	Baccho ke saath sona	To sleep with children	1

Table 9.3   Translations for Orgasm and Digital Penetration

Word in English	Word in Hindi	Back Translation	Number of Respondents
Orgasm	Sambhog	Intercourse	1
	Mazza aata hai	Enjoyment	1
	Anubhav	Experience	1
	Manava uttejana	Human excitement	1
Digital Penetration	Usne Usse chua	Someone touched someone	1
	Koi Cheez Ghusa de	Inserted something	1
	Cheez Daalna	Inserting something	1
	Ungali andar dalna	To insert with finger	1

Dilution of meaning

The Oxford English dictionary defines pornography as printed or visual material intended to stimulate sexual excitement, with its origin from the Greek word 'pornographos' which means 'writing about prostitutes'. Andrea Dworkin (1989) elaborated on the etymology of the word:

> Contemporary pornography strictly and literally conforms to the word's root meaning: the graphic depiction of vile whores. The word has not changed its meaning and the genre is not misnamed. The only change in the meaning of the

word is with respect to its second part, graphos: now there are cameras – there is still photography, film, video (p200).

Dworkin (1989) explains the reference to the understanding of pornography as being bad or dirty in the context of the female body and sexuality being perceived as dirty. This meaning and definition of pornography had been contested as it blurs the sexual subordination of women under the notions of decency and obscenity (Dines et al. 1998). Jensen (2007) calls the process that masks the consumption and the production process of pornography a 'definitional dodge'.

The Hindi words for pornography represent a discourse that dodges the reality of pornography as a system of sexual subordination and oppression (see Table 9.4). The translations for the word were linked to notions of obscenity, nudity and dirty and with no reference to the production and the consumption process.

Table 9.4   Translations for Pornography

Word in English	Word in Hindi	Back Translation	Number of Respondents
Pornography	Ashleel tasveer ya video	Obscene film or video	2
	Nagi Tasveer	Nude pictures	2
	Blue Film	Blue film	2
	Ganda	Dirty	1

Words used as sexual insults

This theme refers to words that are grammatically correct and have a specific meaning in the cultural context in which they operate (see Table 9.5). If they are understood as linguistic labels they are accurate, however, this does not address what is offensive about these words. It is their shared meaning and what it signified for the men and women using and hearing them, that makes it offensive. Dworkin (1989) locates the word and concept of 'whore' within the framework of male sexual domination and their purpose as serving men sexually. Clark (1998) in her study examines reporting from The Sun newspaper about sexual violence against women. She identifies that that it is not just the use of specific words that blame the victim. It is a more sophisticated process whereby words are co-opted within a larger philosophy of victim blaming. In this context, the words and the ideology in which they are located create co-construct the meaning together. According to Black and Coward (1998), sexism is not fixed in meaning encoded by language but the way particular contexts construct meaning.

Table 9.5   Translations of the words used as Sexual Insults

Word in English	Word in Hindi	Back Translation	Number of Respondents
Prostitute	Randi	Whore	4
	Kanjri	Whore	1
Vagina	Choot	Vagina/cunt	5
Penis	Land	Dick	5
Anal Sex	Gand Marna	Anal sex	4

Table 9.6   Shame and Honour in translating Child Sexual Abuse and Rape

Word in English	Word in Hindi	Translation	Number of Respondents
Rape	Izzat loot le	Robbed ones honour	4
	Sharam ho gayi	Brought shame	1
Child Sexual Abuse	Baccho ki Izzat Lootna	To rob a child's honour	1
	Baccho ke saath Besharmi Karna	To do something shameful to a child	1

Shame and Honour

The concept of honour added an additional dimension to the results. The idea of honour is understood to create a hindrance to women seeking help (Gill 2004, Gilligan and Akhtar 2006). In the context of this study, all the respondents were willing to talk about sexual violence and there was an ambiguous sexual vocabulary. For some of the respondents (see Table 9.6) honour and shame provided the labels to name rape and child sexual abuse. They did not silence the sexual violence but rather framed it in a different way. The different facets of Hindi sexual vocabulary would suggest that honour is one of the factors influencing discourse. For a woman willing to disclose, honour is not the only factor creating hindrance. It has been suggested that it is dishonourable to disclose sexual violence (Gill 2009). However, it remains to be explored if honour also silences naming body parts and positive sexual experiences. The results from this study demonstrate that rape and child sexual abuse was translated by a high number of respondents and, in the absence of other words, they used references to honour and shame. The words that had the least number of translations and the words which had a significant ambiguous translation were not framed in sentences that suggested an abusive context. The results would suggest that honour influences the larger discourse; it does not completely silence sexual violence.

Common Ground

The relationship between language and disclosure was discussed with professionals who work with survivors in different settings. The participants spoke about the need for common ground. According to McConnell-Ginet (1989), in linguistic communication the speaker typically takes a common ground with the listener. This could include certain beliefs about the language system, and in particular about familiar connections between linguistic forms (signifiers) and thoughts and concepts (signified). (McConnell-Ginet 1998: 200).

McConnell-Ginet (1998) is referring here to the fact that when a person is talking to another person, the meaning is understood as both of them are from the same speech community where the words have the shared meaning. Speech community is defined as people who speak the same language. In this study, the participants perceived a lack of common ground. The same sexual vocabulary could mean one thing to them and an entirely different thing to the service-user; the thoughts and concepts behind them were not shared. In the professional experience of the participants, sexual vocabulary was reflective of this. Given their different contexts and reasons for coming in contact with survivors, a lack of common ground had different implications for each of them.

One of the participants used the word common ground to explain her work with teenage girls and their parents. For her, not having a shared understanding meant that the same word could mean different things to her and her service user, or not specify the extent of what had actually happened. If a girl is being sexually exploited, then the parents understanding that 'she hangs out with boys' might not have a shared meaning with her as well as their own daughter.

Similarly for the word '*izzat*' (honour), the participants saw this as a very broad term that could mean anything. The available literature on violence against women acknowledges that the concept of '*izzat*' does not have a fixed meaning (Gill 2004; Gilligan and Akhtar 2006; Wilson 1978). Similarly, in the experience of the participants, sex is spoken of as love or the relationship between man and woman. Two of them used the word '*danda*' to translate penis. The literal translation for the word '*danda*' is stick. It is a generic word and unless the listener is familiar or clarifies what the speaker means by '*danda*', the word in itself does not mean penis.

During the preliminary stages of conceptualising the study, I had several discussions at formal and informal networks with fellow practitioners, friends and family. One practitioner who is multilingual and works with survivors of domestic violence illustrated that when one of the service users complained about her violent partner, she used the phrase '*wo jabardasti pilata hai*' (he forces me to drink). On further questioning, they established the meaning of 'he forces me to drink' as being orally raped and being forced to swallow semen (private communication)

The process of establishing common ground and then relaying the Hindi speaking women's experience into another language community has the potential of placing the multilingual professional in a position of power. This study has its limitations, as it has not explored the extent to which the professional context of the participants allows them to create this meaning and their own understanding of sexual violence. However, it opens the discussion about how practitioners in different contexts have the power and can contribute to creating a public discourse of sexual violence.

Conclusions

From the above discussion, it would appear that the Hindi sexual vocabulary is complex and the process of disclosure is a not linear (see Figure 9.1). For a Hindi-speaking survivor willing to disclose sexual violence, getting access to an interpreter would be the first step. The second step would be to use the available Hindi sexual vocabulary, work through the ambiguities, euphemisms and circumlocutions, to establish common ground with the interpreter. The third step would be for the interpreter to relay this meaning into English.

As a fourth step of the translation process, once a Hindi speaking woman's experience has been translated to English, it will come in contact with different discourses and different settings. As discussed earlier, English has been subject to feminist linguistic enquiry. Feminism has shaped how sexual violence is framed, and has attempted to create new definitions where needed. There are also concerns that it is the male definitions of sexual violence that are encoded in law. A Hindi speaking woman's account encoded in English, will possibly come into contact with law enforcement, criminal justice, health, social services, voluntary sector, specialist support organisations. Each of them has English as their official language. Depending on the sensitivity of these organisations, some of these may accommodate her experience and other may not.

At the last stage of disclosure there is the potential of her experience being challenged. Due to not knowing English, she will have to start negotiating from stage one of the process. Each time her experience is challenged she will need access to an interpreter and to negotiate common ground. The intersections of race, class and gender will also play a very significant role in how she is able to respond to the challenge.

Feminism has significantly influenced the discourse on sexual violence. It has also recognised language as a powerful resource where new meanings and women's experiences can be materialised (Cameron 1998a, Cameron 1998b). Feminist linguistic theories emphasise the importance of words as well as of a discourse that shapes the words. Not having a shared meaning is considered representative of a larger context that does not allow women's meanings to shape this discourse (McConnell-Ginet 1998). A larger political context that allows women to reclaim, coin and challenge meaning is considered more important than linguistics labels. My research suggests that this analysis has not been extended to other languages that may have a restricted discourse which co-exist with English. This research identifies a gap in acknowledging the complexity language can add for women seeking to disclose sexual violence.

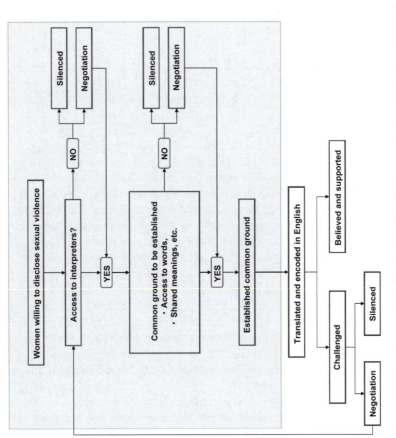

Figure 9.1 Possible processes of silencing and disclosure in Hindi. The contents within the shaded box represent dialogue in Hindi

The study informing this discussion has been carried with a small group of people, but highlights my experience and that of the participants. Nonetheless, it is hoped that it can contribute to a wider discussion about the language and disclosure in languages other than English. It identifies the need to explore the discourse of sexual violence in Hindi with language use analysed from the survivors' perspective as a part of a larger strategy to deal with violence against Asian women.

References

Baker, P. and E. 2000. *Multilingual Capital: The Langauges of London School Children and Their Relevance to Economic, Social and Educational Policies.* London: Batlebridge Publications.

Black, M. and Coward, R. 1998. Linguistic Sexual and Social Relations: A Review of Gale Spender's Man Made Langauge, in *The Feminist Critique of Language, 2nd Edition,* edited by D. Cameron. London: Routledge.

Cameron, D. 1992. *Feminism and Linguistic Theory.* New York: Palgrave.

Cameron, D. 1998a. *The Feminist Critique of Language: A reader.* London: Routledge.

Cameron, D. 1998b. Feminist linguistic theories, in *Contemporary Feminist Theories,* edited by S. Jackson and J. Jones. Edinburgh: Edinburgh University Press.

Cameron, D. 1998c. Gender, Language, and Discourse: A review essay. *Signs,* 23, 945–973.

Chand, A. 2005. Do you speak English? Language barriers in child protection social work with minority ethnic families. *British Journal of Social Work,* 35, 807–821.

Clark, K. 1998. The Linguistics of Blame: Representation of Women in the Sun's Reporting of Crimes of Sexual Violence, in *Feminist Critique of Langauge, 2nd Edition,* edited by D. Cameron. London: Routledge.

Collins, P.H. 1991. Black Feminist Thought. *New York and London: Routledge.*

Crenshaw, K. 1994. Mapping the margins: Intersectionality, identity politics, and violence against women of color, in *The Public Nature of Private Violence,* edited by K.C. Williams. New York.

Dines, G., Jensen, R. and Russo, A. 1998. *Pornography: The Production and Consumption of Inequality.* London: Routledge.

Dworkin, A. 1989. *Pornography: Men Possessing Women,* New York: E.P. Dutton.

Gill, A. 2004. Voicing the silent fear: South Asian women's experiences of domestic violence. *The Howard Journal of Criminal Justice,* 43, 465–483.

Gill, A. 2009. Narratives of Survival: South Asian Women's Experience of Rape, in *Rape Challenging Contempory Thinking,* edited by M. Hovarth and J. Brown. London : Routledge.

Gilligan, P. and Akhtar, S. 2006. Cultural Barriers to the Disclosure of Child Sexual Abuse in Asian Communities: Listening to What Women Say. *British Journal of Social Work,* 36, 1361–1377.

Jensen, R. 2007. *Getting off: Pornography and the End of Masculinity*. New York: South End Press.

Kelly, L. 1988. *Surviving Sexual Violence*. London: Polity.

Kelly, L. and Radford, J. 1990. 'Nothing Really Happened': the invalidation of women's experiences of sexual violence. *Critical Social Policy,* 10, 39.

Mcconnell-Ginet, S. 1989. The sexual (re) production of meaning: A discourse-based theory, in *Language, gender, and professional writing: Theoretical approaches and guidelines for nonsexist usage.*

Sen, P. 2005. Crimes of Honour,Value and Meaning, in *Crimes,Paradigms and Violence Against Women,* edited by L.W.A.S Hossain. London: Zed Books.

Spender, D. 1980. *Man Made Language,* London: Routledge and Kegan Paul.

Wilson, A. 1978. Finding a Voice, in *Teaching ESL*. London: Virago.

Wilson, A. 2006. *Dreams, Questions, Struggles: South Asian Women in Britain*. London: Pluto.

Wyatt, G.E. 1985. The sexual abuse of Afro-American and White-American women in childhood. *Child Abuse and Neglect,* 9, 507–519.

Appendix 1

She is pregnant again.

There are many cases of breast cancer.

Many organizations support survivors of Child sexual abuse.

She hurt her vagina during horse riding.

Working couples get time to have sex only on weekends.

She has no sexual feelings towards him.

Smoking can alter the quality of sperm.

Masturbation is considered unhealthy.

Human orgasm lasts for a few seconds.

She is playing a prostitute in that film.

Anal sex is illegal in some countries.

Size of the penis does not matter.

X was arrested for causing a child to watch sexual act.

She is not obtaining any sexual gratification.

There is a rape scene in that film.

They are investigating if there was any digital penetration.

Pornography is easily available on the internet.

Chapter 10

'True Honour': Domestic Violence, Forced Marriage and Honour Crimes in the UK

Hannana Siddiqui

> The last time I saw Banaz alive was in 2005 ... I wish with all my heart I had taken her with me in 2005 because she would then still be alive ... I find it really hard to say how much her death has affected me. Words just do not say enough. I can honestly say there's not been one night without having nightmares. Banaz herself does not come into my dreams or nightmares, and that upsets me. I would like to see her again ... I cry and become very upset when I think what has happened to her. My life will never be the same again (Bekhal Mahmod).[1]

This chapter follows the cases of two sisters, Banaz and Bekhal Mahmod, as examples of the lives of black and minority ethnic (BME) women who experience gender-based violence: exploring the overlaps between domestic violence, forced marriage and so called 'honour-based violence (HBV), also known as honour crimes. While, in the last decade dramatic cases of 'honour' killings or forced marriage have hit the headlines, women's routine experiences of abuse have received little or no media attention. Yet it is these everyday experiences of abuse which form the continuum of violence experienced by many women over their life time (Kelly 1987). These do not fit neatly in race and gender stereotypes and fail to excite interest stripped of any 'exotic' or dramatic backdrop. While the death of Banaz illustrated how women become the ultimate victims of escalating abuse, the experiences of her sister, Bekhal, reveals the routine experiences of abuse, which if acted upon at an earlier stage, can help women to survive.

BME women live at the intersection between race and gender and other social divisions, which creates multiple discriminations in their lives and tensions in the struggle for equality and freedom (Crenshaw 1991).[2] This chapter, therefore, also charts the journey of the BME women's movement struggle to fight violence

---

1   The words of Bakhal Mahmod on the murder of her sister, Banaz Mahmod, quoted in McVeigh, K. 2001. 'I Wish I'd Taken Her With Me.' 21 July, *The Guardian*.

2   Crenshaw's theory of intersectionality was developed at a time when SBS and some academics were also debating how to adequately conceptualise the intersectional and multiple discriminations faced by BME women in the UK.

against BME women and girls, primarily through the experiences of a leading BME women's organisation, Southall Black Sisters (SBS).[3]

Definitions and Evidence

There is no agreed definition of HBV. The UN Special Rapporteur on violence against women describes honour crimes as taking place in contexts where:

> Honour is defined in terms of women's assigned sexual and familial roles as dictated by traditional family ideology. Thus, adultery, premarital relationships (which may or may not include sexual relations), rape and falling in love with an 'inappropriate' person may constitute violations of family honour.[4]

Honour here is the motivation, excuse or the justification (in some legal contexts, mitigation) for the violence by the perpetrator/s. It is the reason for the abuse, not the act of violence itself, which can include domestic and sexual violence and harmful practices. If the act of violence is on one side of the coin, then honour or the reason for the violence is on the flip side. The terminology of HBV itself has been the subject of much debate, as the definition of honour underpinning it is defined through the perspective of the perpetrator/s. There are widely held notions of personal or group 'honour' which connote integrity, respect for oneself and others: this version of the concept is not contentious. Where codes of 'honour' are used to justify violence and abuse for familial or community respectability, this could be said to be 'dishonourable': an 'honour killing' is murder by another name. The violence within HBV ranges through social ostracism or rejection, emotional blackmail, mental torture and sexual harassment (the most commonly experienced) to rape and sexual abuse, assault and threats to kill, imprisonment and abduction, forced marriage, dowry abuse and female genital mutilation (FGM) and even, at the extreme end, attempted and actual murder (Siddiqui 2005). HBV is, therefore, a concept which encompasses many forms of violence against BME women and girls.

Although some men and boys can be also victims of HBV, the primary victims are women and girls. In this context, notions of honour are gendered; aimed at

---

3   Southall Black Sisters was founded in 1979. It runs a specialist holistic resource centre, providing information, advice, advocacy, counselling and support services on violence against BME women and girls. It has nationally recognised expertise on domestic violence and harmful practices amongst South Asian women. SBS also campaigns, and conducts educational, developmental, policy and research on these issues to change attitudes and practices within BME communities, and to influence law, policy and practice more widely.

4   Report of the Special Rapporteur on violence against women, it causes and consequences, UN Doc. E/CN.4/1999/68 10 March 1999, para 18.

controlling female sexuality and autonomy in male dominated communities where the reputation of the family is believed to rest on women conforming to traditional femininity as good, dutiful and obedient wives, sisters, sister-in-laws, mothers, daughters and daughters-in-laws. These beliefs are supported by conservative cultural and religious value systems, which are often conflated and merged. Women who, or are perceived to, transgress are regarded as 'morally loose' and accused of having brought 'shame' and 'dishonour' on their family. This can result in them being 'punished' by some, or many, members of their extended families and communities, who may perpetrate or collude in HBV (Siddiqui 2005). For Asian women, these prescribed roles are based on the notion of the ideal virtuous Indian womanhood, epitomised by Sita in the Hindu epic Ramayan, who follows her 'true' path as a devoted and obedient wife of Lord Ram. This ideal construct of femininity is found across all religious groups in South Asia, particularly as it also forms part of popular Bollywood culture.

Some argue that HBV is fundamentally different from domestic violence because it involves collective 'punishment' by the community, based on shared value systems and is therefore more dangerous. SBS have argued that HBV is often instigated by the extended family and is, in fact, a form of domestic violence, since notions of shame and honour are part and parcel of the dynamics of, and justifications for, domestic violence within minority communities in the UK.

Domestic violence and HBV can both include forced marriage – a marriage without free and valid consent of one or both parties, involving duress. There is a fine line between arranged and forced marriages, as many arranged marriages involve considerable emotional and social pressure. Both arranged and forced marriage can involve the giving and taking of a dowry, which may include excessive demands for cash, jewellery, property and other goods, resulting in the harassment of women when they are not met. Although contested, FGM may also be considered a form of HBV, since in some contexts it is understood as linked with sexual purity or 'honour' of women (see Roach and Momoh, this volume).

Cultural and religious justifications for VAWG have long histories in many societies. In Britain, for instant, 'shotgun' or forced marriages took place when women became pregnant out of wedlock, or in more aristocratic households, arranged marriages, many no doubt forced, were rife, and a 'dual at dawn' could be arranged to defend the good reputation of a woman without which the family name would be brought into disrepute. However, while men in British society now justify their violent behaviour in terms of an entitlement to ownership of, and respect from, loyal and faithful wives and girlfriends, 'honour' as a justification has diminished, although some have suggested parallels with notions of 'pride' and 'respect' within gang culture (see, for example, Parker, 2007). It remains explicit in conservative sections of some minority communities in the UK, particularly South Asian and Middle Eastern. Although less reported or researched, such codes of honour may also exist in other minority communities, including African,

Chinese, Japanese, Orthodox Jewish and Roma, Gypsy and Travellers, and even in some European communities such as Greek and Italian.

Whilst research data remains weak on violence against BME women and girls, current available information indicates that South Asian and Middle Eastern women and girls are the most likely victims of forced marriage and HBV. In 2011, the Government's Forced Marriage Unit (FMU) dealt with 1468 incidents of forced marriage, of which 78 per cent involved women.[5] The Metropolitan police estimate there are 12 cases of honour killings per year (HASC 2008) and minority and migrant women are disproportionately represented as victims of domestic homicide (Mayor of London 2010). Suicide is up to three times higher amongst South Asian women and higher rates of self-harm have been documented: both have been connected to abusive and oppressive practices in the family (Siddiqui and Patel 2010).

BME Women's Experiences

Honour and shame have been key themes in the lives of most women who have approached SBS for help. Honour is not only the motive for abuse by the perpetrator but fear of dishonour and shame often acts as a barrier to women seeking help. Strong cultural and religious pressures within tight knit, patriarchal minority communities are internal barriers which are reinforced by external barriers including racism, lack of English, insecure immigration status and no recourse to public funds, lack of knowledge about their rights or where to go for help. Those who do reach out may also encounter a refusal by state agencies to take violence against women and girls seriously or a reluctance to intervene in the name of 'cultural sensitivity' and more recently, 'religious sensitivity'. The cases of Banaz and Bekhal below highlight these issues.

Sealed with a Kiss

Banaz Mahmod, an Iraqi Kurdish woman, was only 19 when she died. In April 2006 her body was found in a suitcase buried in the garden of an empty house in Birmingham, three months after being reported missing by her boyfriend, Rahmat Sulemani. Prior to her death, Banaz had reported threats to her life on four occasions, including an attempt on her life by her own father. She had even named the suspects who were later convicted of her murder. In 2007 her uncle, who is a powerful community leader, her father and a man from the Iraqi Kurdish community in South London, were convicted of murder at the Old Bailey. Another two men were later also convicted after being extradited from Iraq, where they had fled to escape justice.

---

5   See http://www.fco.gov.uk/en/travel-and-living-abroad/when-things-go-wrong/forced-marriage/ [online] (Accessed: 2 May 2012)

Banaz had been murdered in a so called 'honour' killing for wanting to divorce her abusive husband and to marry Rahmat. Her family did not approve of him as he was from another tribal group. Her uncle first made threats, and her mother warned her that her life was in danger, when Banaz had been seen kissing her boyfriend outside a tube station. Her fate had been sealed with a kiss. However, her life, even prior to this, was full of abuse and torture. As a child, she suffered at the hands of her strict father, as did her four sisters. Her brother and other male relatives in the extended family also policed their behaviour.

Her older sister, Bekhal, had run away from home as a teenager, following experiences of physical violence and pressure to conform to Islamic and Middle Eastern traditions and values. In an interview, Bekhal said: [6]

> I left home because of the pressure of everything ... you have to get married, you can't have friends outside the family ... there were so many things that were piled on together that it was enough to make anybody do that ... There was (violence) ... I did not want to leave ... I loved my mum and at the time, I loved my dad, but I hated ... how they treated me and dismissed what I say ... [once] my aunty called, and she said "hello, my gorgeous daughter-in-law" ... I said "what are you talking about?" and she said "you are my daughter-in-law". I said "no, I am your niece" ... I was 15 and [the man I was to marry] was 35 years old ... I was in my nappies when he was a teenager ... the last time I saw him, I must have been eight years old ... When I said no, I got a lot of ... harsh beatings.

Bekhal went into a refuge, but soon returned home due to threats to kill her and the family from her father. The second time she left home, she was taken to social services.

> Social services were not very thorough. They were trying their best to take me back home, they were saying that is the best place for you ... because I am young, not making a right decision ... They did not agree with the marriage, but [said that I should] come to terms with my parents ... I returned home because my case worker ... decided to be friendly with my family and pass things back and forth from me to them, from them to me. She decided to record a cassette tape from my dad, where my mum is crying and screaming in the background, my dad is speaking in Kurdish. He is saying "whatever it takes, I will get you back to my house. If you don't come back home, I am going to kill all your sisters, I am going to kill your brother ... I am going to kill myself, and that will be all on you." ... Your dad is your dad ... I see him as a person who will ... follow through what he says, and I did not want to risk anything like that.

---

6   Bekhal Mahmod has given permission to the author to use her story in this chapter.

Bekhal returned home again. The social worker did not speak Kurdish and had not checked the tape. Throughout social services failed to take the risks to Bekhal seriously.

Bekhal eventually left home again. This time permanently when only about sixteen. Although in hiding, Bekhal maintained contact with some of her siblings. On one occasion, she agreed to meet her brother: he took her to a remote area where he attempted to strangle her and hit her over the head with a heavy weight. When Bekhal fought back, he started to cry, saying that his father had told him to kill her saying: "you have to understand, I am the only brother, the only son my dad has got, I am the next in line, being the male, taking over the name, I had to do this, I had to earn my respect from my dad".

Although Bekhal later reported the incident to the police, it did not result in a prosecution. This was a sinister forerunner of events which occurred later to Banaz. Banaz had been pressured into marriage, which later led to a separation. In July 2005 Banaz had accused her husband of domestic violence and rape, and had returned home to her parents in the hope that she would be able to obtain a divorce. On New Year's Eve 2005 Banaz had been asked by her father to bring a suitcase to her grandmother's house which he was clearing. While there, although very disapproving of alcohol, Banaz's father plied her with brandy while he prepared to strangle her. However, Banaz managed to struggle free and ran into the garden, where she tried to summon help by knocking on the neighbour's window. There was no response and she accidently broke the window. She eventually escaped by climbing over a garden fence to a cafe, bleeding and bare footed, where the police were called.

Banaz begged the police to call her boyfriend, who she felt was also in danger and he joined her at the hospital where Banaz explained to the police that her father had attempted to kill her. The officer, however, was dismissive of her claims, treating her concerns as 'melodramatic'. Rahmat recorded Banaz's allegations on his mobile phone. Believing that her mother would protect her, Banaz returned home. The misreading of her situation by the police is further illustrated by their pursuing charging Banaz with criminal damage for breaking the neighbour's window: the case was only discontinued when the neighbour chose not to support this.

The plot to kill Banaz had been hatched after a 'council of war' meeting organised by an uncle, who recruited three men to carry out the murder. On the morning of 24 January 2006, these men tortured, raped and sexually assaulted Banaz for about two hours before strangling her with a bootlace at her parent's home. Her body was then bundled into a suitcase. These men, who were secretly recorded in prison while awaiting trial, laughed and joked about kicking and stamping on her neck "to get the soul out" and raping her "to show her disrespect".[7]

SBS supported Bekhal to give evidence for the prosecution. She did this at great risk to herself, but had been devastated by the death of Banaz, and dismayed and

---

7   McVeigh, K. 2007. 'Honour' Killer Boasted of Stamping on Woman's Neck. 21 July, *The Guardian*.

angry about the failures of the police to protect her. Unfortunately, an investigation into the case by the Independent Police Complaints Commission only resulted in 'words of advice' – minor disciplinary action – against some of the police officers to whom Banaz had turned to save her life.

Bekhal now says:

> (Banaz) still (has not come into my dreams). I am still begging God to help me to have her in my dreams. It may sound really strange, I feel her all over my house … I feel she is there … The first time I left home … she was 14 … she did not understand what I was trying to do … she did not have to make decisions about marriage … she was determined I was doing the wrong thing … The last time I left, she realised what I was doing, and that is when … I realised that I loved her … she was the one that really, really understood me.

The experiences of Bekhal and Banaz illustrate the ways in which forced marriage, domestic and sexual violence, honour and gender inequality interlaced. It was the failure of police and social workers to understand these inter-connections which led them to underestimate the dangers they faced. The fact that both resisted the gendered control their family sought to impose also challenges stereotypes of 'passive' Middle Eastern, Asian and other minority women. SBS and other BME women's organisations have campaigned for over three decades to establish the importance of the state acting as a countervailing power in such contexts: that the practitioners they encountered did not understand this cost Banaz her life and Bekhal her sister.

Multiculturalism and 'Moral Blindness'

While domestic violence and harmful practices have been a daily reality for BME women's groups since the 1970s, public debate on forced marriage only emerged a decade ago when the high profile cases of Rukshana Naz and 'Jack and Zena' hit the national headlines. Rukshana Naz, a 19 year old Asian woman, was killed in 1998 by her brother and mother when she refused to stay in a forced marriage to her cousin in Pakistan, and became pregnant to her lover in the UK. Her family wanted her to return to her husband and have a late abortion. The mother and brother were convicted of murder in 1999. In court, the brother attempted to argue a cultural defence by arguing that he was 'provoked' into killing his sister, who had brought shame and dishonour onto the family. In the case of 'Jack and Zena' we witnessed another extreme example: a white British/Asian couple who went on the run when Zena's family attempted to force her into marriage. They were pursued by 'bounty hunters', private detectives and family members for many years and continue to be at risk. However, despite this, they have publically raised the issue of forced marriage and the right to marry a person of your choice.

It was in the context of these, and other, cases that SBS called for a public inquiry. The Home Office Minister, Mike O'Brien, responded by setting up a Home Office Working Group on Forced Marriage in 1999. This broke from the prevailing government multicultural policy on race and community relations, which recommended non-state interference in minority communities in order to respect cultural difference: to do otherwise was seen as intolerant, even racist. Mike O'Brien advocated a 'mature multiculturalism' to counter this cultural relativist approach, noting "multicultural sensitivity is no excuse for moral blindness" (Hansard 1999). The lobbying of SBS influenced this progressive stance, which, for the first time, recognised the rights of BME women to state protection from abuse from within the family.

SBS were invited to join the Working Group, alongside other women's groups, including a Muslim women's group. It was co-chaired by the Labour Peers, Baroness Uddin and Lord Ahmed. However, just before the Working Group could report, SBS were forced to resign over a disagreement about the use of mediation and reconciliation in tackling forced marriage. Some members of the Working Group, particularly the Islamists, argued this approach was appropriate, since it helped to keep the family together. SBS opposed it on the grounds that it compromised women's safety and that this had been accepted for some time in policies on domestic violence.[8] The dangers inherent in mediation are highlighted by Bekhal Mahmod's experiences with social services discussed earlier.

This disagreement in the Working Group was fundamental. The Islamists regarded forced marriage as an issue to be addressed through education with the community and religious leaders playing a leading role in changing social attitudes and practices. This chimed with government policy at the time. In contrast, SBS argued for greater state intervention to protect women, despite exposing the problems of the community 'warts and all'.

This debate re-played the classic tension between race and gender. For anti-racists, not 'washing our dirty linen in public' was an important principle, while multicultural policies, often supported by more conservative religious and communities leaders, ensured state non-intervention, thus maintaining gender inequality. SBS opposed both the hierarchy of oppression of the anti-racist left, and the 'hands off' approach of the right. We argued that to promote human rights for all, race and gender inequality had to be addressed simultaneously.

Despite our resignation from the Working Group, and the inclusion of mediation as an option, the influence of this position can be seen in final report, *A Choice by Right*, published in 2000. For the first time, the British Government recognised forced marriage as an abuse of human rights, and that the state had some responsibility to tackle it. The FCO set up the Community Liaison Unit to deal with forced marriage, this later became a joint Home Office and FCO

---

8   For a fuller discussion on this see Siddiqui, H. 2003. 'It was Written in her Kismet': Forced Marriage in *From Homebreakers to Jailbreakers; Southall Black Sisters,* edited by R. Gupta. London: Zed Books.

Forced Marriage Unit (FMU). The FMU developed forced marriage guidelines for professional agencies, which SBS ensured did not advocate either non-intervention or mediation and reconciliation as appropriate responses.

'Honour' Killings, Domestic Homicide and Suicide

In 2002, mass media interest in so called 'honour' killings followed the death of Heshu Yonis, a 16-year old Iraqi Kurdish woman killed by her father for having a Christian Lebanese boyfriend. He wanted her to marry a cousin. The labelling as an 'honour' killing meant that the forced marriage intersection was lost and has led to a situation in which most domestic homicides involving South Asian and Middle Eastern women are now defined as 'honour' killings by the media and state agencies. The Metropolitan Police reviewed domestic homicides involving the death of BME women to develop risk assessment tools on HBV. In 2008 the Association of Chief Police Officers (ACPO) also developed an HBV strategy. The Crown Prosecution Service (CPS) also began to develop strategies on forced marriage and HBV but, unlike the police, this was later incorporated into their VAWG strategies. The police and CPS also consulted experts, including SBS, while investigating or preparing cases for trial.

One outcome of these developments in policy and practice was a rapid increase in convictions for such murders, although the prosecution and conviction rate in routine cases of domestic violence, forced marriage and HBV remain low (Greater London Authority/Imkaan et al. 2011). The on-going failures in policing are amply and tragically highlighted in the case of Banaz Mahmod, which could have been regarded as equivalent to the lessons learnt through the racist murder of Stephan Lawrence. Suicides driven by abusive and oppressive practices also continue to be ignored: SBS has dealt with 18 cases of suicide or suspected suicide, most of which were subject to a cursory investigation by the police and the coroner's courts (Siddiqui and Patel 2010).

Forced Marriage Law and Guidelines

In 2005 the government consulted on the criminalisation of forced marriage. The pressure for this came from Ann Cryer MP, later supported by some women's groups including Karma Nirvana. Criminalisation was a contested issue. On the one hand, there was the argument that giving a strong and clear message condemning forced marriage as abhorrent and morally wrong, which attracted criminal sanctions, would both be heard by communities and would ensure a clearer responses from agencies such as the police and social services. On the other hand, women's organisations were aware that a criminal offence could prevent many victims from coming forward: it would exacerbate their ambivalence since many still love and respect their families whilst disagreeing with the decisions being made about their futures. They seek protection of their right to self-determination rather than a prosecution; since they hope, in the long-term, that their parents will come to terms with their decisions. This tension between protection and prosecution requires more debate and consideration within women's movements.

The only comparable law in the UK is the Female Genital Mutilation Act 2003 (which amended the original law introduced in 1985). African women's groups, like Forward, who had lobbied for this law, supported the criminalisation of forced marriage, since in their view it had been the passing of legislation which meant FGM was taken seriously. There have been no convictions under the FGM law, surely this also sends out the wrong message: that perpetrators can 'get away with it'. The problem in relation to forced marriage was the failure of the criminal justice system to act, since in this case – unlike FGM – there were a number of existing criminal offences which could be used: assault, harassment, abduction and false imprisonment.

While others argued against criminalising forced marriage for fear of encouraging racist policing, SBS accepted that criminalisation would send the right message to minority communities. Despite this, on balance, we concluded it was likely to do more harm than good in deterring victims from coming forward and driving the problem underground. Instead, we argued that the forced marriage should be tackled by strengthening civil law, more funding for BME women's services and effective implementation and enforcement of the forced marriage guidelines. In 2005, the government announced that it would not criminalise forced marriage as their consultation showed that the majority of the respondents were opposed to it.

Subsequently, Forced Marriage Protection Orders (FMPOs) were introduced under the Forced Marriage (Civil Protection) Act 2007, proposed by Lord Lester, who worked closely with SBS and lawyers on the Bill. Although the Government originally opposed this and it was rejected for 'demonising' minority communities by some groups, lobbying by SBS and others, including Karma Nirvana, led to a U-turn. The out-going Prime Minister, Tony Blair, it seems, had wanted the criminal law as part of his legacy. The forced marriage guidelines were also put on a statutory footing but no effective inspection and enforcement mechanisms were developed, despite our insistence that these were a vital part of the package of measures.

In December 2011 the new Tory-led Conservative/Liberal Democrat Coalition Government reintroduced consultation on criminalising forced marriage. It also outlined the Government's intent to make a breach of an FMPO a criminal offence. This followed a Home Affairs Select Committee report[9] which, having only taken evidence from two individuals connected to one organisation (Karma Nivrana), recommended that the government should consider criminalisation as the Forced Marriage Act 2007 was not working. Other views appear not to have

---

9   *Forced Marriage: Eighth Report Session 2010-12*, Home Affairs Select Committee, 17 May 2011.

been canvassed. Following protest on the lack of consultation, the Government's immediate response was not to introduce consultation on criminalisation, but to monitor outcomes of the criminalisation of breach of FMPOs in Scotland where it had recently been introduced.[10]

However, despite this official position, David Cameron, the Tory Prime Minister, went ahead with a consultation. The Home Office exaggerated forced marriage figures, estimating that there are 5,000–8,000 cases per year.[11] It seems that politicians in Government are cynically using the 'sexy' issue of forced marriage to gain the woman's vote as more women become disillusioned with their policies. The new criminal law is proposed at a time when the government is introducing severe austerity measures, resulting in cuts in policing and funding for the voluntary sector, particularly frontline BME women's groups. Furthermore, localism is removing central government regulation and inspection regimes, thereby undermining the implementation of the statutory forced marriage guidelines. Criminalisation in this context is both futile and tokenistic, risking undercutting the very purpose behind the proposed reform – protecting victims and giving them the confidence to come forward.

SBS, Imkaan and many other women and BME women's organisations (now also including Forward) responded to the consultation, opposing creating a new criminal offence, but supporting criminalisation of the breach of an FMPO, provided victims retained the choice of also using the civil route of contempt of court. This coalition was supported by many lawyers, some politicians and parts of the media. Karma Nirvana, the Iranian and Kurdish Women's Rights Organisations (IKWRO) and other Middle Eastern women's groups sought criminalisation. They are supported by much of the media and members of the Government. In June 2012, the Government announced its intention to create a criminal offence of forced marriage based on a small majority (54%) who favoured this in response to the consultation. However, responses by individuals were given equal weight to those of organisations, some of which, such as SBS and Imkaan, represented the views of many women's groups, survivors and other experts opposed to criminalisation.[12]

---

10   *The Government Response to the Eight Report from the Home Affairs Committee Session 2010-12 HC 880: Forced Marriage,* Presented to Parliament by Secretary of State for the Home Department, July 2011.

11   *Forced Marriage Consultation,* December 2011, Home Office. Although one study had estimated these figures, most of the other available evidence does not confirm them, including those of the FMU.

12   Home Office, June 2012. *Forced Marriage-Summary of Responses.*

Religion, Social Cohesion and the Parallel Universe

Post 9/11 and the 7/7 London bombings the landscape in which the debates on harmful practices took place changed. Multiculturalism came under attack for breeding segregation and Islamic terrorism. The Government response was to promote social cohesion as the new approach in relation to minority communities. This demanded that minority communities, and Muslims in particular, should adopt core 'British' values to aid social integration. At the same time, the state also promoted 'multi-faithism'. The success of the BME women's movement in empowering women has also created a backlash within the growing fundamentalist and other conservative and patriarchal forces within the community. In some cases, especially in the North and Midlands of England, this has taken the form of more organised networks or gangs of men, 'bounty hunters' and private detectives, who track down women, particularly young women, and force them to return home. Others, more commonly, are pressured to use internal community mechanisms to resolve their problems, such as informal mediation and reconciliation through family or community elders, or increasingly, via formal arbitration by religious courts or Shar'ia Councils. For the state, the need for 'religious sensitivity' under multi-faithism has now, to some extent, overtaken the fear of being regarded as 'culturally insensitive' (Siddiqui 2008, Patel and Siddiqui 2010, and see Patel in this volume).

Within this context the intense interest in forced marriage and HBV has created a parallel universe where all forms of violence within South Asian and Middle Eastern communities are now viewed through the lens of HBV. This returns us to the focus on 'the other', an exoticisation of BME women's experiences, often portrayed in sensationalist terms, sometimes playing into racist stereotypes. For example, a senior prosecutor has often talked about 'hotspots' of HBV correlating with areas with high terrorist activity, without providing any supporting evidence.

Segregating BME women's concerns into HBV fails to locate them within the overarching framework of gender based violence which means that BME women cannot benefit from the positive developments that have taken place in social policy and practice on child protection and VAWG. Had this been the case, Banaz Mahmod may have been saved by the police when she reported threats and attempts on her life by her family and community. The police later argued that the officers did not respond appropriately because they lacked training in HBV, but by the time Banaz's death took place, HBV had already been a subject of public debate and training had been provided to frontline officers. What the police have refused to acknowledge is that Banaz was let down because they failed to treat the matter as a serious crime. Banaz's death also connects to wider failures in policing where women, such as Julia Pemberton,[13] have also been killed after reporting violence; not to mention the recurring stories which document the consequences

---

13   Julia Pemberton and her son were killed by her husband in 2003. Prior to her death, she had turned to the police several times for protection.

of not investigating reports of sexual violence adequately. These cases justify a public inquiry into policing of VAWG.

Responses to women within BME communities are increasingly taking place through the distorting lenses of 'race', 'culture' or 'religion' rather than structural gender inequality. This re-framing is problematic, since it is likely to lead to differential responses from the state, most notably in terms of the introduction of immigration controls in order to tackle issues such as forced marriage. For example, in 2004 the Home Office introduced an age-related policy which required both parties in a marriage involving an overseas spouse to be 18, which was increased to 21 in 2010. This policy was introduced ostensibly to prevent forced marriage of young British nationals so that they would not have to sponsor an overseas spouse into the UK until they were older and more capable of challenging their families.

SBS and others disagreed with this policy as we feared that victims would be forced into marriage regardless of the immigration laws and subjected to greater, not less, pressure and scrutiny to comply for longer periods. Indeed, victims would be taken aboard and forced into marriage and abandoned there. Even if they were allowed to return to the UK, they are likely to be subject to even greater family control and surveillance to ensure they could not leave their partners until they sponsored them into the UK. A lengthy period would also mean that victims are more likely to become pregnant and find it more difficult to separate. The policy, far from protecting victims, placed them at greater risk and, at the same time, prevented family reunification for young couples in genuine marriages, which are more common. In 2001, these arguments were accepted by the Supreme Court in the cases of *Quila and Bibi*, in which SBS intervened. The court overturned the Home Office policy as interfering in the right to family life under the Human Rights Act 1998.

SBS argue that instead of increasing immigration controls to tackle forced marriage, perhaps the Government should be liberalising them so that victims would not be forced into marriage to circumvent the immigration rules. To our dismay, however, in a recent consultation on family migration,[14] the Government announced plans to tighten immigration controls to prevent forced and sham marriages, and to promote social cohesion. One proposal will increase the probationary period for those on spousal visas from two to five years, which will only serve to penalise victims of domestic violence trapped in violent marriages to British husbands.[15] These immigration policies are based on the model of some Scandinavian countries, particularly Denmark and Norway, where forced marriage and the need for greater social integration have been used to justify draconian immigration laws.

---

14   *Family Migration: A Consultation*, July 2011, Home Office.

15   Although SBS has obtained an exemption for victims on spousal visas under the immigration 'domestic violence rule,' many victims will nevertheless stay in violent marriages due to cultural pressures, isolation, ignorance of their rights, and fear of deportation and reprisals.

Where Now?

Spending cuts in a global recession (so conveniently justified in the UK by the Tory 'Big Society' agenda) and de-centralisation through localism policies has accelerated the demise of the BME women's voluntary sector (see also Larasi, this volume), particularly those organised on secular, anti-racist, feminist and human rights principles. BME women are being delivered back into the hands of self-styled, male, conservative community and religious leaders; the 'gatekeepers' between minority and majority communities, who often fail to support BME women's organisation, which are also historically under-funded. This is compounded with growing strong religious identities and fundamentalism amongst young men within BME communities.

Assimilationist social cohesion and paradoxically, multi-faithism, is the way in which the state now engages with minority communities, supporting faith, including Muslim and an increasingly Christian, moral right positions and institutions (see also Patel, this volume). Social cohesion has also added fuel to subtle forms of racism in 'rights for whites' demands, creating competition for funding and resources. Ironically, increased racist immigration controls have been justified in the name of BME women's rights as a route to tackling forced marriage, and promoting social integration of 'backward' migrant communities.

Can the BME and wider women's movement take on these multiple and complex challenges? Future success lies in the unity and consensus amongst BME women's groups and activists in influencing community and state responses, and alliance building with white feminists and other progressive movements. However, the BME women's movement is divided over HBV, immigration and religion. The issue of VAWG within BME communities is increasingly being collapsed into HBV, underpinned by culture rather than gender inequality. Conservative women and community groups argue for self-policing by community and religious leaders or organisations via mediation and religious arbitration. Some BME women's groups have also established faith-based groups or services, which call for varying degree of state intervention, but which may also compromise women's rights as dictated by their particular interpretation of religious doctrine.

While some secular BME women's groups want to promote HBV policies and criminalise forced marriage, with a few also supporting the introduction of immigration controls to address it, others emphasise the need for more resources, education and awareness, and effective implementation of existing policies, guidance and laws within an overarching VAWG framework, acknowledging gendered commonalities with other women. The latter also argue for a more integrated and holistic approach which retains specific policies and services which recognise differences in BME women's experiences based on race.

Recent national VAWG strategies by New Labour and the Coalition Government have introduced reform on BME women's issues, particularly in relation to harmful practices, in a piecemeal fashion, but ignored controversial issues of racism (including subtle forms created by social cohesion policies) and general immigration/asylum controls and no recourse to public funds (NRPFs) problems,[16] the impact of cuts in funding for services and legal aid, the removal of national targets and standards under localism and problems with multi-faith policies, which reinforce the oppression of BME women.

To counter this SBS and the End Violence against Women coalition is developing a UK-wide strategy on violence against BME women and girls embedded within the existing VAWG, equalities and human rights framework. Feminists are increasingly drawing on international human rights treaties and conventions, such as the UN Convention for the Elimination for all Forms of Discrimination against Women (CEDAW) and the Council of Europe Convention on Preventing and Combating Violence against Women and Domestic Violence (CAHVIO) to hold the UK government to account. There is even a growing call for a VAWG Act incorporating the needs of all women in the UK. The increasing polarisation amongst BME women's groups is also being counteracted by a renewal of feminist activism, including a growing number of young BME feminists developing new forums and responses, such as the Black Feminist UK network, Daughters of Eve (working on FGM) and Trafford Rape Crisis' new sexual violence service for BME women.

In the past many differences between BME women's groups were submerged within common struggles for recognition. For example, in 2003 SBS and Middle Eastern groups held a memorial for Heshu Yonis and other victims of honour killings under the common slogan 'there is no "honour" in domestic violence, only shame!' (Siddiqui, 2005). However, by December 2011 IKWRO was giving 'true honour' awards to those fighting HBV and calling for a distinct and separate national strategy on HBV. Internal political differences threaten to distort the intersections between HBV, forced marriage and domestic violence outlined earlier. This is likely to create to confusion amongst policy makers and practitioners attempting to understand of and respond to these issues, since there is no other form of VAWG which defines gendered abuse by motive. It also diverts attention away from pressing issues of racism, poverty and religious fundamentalism where they intersect with VAWG.

In the early 1980s, SBS demonstrated with survivors through Southall to shame the husband of Khrisna Sharma, who had driven his wife to suicide following domestic violence. We sought to subvert the concept of honour by demanding that the community condemn the perpetrator rather than the victim; declaring his abusive behaviour dishonourable and shameful. Perhaps the hope for the future lies in the recognition that as BME women standing at the intersection of race, gender and social class, 'true honour' is not only about personal and community integrity, but also about our united struggles against domestic violence, forced marriage, honour crimes and VAWG. Integrity in struggle, for SBS, can only be

---

16   The exception being the introduction of benefits for domestic violence victims on spousal visas with NRPFs in April 2012, having been won as a result of a momentum created by 20 years of campaigning led by SBS.

strengthened and won through alliances between secular, feminist, anti-racist and other progressive human rights movements.

References

Crenshaw, K. 1991. *Mapping the Margins: Intersectionality, Identity Politics, and Violence against Women of Color.* Stanford Law Review, Vol. 43, No. 6., pp. 1241–1299.

Kelly, L. 1987. The continuum of sexual violence in *Women and Social Control*, edited by Hanmer and Maynard. Basingstoke: Macmillan.

Greater London Authority/Imkaan et al. 2011. *The Missing Link: a Joined up Approach to Addressing Harmful Practices in London.* London: Greater London Authority.

Hansard, 10 February 1999. *House of Commons Adjournment Debate on Human Rights (Women).*

House of Commons Home Affairs Select Committee (HASC). *Domestic Violence, Forced Marriage and "Honour"-Based Violence: Sixth report of Session 2007–8* Vol I. May 2008, page 5 and 17.

Mayor of London. 2010. *The Way Forward: Taking Action to End Violence against Women and Girls. Final Strategy 2010–2013.* London: Mayor of London.

Siddiqui, H. 2005. 'There is no 'honour' in domestic violence, only shame!' Women's struggles against 'honour' crimes in the UK in *Honour*, edited by L. Welchman and S. Hossain. London: Zed Books.

Siddiqui, H. 2008. 'Making the Grade?' Meeting the challenge of tackling violence against ethnic minority women in *Seeing Double: Race and Gender in Ethnic Minority Women's Lives*, edited by Z. Moosa. London: Fawcett Society.

Parker, J. 2007. *Street Gangs: The View from the Street.* Do It Now Foundation. [http://www.doitnow.org/pages/178.html. 2007]. Accessed 26 April 2012

Patel, P and Siddiqui, H. 2010. Shrinking secular spaces in *Violence Against Women in South Asian Communities*, edited by R. Thiara and A. Gill. London: Jessica Kingsley Publishers.

Siddiqui, H and Patel, M. 2011. *Safe and Sane: A Model of Intervention on Domestic Violence and Mental Health, Suicide and Self-harm Amongst Black and Minority Ethnic Women.* London: Southall Black Sisters Trust.

Chapter 11

"It begins with Sister"[1]:
Polygyny and Muslims in Britain

Yasmin Rehman

Polygyny is by far the most common form of polygamy or plural marriage, in which one man is simultaneously married to several wives. It is this practice that will be the focus of this chapter. Polygyny is not limited to Islam but is practiced by many communities across the world. As the prospect of a Mormon entering the White House becomes a possibility, there is increasing attention on the practices of the Church of Jesus Christ of the Latter Day Saints (LDS), the fourth largest religious denomination in the USA with an estimated 14 million members worldwide. The Fundamentalist Church of Jesus Christ of the Latter Day Saints (FLDS) are practising polygynists who have been increasingly presented as the 'family next door' in the HBO television series *Big Love*[2], two reality television series[3] and an opera.[4] President of South Africa, Jacob Zuma, has married six times and currently has four wives. The country he heads is committed to equality principles and yet it has adopted the Recognition of Customary Marriages Act (1998) which purports to regulate plural marriages through addressing the subordinated legal status of African women in such unions. In both the USA and South Africa there is some recognition of polygyny: in the United Kingdom it is rarely discussed and associated only with marginalised communities.

Debates about the integration of Muslims in the West and the implications for social cohesion have increasingly focused on the status of women and the structure of the Muslim family; thus early marriage, forced marriage, honour-based violence and occasionally polygyny have become synonymous with Islam and Muslims.

---

1   The title of this chapter draws on the words of three women interviewed in the research it draws on. Whilst each woman's circumstances were different, their first conversation about polygyny all began with the same word, 'sister' albeit spoken by different people.

2   The series aired between 2006 and 2011 and depicted the lives of Bill Henrickson, his three wives and their nine children living in a suburb in Salt Lake City.

3   *Sista Wives* focuses on a Black polygynist Jacob Jones and his three wives in Utah. *Sister Wives* follows the lives of Kody Brown, his four wives and their 16 children.

4   *Dark Sisters* had its premier in September 2011 and is based on five "sister-wives" in a polygamous Mormon compound, all married to a stern "Prophet".[http://www.huffingtonpost.com/2011/11/08/dark-sisters-nico-muhly_n_1081724.html] Accessed 24 April 2012.

By its very nature, polygyny is a gender issue since it comprises an inherent gender asymmetry in that it is only men who have the right and status to have multiple marriage partners. The threat, possibility and fear that their present or future husband may take another wife is a reality for many Muslim women and undoubtedly influences their perception and management of their relationships. Any attempt to develop an effective policy response requires an analysis of how such marriages affect the lives of women and children. In this chapter I will draw upon original research to explore questions of gender, power and harm. The research involved in-depth interviews with 20 Muslim women and five men, living in the UK, who are or have been in polygynous marriages. Interviews were also conducted with one woman and three men who had grown up in polygynous households. Five expert interviews were undertaken with Islamic scholars, Muslim feminists and representatives from specialist women's organisations. The women had origins in Afghanistan, Bangladesh, Egypt, Ireland, Kenya, Pakistan and India; the men Bosnia, Indonesia, Nigeria, Somalia and Pakistan.

The chapter begins by examining the religious justifications for polygyny as a partial explanation for this continuing practice and concludes by asking why the government and various human rights bodies do not take a more critical stance towards a practice deemed incompatible with gender equality.

Close to Home

In December 2008, Sahar Daftary, a 23 year old model plunged to her death from an apartment block in Salford, Greater Manchester after discovering that her husband Rashid Jamil had another wife and two children. Sahar, a Sunni Muslim, had, a few months prior to her death, undergone a religious marriage ceremony with Rashid Jamil unaware that he was already married. Many newspaper reports at the time[5] predicted that Sahar's death would shine a light on polygynous marriages in Britain. However, unlike the cases of forced marriages and 'honour' killings, polygyny failed to capture the same degree of media, public or political attention even within BME women's organisations.

Addressing polygynous marriages amongst Britain's Muslim population will raise difficult, complex and uneasy questions for supporters and opponents of the practice. As many Muslims adhere to classical interpretations of Islam which allows men to marry up to four wives, it could be argued that any prohibition of the practice would be seen as a direct violation of their freedom of religion. Further, as many Muslims believe that Shari'a law supersedes secular law some followers will continue to enter into polygynous unions. Opponents will have to address tensions between freedom of religion, gender equality and the definition of violence against women and girls.

---

5   http://www.muslimparliament.org.uk/SaharDaftary.html. Accessed 24 April 2012.

Defining a Polygynous Marriage

The problems associated with defining polygyny impact our knowledge about such practices (Zeitzen, 2008). Polygynous marriages between foreign nationals living in Britain and/or British nationals and foreign nationals who were married in jurisdictions where polygyny is permitted are less difficult to identify. However, identifying polygynous marriages entered into under religious law in Britain is much more problematic as these are neither recognised nor recorded as legal marriages. Thus estimates of the possible numbers range from 1,000[6] to 20,000[7] for polygynous unions in the United Kingdom with minimal discussions about how these figures are arrived at.

We thus have to 'grapple with the practical problem of identifying such 'irregular' and perhaps "invisible" unions' (Zeitzen, 2008: 5). Among the women interviewed some shared a common spouse (the husband) but lived in separate households, for others the marital arrangements were less clear with the husband not living with any wives, and in some cases there being no public acknowledgement of the relationship. Rani in her mid-thirties, a divorcee, British born and educated, elected to become a second wife after many years as a single parent.

> I am lonely and want to be with someone. This is my choice. I get to keep my children, stay in my home, keep my job and get a husband. He doesn't live with us all the time but stays here for a couple of nights a week. It's a good arrangement. The only thing is – I don't know how to tell my friends. They won't approve. They'll think I'm no better than a souten[8]. What choice do I have? It's this or no one. I do not want to spend the rest of my life alone. I can't and won't marry out of my faith. Women aren't allowed to. Islam gives us both the right to be happy (Rani).

How this arrangement fits within current understandings of the family and what constitutes marriage is not just an academic but also a policy question.

Various forms of marriage are permitted in Islamic doctrine ranging from a model of monogamous marriage that echoes Christian ideals, to a number of forms of temporary marriage, which are contested by academics and theologians.[9] These

---

6   Government figures in response to Parliamentary question in 2007.

7   Quote from BME project leader in Lancashire http://www.dailymail.co.uk/news/article-2041244/Polygamy-Investigation-Muslim-men-exploit-UK-benefits-system.html. Accessed 24 April, 2012.

8   Urdu - Hindi word for co-wife, mistress or 'the other woman'.

9   The practice of temporary marriages, such as mut'a marriages,have re-emerged in recent years in Iran following a *fatwa* by the late Ayatollah Khomeini. These temporary marriages can last from a few hours to a period of many years but do require the woman to waive many of the rights she would have if the marriage was conducted under the usual nikaah form. This practice is specific to Shi'a Muslims and not permitted by other Muslim

temporary marriages lend themselves to great scrutiny not least of which being their impact upon the status of an existing marriage. If disclosed to an existing wife does this become a polygynous marriage? If the 'wife' is not aware of the temporary marriage is her marriage still monogamous? Many of the women I interviewed did not know that their husband had taken another wife.

> I didn't know he had married again. It was awful when I found out. I had gone to a women's group about trouble at home and met this woman there. We were talking about stuff – you know families, kids, husband – then it dawned on us that we could be talking about the same man. We were! I lost it there and then. The workers had to pull us apart. How could he do it to me … and to her? (Zarina)

A Question of Interpretation

The religious justification for polygyny is derived from the Qur'an, religious texts and the life of the Prophet. Muslim feminists and activists such as Musawah[10] and Sisters in Islam[11] have challenged polygyny as one of the traditional practices within Islam that (re)produce women's unequal status.

It is worth noting that polygynous practices pre-date Islam, however, it was in response to a particular set of circumstances that the letter and spirit of the verse on polygyny emerges. Polygyny is mentioned only once in the Qur'an in Surah An-Nisa (The Woman) 4:3 in response to the number of deaths of Muslim men following the Battle of Uhud.

> If you fear that you shall not be able to deal justly with the orphans, marry women of your choice, two, or three, or four; but if you fear that ye shall not be able to deal justly (with them), then only one …

This verse permitted limited polygyny (four wives) within a responsibility to a large group of widows and orphans. It could be argued that there is simultaneously a preference for one wife in order to avoid 'injustice' reinforced in a later verse 4:129: '*you are never able to do justice between wives even if it is your ardent desire*'. Thus, polygyny was envisaged as a solution to a particular set of circumstances, with caveats and concerns which bear further reflection.

Many Muslim feminists have pointed out 'injustice' is subjective and therefore difficult to define. What does 'justice' mean within marriage?

---

sects. It has been used to legitimise prostitution. [see, for example, http://www.motherjones.com/politics/2010/03/temporary-marriage-iran-islam]. Accessed 27 April, 2012.

10　　A global movement for equality and justice within the Muslim family.

11　　An organisation promoting an understanding of Islam that embraces the principles of justice, equality, freedom and dignity.

> If a man marries four wives, even if he treats them equally, it still means that each woman among them has only a quarter of a man, whereas the man has four women. The women here are only equal in the sense that they suffer an equal injustice... This can in no way be considered equality or justice or rights for women (El Sadaawi, 1980: 140).

If subsequent wives are not legally recognised under the laws of the State then by definition they cannot be treated justly or equally as is required by verse 4:3. The concept of maintenance is also significant. In Shari'a *nafaqa* is defined as an obligation of material support for a wife. This is a gendered concept reinforcing the role of men as providers.

> Men are protectors and maintainers of women because God has given them the one more than the other, and because they support them from their means (Quran 4:34).

Once a marriage is consummated a husband becomes responsible for providing for his wife (and children). The men I interviewed argued that to be a just husband they ensured that each wife and her children were treated equally with respect to food, clothing and shelter. In contemporary times, rather than the original example of polygyny providing material support to those widowed in war, men are entering into polygynous unions with young, virgin brides, justified through a self-serving reading of religious texts.

Further justifications include that a first wife is infertile, or that she has failed to produce a male child, or that she is ill and can no longer fulfil her marital duties. All of these arguments both reflect and reinforce the subordinate position of women: failure to produce children or a male child mean a woman can face the threat of divorce and abandonment or be forced to accept that her husband takes another wife.

What marital duties constitute is unclear – is this taking care of the home, producing children, making herself sexually available or indeed all three and perhaps more? If marital duties are, as raised above in relation to maintenance, based on sexual availability, then many Islamic jurists would agree that refusal or inability to provide sexual access could result in the taking of an additional wife and/or the suspension of maintenance. But what about the emotional and sexual lives of women within polygynous unions?

> I was 29 years old when he married another woman. We had children – two boys and a girl. I thought we were happy. He never gave me any warning or sign that he was not happy with me. Afterwards he simply told me that he could do this because our religion allows it. He provides for the children and comes to see them but I am invisible to him. He barely speaks to me and never stays with me. I am dead to him. It's been 10 years now (Aliyah).

The Prophet as exemplar

Support for polygyny often refers to *sunnah*: the customs and practices of the Prophet and His Companions that are to be emulated by all Muslims. The Prophet Muhammad is reported to have married up to eleven times. The first marriage to Khadija lasted for 27 years and was monogamous until her death. The subsequent marriages were to women who had been married and were divorced or widowed as a result of conflicts with other tribes. The exception was A'isha, the daughter of his closest companion Abu Bakr. A'isha, a virgin wife, is widely acknowledged as his favourite. Although it is reported that all wives were treated justly and equally in material terms, emotionally the Prophet's feelings for A'isha were different. In addition there is a hadith[12] that the Prophet forbade his son-in-law Ali from marrying another woman unless he first divorced his existing wife, the Prophet's daughter Fatima. This could be seen as additional support for an interpretation of verse 4:3 (see above) as limiting polygyny to specific contexts, rather than offering a general permission.

She Who Must Be Controlled

Islam places a strong emphasis on sexual relationships as both a 'natural' human need and a foretaste of the delights of Paradise, whilst simultaneously requiring regulation. Some interpretations stress the classical Arab view of women as seductive, manipulative, cunning and dangerous who ensnare men. This can be seen in references to *fitna* (chaos): traditional interpretations suggest chaos will ensue if women and their sexuality are not controlled, supported by many *hadith*. How is the tension between sex as one of the pleasures of life and yet containing the danger of *fitna* to be resolved? Male responsibility to protect and control women and limiting sex to inside marriage, have been presented as the bulwarks against chaos. Fatima Mernissi (2003) argues that within this discourse women become the symbol of disorder (*fitna*) and therefore must be controlled. Alongside the limitations for women are parallel permissions for men: that it is preferable for them to meet essentialised needs and desires through polygyny rather than extra marital sex. Haqqi (2005), for example, states that polygyny is a just system that limits under age and extra marital sex, unwanted pregnancies and offers Muslim women the protection and status of being married, rather than the uneasy position of a mistress.

---

12   Reports of the sayings or actions of the Prophet Muhammad.

Lawful Wives or Mistresses?

In April 2010, France introduced legislation banning the wearing of the burqa in public. This, coincidentally, raised the issue of polygyny when the wife of a French Algerian man, Lies Hebbadj, was arrested and fined for wearing the niqab[13] whilst driving. The investigation revealed that he had four wives and up to 15 children. The debate which followed included calls for the withdrawal of French citizenship in cases of polygyny, female genital mutilation and honour-based violence. Such drastic and far-reaching proposals did not come from the far right parties but from the then President Sarkozy and the French Interior Minister Brice Hortefeux. President Sarkozy has been quoted in a number of French newspapers linking polygyny to anti-social behaviour including rioting, social security fraud and low levels of educational attainment amongst French Muslims.

Meanwhile, the French authorities were investigating Hebbadj's relationship with the four women and their individual claims for welfare benefits. The official line is that he has attempted to circumvent French bigamy laws by entering into religious marriages.[14] If the accounts in French newspapers are accurate, Hebbadj has effectively denied his wives and children the protections of marriage: within extreme interpretations of Islamic marriage law to define the women as 'mistresses' exposes them to accusations which are punishable by death. Here we see a reversed self-serving justification in a cynical manipulation of state laws and French 'custom' for his own ends.

Is Polygyny Harmful to Women?

In 2011 the Polygamy Reference Case, brought by the British Columbia government, sought to test the constitutionality of the law before taking legal action against members of a breakaway Mormon sect that practises polygamy at their Bountiful settlement. The British Columbian authorities had been wary of prosecuting members of Fundamentalist Church of Jesus Christ of Latter-Day Saints out of fear the nineteenth century prohibition on polygny being ruled a violation of the guarantee of freedom of religion as stated in the Canadian Charter of Rights and Freedoms. A central issue in the case has been the question of whether the practice of polygyny involves the potential for abuse of women and children. British Columbia Supreme Court Chief Justice Bauman upheld Canada's 120 year old prohibition of polygyny stating:

> ... the harms associated with the practice are endemic; they are inherent. This conclusion is critical because it supports the view that the harms found in

---

13   Full face covering.

14   http://www.religionnewsblog.com/24266/french-muslim-i-have-mistresses-not-multiple-wives. Accessed 23 April 2012.

polygynous societies are not simply the product of individual misconduct; they arise inevitably out of the practice.[15]

Polygyny is a complex practice and raises many questions about power, harms and choice. What does it mean if one or more women in a polygynous household are being abused and another woman in that same household is not?

Many women state that they have willingly entered into polygynous relationships. However, as the research interviews show, women who claim such choice do so in a context of limited options. First wives face loss of status and maintenance if they refuse to agree to their marriage becoming polygynous. For second and subsequent wives, their decisions are shaped by religious, social and cultural forces. One woman was clear that being a third wife was a test of her faith.

> My husband has two other wives. It is his right. I do find it difficult but Allah gives me strength. I am a Muslim, my religion is everything to me and about me – the way I dress, what I eat, how I live and who I marry. It's not a problem (Anissa).

The phrase "Allah allows this" recurred as a legitimation, which in turn meant women struggled to name their experience of polygyny as abuse, since to do so would place their sense of being harmed and damaged at odds with religious teachings. This tension was resolved by attributing the pain and hurt they experienced to not being a good enough Muslim.

> I love Allah and if he says it is my husband's right to do this what right do I have to say no? I love Allah but why has he given me and my children such pain? If I were a better Muslim I would be able to cope with this. I keep praying for peace. (Tehmina)

The men interviewed also referred to polygyny as both permissible and a religious right and as such it could *not* be harmful to women.

> Sister you forget we are Muslims we cannot question Allah. This is my duty and my right. (Talal)

Naming one's experience is the first step in defining it as violence or abuse (Kelly, 1988). Whilst many of the women interviewed experienced their husband's behaviour as abusive, they saw this as part of their personal experience, a lack of faith or inability to cope.

---

15   http://jurist.org/forum/2011/12/nicholas-bala-canada-polygamy.php Accessed 23 August 2012.

It is the lack of a *social definition* that is crucial. A social definition/name makes clear that others may share this experience, thereby undermining the isolation of feeling that you are the only one. A social definition also suggests the possibility of a social cause (Kelly, 1988: 141).

Defining violence

Article 1 of the 1993 Declaration on the Elimination of Violence against Women adopted by the United Nations Assembly offers the following definition:

> ... any act of gender-based violence that results in, or is likely to result in, physical, sexual or psychological harm or suffering to women, including threats of such acts, coercion or arbitrary deprivation of liberty, whether occurring in public or private life.

It is important to recall this definition of violence against women in relation to polygyny: a discriminatory practice which has very real consequences for women and children. The women (and some of the men) interviewed spoke movingly about the impact of polygyny on their lives, including their status in the community and in the home, on their economic circumstances, and on their health. They also spoke of incidents of physical, psychological and sexual abuse directly linked to the issue of polygny – either due to resisting it or the dynamics within polygynous unions.

Shamim was subjected to repeated violence for refusing to give her permission for her husband to take a second wife. Bilqis, a young Afghan woman, is the second wife in the household but has suffered violence at the hands of her husband, his first wife and their children.

> I don't know why he married me. He was already married and she has the control so why marry me? He beats me if I complain too much about her. I am silent now. She beats me if I haven't done the housework or cooked the food. The children are horrible to me. I want to leave but where can I go? It would be better to just die than live this life (Bilqis).

The emotional and psychological impact of polygyny on women is significant: "It is the spectre that haunts every Muslim woman" (Brooks, 1994:33). The threat alone is often used by men to control their wives. The vast majority (85%) of the women interviewed reported suffering from depression after discovering their husbands had taken another wife. Some felt they must have somehow failed as a wife, others were burdened by the shame of being a first wife as they knew they were being pitied at one level and judged at another. The hierarchy of wives and ensuing competition for the attention of their husbands places a huge strain on women.

Polygyny is a means by which men make themselves valuable by simply creating a competitive situation between females (Mernissi, 2003: 115).

I had never been depressed before. I had no reason to be. I thought we were happy and then he does this to me. I couldn't eat or sleep. I just sat here, crying all the time. I loved him but he didn't love me. It got so bad that the school began to ask questions about the children as I wasn't looking after them well. I stopped cooking too. It got so bad I called the hospital and asked them to take me away from all this. I just wanted to die. I was in hospital for many weeks. The children had to go to foster care. But what could I do? I was broken. The children do not understand what has happened to me, they are too young. I still want to die but what can I do? (Nusrat)

The financial impact of polygyny leaves many women facing increasing financial hardships as their husbands fail to maintain multiple wives and children. Left without any support from their husbands, women are forced to claim state benefits or take on additional work, as they assume sole responsibility for themselves and their children.

I don't know why he married me or the other wives. I am a single parent but I still have a husband. It's hard making ends meet. The children need things and I ask him to help but he doesn't. I have spoken to my brother about it but he just tells me to keep quiet and not upset my husband anymore and then maybe he will help me and the children. My brother is worried my husband will divorce me. I wonder what difference it would make anyway. I know people talk about us and the fact he has three wives (Sara).

Tehmina resigned from her job, as a form of protest, after finding out her husband had taken another wife.

Why should I help him? If he wants to support two wives then he must work. It's hard and there is a lot less money than before, but this is his fault. He chose this for us.

The sexual arrangements within polygynous marriages arouses a great deal of prurient interest, but rarely explored is the enforced celibacy for some women or the burden of always being sexually available according to a husband's demands. According to Imam Bukhari, a Muslim woman who refuses sexual access to her husband will be punished on earth and in heaven – on earth the husband has the right to withhold maintenance.

I have to keep him happy. I am his third wife. He could take another if he chooses. But if I keep him happy he won't. I am disgusted with myself when I think of what I have to do. Men need sex – it's so important to them (Ghadah).

Polygyny enables older men of wealth and status to gain sexual access to young women for marriage.

> My parents said it was better for us all for me to marry this old, rich man as a second wife than to be the first wife of a nobody. I don't love him or like him but I have to stay for my family's sake. (Meher)

A number of women interviewed felt they were being exploited by their husbands.

> I am just a slave for them. My husband's parents are old and they need to be looked after. I cook, clean, look after them and I work. I go to clean other people's houses to earn extra money but he takes this from me. He has his own life. I don't know what he does or where he goes. I know he has a wife not a slave like me. I want to leave but where can I go? What can I do? This is my fate? This is what Allah has chosen for me (Zarina).

Eileen's story was of particular interest. She married a Muslim man in the 1960's and knowingly became his second wife.

> I knew he had a wife and children in Pakistan. I love him, what can I say. It hasn't been easy. I worked so hard for years. We lived on my money and Kamal sent his back to her. Then we helped her come to England. She couldn't work as she was depressed and couldn't speak English. Nothing changed for me. I kept on working to help him support his first family. I loved the boys (Kamal's children from his first marriage) but they never loved me. They just blamed me for taking their father from them. They don't really get on with my children. It's so sad. Kamal loved me but we all suffered (Eileen).

Unhappiness, humiliation and pain were recurrent themes in women's accounts, almost regardless of whether they were first, second or other order wives.

Children

Children are witness to the impact of their father's subsequent marriage on their mothers.

> I watched Mum disappear before my eyes. She just gave up, stopped eating, sleeping, speaking even. He would come and visit sometimes but we all knew his new family were more important now. He looked at Mum like she was crazy. She was, because he made her that way. First he beat her and said he never wanted to marry her in the first place and that his family made him marry her. That didn't stop him having children with her or getting her to look after him and his family. Then he goes and marries another woman. I know Mum wanted

to keep going for us but she couldn't anymore. And then she died. She killed herself. She just couldn't take it anymore. I miss her so much (Rabiya).

Here the desire to die, which other women cited earlier became a reality: it is an open question as to how much of the higher suicide rate amongst Asian women (Southall Black Sisters, 2011) is connected to polygny.

Dawud is shouldering the financial implications of his father's repeated marriages. His father had married several women: Dawud is the eldest son from the first marriage.

My father is old and is now retired but he has young wives and young children. Because he no longer works it is now my responsibility to support my younger brother's and sisters in Somalia. I am married with children of my own now but I have all these responsibilities. Men do not think about the children they may have when they marry when they are old. It's ok for them as someone else has to take the responsibility (Dawud).

Jibran is still coming to terms with feelings of rejection, loneliness and being unloved.

My mother is the first wife. My father no longer wanted her or us. He barely spoke to us after he got married again. It really hurt when he would buy presents for his new wife and children and forgot about us. Even now it hurts me. It (polygyny) is not good for the children (Jibran).

There were no accounts in the interviews of happy households in which co-wives worked together, sharing domestic chores and raising their children with a loving and caring patriarch at the head of the family. Rather the reality was lives blighted by violence, abuse, rejection, neglect and humiliation.

Mixed Messages

Polygyny has been a matter of muted concern to the UK government. The Immigration Act 1988 contained a refusal to recognise the validity of a polygynous marriage, thus effectively placing a ban on the entry of second wives. This ban, however, even when combined with the continuing non-recognition of polygynous marriages under religious law in the UK has neither eliminated nor halted the practice between British citizens and British citizens and foreign nationals (Shah, 2003).

In February 2009, the issue of polygyny was the focus of media attention as Baroness Warsi,[16] at the time Shadow Minister for Community Cohesion, accused

---

16   http://news.bbc.co.uk/1/hi/7900779.stm. Accessed 23 April, 2012.

the Government of ignoring polygny among British Muslims due to 'cultural sensitivity'. In response the Ministry of Justice confirmed that government policy was to prevent the formation of polygynous households in the UK, whilst noting "It is not the role of government to take a position on the rites, beliefs or practices of any particular religious faith".[17] This appears to be something of a policy fudge.

Baroness Warsi has added her voice to calls for the registration of all religious marriages to ensure compliance with the marriage laws of the United Kingdom. This would place polygynous marriages in the same category as bigamous marriages and therefore subject to the same legal sanctions. Many in the Muslim community have supported this call. In 2008, the Muslim Institute launched the Muslim Marriage Contract[18] as a result of concerns that women were entering religious marriages unaware of the potential consequences of being party to an unregistered marriage. The contract is envisaged as a means for both parties to negotiate the terms and conditions of their union and to make them aware of their obligations under both Shari'a and civil law.

In September 2011, Baroness Flather linked polygynous practices to benefit fraud arguing that Pakistani men were exploiting the benefits system: "The wives are regarded by the welfare system as single mothers, and are therefore entitled to a full range of lone parent payments".[19]

In none of the parliamentary debates or media reports has the impact of such practices on women and children been the central concern.

For all to see

Women faced with the dissolution of a polygynous marriage are left to seek redress through religious tribunals (see also Patel, this volume). As one scholar and activist interviewed in the research pointed out:

> The Shari'a tribunals in Britain deliver some of the most conservative and fundamentalist judgements I have come across in the Muslim world. These tribunals will not be acting in the best interests of women and children but in maintaining the position of the family.

A Muslim scholar interviewed found the continuation of the practice of polygyny disappointing.

> I am very surprised that this is happening today with Muslims born in this country. I thought it (polygyny) would die out as Muslims became more settled. It is very sad to see it is happening still.

---

17 Op cit.

18 http://www.muslimmarriagecontract.org/. Accessed 25 April, 2012.

19 http://www.dailymail.co.uk/news/article-2037998/UK-immigration-Polygamy-welfare-benefits-insidious-silence.html. Accessed 24 April, 2012.

Some see its re-emergence as linked to an increasingly exclusivist, literalist interpretation of Islam and Islamic scriptures, propagated by Saudi Wahhabism. This profoundly gendered teaching is also implicated in the resurgence of practices such as wearing of the burqa and seclusion of women.

Some Muslims organisations are also drawing attention to polygyny as a positive solution to what is viewed as the breakdown of the family. The launch of the Obedient Wives Club (OWC), also known as the Global Polygamy Club,[20] in London in November 2011, was a significant and public move to promote plural marriage amongst Muslims in Britain. The OWC, known to have links to the Muslim Brotherhood,[21] presents polygyny as an Islamic response to prostitution, family breakdown and even to trans-national marriages as additional wives could be found within the UK.

Human Rights, Violence against Women and Marriage Practices

With regard to human rights standards polygyny is incompatible with, and contravenes, the fundamental human rights principle of equality between men and women. CEDAW General Recommendation 21 states:

> Polygynous marriages contravene women's right to equality with men and can
> have serious emotional and financial consequences for her and her dependants
> that such marriages ought to be discouraged and prohibited.[22]

However, international human rights committees have refrained from calling for the abolition of polygyny as "government experts … were of the view that the abolition of the practice would be unfair to those women already in existing marriages" (Banda, 2008:92). Are attempts to protect women in existing polygynous marriages leaving future generations at risk of harm from such practices?

Harmful traditional practices or harmful marriage practices

The United Nations concept of harmful traditional practices is aimed at identifying practices that are condoned by culture, and increasingly religion, as forms of violence against women. A 1995 United Nations Fact Sheet offers the following expanded definition of harmful traditional practices:

---

20   http://www.bbc.co.uk/news/uk-england-london-15869796. Accessed 23 April, 2012.

21   The Muslim Brotherhood is an international organisation founded in 1928. It is believed to have influenced and shaped the views of generations of Islamists. A potent political force in many countries they are said to wish to extend Shari'a law as far as possible.

22   CEDAW General Recommendation 21 para. 14.

... female genital mutilation (FGM); forced feeding of women; early marriage; the various taboos or practices which prevent women from controlling their own fertility; nutritional taboos and traditional birth practices; son preference and its implications for the status of the girl child; female infanticide; early pregnancy; and dowry price (UN, 1995: 3–4).

Polygyny is notably absent from this list. A 2010 report by the United Nations Assistance Mission in Afghanistan on violence against women also excludes polygyny from its list of harmful traditional practices. The list includes forced marriage, *baad* (giving away girls to settle disputes), *baadal* (exchange marriages), dowry and bride price, child marriage. These marriage practices are deemed to be cultural practices which cause harm and reinforce the inequality of women and girls; polygyny escapes due to its association with religious belief. But since polygyny, like female genital mutilation and forced marriage, pre-date Islam it should surely also be understood as a harmful practice based on cultural traditions, and is already understood as a cause and consequence of gender inequality.

> The balance of power within a marriage and in the community is important to understand. Women use culture to explain the constraints, both real and psychological, whilst men use culture to maintain power and control (Patel, 2003: 249).

Perhaps one way out of these contradictions is to develop the concept of 'harmful marriage practices' which would not only include polygyny but as importantly recognise the links between it and early and forced marriage. Moreover, if polygyny is included in such a concept should it not also be incorporated as part of the continuum of violence against women and girls? Here too there are connections to be made with domestic violence, sexual violence, child abuse, and whether polygyny constitutes a conducive context (Kelly, 2008) for violence against women and children.

In conclusion, polygyny is a complex and challenging issue. Legislative and policy responses must take into account the impact on women and children. There is a need to develop more complex feminist analyses of harmful marriage practices including how such practices (re)produce gender inequality.

References

Agosin, M. (Ed). 2002. *Women, Gender and Human Rights: A Global Perspective.* New Jersey: Rutgers University Press.

Ahmed, L. 1992. *Women and Gender in Islam.* New Haven: Yale University Press.

Ali, K. 2006. *Sexual Ethics and Islam: Feminist Reflections on Qur'an, Hadith, and Jurisprudence.* Oxford: One World Publications.

Armstrong, K. 2001. *Islam: A Short History.* London: Phoenix Press.

Banda, F. 2008. *Project on a Mechanism to Address Laws that Discriminate Against Women* [http://www.ohchr.org/Documents/Publications/laws_that_ discriminate_against_women.pdf]. Accessed 23 April, 2012.

Brooks, G. 1995. *Nine Parts of Desire: The Hidden World of Islamic Women.* London: Penguin Books.

Campbell, A. , Bala, N., Duvall-Antonacopolous, K., Macrae, L., Paetsch, J.J., Bailey, M., Baines, B., Amani, B., and Kaufman, A. 2005. *Polygamy in Canada: legal and Social Implications for Women and Children. A Collection of Policy Reports.* [http://www.vancouversun.com/pdf/polygamy_021209. pdf] Accessed April 22 2012.

Chapman, S. 2001. *Polygamy, Bigamy and Human Rights Law.* Bloomington: Xlibris Corp.

El Saadawi, N. 1980. *The Hidden Face of Eve: Women in the Arab World.* London: Zed Books.

Engle Merry, S. 2006. *Human Rights and Gender Violence: Translating International Law into Local Justice.* Chicago: University of Chicago Press.

Goodwin, J. 1995). *Price of Honour: Muslim Women Lift the Veil of Silence on the Islamic World.* London: Warner Books.

Haqqi, K. 2005. *Polygamy: Lawful Wives or Unlawful Girlfriends.* London: Al-Firdous.

Human Rights Council. 2006. *Report of the Special Rapporteur on Violence against Women, its causes and consequences; Intersections between culture and violence against women.* [pub http://www.crin.org/docs/SRVAW_07] Accessed 21 April, 2012.

Husseini, R. 2009. *Murder in the Name of Honour; The True Story of One Woman's Heroic Fight Against An Unbelievable Crime. Oxford*: One World Publications.

Kandiyoti, D. 1991 *Women, Islam and the State.* London: Macmillan Press.

Kelly, L. 1988. *Surviving Sexual Violence.* Cambridge: Polity Press.

Kelly, L. 2008. A conducive context: trafficking in persons in Central Asia. In M Lee (Ed) *Human Trafficking.* Cullomton, Willan, pp. 73–91.

Khan, M.A. 2006. *Women and Human Rights.* New Delhi: SBS Publishers.

Khan, T.S. 2006. *Beyond Honour: A Historical Materialist Explanation of Honour Related Violence.* Karachi: Oxford University Press.

Mernissi, F. 2003. *Beyond the Veil: Male-Female Dynamics in Muslim Society* London: Saqi Books.

Mir-Hosseini, Z. and Hamzic, V. 2010. *Control and sexuality: The Revival of Zina Laws in Muslim Contexts.* Nottingham: Russell Press.

Mojab, S. and Abdo, N. (Eds). 2004. *Violence in the Name of Honour: Theoretical and Political Challenge.* Istanbul: Bilgi University Press.

Peters, J. and Wolper, A. (Eds). 1995. *Women's Rights, Human Rights: international Feminist Perspectives.* New York: Routledge.

Phillips, A. 2010. *Gender and Culture.* Cambridge: Polity Press.

Pickup, F., Williams, S. and Sweetman, C. 2001. *Ending Violence against Women: A Challenge for Development and Humanitarian Work.* Oxford: Oxfam Publications.

Qur'an, The Holy n.d. Medina: King Fahd Holy Qur'an Printing Complex.

Ramadan, T. 2004. *Western Muslims and The Future of Islam.* New York: Oxford University Press.

Ramadan, T. 2007. *The Messenger: The Meanings of the Life of Muhammad.* London: Oxford University Press.

Rosen, L. 1989. *The Anthropology of Justice: Law as Culture in Islamic Society.* Cambridge: Cambridge University Press.

Sahih Al-Bukhari Riyadh: Dar us Salam Publications. Translated by Dr Muhammad Muhsin Khan.

Siddiqui, H and Patel, M. 2011. *Safe and Sane: A Model of Intervention on Domestic Violence and Mental Health, Suicide and Self-Harm Amongst Black and Minority Ethnic Women.* London: Southall Black Sisters.

Sisters in Islam, 2011. *CEDAW and Muslim Family Laws: In Search of Common Ground.* Selangor, Musawah.

Thiara, R. and Gill, A. 2009. *Violence Against Women in South Asian Cultures: Issues for Policy and Practice.* London: Jessica Kingsley.

Warraich, S.A. and Balchin, C. 2006. *Recognising the Un-Recognised: Inter-Country Cases and Muslim Marriage and Divorces in Britain. A Policy Research by Women Living Under Muslim Laws.* Nottingham: Russell Press.

Welchman, L. (Ed). 2004. *Women's Rights and Islamic Family Law: Perspectives on Reform.* London: Zed Books.

Welchman, L. and Hossain, S. (Eds). 2005. *Honour: Crimes, Paradigms and Violence Against Women.* London: Zed Books.

Zeiten, M. 2008. *Polygamy: A Cross-Cultural Analysis.* Oxford: Berg.

PART III
Interventions and Responses

Chapter 12

Finding a Voice: African and Caribbean Heritage Women Help Seeking[1]

Ava Kanyeredzi

I am interested in and currently researching why black women of African and Caribbean heritage appear to delay disclosure and or seek help in the aftermath of violence. This chapter will review the literature on seeking and receiving help for black women. The knowledge base on black women in the UK is very limited. Therefore findings from studies that have been carried out in the USA will be used to pinpoint possible gaps in what we know here in the UK. Many of the studies cited are small and qualitative and raise issues that require further exploration. The chapter is organised through a set of key themes that offer possible explanations for why black women may delay help seeking or choose not to disclose.

The themes are outlined here. Because black women are socially located at the intersections of gender and race, within their lived experiences some may already feel inadequately treated by a range services from education, social services, healthcare to employment, making accessing support services for violence seem counter-intuitive. A historic continuum of violence that encompasses experiences of racism and marginalisation in some black women's lives can normalise violence to the extent that women struggle to identify as victimised and in need of assistance. Related to this, is the theme of being entrapped by a socialisation that encourages black women to protect or overvalue black boys/men, where some may decide not to report the violence from their minoritised partners. Internalised cultural messages such as, black women are hypersexual, or inordinately strong, can also act as barriers to disclosure and seeking help.

Those who do seek help may encounter service practitioners who believe them to be either, stronger and more able to cope or less authentic victims, especially in relation to sexual violence. The cultural discourse of black female resilience typified by the 'strong black woman' also enables a coping and survival strategy for individual women. However self-identifying as a strong black woman can also constrict the space to acknowledge the impact of violence and seek help in its aftermath and could have far reaching consequences for women's mental well being. These themes are challenges which practitioners should address if they are to better respond to the needs and experiences of black women.

1   Thank you to my PhD supervisor Professor Liz Kelly for her insightful comments and patience especially during the earlier drafts of this chapter.

Language and Black Women in the UK

The terms black, black women of African and Caribbean heritage, African, Caribbean, black British, African-American, and where a parent is from another racial background such as white English or Asian; dual heritage, are used here to reflect the variety of ways women self-identify and are identified, geographically, socially and politically. Self-identifying as black for individual women may be nuanced, complex and related to particular contexts (Hall, 1991).

For example the term 'black women' is descriptive of skin colour (Fernando, 2009), post-colonial legacies of slavery, racist treatment and migration histories (Brice-Baker, 1994; Maginn et al. 2004; Phoenix 2010; Reynolds, 2005). Yet, a racial category may not be the most salient aspect of individual women's identities (Fernando, 2009).

Nigerian author Chimamanda Adichie has written about the danger of telling 'a single story' as the only point of reference whenever we are making accounts of people's experiences (Adichie, 2009). In social science research in the UK, the narratives of black women of African and Caribbean descent are so few, that those that do exist inadvertently represent a limited repertoire of voices despite the rich and many voiced or polyvocal experiences (Henry-Waring, 2004). Black women have a longer history of residence in the UK than their counterparts in the USA, yet there is little historical or any other research on their presence and lived experiences (Dabydeen, Gilmore and Jones, 2010; Henry-Waring, 2004; Lees, 1997; Reynolds, 2002). This is not to say that there are no positive representations of black women in the media or in other social and cultural spaces, nor that some black women are not professionally successful in the UK. It is to say that in social science the range of representations is somewhat restricted (Phoenix, 1996; Phoenix and Husain, 2007).

Key Concepts

In this section, I set out the key concepts underpinning my work and how they are used in this chapter.

Help seeking

Seeking help is defined as the point where an individual reaches out and asks for assistance either from the people within their informal network, or more formal statutory sources such as the police, a general medical practitioner (GP), or voluntary sector specialised services (Foster, 2000; Nadler, 1997; Ullman, 2007). Help seeking is one of the many strategies women use to end violence within their intimate relationships (Dutton, Orloff and Hass, 2000) or to move on with their lives after having had experiences of sexual violence as children, or as adults.

Intersectionality

Kimberle Williams Crenshaw (1991) used the term intersectionality to illustrate how differences in socio-cultural locations enable or limit women's options in their decision-making processes after experiences of violence. For example poor African-American women find it much harder to move on with their lives after experiencing intimate partner violence, because of structural inequalities which affect their access to jobs, suitable housing and social support.

Intersectionality is used here as a tool to think not only about how some black women are marginalised, but to argue that marginalisation is never totalised, without opportunities albeit constrained, to resist. This also means that black women may not be equally marginalised because of differences in socioeconomic status between them (Cramer and Plummer, 2009; Hill Collins, 2000; hooks, 1984; Nash, 2008).

Continuum of violence

Locating experiences of violence in women's everyday life contexts enables an understanding not only of the forms, but the meaning of the violence for individual women (Briere and Jordan, 2009; Sokoloff and Dupont, 2005) and the complex terrain of choices, opportunities and limitations women have to negotiate. Feminist academic Liz Kelly (1988) analysed violence by men towards women on a continuum of behaviours that range from sexual harassment, name calling, sexual banter, sexual touching, fondling, to rape and physical assault. These experiences can occur to the same woman or different women over their lifetime and are experienced variously as everyday annoyances to life-threatening: some women, for example, might describe an offensive and or abusive act by saying 'nothing really happened' (Kelly and Radford, 1996). These experiences are not limited to the specific domains of the home or public spaces and are viewed as part of women's everyday relationships with men they know and those they do not, albeit that violence is most often committed by men they know (Kelly, 1988; Stanko, 1985).

Understanding black women's lived experiences through an exploration of slavery, colonialism and racism as patterns of marginalised experiences, especially outlined in the studies carried out in the USA, may be important to individual women (Adkison-Bradley, 2007 in Adkison-Bradley et al. 2009) highlighting not only intersectional differences, but also how epithets of strength are interwoven with women's narratives of survival. Anthropologist Srila Roy (2008) extends Liz Kelly's (1988) continuum of sexual violence to include everyday, political, structural and symbolic violence (Bourdieu, 2001; Bourdieu and Wacquant, 1992), which results in individuals "mourning some forms [of violence] ..." mainly everyday and political violence against men, whilst "... and silencing others' usually sexual violence against women (Roy, 2008: 330). Roy builds on the argument made by Michele Wallace (1979) in *Black Macho and the Myth of the*

Superwoman who explicated the contradictory nature of arguing for civil rights for black men within Black Power movements in the USA during 1960's, while simultaneously restricting the black women within the movements to traditional gendered roles. The revolution became a dialogic bargain between men where the women were positioned in supportive roles. Roy (2008) theorizes that during times of revolution or political bargaining for rights, women may feel that their freedom is within view, yet while working with their male comrades are targeted for sexual violence; when this is raised as an issue, it is defined by the male leaders as a minor sacrifice for the revolution (see also Cone, 2003; Morgan, 1985).

What We Know about Black Women's Help Seeking

In studies on help seeking carried out in the USA, comparisons are often made between women from different racial categories such as white, Hispanic, Asian and African-American or simply, white and minority. The large quantitative studies carried out in the USA on help seeking show that although African-American women do seek help from a range of services they stay longer in relationships with partners who are violent towards them (Bell, Goodman and Dutton, 2009; Fugate et al. 2005; Lipsky et al. 2006; Rennison and Welchans, 2000). This results in a higher risk of homicide especially for women aged 16–24 (Plass, 1993).

At the same time white, Hispanic women and African-American women most commonly disclose intimate partner violence to their informal network of family and friends. African-American women seek help particularly from the police as much as, or even more, than white women, but less than women from Hispanic backgrounds (Bachman and Coker, 1995; Few, 2005; Hutchinson, Herschel and Pesackis, 1994; Lipsky et al. 2006). The explanation offered for this pattern of help seeking is the intersection between violence, poverty and racial category: African-American women are heavily concentrated in the lower socioeconomic strata, which often results in the over surveillance of social services and women fear that their children will be taken from them (Bent-Goodley, 2004; Nicoliadis et al. 2010; Richie, 1996; Taft et al. 2009). Smaller qualitative studies reveal that middle class African-American women experiencing intimate partner violence may be encouraged to stay to counter the image of black families in crisis and also to maintain their middle class status (Nash, 2005; Nash and Hesterberg, 2009; Potter, 2007; 2008).

African-American women have been also found to stay silent for longer about experiences of sexual violence because of internalised concepts of female strength: since disclosing or showing distress runs counter to this discourse some women choose self-help, including using substances, to cope (Campbell et al. 2001; Fine, 1984; Frazier, Rosenberg and Moore, 2000; Nicolaidis et al. 2010).

African-American woman are thus found to be less likely to seek help from counselling or mental health services in the aftermath of sexual violence, unless they are severely distressed (Amstadter et al. 2008; Nicolaidis et al. 2010). Several studies also suggest a perception that they will not be considered legitimate victims of sexual violence by service providers connected to historical stereotypes of black women as promiscuous (Bell and Mattis, 2000; Wyatt, 1992; Kaukinnen and Demaris, 2005; Kaukinnen and Demaris, 2009; Ullman, 2007; Wyatt, Notgrass and Newcomb, 1990). Campbell and Raja (1999) found that minority women were less believed than white women by mental health professionals when they disclosed sexual assault. Ullman and Filipas (2001) found in their study of 323 women who had experienced sexual assault that among the women from minority backgrounds, they had received more negative social reactions from family and friends than white women and these reactions impacted negatively on their mental health. This was in contrast to the findings by Abney and Priest (1995) who concluded black girls disclosed to their families more readily because they felt they would not be rejected.

Projected and Internalised Cultural Messages

Poverty, racial category and violence against women may intersect with cultural messages about African-American women to delay their disclosure, or protract their help seeking. The perpetuation of sexualised discourses about African-American women's bodies in social and cultural spaces have been seen to intimate that black women are either unrapeable, or to blame for their experiences of rape (West, 1995; 2006) and such cultural messages may be internalised. Gail Wyatt (1992) in her study on the aftermath of child sexual abuse for African-American, Hispanic and white women noted African-American women drew on racialised stereotypes and the stories of rape handed down from family members and internalised the meaning of these cultural constructions as part of the embodied experience of being black and female. This was also a theme in Patricia Washington's (2001) study. Both suggest possible explanations for why the women took longer to seek help.

Research on racial differences in help seeking after experiences of sexual violence or violence in intimate partner contexts has not been replicated in the UK, making comparisons difficult. It is unclear how in the UK lower socioeconomic status among black women intersects with their help seeking decisions in the aftermath of violence and whether they stay silent for longer than women from non-black minority ethnic backgrounds.

The Continuum of Violence in Black Women's Lives

Black women may experience a continuum of violence where everyday racism, sexual violence and violence within intimate partner contexts intersect within their lived experiences (Davis, 2000). In Hilary Potter's (2008) study of 40 African-American women with experience of intimate partner violence, she described the women as 'dynamic resistors' whose view was that sexual and physical violence was just one of the multiple burdens that they had to carry (see also Garfield, 2005; Geller, Miller and Churchill, 2006) and relied primarily on their network of family members and friends especially mothers for respite and childcare support.

Similarly in the UK, Kalathil et al. (2011) in a study of 27 women of African, Caribbean and South Asian descent recovering from mental distress, found that the participants of African and Caribbean descent attributed their mental distress to living through long periods with multiple incidences of racism, prejudice and undisclosed sexual violence. One woman described the isolation and invalidation she felt when she disclosed racial assaults which frequently evoked a common retort of her being 'oversensitive' (see also Alleyne, 2004). Another theme was that women who were of dual heritage felt displaced by a sense of not belonging either to the black, or white communities of their parents.

In Tracey Reynolds' study (2005) of 40 black Caribbean mothers, whilst sexual violence was a minor theme – racism in schools being the most pressing concern – women voiced concerns that sexualised discourses about black women might result in their teenage daughters being harassed by men in public spaces. A recent study on sexual harassment in UK offices (Fielden et al. 2010) found that women of African and Caribbean descent thought that both black and white men perceived them as more sexually accessible and thus more legitimate targets and this was an everyday normalised concept.

While the women in Kalathil et al. (2011) could distinguish between forms of violence, they made sense of these experiences as a continuum of violence to the self, which resulted in mental distress. Extending the continuum of sexual violence to encompass the everydayness of a wider variety of intrusive acts within some black women's experiences (see Essed, 1991 on everyday and gendered racism; Garfield, 2005) can address these practices and may also offer routes to exploring whether black women are also constructed as the least deserving of help when they disclose and/or are expected to be stronger and cope better in the aftermath.

Resilience and the Strong Black Woman

Some black women's apparent resilience might reflect the normalisation of coping with extraordinary burdens and a sense of personal achievement for this skill, masking any distress caused. Tamara Beauboeuf-Lafontant (2008; 2009) carried out interviews with 58 African-American women experiencing depression and over-eating, finding they referred to themselves using this construct, which she linked to black female exploitation in domestic work during and after slavery. She argues that many women coped with sexual violence, the pressures of the emotion work (Hochschild, 1983) looking after other women's children in rich white households in the Southern states in America for limited financial rewards, by a 'self-imposed invisibility', or a closing down of the self for protection (see also Clark-Hine, 1989; Washington, 2001). For Beauboeuf-Lafontant, the strong black woman is a 'controlling image', drawing on Patricia Hill Collins (2000) who defined 'controlling images' as discourses about marginalised people that may be experienced as overwhelming, reproduce self-regulated bodies and reinforce existing power differentials. Other controlling images of African-American women for example, are the 'Mammy', a woman who is primarily a caretaker of others, overweight, overeating food to cope with the stresses of life. 'Sapphire' is a dark-skinned woman who is angry, aggressive and emasculates black men and the 'Jezebel' a light-skinned woman who is easily sexually aroused and promiscuous. These racialised and sexualised discursive constructs appear to describe archetypical behaviour and physical characteristics of black women in such a derogatory manner, some might want to distance themselves from their experiences of violence to resist being further stigmatised (Bell and Mattis, 2000; Brice-Baker, 1994). Arguably, those who view themselves through these discursive constructs, could be subjected to deleterious consequences. For example, when African-American women internalize the 'Jezebel' discourse, they are more likely to blame themselves for being raped and may suffer more mental distress (West, 1995; see also Hill Collins, 2005). The contemporary construction of the strong black woman may enable some African-American women to cope with little support while simultaneously creating the illusion that the multiple social injustices they contend with, can be overcome through individual psychological resolve.

Self-identifying as a 'strong black woman' holds a bay recognition of the desperation an individual may feel about her situation (Beaubeouf-Lafontant, 2008). The more a woman self-identifies as a strong black woman, the less likely she is to ask for help (Hill Collins, 2000). Patricia Washington (2001) found a connection between the strong black woman construct and delayed disclosure and help seeking for sexual violence.

The double bind of being expected to be strong and resilient while experiencing distress, results in no space to express these feelings as exemplified by the participant below.

> There are these strange coping skills that help you sort of get through your life, and then all of a sudden, one day, you just can't do it anymore. You can't get out of bed. You can't look at anything without crying. The whole world's falling apart ... and you just think you're losing your mind (Washington, 2001:1271).

Washington also found that practitioners perceived black women as more resilient, a finding echoed in later studies (Garfield, 2005; Gillum, 2008; 2009; Potter, 2008), with one making connections between experiences of violence, depression and notions of inner strength (Nicolaidis et al. 2010). In the UK, Dawn Edge (2007; 2008; 2010) has consistently found black women of Caribbean heritage score highest on measurements for perinatal and postnatal depression. However, the women felt unable to admit to being depressed and with the discourse of strong black woman making it appear that to do so would be a threat to their identity (see also Brown et al. 2011, Maginn et al. 2004).

Whilst we lack the depth of research in the UK on the intersection of sexual violence or violence in intimate partner contexts and black women's mental distress, there are some important studies. In Kalathil et al. (2011) violence was present in all of the women's narratives. As in Beaubeouf-Lafontant (2008; 2009) women discussed inter-generational handing down of epithets of strength and this was in turn associated with taking longer to seek help. Additionally, some women bemoaned the contradiction between being expected to be strong enough to cope with the stresses of life, childcare, employment and abuse, whilst subservient in relation to the men in their lives.

> Oh yeah, women of colour, African Caribbean, African, whoever they are, there is a stigma attached. They are not supposed to have breakdowns. We are supposed to be strong black women. Put up an appearance and take care of the house and so on. How are you going to do those things? (Kalatihil et al. 2011:36).

Notions of resilience can also influence how black women are constituted in the courts. Feminist journalist Julie Bindel reported on three cases of women who killed their partners. In one of cases where the woman was black, pseudonym Alicia Crown, the defence argued that the woman was 'incredibly resilient' because she had escaped poverty and abuse in Jamaica. Feminist practitioner Marai Larasi who gave expert testimony for Alicia Crown in court commented:

> [The] failure to look beyond Ms Crown's 'resilient' exterior is not unfamiliar … In my experience black women are particularly susceptible to being viewed as 'strong', able to cope and somehow not vulnerable (cited in Bindel, 2009).

The construct of the strong black woman, therefore, is relevant to the experiences of African Caribbean heritage women in the UK. It may form part of the explanation for why they delay seeking help and as a consequence may suffer abuse or its aftermath for longer. This may also explain some of the elevated levels of depression and mental health problems elucidated by research.

Intersections of Gender and Race: Gender Entrapment

The socialisation of black women within their families of origin can contribute to how they respond to intimate partner violence. Beth Richie (1996) conducted life history interviews with 37 women at Rikers Island Prison in New York between 1992–1994. The women were divided into three groups; black with partners who were violent, black without partners who were violent and white with partners who were violent. Richie theorised that victimised black women were entrapped by culturally determined gender roles, social conditions, race/ethnicity, institutional hierarchy and discriminatory practices within the criminal justice system. The process of what she calls 'gender entrapment' begins with socialisation into a femininity in which women are expected to service the men and boys in their homes, this is accentuated through a sensitivity to the location of black men in US society and an expectation that black women must position themselves in supportive roles.

For those who become gender entrapped, their primary aspiration is to middle class status in the form of a partner and children. The antithesis to this was to be a "battered single mother", or single woman, "a poor woman, an unsuccessful woman, and a bad mother" (Richie, 1996:139). Having a man and a family elevated their own status within their families of origin, gained them admiration from peers and the social status of having a 'real family'. The more marginalised the women became, the more traditional and 'patriarchal' their family model, which resulted in their entrapment in violent and abusive relationships.

This in turn meant they were more likely to excuse their abusers who they constructed as "the most oppressed sector of the community" (Richie, 1996:140) and in some cases even led to them serving prison sentences for crimes committed by their male partners. In contrast although the white and black women who were not gender entrapped felt loyalty to their families and communities, they did not share a philosophical alignment with their male partners. Gender entrapment devalues black girlhood/womanhood and overvalues black boyhood/manhood (see also Wallace, 1979 for an early version of this thesis). One direct consequence is to limit black women's disclosure of sexual and or physical violence and may mean they remain longer in violent relationships.

Studies in the UK show some support for the finding that black women protect their minoritised black partners by not reporting their violence to the police, to counter discourses of being a part of a pathologised pairing (Mama, 1989; Humphreys and Thiara, 2003; Wilson, 1993). However, Jane Mooney (1993) found black women to be more likely to report intimate partner violence to the police than white women in her mixed methods study of 571 women and 429 men, and Sue Lees (1993) found that black female students would be more likely to call the police for intimate partner violence, because they believed the police would take action against black men. This finding possibly reflects a strategic use of police racism (Grewal et al. 1998; Mama, 1989; Rai and Thiara, 1997) by some to escape men who are violent towards them.

Whilst the overvaluing of black boyhood/manhood may not be as strong in the UK, it may still influence some black women's decisions to report violence. Others[2] have noted that we currently know little about how black women, whose partners are not black, or male, disclose and seek help (see also Nixon and Humphreys, 2010).

---

2   Findings from expert interviews for my PhD research.

Devalued Womanhood

Help seeking may be further complicated if a systematic bodily/self devaluation forms a part of a black woman's lived experience. Gail Garfield (2005) in her study of nine black women with experience of sexual violence and violence in an intimate partner context, found that the devaluation of black women starts very early in childhood and may be reinforced in peer groups, school and later on at work. Black girls may be socialised to feel 'less than' because of the texture of their hair, the tone of their skin, the shape of their bodies and gradually the devaluation of these putative characteristics may have an enduring impact on women's sense of self worth. If violence is a part of their lived experience, it may be appraised as confirmation of existing bodily/self devaluation. Hence the women in Garfield's study felt that they must continue to fight metaphorically, politically and physically to resist violence and to re-establish their self worth as women.

Charlotte Pierce-Baker (2000) in her study of the aftermath of rape for seven black women and their male partners also found an internalised acceptance of devalued girlhood/womanhood. Even counsellors seemed to have a view that black girls are used to being sexually assaulted and black women live in loveless families (Pierce-Baker, 2000).

> ... one of my frustrations is knowing that we black women accept being raped and middle class black women don't talk about rape. We support society in viewing us as not important victims (Pierce-Baker, 2000:91).

This leads her to argue that some black women may unwittingly "sacrifice their own souls" on the altar of racial pride (Pierce-Baker, 2000:84). Few and Bell-Scott (2002) interviewed six college women who had been raped and found that the women were advised to keep silent and stay with their partners by their colleagues who also had abusive experiences (see also Taylor, 2002).[3] The association between devalued girlhood/womanhood and help seeking and how that may intersect with black women's decision-making in the aftermath of sexual violence requires exploration in the UK context, it has implications not only for how organisations might seek to encourage help seeking, but also the issues women might be struggling with in its aftermath.

---

3   One of the experiences which informed Kimberle Williams Crenshaw's (1991) theory of intersectionality was the culture of silencing she encountered when she was raped on campus by a black boyfriend and spoke with friends about reporting him. They advised against this on the grounds it would damage his future employment prospects.

Help Receiving

Most of what is available on black women's experience of receiving help is from violence against women support services. In her ground-breaking study of help receiving after intimate partner violence among 113 women of African, Caribbean, South and far East Asian heritage, Amina Mama (1989) found that the women of African and Caribbean heritage were often criminalised by police when investigation of immigration issues was prioritised over the details of the intimate partner violence incident (Mama, 1989; see also Joseph, 2006). If the women had insecure immigration status their partners might collude with the police to get them deported (Mama, 1989), and subsequent research, primarily with South Asian women (Thiara and Gill, 2010), has noted how men who are abusive to their partners use immigration status as a form of control. These abusive practices acted as barriers to seeking help, lengthening the number of years women spent in relationships with intimate partners who are violent (Mama, 1989).

Reflecting on the findings of her 1989 study Mama (2000) argues that black women's experiences of violence are compounded by poor treatment by statutory agency staff who also prioritise child protection issues and bounce the women from agency to agency for a number of years. More contemporary explorations of black women's experiences of receiving help from statutory agencies would add to this knowledge base.

When receiving help for sexual violence, or violence within the context of an intimate relationship, black women are often limited by the availability of specialised services and there is even less culturally specific/sensitive provision (Coy, Kelly and Foord, 2009; Kalathil et al. 2011; Rai and Thiara, 1997; Wilson, 2008 cited in Topping, 2008). Receiving help from culturally specific/sensitive services for some black women made them more comfortable and they were able to build closer relationships with black female staff (Batsleer et al. 2002; Rai and Thiara, 1997). In Kalatihil et al.'s (2011) study culturally sensitive services relieved black women of the burden of having to explain and differentiate the minutiae of their culture whilst disclosing their experience of abuse and distress.

> My care co-ordinator was an African woman. [This] made a big difference because suddenly my job of trying to explain where I was coming from, I did not have to explain that part of it to her, you know … about being a black woman, about being a black mother, about black culture … and because she was a black woman, she recognized certain things as well, about what I need, you know, what my anxieties might be as well. I did not have to spell them out (Kalathil et al. 2011:38).

Melba Wilson (1993) also found that counsellors intimated that their black women clients with experience of child sexual abuse benefited from having culturally relevant interventions that recognised their social locations.

Conclusion

This chapter has explored the question of delayed help seeking among black women, contrasting findings from the USA with what little is known from studies carried out in the UK. Srila Roy's (2008) extension of Liz Kelly's (1988) continuum of sexual violence was used to argue that a historic continuum of violence in some black women's lived experiences, which could include marginalisation and racism, can be so normalised as to limit their identification as women who have been victimised. Beth Richie's (1996) concept of gender entrapment was used to map how violence against women may be reprioritised by the protecting, or overvaluing of black boys/men or through the systematic bodily devaluation of black girls/women. Both hinder disclosure and help seeking. How far a continuum of violence and gender entrapment impacts on black women's help seeking and decision making in the UK, requires further exploration and is a theme in my ongoing research.[4]

Another possible influence is the perceived need to maintain intact black families to counter images of pathology. The strong black woman construct was a recurring theme, found to be both a coping strategy in the absence of other support and a silencer when it is part of an internalised or projected identity. Culture plays a role in receiving help with studies showing black women wanting the context of their lives to be acknowledged and for helping professionals not to assume strength and resilience. This research overview suggests service providers need to engage black women who identify as strong black women in a dialogue to unpack what strength means to them, while recognising their testimony of survival. This might involve keeping strength as a form of resistance and a reasonable response to personal attack whilst proposing that the normalisation of violence and its impacts might be damaging to black women's self-concept. What support would make it possible for women who identify as strong black women to express vulnerability? Who is best to do this work? Do women who do not self-identify as strong black women access more support services and earlier? These are critical questions which research and practice should offer new information and insights if we are to better respond to black women's needs and experiences.

---

4   My PhD research 'Knowing what I know now ... black women talk about violence inside and outside of the home', is being undertaken at the Child and Woman Abuse Studies Unit, London Metropolitan University and examines how black women seek help for violence and explores the impact of violence on their everyday experiences of embodiment in places, spaces and objects.

References

Abney, V. D. and Priest, R. 1995. African-Americans and Child Sexual Abuse, in *Sexual Abuse In Nine North American Cultures, edited by* L. A. Fontes. Thousand Oaks, CA: Sage, 11–30.

Adichie, C. 2009. *The Danger of a Single Story.* TED Global. Available at: http://www.ted.com/talks/chimamanda_adichie_the_danger_of_a_single_story.html [accessed: 20 June 2011].

Adkison-Bradley, C. 2007. African-American Women and Depression, in *Mental Health Care in the African-American Community*, edited by S. Logan, R. Denby and Gibson, P. Binghamton. New York: Haworth Press, 77–88.

Adkison-Bradley, C., Maynard, D., Johnson, P. and Carter, S. 2009. British African Caribbean Women and Depression. *British Journal of Guidance and Counselling*, 37(1), 65–72.

Amstadter, A.B., McCauley, J.L., Ruggiero, K.J., Resnick, H.S. and Kilpatrick, D.G. 2008. Service Utilization and Help Seeking in a National Sample of Female Rape Victims. *Psychiatric Services (Washington, D.C.)*, 59(12), 1450–1457.

Bachman, R. and Coker, A. 1995. Police Involvement in Domestic Violence: the Interactive Effects of Victim Injury, Offender's History of Violence and Race. *Violence and Victims,* 10(2), 91–106.

Batsleer, J., Burman, E. Chantler, et al. 2002. *Domestic Violence and Minoritisation: Supporting Women to Independence.* Manchester: Women's Studies Research Centre, MMU.

Beauboeuf-Lafontant, T. 2008. Listening Past the Lies That Make us Sick: a Voice-Centered Analysis of Strength and Depression among Black Women. *Qualitative Sociology,* 31, 391–406.

Beauboeuf-Lafontant. T. 2009. *Behind the Mask of the Strong Black Woman: Voice and the Embodiment of a Costly Performance.* Philadelphia, USA: Temple University Press.

Bell, C. C., and Mattis, J. 2000. The Importance of Cultural Competence in Ministering to African-American Victims of Domestic Violence. *Violence Against Women,* 6(5), 515–532.

Bell, M. E., Goodman, L. A. and Dutton, M. A. 2009. Variations in Help-Seeking, Battered Women's Relationship Course, Emotional Well-Being, and Experiences of Abuse Over Time. *Psychology of Women Quarterly*, 33(2), 149–162.

Bent-Goodley, T. B. 2004. Perceptions of Domestic Violence: A Dialogue with African-American Women. *Health and Social Work* [Online], 29(4), 307–16. Available at: http://www.ncbi.nlm.nih.gov/pubmed/15575458, [accessed: 22 June 2011].

Bindel, J. 2009. Driven to Kill. *The Guardian Newspaper*, [Online 26 June]. Available at: http://www.guardian.co.uk/lifeandstyle/2009/jun/26/women-kill-violent-partners-law [accessed: 22 June 2011].

Bourdieu, P. 2001. *Masculine Domination,* translated by R. Nice. Cambridge: Polity.

Bourdieu, P. and Wacquant, L.J.D. 1992. *An Invitation to Reflexive Sociology.* Cambridge: Polity.

Brice-Baker, J.R. 1994. Domestic Violence in African-American and African-Caribbean Families. Special Issue: Multicultural Views on Domestic Violence. *Journal of Social Distress and the Homeless*, 3(1), 23–38.

Briere, J., and Jordan, C.E. 2009. Childhood Maltreatment, Intervening Variables, and Adult Psychological Difficulties in Women: an Overview. *Trauma, Violence and Abuse*, 10(4), 375–88.

Brown, J.S.L., Casey, S. J., Bishop, A.J., Prytys, M., and Whittinger, N. 2011. How Black African and White British Women Perceive Depression and Help-seeking: a Pilot Vignette Study. *International Journal of Social Psychiatry*, 57(4), 362–374.

Brownmiller, S.L. (1975). *Against our will: men, women and rape.* New York: Simon Schuster.

Campbell, R., and Raja, S. 1999. Secondary Victimization of Rape Victims: Insights from Mental Health Professionals who Treat Survivors of Violence. *Violence and Victims*, 14, 261–275.

Campbell, R., Wasco, S.M., Ahrens, C.E., Sefl, T., and Barnes, H.E. 2001. Preventing the "Second Rape": Rape Survivors' Experiences with Community Service Providers. *Journal of Interpersonal Violence*, 16, 1239–1259.

Hine, D.C. 1989. Rape and the inner lives of black women in the Middle West: preliminary thoughts on culture and dissemblance. *Signs*, 14(4), 912–920.

Cone, J. 2003. Black Theology, Black Churches and Black Women, in *Out of the Revolution: The Development of Africana Studies*, edited by D.P. Aldridge and C. Young. Oxford, UK: Lexingham Books, 407–426.

Coy, M., Kelly, L., and Foord, J. 2009, *Map of Gaps 2: The Postcode Lottery of Violence Against Women Support Services in the UK*. London: EVAW.

Cramer, E.P. and Plummer, S.B. 2009. People of Color with Disabilities: Intersectionality as a Framework for Analysing Intimate Partner Violence in Social, Historical and Political Contexts. *Journal of Aggression, Maltreatment and Trauma*, 18, 162–181.

Crenshaw, K. 1991. Mapping the Margins: Intersectionality, Identity Politics, and Violence Against Women of Color. *Stanford Law Review*, 43(6), 1241–1299.

Dabydeen, D., Gilmore, J. and Jones, C. (eds.) 2010. *The Oxford Companion to Black British History (Oxford Companions)*. Oxford: Oxford University Press.

Davis, A. 2000. *The Color of Violence Against Women.* Keynote Address. The Color of Violence Conference, Santa Cruz, USA, October 10 2000. Available at: http://www.arc.org/c_lines/clarchive/story3_3_02.html [accessed 08 01 2012].

Dutton, M.A., Orloff, L.E. and Hass, G.A. 2000. Characteristics of Help-Seeking Behaviors, Resources and Service Needs of Battered Immigrant Latinas: Legal and Policy Implications. *Georgetown Journal On Poverty Law and Policy,* 7(2), 247–303.

Edge, D. 2007. Ethnicity, Psychosocial Risk, and Perinatal Depression–A Comparative Study Among Inner-City Women In The United Kingdom. *Journal of Psychosomatic Research,* 63(3), 291–295.

Edge, D. 2008. 'We Don't See Black Women Here': an Exploration of the Absence of Black Caribbean Women from Clinical and Epidemiological Data on Perinatal Depression in the UK. *Midwifery,* 24, 379–389.

Edge, D., and Mackian, S.C. 2010. Ethnicity and Mental Health Encounters in Primary Care: Help-Seeking and Help-Giving for Perinatal Depression Among Black Caribbean Women in the UK. *Ethnicity and Health,* 15(1), 93–111.

Essed, P. 1991. *Understanding Everyday Racism: and Interdisciplinary Theory.* Newbury Park, CA: Sage.

Fernando, S. 2009. Terminology of 'Race' and Culture, in *Mental Health in a Multi-Ethnic Society: a Multidisciplinary Handbook,* edited by Fernando, S. and Keating, F. 2nd edition. London: Routledge, 13–18.

Few, A.L. 2005. The Voices of Black and White Rural Battered Women in Domestic Violence Shelters. *Family Relations,* 54(4), 488–500.

Few, A.L and Bell-Scott, P. 2002. Grounding Our Feet and Hearts: Black Women's Coping Strategies In Psychologically Abusive Dating Relationships, in *Violence in the Lives of Black Women: Battered Black and Blue,* edited by C.M. West. New York: Haworth Press, 59–77.

Fielden, S.L., Davidson, M.J., Woolnough, H., and Hunt, C. 2009. A Model of Racialized Sexual Harassment of Women in the UK Workplace. *Sex Roles,* 62(1–2), 20–34.

Fine, M. 1984. Coping with Rape: Critical Perspectives on Consciousness. *Imagination, Cognition, and Personality,* 3, 249–267.

Foster, M. 2000. Positive and Negative Responses to Personal Discrimination: Does Coping Make A Difference? *Journal of Social Psychology,* 140, 93–106.

Frazier, P., Rosenberger, S. and Moore, N. 2000. Correlates of Service Utilization among Sexual Assault Survivors. Poster presented at the Annual Meeting of the American Psychological Association., Washington, DC, in *Ullman 2007.*

Fugate, M., Landis, L., Riordan, K., Naureckas, S., and Engel, B. 2005. Barriers to Domestic Violence Help Seeking: Implications for Intervention. *Violence Against Women,* 11(3), 290–310.

Garfield, G. 2005. *Knowing What We Know: African-American Women's Experiences of Violence and Violation.* New Brunswick New Jersey: Rutgers University Press.

Geller, J.A., Miller, J. and Churchill, P. 2006. Triple Trouble; Battered Women of Color: 'Being Black, Being Battered and Being Female …'. *Journal of Emotional Abuse,* 6(2–3), 77–96.

Gillum, T. L. 2009. Improving Services to African-American Survivors of IPV: from the Voices of Recipients of Culturally Specific Services. *Violence Against Women,* 15(1), 57–80.

Gillum, T. L. 2008. Community Response and Needs of African-American Female Survivors of Domestic Violence. *Violence Against Women,* 23(1), 39–57.

Gillum, T.L., Sullivan, C.M., and Bybee, D.I. 2006. The Importance of Spirituality in the Lives of Domestic Violence Survivors. *Violence Against Women, 12*(3), 240–50.

Grewal, S., Kay, J. and Landor, L. et al. (eds.) 1988. *Charting the Journey: Writings by Black and Third World Women.* London: Sheba.

Hall, S. 1991. Old and New Identities, Old and New Ethnicities, in *Culture, Globalization and the World-System*: contemporary conditions for the representation of identity, edited by King, A.D. Basingstoke: Palgrave-Macmillan, 41–68.

Henry-Waring, M.S. 2004. Moving Beyond Otherness: Exploring the Polyvocal Subjectivities of African Caribbean Women across the United Kingdom. *Hecate* (30)1, 31–41.

Hill Collins, P. 2005. *Black Sexual Politics; African-Americans, Gender and the New Racism.* London: Routledge.

Hill Collins, P. 2000. *Black Feminist Thought: Knowledge, Consciousness and the Politics of Empowerment.* 2nd Edition. London: Routledge.

Hine, D.C. 1989. Rape and the Inner Lives of Black Women in the Middle West: Preliminary thoughts on Culture and Dissemblance. *Signs* 14(4), 912–920.

Hochschild, A. 1983. *The Managed Heart: Commercialization of Human Feeling.* Berkeley: University of California Press.

hooks, b. 1984. *Feminist Theory from Margin to Center.* South Boston: Southend Press.

hooks, b. (1981). *Ain't I a Woman: Black Women and Feminism.* South End Press, Boston, MA : LA.

Humphreys, C. and Thiara, R. 2003. Mental Health and Domestic Violence: "I Call It Symptoms of Abuse." *British Journal of Social Work*, 33(2), 209–226.

Hutchinson, I., Hirschel, J.D., and Pesackis, C. 1994. Family Violence and Police Utilization. *Violence and Victims,* 9(4), 299–313.

Kalathil, J., Collier, B., Bhakta, R., Daniel, O., et al. 2011. *Recovery and Resilience: African, African-Caribbean and South Asian Women's Recovery From Mental Illness*. Mental Health Foundation. Available at: http://www.mentalhealth.org. uk [accessed 09 June 2011].

Kaukinen, C. 2004. The Help-Seeking Strategies of Female Violent-Crime Victims: the Direct and Conditional Effects of Race and the Victim-Offender Relationship. *Journal of Interpersonal Violence*, 19(9), 967–90.

Kaukinen, C., and Demaris, A. 2009. Sexual Assault and Current Mental Health: the Role of Help-Seeking and Police Response. *Violence Against Women*, 15(11), 1331–1357.

Joseph, J. 2006. Agency Response to Female Victims of Domestic Violence: The British Approach. *Criminal Justice Studies,* 19(1), 45–60.

Kelly, L. 1988. *Surviving Sexual Violence.* Cambridge: Polity Press.

Kelly, L. and Radford, J. 1996. "Nothing Really Happened": the Invalidation of Women's Experiences of Sexual Violence, in *Women Violence and Male Power*, edited by Hester, M., Kelly, L. and Radford, J. Milton Keynes: Open University Press.

Lees, S. 1993. 'Judicial Rape', *Women's Studies International Forum*, 16(1), 11–36.

Lees, S. 1997. *Carnal Knowledge: Rape On Trial*. 2nd edition. London: Penguin.

Lipsky, S., Caetano, R., Field, C.A. and Larkin, G.L. 200). The Role of Intimate Partner Violence, Race, and Ethnicity in Help-Seeking Behaviors. *Ethnicity and Health*, 11(1), 81–100.

Mama, A. 1989. *The Hidden Struggle: Statutory and Voluntary Sector Responses to Violence Against Black Women in the Home.* 2nd edition. London: Whiting and Birch.

Mama, A. 2000. Violence Against Black Women in the Home, in *Home Truths about Domestic Violence; Feminist Influences on Policy and Practice: a Reader*, edited by J. Hanmer and C. Itzin. London and New York: Routledge, 44–56.

Maginn, S., Boardman, A.P., Craig, T.K, Haddad, M., and Stott, J. 2004. The Detection of Psychological Problems by General Practitioners. *Social Psychiatry and Psychiatric Epidemiology,* 39, 464–471.

Mooney, J. 1993. The Hidden Figure: Domestic Violence in North London. London: Middlesex University Centre for Criminology.

Morgan, R. 1985, *Sisterhood is Global: the International Women's Movement Anthology*. Middlesex, UK: Penguin Books, 23–25.

Nadler, A. 1997. Personality and Help Seeking: Autonomous versus Dependent Help Seeking, in *Sourcebook of Social Support and Personality*, edited by G. Pierce, B. Lakey, I. Sarason, and B. Sarason. New York: Plenum Press, 379–407.

Nash, J. C. 2008. Re-Thinking Intersectionality. *Feminist Review,* 89, 1–15.

Nash, S.T. 2005. Through Black Eyes: African-American Women's Construction of their Experiences with Intimate Partner Violence. *Violence Against Women,* (11)11, 1420–1440.

Nash, S.T., and Hesterberg, L. 2009. Biblical Framings of and Responses to Spousal Violence in the Narratives of Abused Christian Women. *Violence Against Women*, 15(3), 340–61.

Nicolaidis, C., Timmons, V., Thomas, M., Waters, A.S., Wahab, S., Mejia, A., et al. 2010. "You Don't Go Tell White People Nothing": African-American Women's Perspectives on the Influence of Violence and Race on Depression and Depression Care. *American Journal of Public Health*, 100(8), 1470–1476.

Nixon, J. and Humphreys, C. 2010, Marshalling the Evidence: Using Intersectionality in the Domestic Violence Frame Social Politics. *International Studies in Gender, State and Society*, 17(2), 137–158.

Pierce-Baker, C. 2000. *Surviving the Silence: Black Women's Stories of Rape*. New York: W.W. Norton.

Phoenix, A. 1996. 'Social Constructions of Lone Motherhood: a Case of Competing Discourses', in *Good Enough Mothering?: Feminist Perspectives on Lone Motherhood,* edited by E.B. Silva. London: Routledge, 175–190.

Phoenix, A. 2010. Adult Retrospective Narratives of Childhood Experiences of Serial Migration and Reunification with Mothers. *Finnish Journal of Ethnicity and Migration,* [Online] 5(2), 70–78. Available at: http://www.etmu.fi/fjem/pdf/fjem_2_2010.pdf [accessed: 05 May 2011].

Phoenix, A. and Husain, F. (2007). *Parenting and Ethnicity.* York: Joseph Rowntree Foundation.

Plass, P. S. 1993. African-American Family Homicide: Patterns in Partner, Parent, and Child Victimization, 1985-1987. *Journal of Black Studies,* 23, 515–539.

Potter, H. 2008. *Battle Cries: Black Women and Intimate Partner Abuse.* New York: New York University Press.

Potter, H. 2007. Battered Black Women's Use of Religious Services and Spirituality for Assistance in Leaving Abusive Relationships. *Violence Against Women,* 13(3), 262–284.

Rai, D. and Thiara, R. 1997. *Re-Defining Spaces: the Needs of Black Women and Children in Refuge Support Services and Black Workers.* Bristol: Women's Aid Federation of England.

Richie, B.E. 1996. *Compelled To Crime: The Gender Entrapment of Battered Black Women.* New York: Routledge.

Rennison, C.M. and Welchans, S. 2000. *Intimate Partner Violence. (*NCJ 178247). U.S. Department of Justice Office of Justice Programs. Available at: http://bjs.ojp.usdoj.gov/content/pub/pdf/ipv.pdf [accessed 01 June 2011].

Reynolds, T. 2002. Re-Thinking a Black Feminist Standpoint. *Ethnic and Racial Studies,* 25(4), 591–606.

Reynolds, T. 2005. *Caribbean Mothers: Identity and Experience in the U.K.* London: Tufnell.

Roy, S. 2008. The Grey Zone: the "Ordinary" Violence of Extraordinary Times. *Journal of the Royal Anthropological Institute (N.S.)* 14, 316–333.

Sokoloff, N. J., and Dupont, I. 2005. Domestic Violence at the Intersections of Race, Class, and Gender: Challenges and Contributions to Understanding Violence Against Marginalized Women in Diverse Communities. *Violence Against Women,* 11(1), 38–64.

Stanko, E.A. 1985. *Intimate Intrusions: Women's Experience of Male Violence.* London: Unwin Hyman.

Taft, C.T, Bryant-Davis, T., Woodward, H.E et al. 2009. Intimate Partner Violence against African-American Women: an Examination of the Socio-Cultural Context. *Aggression and Violent Behavior 14,* 50–58.

Taylor, J.L. (2002). "The Straw that Broke the Camel's Back": African-American Women's Strategies for Disengaging from Abusive Relationships. *Women and Therapy,* 25(3 & 4), 79–94

Thiara, R., and Gill, A. 2010. *Violence Against South Asian Women: Issues for Policy and Practice.* London: Jessica Kingsley.

Topping, A. 2008. Threats from all Directions Specialist Refuges for Abused Black and Minority Ethnic Women say they are at risk as Councils strive to slash Budgets: Funding Crisis for Women's Services. *The Guardian Newspaper* [Online 13 February]. Available at: http://www.guardian.co.uk [accessed 20 November 2010].

Ullman, S.E. 2007. Mental Health Services Seeking in Sexual Assault Victims. *Women and Therapy*, 30(1), 61–84.

Ullman, S.E., and Filipas, H. 2001. Predictors of PTSD Symptom Severity and Social Reactions in Sexual Assault Victims. *Journal of Traumatic Stress*, 14, 393–413.

Wallace, M. 1979. *Black Macho and the Myth of the Superwoman.* 2nd edition. London: Verso.

Washington, P.A. 2001. Disclosure Patterns of Black Female Sexual Assault Survivors. *Violence Against Women,* 7, 1254–1283.

West, C.M. (1995). Mammy, Sapphire and Jezebel: Historical Images of Black Women and their Implications for Psychotherapy. *Psychotherapy,* 32(3), 458–466.

West, C.M. (2006). Sexual Violence in the Lives of African-American Women: Risk, Response, and Resilience. *VAWNet: The National Online Resource Center on Violence Against Women.* Available at: http://www.vawnet.org [accessed: 20 November 2010].

Wilson, A. 2008. In *Topping 2008.*

Wilson. M. 1993. *Crossing the Boundary: Black Women Survive Incest.* London: Virago Press.

Wyatt, G. E. 1992. The Sociocultural Context of African-American and White American Women's Rape. *Journal of Social Issues,* 48, 77–91.

Wyatt, G.E., Notgrass, C.M., and Newcomb, M. 1990. Internal and External Mediators of Women's Rape Experiences. *Psychology of Women Quarterly*, 14, 153–176.

Chapter 13

Women Seeking Asylum
– Failed Twice Over

Debora Singer

Introduction

This chapter focuses on women asylum seekers. An asylum seeker is someone seeking protection from human rights abuses they sustained, or are at risk of sustaining, in their country of origin. To be recognised as a refugee they have to be outside their country of origin and demonstrate that they are in fear of persecution for one of five reasons (political opinion, religion, race, nationality or membership of a particular social group) and that their state is unwilling or unable to protect them (UN Refugee Convention 1951: article 1A(2)).

Women asylum seekers seek protection from a range of human rights abuses in their home countries. A woman may claim asylum because she is persecuted by the state. For example, she may have been involved in political activities and been detained as a result. Whilst detained she may also have been subjected to torture and rape by state officials. Alternatively, a woman may have been persecuted by her family or community, and found that state authorities either lacked adequate laws to prevent this persecution or failed to enforce these laws. Some forms of persecution are particular, although not exclusive, to women. They include domestic violence, rape, forced marriage, honour crimes and female genital mutilation. All these forms of harm are gender-related persecution (UNHCR 2002).

This chapter focuses on the experience of women whilst their asylum claim is being assessed through the refugee status determination process, drawing on the practice experience of the author. It does not include discussion of the rights of women once they obtain refugee status or some other form of leave to remain.

The framework of intersectionality allows us to look at the multiple cross-cutting ways in which different strands of discrimination and oppression interact. Such discrimination can result from:

> ... a combination of factors such as gender, race, caste, class, ethnicity, culture, religion, sexual orientation, nationality, language, age, status as indigenous peoples, health status, disabilities, status as refugee/displaced people (Centre for Women's Global Leadership 2001).

The asylum system is one site where intersecting forms of discrimination in women's lives are evident. Firstly, women's experiences are marginalised because the Refugee Convention is written from a male perspective. Secondly, violence against women (VAW) strategies in the UK have not been extended sufficiently to protect women fleeing from VAW they experienced in their country of origin. Women seeking asylum therefore face double discrimination – due to their gender and due to their status as asylum seekers. The lack of inclusion of women asylum seekers in VAW strategies then leads to differential standards of treatment for them compared to women who are affected by VAW in other countries who benefit from international development projects and compared to women who are settled in the UK (i.e. British citizens and those with some form of leave to remain).

In the women's sector the term violence against women (VAW) is used to denote:

> Any act of gender-based violence that results in, or is likely to result in, physical, sexual or psychological harm or suffering to women, including threats of such acts, coercion or arbitrary deprivation of liberty, whether occurring in public or in private life (United Nations 1993).

This is also the definition used by the UK government.

In the refugee sector the term gender-related persecution is used to denote acts including those:

> of sexual violence, family/domestic violence, coerced family planning, female genital mutilation, punishment for transgression of social mores, and discrimination against homosexuals (UNHCR 2002: 1).

VAW and gender-related persecution are overlapping concepts although the definition of gender-related persecution encompasses discrimination on the basis of sexual orientation. Despite this overlap the strategies on VAW published by the Westminster government include only a limited mention of women seeking asylum (HM Government 2009, 2010).

VAW in the International Context

In launching his 2008 campaign, UNite to End Violence Against Women, UN Secretary-General Ban Ki-moon observed that "at least one out of every three women is likely to be beaten, coerced into sex or otherwise abused in her lifetime". He continued to outline the scale of the problem and barriers to women seeking and receiving support.

> Women continue to be victims of rape and sexual violence, perpetrated by intimate partners as well as non-partners, in many settings. They are at particular

risk in certain situations, including in conflict and post-conflict settings. Studies indicate, however, that only a small percentage of such crimes come to the attention of the police, and an even smaller number result in convictions. Shame, fear of retaliation from their families or communities, as well as fear of being re-victimized by the criminal justice system, often prevents women from seeking redress (UN Secretary-General 2008).

The most recent VAWG strategy issued by the UK coalition government recognises the international nature of VAW and its effects.

> Tackling violence against women and girls does not stop at the borders of the United Kingdom. This violence stops progress towards the Millennium Development Goals (MDGs) when women are unable to contribute to society and benefit fully from health, education, economic opportunities and other services due to physical suffering or fear of being attacked ... Women and children are disproportionately affected in situations of conflict and post-conflict where they face high risk of sexual violence. Rape is increasingly used as a weapon of war. Entrenched social and cultural attitudes and gender biased criminal justice and informal justice mechanisms mean that most victims suffer in silence with little or no recourse to justice, care or support. Moreover, the institutions which are supposed to protect citizens, such as police and armed forces, are often key perpetrators of abuse (HM Government 2010: 21–22).

Refugee women are amongst groups of women most affected by VAW. Having escaped VAW in their country of origin, women are at risk of sexual violence and trafficking in transit, in refugee camps or on arrival in destination countries (Refugee Council 2009: 4–5).

Refugees and VAW: International Law and Policy

Early international human rights treaties referring to refugees failed to mention the specific needs of women or the particular forms of persecution they may face (UN Universal Declaration of Human Rights 1948: article 14, UN Refugee Convention 1951). In fact the Refugee Convention's grounds for persecution, which must be met for a refugee claim to be successful, do not include gender. The possibility of including gender as a reason was discussed only once during the drafting of the Convention but was dismissed partly because doubts were raised whether there would be any such cases (UNHCR 1951: 9–10), reflecting the lack of understanding of gender inequality prevalent at that time. The consequence of this omission was that the male experience was established as the norm of international refugee law and policy, with women and women's experiences relegated to the margins (Crawley 2001, Edwards 2010: 23).

As a consequence, asylum systems tended to interpret persecution through this framework of male experiences, requiring a process of lobbying for the Refugee Convention to address gender (UNHCR 2002: 1–2). This has involved over two decades of work to establish that gender-related persecution can fall within the Refugee Convention, that non-state actors can be perpetrators of persecution and that where there is no state protection from such persecution, a person might be eligible for refugee status. This has taken place through parallel processes within the UN Refugee Agency (UNHCR) and through the reading of VAW into UN gender equality policies including the Convention on the Elimination of all Forms of Discrimination Against Women (CEDAW).

It was in 1985 that the UNHCR first referred to the fact that "women asylum seekers who face harsh or inhuman treatment due to their having transgressed social mores of the society within which they live" may fit within the refugee definition (UNHCR 1985: para k), but there was slow progress. It took until 2000 for there to be widespread acceptance that gender can "influence, or dictate, the type of persecution or harm suffered and the reasons for this treatment" (UNHCR 2002: above n.4, para 6). By 2006 the UN General Assembly recommended that States "adopt a gender-sensitive approach to the granting of asylum" (United Nations 2006: para 382, 107).

The United Nations first specifically recognised the plight of women refugees in 1979 when the General Assembly added an item on the situation of women refugees to the provisional agenda for the World Conference of the UN Decade of Women (United Nations 1979: para 34/159, 182). Again progress was halting but under the Beijing Platform for Action of 1995, actions to be taken regarding women refugees focus mainly on women in flight and as displaced persons in camps. Women seeking asylum are only briefly mentioned in relation to the need to consider recognising gender-related persecution, provide access to specially trained officers, including female officers and to disseminate and implement UNHCR guidelines on the protection of refugee women (United Nations 1995: paras 136, 147–8). Ten years later, in its updated UK-based call for action, the Women's National Commission stated that the UK must champion enforceable gender guidelines for women refugees into the EU (Women's National Commission 2005: 4).

In 2000, the first UN Special Rapporteur on violence against women, Radikha Coomaraswamy, stated that government bodies must "adopt and implement guidelines recognising gender-related persecution as a basis for women to claim refugee status" (Coomaraswamy 2000: para 122(f)). In 2009, in her review of the work and progress of the mandate throughout its 15 years, the second Rapporteur Yakin Ertürk recognised that "work remains to be done to establish gender as independent grounds for claiming asylum as a refugee" and stated further that:

> ... it would seem important for the mandate to dedicate a thematic report on [concerns relating to gender forming a basis for refugee status] for standard setting, providing an analysis of trends, and addressing aspects of gender

guidance, fast track asylum determination procedure, internal flight alternative, detention, forced removal and destitution (Ertürk 2009: para 126, 59).

In recent years, the CEDAW committee has specifically called on governments (including the UK, see later) to implement gender-sensitive asylum procedures (Edwards 2009: 53) The link was made between international instruments regarding refugees and VAW when, on the 60th anniversary of the Refugee Convention, the CEDAW committee called on all State parties to CEDAW to ensure that their laws, policies and practices do not discriminate against refugee women and girls. The committee also asked States to ensure that women have equality of access to all stages of the asylum process and to recognise gender-based persecution as grounds for an asylum claim (CEDAW Committee October 2011).

Refugees and VAW: the National Context

Despite key case law going back to 1999 (*Islam v SSD, R v IAT* 1999) there is considerable evidence that the UKBA does not interpret the Refugee Convention in a gender-sensitive way on a systematic basis (UKBA 2011a, Asylum Aid 2011, UNHCR 2008). In its report to the CEDAW committee in 2007, the UK failed to include its own asylum gender guidelines as an example of good practice until reminded to do so by Asylum Aid (*Women's Asylum News* June/July 2007: 4). The UK's most recent report to the CEDAW committee (UK Government June 2011: 29–31) does include a range of policies and practice developed in response to persistent lobbying under the Charter of Rights of Women Seeking Asylum (Asylum Aid 2008) but still omits many key developments. In contrast, since 2004, activists in the VAW sector, the women's sector and the refugee sector in the UK have ensured that the rights of women seeking asylum are included in shadow reports to the CEDAW committee (Sen et al 2004, Sen and Kelly 2007, Women's National Commission 2008). This has resulted in the CEDAW committee highlighting the need for gender guidelines regarding asylum decisions to be implemented in its concluding observations to the UK government (CEDAW committee 2008: para 47–48).

The issue of women asylum seekers has limited mention in UK government VAW strategies. Without the intervention of NGOs, it would have been omitted completely from the strategies of both the Coalition Government (*Women's Asylum News* November 2010: 5) and the previous Labour Government (Asylum Aid 2009, Refugee Council 2009a). Within 100 pages focusing on VAW and the criminal justice system, the Labour Government's integrated VAW strategy devoted less than a page to the rights of women seeking asylum and simply confirmed that gender issues should be taken into account in the assessment of the asylum claim (HM Government 2009: 52–53). Similarly, in a 30-page document the Coalition Government gives one paragraph to women seeking asylum, which recognises only that women may have experienced gender-specific violence and stating that the UK Border Agency (UKBA) is dedicated to being as gender-sensitive as possible throughout the asylum process (HM Government 2010: 15–16).

Despite its VAW strategy the Coalition Government has failed to opt-in to some key European instruments that would demonstrate its commitment to protecting women from violence. Firstly, the UK has decided not to opt-in to the recast EU Qualification, Procedures and Reception Conditions Directives developed as part of the EU harmonisation process and will therefore continue to be bound by previous Directives which have far more limited reference to gender (Green 2011). Secondly, the government delayed signing the Council of Europe Convention on Preventing and Combating Violence Against Women and Domestic Violence which was finalised in Istanbul in May 2011 (HM Government 2011: 27). The convention includes strong provisions on women asylum seekers, requiring signatories to: recognise gender-based violence as a form of persecution within the Refugee Convention; provide a gender-sensitive interpretation of the Refugee Convention grounds; develop gender-sensitive reception procedures and support services for asylum-seekers; and have gender guidelines and gender-sensitive asylum procedures (Articles 60.1–3). Just before the convention was finalised, the UK put forward new amendments, one of which would have made it possible for Member States to make reservations to Article 60.3. This was rejected since the proposals were made so late in the process. In fact, the convention does not appear to require the UK to do much more than it has already committed to through its own VAW strategy. The government finally signed the convention on 8th June 2012 (Council of Europe 2012).

VAW strategy on International Work

> We are very clear that our obligations to help women who are being abused do not stop at our borders so, for the first time, our strategy to tackle violence against women and girls also includes the innovative work we are doing internationally on this global problem (Verma 2011).

As stated by Baronness Verma above, the Government's own VAW strategy recognises that VAW is a global phenomenon and that state protection can be lacking.

The Department for International Development (DFID) prioritises VAW as an issue. One of the four pillars of DFID's strategic vision for stopping poverty is to prevent violence to girls and women. In this strategy DFID states it will help 10 million women to access justice through the courts, police, and legal assistance. This will include supporting survivors of violence to seek legal redress, alongside resolving disputes over issues such as land and inheritance. DFID aims to work in at least 15 countries to address physical and sexual violence against girls and women – increasing the numbers of survivors who have access to treatment and advice, and whose cases are satisfactorily investigated. Innovative approaches to creating safe spaces for girls and women will be explored, along with work to support behaviour change by challenging social attitudes and perceptions (DFID 2011).

It is women who have suffered such violence who flee and arrive in the UK and claim asylum. Yet successive governments have failed to make the link between the UK's commitments to dealing with VAW in the context of international development and any concerns for the women who arrive here fleeing VAW. Thus whilst the UK government works through DFID to tackle VAW overseas, the UKBA may refuse to protect women who reach the UK despite their having been affected by VAW and having been denied state protection in their country of origin.

Women Seeking Asylum in the UK

One third of people applying for asylum in the UK each year are women: a proportion that has remained constant since 2003.[1] In 2010, 5,329 women claimed asylum in their own right, as did 12,571 men. One fifth of all women applying in their own right were from Zimbabwe, with other significant numbers coming from Pakistan, China, Nigeria and Iran,[2] countries where there are particular concerns about lack of state action to protect women from VAW.

Statistics published by the Home Office do not include the types of claim which asylum seekers make so there is a lack of information on how often gender-based persecution is the basis of a woman's claim.[3] However research shows that between one half and three quarters of women asylum seekers have experienced VAW either in their country of origin, during transit to the UK, or once in the UK (Scottish Refugee Council and London School of Hygiene and Tropical Medicine 2009, Refugee Council 2009b).

Standards for Women Asylum Seekers Compared with Women who are Settled in the UK

Because women seeking asylum have limited inclusion in VAW strategies, the standards of treatment they experience are different from those experienced by settled women. Thus there is a marked disparity between the experiences of female victims of sexual and domestic violence going through the criminal justice process in the UK and that of women who have experienced the same abuses in their country of origin going through the asylum process. Whilst the purposes of

---

1   Home Office Immigration Statistics April to June 2011.

2   Home Office Asylum data tables Immigration Statistics July – September 2011 Volume 1.

3   Home Office Asylum data tables Immigration Statistics July – September 2011 Volume 1.

the two processes are not the same – one is to investigate a crime and the other is to determine refugee status – the sensitivities required are similar. Similarly there is a disparity between how women are dealt within residential institutions, notably a comparison can be made between women's prisons and Immigration Removal Centres where women asylum seekers are held. Finally the rights of women in relation to support and benefits vary widely depending on their immigration status (Women's Asylum Charter 2009).

Comparison of asylum and criminal justice systems in relation to VAW

Over the past ten years the way the criminal justice system deals with domestic and sexual violence in the UK has been transformed. A number of legislative reforms have been introduced, some of which change the way offences are defined, and sit alongside a series of policies designed to improve the investigation, prosecution and provision of support in cases of VAW. Some of the changes on sexual violence are intended to limit the ways police, prosecutors and judges rely on stereotypes relating to a woman's credibility. While no panacea, there is little doubt that these reforms have brought some benefits to some women (Baillot et al. 2009). Whilst major problems remain for settled women who experience VAW, demonstrated for example by attitudes to rape and by the low conviction rates, there is at least recognition by the government and by service providers that this is a problem.

Treatment of VAW in general

Despite a strong Asylum Instruction on Gender (UKBA, 2010), the UKBA's policy does not always recognise the underlying sensitivities. As just one example, the police recognise the importance of providing a specially trained officer to support a victim of rape throughout an investigation (ACPO et al., 2010: 130–31). Conversely a woman asylum seeker's case will routinely be dealt with by more than one decision-maker as the policy does not reflect the need to prevent her having to repeat her story and to develop trust in the person interviewing her (Asylum Aid 2011: 34–35).

The key reason why women are refused asylum is because they are not believed by the UKBA's decision-makers (Asylum Aid 2011). Women not being believed when they report gender-based violence has also been recognised as a concern in the criminal justice system. When the new Sapphire Unit opened in 2010, Commander Simon Foy at the Serious Crime Directorate of the Metropolitan Police stated that it was "completely victim-based … when victims come forward we believe them and take their allegations seriously. That is our mantra" (Davenport 2010). Whilst this has not always been translated into practice, it contrasts with the UKBA where accusations of a culture of disbelief (Asylum Aid 2011, UNHCR 2008) have generally been refuted until late 2011, when the UKBA said that they would like to attain a culture of objectivity and neutrality (UKBA 2011c).

The poor outcomes for women asylum seekers continue when comparing treatment in the courts. Judges in the criminal justice system have received training on sexual offences and guidance on sexual and domestic violence (Judicial Studies Board 2009: chapter 6). There are specialist domestic violence courts in some areas of the country. In contrast, Immigration Judges have not had any gender guidance since the Immigration Appellate Authority's Gender Guidelines were withdrawn by the Asylum and Immigration Tribunal in September 2006 (Women's Asylum News January/February 2007: 8). The new Immigration and Asylum Chamber's Guidance on Vulnerable Witnesses (Immigration and Asylum Chamber 2010) is limited to ensuring that vulnerable individuals understand and are able to participate in proceedings and fails to take into account the nature of the claim for asylum itself (Querton 2012: 27).

One striking comparison relates to late disclosure of a rape complaint. In the criminal courts judges should direct juries when they 'sum up a case' at the end of a criminal trial that a late complaint should not be interpreted as a false complaint. The Court of Appeal explained "… the fact that the trauma of rape can cause feelings of shame and guilt which might inhibit a woman from making a complaint about rape is sufficiently well known to justify a comment to that effect" (*R v Doody* 2008). At the asylum appeal tribunal, the late disclosure of information about gender-based persecution is used against women, with appeal determinations by Immigration Judges suggesting that the disclosure has been made up to aid the asylum claim. This is despite the UKBA's own gender Asylum Instruction and case law stating that late disclosure should not affect credibility.

Specific types of VAW

In the criminal justice system both rape and domestic violence are dealt with through legislation and policy that covers prevention, protection, investigation, support, prosecution and compensation. In the asylum system, the gender Asylum Instruction reflects the fact that rape is in principle accepted as a form of persecution, if perpetrated by the State or by non-state actors in the absence of state protection (UKBA September 2010: para 2.2). However, refusal letters from the UKBA have argued that even when the rape took place in detention this was the action of a private individual and not the state (Querton 2012: 29). In the asylum system it is accepted that domestic violence can amount to persecution where there is an absence of state protection (*Islam v SSD, R v IAT* 1999). However, despite the VAW definition including psychological abuse, there is evidence that UKBA decision-makers sometimes fail to accept that psychological abuse could amount to domestic violence (Asylum Aid 2011: 57).

In relation to honour-based violence progress has been made within the UK in recent years within the criminal justice system, and the Association of Chief Police Officers (ACPO) strategy document includes a vision of victims of honour-based violence having confidence and trust in the police service to provide an appropriate response (ACPO 2008). In relation to asylum, the Gender Asylum

Instruction refers to crimes in the name of honour (harm or risk of harm for having offended the honour of your family or community or transgressed social mores) as harm which is predominantly gender-specific (UKBA 2010: para 2.2). However, it may be difficult to show that honour crimes as opposed to honour killing amount to persecution and it is very difficult to establish the risk from the family or establish the required level of risk (Querton 2012: 29). In research on the quality of decision-making in women's asylum claims, it appeared that all claims examined which were based on a fear of honour killing were found not to engage the Refugee Convention (Asylum Aid 2011: 50–51).

If a British woman is forced into marriage or is at risk of being forced into marriage she is able to access protection under the Forced Marriage (Civil Protection) Act 2007 and the statutory guidance issued under it (Foreign and Commonwealth Office, 2010). If a British woman is taken abroad to be forced into marriage the Foreign and Commonwealth Office may rescue her and offer her assistance to return her to the UK (Foreign and Commonwealth Office 2011). In June 2012 the government announced plans to criminalise forced marriage (Baksi 2012). Given the prominence of UK domestic initiatives on forced marriage it is notable that the number of UK asylum cases involving forced marriage is very low and those cases demonstrate a deep and on-going resistance to accepting forced marriage as the basis for refugee claims in the UK in comparison with Canada and Australia (Dauvergne and Millbank 2010).

Since 1985 it has been illegal to subject a girl or woman to female genital mutilation (FGM) in the UK (Prohibition of Female Circumcision Act 1985) and since 2003 it has been illegal to take her abroad to do this (Female Genital Mutilation Act 2003). FGM is considered a form of persecution in UK asylum case law but in this landmark case the woman concerned (who claimed that if she were returned to her country of origin she would be subjected to FGM) had to go all the way to the House of Lords to gain refugee status (*SSD v K, Fornah v SSD* 2006). However, where a woman has already been subjected to FGM which might be an indication of related risks such as having FGM redone after childbirth, the UKBA does not consider that she would face a risk of persecution in the future (Querton 2012: 28).

The starkest contrast between how women are treated in the criminal justice system and in the asylum system is demonstrated by cases of women who have been trafficked into the UK from abroad. In this situation the same woman can go through both systems either simultaneously or within a very close time period. In these cases, the UKBA undertakes the National Referral Mechanism (NRM) procedure to make a formal designation as to whether someone is a victim of trafficking.

> There have been cases where women have been cooperating with the police, so where there is a potential prosecution and yet have been issued negative decisions [under the NRM]. This is despite the fact that the police authorities were treating them as credible victims (Montier, S. 2012: private communication).

Detention in the Asylum and Criminal Justice Systems

Women asylum seekers in immigration detention and women in prison are all women detained involuntarily in a residential institution: detention centres have been described as 'essentially prisons' by the Home Affairs Select Committee (House of Commons Home Affairs Committee 2009).

In the main, women in prison are held because they have been charged with or convicted of a criminal offence. Asylum seekers are detained in Immigration Removal Centres (IRCs) under administrative powers – claiming asylum is not a criminal offence. Their detention is indefinite and not subject to automatic judicial oversight. Some women seeking asylum are detained on arrival in the UK, others after their asylum claim has been refused often with a view to removing them to their country of origin.

The prison service has many policies relating to women including a national service framework for women offenders (HM Prison Service 2008a) and policies concerning searching (HM Prison Service 2009–10), gender-specific standards (HM Prison Service 2008b), gender equality impact assessments (HM Prison Service 2007) and staffing ratios (HM Prison Service 2001). The Detention Service Operating Standards which collates all the standards for IRCs introduced since December 2002 includes one page on female detainees and two references elsewhere to searching women (UKBA undated).

Not every policy relevant for women in prison will be relevant for women in immigration detention; however as standards for women in prison are far more developed, they can be used as a starting point to inform standards for women in immigration detention. Following lobbying by endorsers of the Women's Asylum Charter, the UKBA undertook a comparative study between Prison Service policies and Detention Services policies (UKBA 2011b: 6).

Despite this, there is a lack of relevant asylum policies relating to women. For example, the Prison Service's policy states that an appropriate ratio is generally considered to be 60:40 female to male staff because "women who have been abused by men may feel safer in a predominantly female environment" and 'there are also issues of decency and security that need to be dealt with by women staff' (HM Prison Service 2001: 52). The UKBA does not have a policy about staffing ratios at IRCs for women although the HM Inspectorate of Prisons recommended that there should be a considerably higher proportion of female staff at Yarl's Wood IRC, the main IRC for women (HMIP 2011).

The UKBA can determine asylum claims in the detained fast track (DFT) if they believe a claim can be decided 'quickly' (UKBA 2009: para 2.2.1). In 2010, 530 women were placed in Yarl's Wood for their claims to be dealt with in the DFT (men's claims are dealt with at Harmondsworth). Women's DFT cases made up one fifth of the total.[4] Women may be placed in the DFT on the basis of lack of credibility during the UKBA screening process (Human Rights Watch 2010:

---

4   Home Office, Immigration Statistics July – September 2011 Volume 3.

38). Torture and trafficking claims come within the UKBA's exclusion criteria for the DFT (UKBA 2009: para 2.3) but claims based on sexual and gender-based violence do not. Women who claim that they have suffered gender-based violence are still placed into the DFT (Vine 2012).

However it can be argued that such cases of gender-related persecution cannot be decided quickly. They are complicated for two reasons. Firstly, asylum claims based on violence inflicted by family or community can be harder to prove and the lack of protection by the state also has to be evidenced. Secondly, these types of claims require sensitivity, time to build a basic level of trust between the woman and the decision-maker, knowledge of women's rights in countries of origin and knowledge of how women react to trauma (Human Rights Watch 2010).

Women are placed in the DFT despite a non-detained option being available through the New Asylum Model, where initial decisions are expected to be made promptly. In November 2009, the Home Affairs Committee concluded that time, effort and money spent on improving Yarl's Wood IRC would be better spent reforming the asylum process to reduce the need for detention (House of Commons Home Affairs Select Committee 2009).

Because of its arbitrary nature, detention has particular impacts on women's psychological well-being.

> The unpredictable nature of detention, the fear of being arbitrarily moved around the country and never knowing when they were going to be released or removed, in addition to the often violent removal attempts they were subjected to or witnessed, increased the stress experienced by these women (Cutler and Ceneda 2004: 89).

Women who get out of detention and go back to live in the community continue to experience a fear of being re-detained (Cutler and Ceneda 2004).

Destitution

Eligibility for financial support and accommodation for a woman claiming asylum depends on the stage she has reached in the asylum process. If she is in the process of claiming asylum she will be given no-choice accommodation and financial support that is only 70 per cent of income support. There have been instances of sexual harassment or bullying between male staff and female asylum seekers in UKBA accommodation, as well as concerns about staff entering women's rooms unannounced.

Unlike many women with uncertain immigration status, women seeking asylum do have recourse to public funds if they are affected by domestic violence whilst living in UKBA accommodation (UKBA 2004). However the fact that they are entitled to a bed in a refuge funded by the UKBA is not well known by those working in women's refuges, even those in refuges catering particularly for black and minority ethnic women.

If a woman is refused asylum and does not have children she will only be given accommodation and support in exceptional circumstances, e.g. if she is unable to leave the UK due to a physical impediment to travel to her country of origin. The accommodation will again be no-choice and the support will be in the form of a card which allows her to spend a limited amount of money, and only on certain produce and in certain shops. There is no money for transport and the shops involved do not provide the cheapest goods, nor culturally specific foods.

If she has neither children nor exceptional circumstances a woman whose asylum claim and appeals have been refused will have her accommodation and support withdrawn by the UKBA. This can leave her destitute. Women may face destitution because of gender-related reasons. Pregnancy or the birth of a child is the most common reason for women having to move out of accommodation provided by family or friends. Domestic violence and sexual exploitation are other causes of women being forced out of their accommodation. Yet decision making on support provision fails to take adequate account of such vulnerability. The poor quality of decision making is demonstrated by the high proportion of decisions regarding support being overturned on appeal (Asylum Support Appeals Project 2011).

A destitute woman asylum seeker will have to rely on the goodwill of friends or on food parcels from churches; she may become homeless and have to sleep on the street. She will be vulnerable to sexual violence and exploitation and women in this situation are known to engage in transactional activity including sexual activity to get a roof over their head (Crawley et al. 2011: 49, 52). Despite the Government's VAW strategy's emphasis on protection, destitute women asylum seekers are thus not protected from VAW.

A destitute woman who becomes pregnant is not normally entitled to accommodation and support until six weeks before her due date. This is despite evidence that 12 per cent of maternal deaths are to refugee and asylum seeking women (Confidential Enquiry into Maternal and Child Health 2007). If a woman is given accommodation this is likely to require moving to a different region, resulting in the loss of continuity in antenatal care. UKBA policy fails to take account of specialist advice emphasising the importance of continuity of care and effective risk management (Royal College of Obstetricians and Gynaecologists 2011, Maternity Action 2010).

Conclusion

Women seeking protection from violence against women abroad and who claim asylum in the UK face the double hurdle of being both women and asylum seekers. The intersection of discrimination on the grounds of their gender and of their status as asylum seekers creates a number of ironic comparisons.

One of the most obvious ironies is the current government's increased focus on VAW within international development work when the UK does not provide protection to those same women if they claim asylum in the UK. There is an irony too in the UK laws and government departments providing British women with protection from honour crime, forced marriage and FGM whilst regularly failing to offer protection to women fleeing from those practices in other countries. Last, but not least, the practices of UKBA result in women becoming destitute and therefore vulnerable to further sexual exploitation and VAW whilst living in the UK.

Thus VAW that is recognised as a problem in the context of international development stops being a problem when the woman arrives in the UK. VAW that is recognised as a problem for a British woman in the UK is not recognised as a problem if it happens to a woman abroad who then seeks protection here. Women seeking asylum can be said to be failed by both the asylum system and current VAW policies.

References

Association of Chief Police Officers. 2008. *Honour Based Violence Strategy*. [online] Available at http://www.acpo.police.uk/documents/crime/2008/200810CRIHBV01.pdf [accessed: 20 August 2012].

Association of Chief Police Officers and Crown Prosecution Service. 2010. *Guidance on investigating and prosecuting rape cases* (abridged version). Bedfordshire: National Policing Improvement Agency.

Asylum Aid. 2008. *Charter of Rights of Women Seeking Asylum*. [online] Available at http://www.asylumaid.org.uk/data/files/charter.pdf [accessed 20 August 2012].

Asylum Aid. 2009. *Response to HM Government's Consultation Paper: Together We Can End Violence Against Women And Girls*. [online] Available at http://www.asylumaid.org.uk/data/files/publications/104/VAW_integrated_ strategy_Asylum_Aid_response_2009.pdf [accessed: 20 August 2012].

Asylum Aid. 2011. *Unsustainable: the quality of initial decision-making in women's asylum claims*. London: Asylum Aid.

Asylum Aid. 2012. *The Women's Project*. [online] Available at http://www. asylumaid.org.uk/pages/the_projects_purpose.html [accessed   20 August 2012].

Asylum Support Appeals Project. 2011. *No credibility: UKBA decision making and section 4 support*.   London: ASAP.

Baillot, H., Cowan, S. and Munro, V. 2009. *Rape narratives and credibility assessment (of female claimants) at the AIT*. Nuffield Research Proposal.

Baksi, C. 2012. Forced marriage to be criminalised. *Law Society Gazette,* 8 June. CEDAW Committee. 2008. *Concluding Observations of the Committee on the Elimination of All Forms of Discrimination against Women: United Kingdom of Great Britain and Northern Ireland*. [online] Available at http://daccess-dds-ny.un.org/doc/UNDOC/GEN/N09/555/92/PDF/N0955592.pdf?OpenElement [accessed: 20 August 2012].

CEDAW Committee. 2011. *Statement on the Anniversaries of the 1951 Convention Relating to the Status of Refugees and the 1961 Convention on the Reduction of Statelessness* [online] Available at http://www.unhcr.org/refworld/docid/4ea13f012.html [accessed: 20 August 2012].

Centre for Women's Global Leadership. 2001. *A Women's Human Rights Approach to the World Conference Against Racism.* [online] Available at http://www.cwgl.rutgers.edu/globalcenter/policy/gcpospaper.html. [accessed: 15 March 2012].

Confidential Enquiry into Maternal and Child Health. 2007. *Saving mothers' lives: reviewing maternal deaths to make motherhood safer- 2003- 5.* London: CEMACH.

Coomaraswamy, R. 2000. *Integration of the human rights of women and the gender perspective, violence against women*: UN doc. E/CN.4/2000/68. New York: United Nations.

Council of Europe. 2012. *Convention on preventing and combating violence against women and domestic violence.* Available at http://www.coe.int/t/dghl/standardsetting/convention-violence/default_EN.asp [accessed: 20 August 2012].

Crawley, H. 2001. *Refugees and Gender: Law and Process.* Bristol: Jordans.

Crawley, H. et al. 2011. *Coping with destitution, survival and livelihood strategies of refused asylum seekers living in the UK.* Oxford: Oxfam.

Cutler, S. and Ceneda, S. 2004. *'They took me away': Women's experiences of immigration detention in the UK.* London: Bail for Immigration Detainees and Asylum Aid.

Dauvergne, C. and Millbank, J. 2010. Forced Marriage as Harm in Domestic and International Law. *The Modern Law Review*, 73(1), 57–88.

Davenport, J. 2010. Met will boost its sex crime squad as rape reports rocket. London *Evening Standard*, 15 October.

Department for International Development. 2011. *A new strategic vision for girls and women: stopping poverty before it starts* [online] Available at http://www.dfid.gov.uk/Documents/publications1/strategic-vision-girls-women.pdf. [accessed: 20 August 2012].

Edwards, A. 2009. *Displacement, Statelessness and Questions of Gender Equality under the Convention on the Elimination of All Forms of Discrimination against Women, Legal and Protection Policy Research Series.* Geneva: UNHCR.

Edwards, A. 2010. Transitioning Gender: Feminist engagement with international refugee law and policy 1950–2010, *Refugee Survey Quarterly*, 29(2), 21–45.

Ertürk, Y. 2009. *15 years of the United Nations Special Rapporteur On Violence Against Women, Its Causes and Consequences.* Geneva: United Nations.

Foreign and Commonwealth Office. 2010. *The right to choose: multi-agency statutory guidance for dealing with forced marriage.* [online] Available at http://www.fco.gov.uk/resources/en/pdf/travel-living-abroad/when-things-go-wrong/fmu-right-to-choose.pdf [accessed: 20 August 2012].

Foreign and Commonwealth Office. 2011. *What is a forced marriage?* [online] Available at http://www.forcedmarriage.net/whatis.html [accessed: 20 August 2012].

Green, D. 13 October 2011. Written Ministerial Statements [online] Available at http://www.publications.parliament.uk/pa/cm201011/cmhansrd/cm111013/wmstext/111013m0001.htm#11101330000114. [accessed: 20 August 2012].

HM Government. 2009. *Together We Can End Violence Against Women And Girls.* [online] Available at http://webarchive.nationalarchives.gov.uk/20100419081706/http://homeoffice.gov.uk/documents/vawg-strategy-2009/index.html [accessed: 20 August 2012].

HM Government. 2010. *Call to End Violence Against Women and Girls.* [online] Available at http://www.homeoffice.gov.uk/publications/crime/call-end-violence-women-girls/vawg-paper?view=Binary [accessed: 20 August 2012].

HM Government. 2011. *Ending Violence Against Women and Girls: Action Plan Progress Review.* [online] Available at http://www.homeoffice.gov.uk/publications/crime/call-end-violence-women-girls/action-plan-progress-review?view=Binary [accessed: 20 August 2012].

HM Inspector of Prisons. 2011. *Report on an announced inspection of Yarl's Wood Immigration Removal Centre 4–8 July 2011.* London: Her Majesty's Inspectorate of Prisons.

HM Prison Service. 2001. *Establishing an Appropriate Staff Gender Mix in Establishments, Prison Service Order (PSO) 8005.* London: HM Prison Service.

HM Prison Service. 2007. *Gender Equality Impact Assessments (Prisoners), PSO 40/2007.* London: HM Prison Service.

HM Prison Service. 2008a. *National Service Framework for Women Offenders.* London: HM Prison Service.

HM Prison Service. 2008b. *Women Prisoners, PSO 4800.* London: HM Prison Service.

HM Prison Service. 2009–2010. *New Full Searching Arrangements for Women Prisoners, PSO 1000.* London: HM Prison Service.

Home Office, Asylum data tables, Immigration Statistics, July - September 2011, Volume 1. [online] Available at http://www.homeoffice.gov.uk/publications/science-research-statistics/research-statistics/immigration-asylum-research/immigration-tabs-q3-2011/asylum1-q3-11-tabs [accessed: 20 August 2012].

Home Office, Immigration Statistics, April to June 2011: Asylum, Table as.03: Asylum applications from main applicants by age, sex and country of nationality. [online] Available at http://www.homeoffice.gov.uk/publications/science-research-statistics/research-statistics/immigration-asylum-research/immigration-tabs-q2-2011v2/asylum1-q2-11-tabs [accessed: 20 August 2012].

House of Commons Home Affairs Committee. 2009. *The detention of children in the immigration system, HC73.* [online] Available at http://www.publications.parliament.uk/pa/cm200910/cmselect/cmhaff/73/7302.htm [accessed: 20 August 2012].

Human Rights Watch. 2010. *Fast tracked unfairness: detention and denial of women asylum seekers.* New York: Human Rights Watch.

Immigration and Asylum Chamber. 2010. *Joint Presidential Guidance Note No 2, Child, vulnerable adults and sensitive appellant.* [online] Available at http://www.justice.gov.uk/downloads/tribunals/immigration-and-asylum/lower/ChildWitnessGuidance.pdf [accessed: 20 August 2012].

Judicial Studies Board. 2009. *Equal Treatment Bench Book.* [online] Available at http://www.judiciary.gov.uk/publications-and-reports/judicial-college/Pre%20 2011/equal-treatment-bench-book [accessed: 20 August 2012].

Maternity Action. 2010. *Notes on the timing of dispersal during pregnancy and following the birth.* [policy document]

Querton, C. 2012. *"I feel like as a woman I'm not welcome": A gender analysis of UK asylum law, policy and practice.* London: Asylum Aid.

Refugee Council. 2009a. *Response to HM Government's Consultation Paper: Together We Can End Violence Against Women And Girls.* [online] available at http://www.refugeecouncil.org.uk/Resources/Refugee%20Council/ downloads/policy_responses/RC%20response%20to%20VAWAG%20 consultation%20May%202009.pdf [accessed: 20 August 2021].

Refugee Council. 2009b. *The vulnerable women's project: refugee and asylum seeking women affected by rape or sexual violence – literature review.* London: Refugee Council

Royal College of Obstetricians and Gynaecologists. 2011. *Response to the UKBA's Healthcare Needs Dispersal Guidance consultation.* [online] Available at http://www.rcog.org.uk/files/rcog-corp/RCOG%20policy%20briefing%20 -%20RCOG%20response%20to%20UKBA%20-%20final.pdf [accessed: 20 August 2012]

Scottish Refugee Council and London School of Hygiene and Tropical Medicine. 2009. *Asylum seeking women, violence and health.* [online] Available at http:// genderviolence.lshtm.ac.uk/files/2009/10/Asylum-seeking-Women-Violence-and-Health.pdf [accessed: 20 August 2012].

Sen, P., Humphreys, C & Kelly L. 2004. *Violence against Women in the UK, Shadow thematic report for CEDAW.* London, Womankind.

Sen, P. & Kelly, L. 2007. *Violence against Women in the UK, Shadow thematic report for CEDAW.* London, Child and Woman Abuse Studies Unit.

UK Border Agency. 2004. *Asylum Support Policy Bulletin 70: Domestic Violence.* [online] Available at http://www.ukba.homeoffice.gov.uk/sitecontent/ documents/policyandlaw/asylumsupportbulletins/accesstosupport/ [accessed: 20 August 2012].

UK Border Agency. 2009. Detained fast track processes [online] Available at http://www.ukba.homeoffice.gov.uk/sitecontent/documents/ policyandlaw/asylumprocessguidance/detention/guidance/detained_fast_ processes?view=Binary. [accessed: 20 August 2012].

UK Border Agency. 2010. *Asylum Instruction on Gender Issues in the Asylum Claim.* [online] Available at http://www.ukba.homeoffice.gov.uk/sitecontent/ documents/policyandlaw/asylumpolicyinstructions/ [accessed 20 August 2012].

UK Border Agency. 2011a. *Quality and Efficiency Report: Thematic Review of Gender Issues in Asylum Claims.* [internal document]

UK Border Agency. 2011b. *Gender issues in the asylum claim action plan.* [internal document]

UK Border Agency. 2011c. *Minutes of National Asylum Stakeholders Forum Quality Group.* [internal document]

UK Border Agency. undated. *Detention Service Operating Standards for Immigration Service Removal Centres* [online] Available at http://www. ukba.homeoffice.gov.uk/sitecontent/documents/managingourborders/ immigrationremovalcentres/. [accessed: 20 August 2012].

UK Government. 2011. *United Nations Convention on the Elimination of all Forms of Discrimination against Women (CEDAW): United Kingdom's Seventh Periodic Report.* [online] Available at http://www.homeoffice.gov.uk/ publications/equalities/international-equality/7th-cedaw-report [accessed: 20 August 2012].

UN Secretary-General. 2008. *Report of the Secretary-General on eliminating rape and other forms of sexual violence in all their manifestations, including in conflict and related situations.* UN Doc. A/63/216. New York: UN [online] Available at http://daccess-dds-ny.un.org/doc/UNDOC/GEN/N08/449/78/ PDF/N0844978.pdf?OpenElement [accessed: 20 August 2012].

UNHCR. 1951. *Conference of Plenipotentiaries on the Status of Refugees and Stateless Persons: Summary Record of the Thirty-second Meeting, Travaux préparatoires,* UN Doc. A/CONF.2/SR.5.

UNHCR. 1985. *Executive Committee of the High Commissioner's Programme. Conclusion No 39 (XXXVI) on refugee women and international protection.*

UNHCR. 2002. *Guidelines on International Protection: Gender-Related Persecution within the context of Article 1A(2) of the 1951 Convention and/or its 1967 Protocol relating to the Status of Refugees.* [online] Available at http:// www.unhcr.org/3d58ddef4.pdf [accessed: 20 August 2012].

UNHCR. 2008. *Quality Initiative Project Fifth Report to the Minister.* London: UNHCR.

United Nations. 1951. 1951 *Convention relating to the Status of Refugees and its 1967 Protocol relating to the Status of Refugees.* [online] Available at http:// www.unhcr.org/3b66c2aa10.html [accessed: 20 August 2012].

United Nations. 1979. *Resolution adopted by the General Assembly during its thirty-fourth session: Women refugees*: UN doc. A/RES/34/161, 17 December 1979 [online] Available at http://www.un.org/documents/ga/res/34/a34res161. pdf [accessed: 20 August 2012].

United Nations. 1995. *Beijing Declaration and Platform for Action, Fourth World Conference on Women*, A/CONF.177/20 1995 and A/CONF.177/20/Add.1 1995.

United Nations General Assembly. 2006. *In-depth study on all forms of violence against women*: UN doc. A/61/122/Add.1, 6 July 2006 [online] Available at http://daccess-dds-ny.un.org/doc/UNDOC/GEN/N06/419/74/PDF/N0641974.pdf?OpenElement. [accessed: 20 August 2012].

United Nations. 1993. *Declaration on the elimination of violence against women.* [online] Available at http://www.un.org/documents/ga/res/48/a48r104.htm [accessed: 20 August 2012].

United Nations General Assembly. 1948. *Universal declaration of human rights.* [online] Available at http://www.ohchr.org/EN/UDHR/Documents/UDHR_Translations/eng.pdf [accessed: 20 August 2012].

Verma, Baroness. 2011. *Hansard, House of Lords*, Violence against women, 15 Nov 2011: Column GC238.

Vine, J. 2012. *Asylum: a thematic inspection of the detained fast track, July – September 2011.* London: Independent Chief Inspector of the UKBA.

Women's Asylum Charter. 2009. *Every Single Woman: a comparison of standards for women in the asylum system with standards for women in the criminal justice, prison and maternity systems in the UK.* London: Asylum Aid.

Women's Asylum News. January /February 2007. Gender guidelines no longer Appeals Tribunal policy. *Women's Asylum News,* issue 66.

Women's Asylum News. June/July 2007. Gender guidance added to CEDAW report. *Women's Asylum News,* issue 67.

Women's Asylum News. November 2010. 'Call to end violence against women'. *Women's Asylum News,* issue 97.

Women's National Commission. 2005. *Having it all.* London: Women's National Commission.

Women's National Commission. 2008. *Submission to the UN Committee on CEDAW.* London: Women's National Commission.

Cases

Islam v Secretary of State for the Home Department; R v Immigration Appeal Tribunal and Another, ex parte Shah [1999] UKHL 20, 25 March 1999.

R v Doody [2008] EWCA Crim 2394.

Secretary of State for the Home Department v K; Fornah v Secretary of State for the Home Department [2006] UKHL 46, 18 October 2006.

Chapter 14

Working Trans-culturally with Domestically Violent Men

Phil Price

In this chapter, I want to explore the particular difficulties involved in providing a mainstream domestic violence perpetrator programme (DVPP) to male abusers from ethnic minority communities. My aim is to do so within a wider discussion of what is currently understood in the field as safe working practice when delivering such programmes, and the wider partnership response in which such work takes place. Specifically, I draw on my practice experience of facilitating programmes at the Domestic Violence Intervention Project (DVIP) for male perpetrators of domestic violence from a non-English speaking community in a London borough, and the questions this work raises about developing more appropriate responses to particular client groups.

The chapter is not based on research or any form of 'scientific' or psychological certainty, nor is it a description of 'how to' deliver this work. Rather, it is a exploration of what programmes should aim for, what can be achieved and an account of what I consider to be the appropriate model for delivering perpetrator work. Most importantly, it raises questions that I, my organisation, and the sector as a whole needs to be asking in terms of working with violent men from a range of cultural backgrounds.

Perpetrator Programmes

Domestic Violence Perpetrator Programmes (DVPPs) are community based organisations, delivering group-work programmes with perpetrators with the aim of changing their behaviour and stopping further abuse, alongside a range of other services. Respect[1], the UK membership association for DVPPs, stipulates the following (minimum) accreditation standards for such programmes, which should:

- provide proactive partner contact for current, former and new partners of programme participants via a dedicated Integrated Support Service (ISS);
- carry out risk assessments and case management to protect victims and children;

---

1   See www.Respect.net.uk.

- deliver group work programmes of sufficient length and quality to ensure the best possible opportunities for change;
- take referrals from Family Courts, Social Services, health professionals, voluntary sector agencies and perpetrators themselves.

Perpetrator work is now considered an essential component of any coordinated community response to domestic violence, the foundation of current government responses (Home Office, 2011). Whilst research findings remain equivocal on the effectiveness of perpetrator programmes, there is some evidence that they can prevent further harm by placing the responsibility for domestic abuse where it belongs: with the perpetrators. DVIP has been part of two evaluations – one internal and one external (Burton et al., 1998) – that show a 70 per cent cessation of violence for men completing significant amounts of the programme over a two year follow-up period. Other larger and more extensive evaluations, over four years and upwards across multiple sites, demonstrate similar results for men completing programmes (Gondolf, 2002). While these might be seen as impressive outcomes for any form of psycho-educational offending behaviour programme, the findings need to be balanced against the reality that often less than a third (30%) of men referred will complete a programme. Also, from within the group of men who do stop their violence, a significant number have been shown to still be using other forms of coercive and controlling behaviours (Dobash 1999; Pence and Paymar, 1993; Price et al., 2008).

What this means is that perpetrator programmes by themselves form only a part of the interventions required to address domestic violence. As highlighted in the Respect frameworks and criteria, programmes need to view themselves as embedded within a wider co-ordinated partnership response to domestic violence. Programmes can, with accurate monitoring and risk management information from (ex-)partners, link in with social care agencies, children's services and local community safety boards. A recent Respect briefing paper (Respect, 2010) drew a sample of perpetrators from membership programmes in the UK, showing the levels of risk posed by men attending and noting that most were not linked into any other form of risk management process or statutory agency.

With these caveats in mind, the challenge lies in making the range of interventions more effective, responsive and accountable: safer for women and children and accessible to a wider range of perpetrators.

The DVIP Approach

DVIP have been at the forefront of developing and delivering multi-faceted interventions that address the use of violence and abuse in intimate relationships since its inception in 1992. Alongside the perpetrator programme and integrated victim support services, we provide a specialist risk assessment service for the family courts in private and public law and a 'high vigilance' contact centre for cases where domestic violence is the primary concern identified by Children's Services. The core aims of all DVIP's services are presented below.

1. To increase the safety of women and children

Referral onto a perpetrator programme can sometimes result in an elevated level of risk for a man's partner or ex-partner. This is because some women who might otherwise have left the relationship will choose to remain – or reconcile – with the abusive partner in the hope or belief that he will change.

To mitigate these risks, an integrated and fully resourced women's support service is essential to provide safety planning and safety-focused support for women and children. DVIP do not work with men unless we are able to provide feedback and support to the women who are or were at risk of his violence.

2. To empower women to make safer choices for themselves and their children

The work of the women's support service (WSS) is accessible, varied, women-focussed and on-going. The service recognises that information provided by perpetrators of domestic violence can be both misleading and manipulative, and may raise 'false hope' or unrealistic expectations on the part of the victim. It recognises the isolating effects of domestic violence, makes pro-active contact and names the domestic violence for what it is by holding the perpetrator to account.

3. To help perpetrators stop their use of violence and controlling behaviour

The DVIP model considers violence and abuse to be learned behaviours which can be unlearned; and holds abusers "100% responsible" for their behaviour. It also considers that domestic violence perpetrators can be helped to stop damaging their partners, their children and themselves, through engagement with interventions that challenge, support and encourage them to make positive changes and to begin to engage in respectful relationships.

The vast majority of domestic violence does not result in prosecution of the perpetrator, much less their access to programmes to address their behaviour. In recognition of this fact, DVIP's services are designed to be accessible to perpetrators outside current criminal justice programmes. We accept self-referrals as well as referrals from the family courts, criminal justice system and, of particular note in terms of the work described below, referrals from children's services.

Experiences in East London

DVIP's East London perpetrator programme is award winning and was commissioned in partnership by three East London Boroughs (Newham, Barking and Dagenham and Waltham Forest) in 2007.

The profiles of the perpetrators referred into this programme tend to match the demographics of their respective boroughs. Black, Asian and Minority Ethnic backgrounds or Refugees (BAMER) constituted approximately 60 per cent of Newham's referrals for example, whereas the majority of referrals from Barking and Dagenham identified themselves as White/Caucasian. The diversity of the client group allowed us to compare and contrast the different presentations of men using intimate partner violence. Within the non-English speaking group – largely from South Asian backgrounds living in Newham – we provided one to one treatment via interpreters. English speaking men referred from Barking and Dagenham were treated on the group-work programme. Before going on to talk in more detail about my observations in practice, an overview of the model of intervention which informs this is needed.

Programme model

DVIP perpetrator programmes are based on the power and control model of domestic violence and abuse, pioneered by the Duluth DAIP Programme in Minnesota (Pence and Paymar 1993). This model was developed in consultation with victims, and proposes that intimate partner violence is not the result of one-off 'explosions' of anger, or a release of psychological tension and frustration that has built up in a relationship. Rather, violence is used to create an atmosphere of threat, fear, punishment and humiliation, and is rooted in power and control.

The power and control wheel (see Figure 14.1) – also developed in consultation with victims – sections out the different forms of abuse that a perpetrator may use, and depicts these as sections of a pie, encircled by an outer ring labelled 'sexual and physical violence'. In group work this offers a message to perpetrators that it's not just that you shout, or slam the door, or call her names; it's that every- time you use abusive behaviour, it carries with it the reality and the threat of previous violence. At the centre of this wheel is a circle entitled 'power and control', communicating that all the violence, all this noise and all this hurt is instrumental: it is targeted at preventing a victim from being who she is, from doing what she wants, from expressing her anger, or challenging his.

The power and control wheel is now used in conjunction with two others: the equality wheel, which offers a framework for respectful, egalitarian relationships; and a wheel that highlights the wider social and institutional supports for violence against women (see Figures 14.2 and 14.3). This latter wheel sets the context for men's violence to women: the pervasive drip, drip of gender oppression; the 'it's just a domestic' dismissal by the police; the focus on her "failure to protect her children" from social services; her nagging, craziness or infidelity as a discursive justification in media reporting; the belief that men are *this*, masculinity is *this*; women are *this,* femininity is *this*. This wheel makes clear that domestic violence is culturally syntonic and – from this perspective – it is chosen and men can choose otherwise.

The power and control wheels have often been read as a political framework rather than a treatment model, but in ten years of delivering programmes with abusers, I have come to see the notion of 'power and control' as something that speaks to the heart of men's violence to women, and – importantly – it is not feminism 'put onto men' (as a training delegate put it recently), but when well delivered, can explain the unexplainable to men who are being required to talk about some of the worst parts of themselves.

Power and control

Perpetrator programmes are not anger management or counselling groups. They are treatment groups specifically designed to address intimate partner violence. They draw upon a wide range of approaches including cognitive-behavioural theory, social learning theory, psychodrama, psychotherapeutic and relationship skills teaching. They work to create a challenging environment whilst offering support for personal change. They address issues of masculinity, sexual respect, the instrumental and systematic nature of intimate partner violence, and the failure of intimacy for the men. DVIP have, in addition, built a specific and detailed set of modules around the impact of domestic violence on children, considering post-violence parenting, fear and shame based parenting, attachment, post-separation abuse and letting go.

When the programme works at its best, we create a space from which men can become more open to themselves, their internal worlds, the historical basis for some of the worst of their behaviour and, from here, help them to build empathy and intimacy with the women and children that will have suffered at their hands. In my view, even when effective empathy is an unrealistic treatment goal, teaching the language of responsibility and the effects of their violence can work as a form of cognitive 'self-statement' which may mitigate against further violence.

Within this, however, it is important not to lose sight of the reality at the centre of this model, built, as it is, from the words and experiences of the victims of this abuse, and the notions of power and control. As a treatment provider, it is vital we remember that the centre of the power and control wheel is not his self-esteem issues, substance use history, historical patterns of attachment, 'mutual malignancy', or his exposure to violence as a child or young man. Some or all of these issues are crucial in terms of treatment plans, risk and case management, but it is necessary to keep the use of violence in mind, and be aware that it makes sense to men, it is a learned behaviour, it is rooted in historical gender expectations, and perpetrators always have a choice as to how they do or do not behave.

Working with Difference

When working 'trans-culturally' in any setting, it is important to bear in mind some of the specific dynamics that can be present, or more emphasised, in the relationship between worker, material, client and organisation. For example, NHS mental health and psychological provision focuses on the need for 'cultural competency' amongst practitioners – for the professional to be able to understand his/her own world views and those of the patient, while avoiding stereotyping and misapplication of scientific knowledge in the client/practitioner encounter.

Cross et al. (1989) list five essential elements that contribute to an institution's or agency's ability to become more culturally competent:

- valuing diversity;
- having the capacity for cultural self-assessment;
- being conscious of the dynamics inherent when cultures interact;
- having institutionalized cultural knowledge;.
- adaptation of service delivery reflecting an understanding of cultural diversity.

These elements notwithstanding, the concept of 'cultural competency' has been criticised for being 'race neutral' in that it glosses over the power dynamics at work in any trans-cultural encounter: the racism; the history of imperialism, violence and dominance of one culture over another (see, for example, Areán 1998).

Applying these ideas to treatment D'Ardenne and Mahanti (1999) speak about the power dynamics, assumptions and institutional racism that can form the experiential core of therapy for men and women seeking help in a UK or other 'westernised' context. They explore what they perceive to be the Eurocentric, individualised, inward looking and goal orientated assumptions underpinning the notion of individual therapy, whilst simultaneously warning against narrow and excluding definitions of culture.

Another important emphasis in the writing about psychotherapy from a trans-cultural perspective is the need for the therapist to be aware of, and actively working on, the assumptions and prejudices that can (and will) form a part of the therapeutic encounter. This includes being: actively engaged in working against the power dynamics enacted in the 'therapeutic encounter'; consistently mindful of the assumptions, guesses and supposed 'intuitions' they are making; and aware of how easily they could be re-enforcing a set of biased or downright oppressive ideas.

We know, for example, that from the perspective of the anti-violence against women movement, notions such as 'honour based violence' or 'forced marriage' can serve to 'otherise' certain cultures and to distance a majority culture from its own issues with regards to the patriarchal nature of domestic violence, or generalised violence against women (Thiara and Gill, 2010). Khanum (2008) is also very clear that honour based violence exists in a range of cultures including the South Asian, Turkish, Eastern European, Afro-American, and rural communities in Western Europe. She also talks about parallel notions of 'honour' at work in gang cultures when considering violence against known women. In fact, when viewed from a distance, what does honour actually mean other than an act which goes against normative expectations of what a woman is 'allowed and supposed' to do?

In my day to day practice and clinical experience, it is unhelpful to think in terms of 'culture' as causal from the perspective of any specific group, country, ethnic or religious background. In terms of domestic violence perpetrators, the supports for the violence are often 'trans-cultural', for example the perpetrator's sense of his entitlement to power and control within relationships, and his justification in using violence if his demands are not met.

Delivering programmes

Domestic violence is gender based, and when men come on to a perpetrator programme, we hope and expect that at the very least: it is the safest possible option; that the agencies involved with the family are fully aware of the risk of further harm; and that the treatment is viable. Equally, having agreed that domestic violence occurs in all cultures, and treatment for men needs to be considered as such, it does not mean that we can become complacent. There are some general observations I want to make in terms of the need to deliver perpetrator work with Black, Asian and Minority Ethnic backgrounds or Refugee (BAMER) men, and to address harmful traditional practices such as honour based violence and forced marriage.

First and foremost, the power and control model, especially with its focus on societal and institutional supports, seems an entirely appropriate model from within which to be working with any group of men. The wheel places their behaviour in context, and does seem to be easily grasped.

The wider societal and social supports for violence can easily become lost in a more individualistic treatment culture which focusses on feelings, insecurities, fears and 'self-esteem' rather than the wider meaning – and supports – for what they do. Groups can easily digress into discussions of vulnerability, self-esteem or attachment which in turn can minimise, downplay or otherwise distort the basic and gendered aspect of the violence. These men, when entering into treatment, have the sense that their partners are responsible for both the physical and metaphorical housework within the relationships, with a more 'self' oriented treatment population their core beliefs – expectations of authority and service, feelings of entitlement and the fear of abandonment or of shame which places the locus of control for his feelings with his partner – can remain unchallenged.

Whether White, South Asian, Pakistani or African, all of the men I have worked with in the East London programme recognised the 'cultural supports' for their violence from within their own personal social and societal context. It is a very interesting phenomenon to work with clinically, as most men minimise and deny their own behaviour, but recognise instantly how it is supported in the society they are asked to describe: – 'of course it makes sense, it is everywhere, men are abusive to women but *I'm not that bad'*.

Creating a dialogue

In the end, however, it is how you can make sense of these links and differences with an individual man that is important. Practitioners have to make this treatment work, or at least make sure we can evidence a reduction in the harm and a decrease or cessation of violence over the alternatives or we may as well give up.

Programmes, whether in group or individually, are designed to widen the men's context and understanding of their behaviour, to increase their awareness of what is abusive and controlling, and to focus on finding whatever message and underlying meaning is most likely going to make sense for each individual. Men who struggle with their partner's ambivalence or anger need to be exposed to experiences of conflict, contained within the safe setting of the group. They also need to understand the amount of conflict they are trying to avoid, the aggression they use to 'shut her up'. Men that are so damaged and damaging they can only think in terms of their own needs can be taught awareness of how their behaviour harms them, and the skills to self-regulate difficult emotions. We try to build affective and cognitive empathy with all clients, and we try to plan for conflict and relate his own experiences of being a child to his behaviour as a parent.

DVPPs seek to teach men what it means to be in a 'relationship' with a real, feeling and thinking human being (as opposed to an object), how to accept responsibility for their behaviour, to find the narrative for who they have come to be and how they can take responsibility for their lives.

Establishing the power and control basis of a man's violence is a fairly easy task. Ask any violent man about grabbing his partners throat (they almost all have) and then ask him to scale this act, from 1 to 10, from as hard as physically possible, to barely 'holding her'. Most will say it was a 5, or a 6 or a 7. From here we can say clearly, that no matter how angry you were feeling, no matter how raging, humiliated or diminished, it is still possible to set a limit for yourself, and if you can set a limit at a 6, or a 7, then you can set a limit a long way before then, a limit before the argument escalates, or a limit in terms of what you expect from yourself or your partner. At the same time as clarifying how much control and choice he has, it is also crucial to make the point that there is no way his partner can know this, he is using extremely dangerous behaviour and putting her in fear for her life.

The power and control model, by making the wider supports visible, can in some ways, make it easier for the men by 'normalising' or explaining their use of violence. That said, providing an 'explanation' or account of the violence means they have to take responsibly which can produce a resistance of its own; it is easier to be mad rather than bad. It is more comfortable for this not to make sense.

Of course, trying to deliver some of this normalisation and accountability 'trans-culturally' can produce deeper difficulties when discussing an individual's behaviour in more than just vague and general terms. A group of BAMER men, while abusing their partners, may also have experienced racism, dismissal, invisibility, loss of status, dislocation and oppression. In practice, no matter how much I might try and normalise, and link the wider, hidden supports for violence in my own culture, or how much curiosity I express (and I am genuinely curious as to how any man ends up in a session at DVIP), the fact remains that the questions designed to elicit reflection on the narrative of a man's violence from a sociological point of view can feel blaming and lead to defensive reactions.

Interestingly, of all the men assessed over two years in the East London site, only 20 per cent of the Asian cohort disclosed experiencing or witnessing domestic violence as children. This compares to 60 or 70 per cent of the White UK men assessed in the same project. Does this mean then that Asian males have seen and heard less domestic violence? Or could it be that this discrepancy reflects a socialised and healthy emphasis on respect and protection for the family or issues of social shame (Shweder 1991); enacting in the therapeutic relationship the wider psycho-social conflict between an 'egoentric' majority culture and a 'socio-centric' minority one? Might there be elements of a member of an oppressed group resisting the threat of the casual and racist pathologising of their personal experience? Perhaps, in practice, these experiences reflect a wider difficulty in providing programmes trans-culturally.

Powerlessness

In her book, *Slow Motion: Changing Masculinities, Changing* Men (1990) Lynne Segal raises interesting questions around the extent and severity of male violence in the USA's African-American communities, relating this to the legacy of the violence and denigration of the slave trade. How does such powerlessness in the face of state-sanctioned oppression relate to intimate partner violence and child abuse, and an individual's attempt to create his own empire in the home? Certainly, some of the most moving work I have witnessed has been with young black men who, in coming to terms with their own violence, have spoken about their fathers' violence and their own attempt to reach some kind of reparation with the men they loved and feared, placing that violence in the wider context of racist oppression and violence.

This level of nuance, around an individual's narrative and social context, is difficult and yet necessary to address within any 'model of intervention' and is something that I believe needs considerable effort from within my own sector.

Other barriers

There are some straightforward blocks to delivering perpetrator work trans-culturally. Working with interpreters, for example, can make it difficult to judge how the material is being heard, understood or even translated. At DVIP we are always careful to meet with new interpreters before starting any work, not only to explain the model but also to try and gauge interpreter's own expectations of men and women in relationships. Again, delivering the work from this potentially 'outsider' context invites resistance. I have certainly experienced interpreters wanting to explain a service user's 'culture' to me as I am trying to deepen or explore a service user's account. Very occasionally, an interpreter will respond 'yes that's what he said' when I have paraphrased a man's statement in order to allow him to expand on what he has told me.

Also, what of the experience of the non-white men in what will be a largely white group at any given time? I hear very little overt racism expressed within the group that I am present at, but what about the 'anti-group' (Nitsun, 1996) – the group that goes on in the breaks, the before and after of the formal treatment time and in the unspoken group process. Overt racism can be challenged, either shut down via the group rules or even explored in terms of the objectification involved and how closely that mirrors the permission men have given themselves for their violence towards their partners. But there is also covert racism in terms of what gets explicitly addressed or left out in the programme itself: the material delivered from within an organisation's own 'Eurocentric' process of exploration and focus, our case scenarios, our constructions of the family. And of course, all of the issues that I feel we are not always fully conscious of exploring in the groups we run - many of the issues highlighted in the wider context of this book.

At DVIP we have a structured organisational framework for case management, treatment management and clinical supervision for programme staff. Within this structure, we actively encourage programme staff to reflect on the counter-transference at work in any programme encounter, and this will include the potential for any oppressive and excluding practice. But as I reflect on the material and the organisational discourse we have around the work we deliver to abusive men, I am aware of how (appropriately) conscious and directed our discussions around what it means to be a woman in the group-room are. But also, how much less explicit and pro-active our attempts are to explore what it might mean for any BME staff delivering the programme interventions to violent men.

Final Thoughts

As the chapter from the Al-Aman project at DVIP (Abdalla Ballela, this volume) shows, programmes set up to deliver interventions with specific minority groups have their own struggles, but can and do have an important impact. The anti-domestic violence messages and programmes in Al-Aman are delivered by practitioners who share a cultural context with the men attending, which may remove some of the blocks and denial that can come in to play when the majority culture is delivering 'psycho-educational' programmes from the 'outside'; preventing the intervention becoming a model imposed on already marginalised groups.

At the same time, men were referred appropriately to the East London project and I believe the work needs to be done. I believe that at the very least, good programme content can re-enforce the consequences of the man's violence to himself, and at best, I have borne witness to some men really opening up about their feelings and experiences. Here I would note unprompted discussions about the fear of building egalitarian relationships, or the need to 'make friends' with their children and learn to express the love and care from which they have cut themselves off to their partners and children. The experiences in East London show that children's services can offer an effective pressure for perpetrators to attend treatment and we need to work harder to make these programmes appropriate and relevant to the men required to attend.

The wider content of this book I realise is difficult to explore. Our risk assessment tools do consider 'honour based violence' from a power and control perspective, but we need to improve our understanding and awareness around notions such as bride price, other harmful practices, and shame, powerlessness and oppression for minority men. We must seek to improve our own and our clients' understanding of the oppression of their partners in terms of family status or religion, what it means to him to be a man when females are explicitly considered to be less valuable than their male counterparts. These challenges notwithstanding, there can be real benefits to the men who attend perpetrator programmes when they can begin to take on the language of responsibility, closeness and accountability.

This is often not enough, and the harm done in many relationships is too great for there to be any going back. Even when this is the case a perpetrator programme, working with an integrated women's support service, can help a couple separate as safely as possible. Reducing a man's dangerousness, and increasing a woman's confidence, self-efficacy and options to the point where she feels safe enough to leave constitutes, in some cases, the best work we do as an organisation. But when I think back over the non-English speaking group I worked with in the East London programme, most of those men were going to go back home at some point, and most of their partners, at least explicitly, made clear that they were planning to reconcile when the level of statutory involvement was reduced. This of course places great responsibility on the 'community' and community based programmes of support and intervention.

In conclusion there are a number of implications of transcultural work that DVPPs need to be more mindful of.

- Intimate partner violence occurs across cultures, and the power and control model accurately provides an account, at least in sociological terms, which men can apply to their own histories and cultural contexts.
- Perpetrator programmes can work, especially when embedded in an appropriate risk management and women's support context. They have been shown to reduce risk, end the violence and abuse of some and place the responsibility for this harm where it belongs – with the abuser.
- Such programmes do however have a clear responsibility to gain a greater understanding of all groups of men coming into treatment who seek to understand and change their behaviour.
- Agencies such as Children's Services can offer an effective referral and re-enforcement source and we can, at the very least, offer the option of a programme in cases where domestic violence places children at risk.
- Al-Aman remains the only culturally specific perpetrator service in the UK

– this seems something of a dereliction of duty on the part of the whole of the sector.

• Working 'trans-culturally' can offer some of the answers – the work needs to be done, the men need to be seen and the violence needs to end. This requires conscious intent and engagement, and a genuine, effortful, curious and committed attempt to make sense of this violence to the men who are using it. This is the challenge to practitioners – to both work with the knowledge that the power and control perspective makes sense to most men, whilst recognising the particularities of their cultural contexts which frequently includes lived experiences of marginalisation and vulnerabilities. In short, DVPPs need to further explore the range of violent masculinities.

Figure 14.1   The Power and Control Wheel

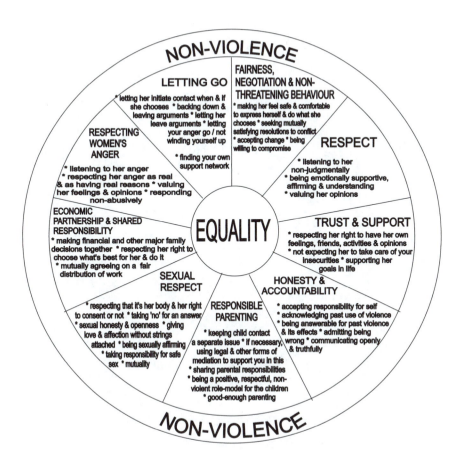

Figure 14.2   The Equality Wheel

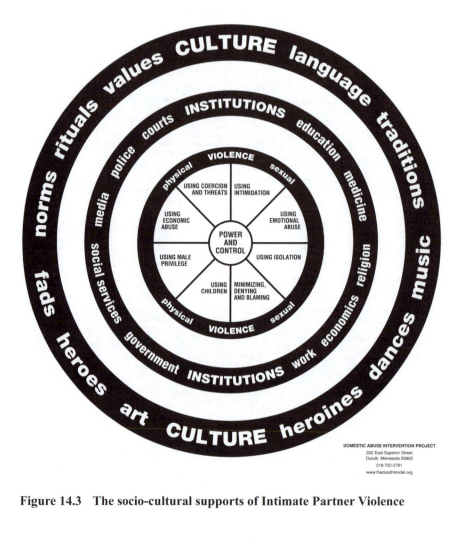

DOMESTIC ABUSE INTERVENTION PROJECT
202 East Superior Street
Duluth, Minnesota 55802
218-722-2781
www.theduluthmodel.org

Figure 14.3   The socio-cultural supports of Intimate Partner Violence

References

Areán, J C 2000. *Beyond Cultural Competence. Futures without Violence* [available at: http://toolkit.endabuse.org/Resources/Beyond.html] Accessed 10 April 2012.

Burton, S, Regan, L & Kelly L (1998). *Supporting Women and Challenging Men.* Bristol, Policy Press.

Cross T et al. (1989). *Towards a culturally competent system of care, volume I.* [online] [available at: http://gucchd.georgetown.edu/72808.html] accessed 9 April 2012.

D'Ardenne, P and Mahanti, A.1999. *Trans-Cultural Counselling in Action.* London: Sage.

Dobash, R.E., Dobash, R.P., Lewis, R. and Cavanagh, K. 1999. *Changing Violent Men.* London: Sage.

Gondolf, E. 2002. *Batterer Intervention Systems: Issues, Outcomes and Recommendations.* London, Sage.

Home Office. 2011. *Call to End, Violence Against, Women and Girls: Action Plan.* [available at: http://www.homeoffice.gov.uk/publications/crime/call-end-violence-women-girls/] accessed 10 April, 2012.

Khanum, N. 2008. *Forced Marriage, Family Cohesion and Community Engagement: national learning through a case study of Luton.* Luton: Equality in Diversity.

Nitsun, M. 1996. *The Anti-Group: Destructive Forces in the Group and their Creative Potential.* London: Routledge.

Pence, E. and M. Paymar. 1993. *Education Groups for Men Who Batter: The Duluth Model.* New York: Springer.

Price, P., Rajagopalan, V., Langeland, G. and Donaghy P.. 2008 *Improving Women and Children's Safety.*[available at http://mgov.newham.gov.uk/mgConvert2PDF.aspx?ID=19298] Accessed 16 April 2012.

Respect. 2010. E*vidence of the effects of perpetrator programmes on women's safety.* [available at http://www.respect.uk.net/data/files/resources/respect_briefing_paper_on_the_evidence_of_effects_of_perpetrator_programmes_on_women_revised_18th_march_10.pdf] accessed 15 April 2012.

Segal, L. 1990. *Slow Motion: Changing Masculinities, Changing Men.* London: Virago.

Shweder, R. 1991. *Thinking Through Cultures.* Cambridge, MA: Harvard University Press.

Thiara, R and Gill, A. (2009). *Violence Against Women in South Asian Communities: Issues for Policy and Practice.* London. Jessica Kingsley.

Chapter 15

Challenging Domestic Abuse in the Arabic Speaking Community: The Experience of Al-Aman

Mohamed Abdalla Ballela

Al-Aman is the Arabic speaking project of the Domestic Violence Intervention Project (DVIP). The project was established in 2000 to provide services to Arabic speaking clients in their own language including a perpetrator programme and an integrated women support service. The project attempts to provide culturally sensitive and effective solutions to issues of domestic abuse in the Arabic speaking community.

Al-Aman has made huge strides since its establishment, with the number of male perpetrators who come through the perpetrators programme significantly increasing over the years, and the majority of women who used the project reporting an increase in safety for them and their children. Al-Aman is also an award winning project that has established itself within a specific community, building alliances with religious leaders and forging links with other agencies and organisations working in the field.

The main aim of this chapter is to share some of our experiences in Al-Aman of offering a perpetrator programme for Arabic speaking men in London, and the associated work in the community. Although the Arabic speaking community in London is multi-faith, it is predominantly Muslim: whilst the two major doctrines – Sunni and Shia – disagree on some Islamic interpretations, they adopt similar positions on women's status and rights. These Islamic Arab values are sometimes in tension with contemporary British gender relations.

Al-Aman is a groundbreaking project as it challenges practices that are deeply embedded in cultural and religious traditions. The issue of domestic abuse was formerly unchallenged and still has a wall of silence surrounding it. As a consequence most men in the Arabic speaking community refuse to accept the existence of domestic violence and abuse, since the maltreatment of women can be rooted in cultural and religious understandings whereby it is the responsibility of the husband to control and guide the family, especially his wife and female relatives. This reflects longstanding conventions, moral and religious teachings from countries of origin in the Middle East and North Africa.

Challenges that Face the Programme

Among the many challenges that face us in working with perpetrators of domestic abuse in the Arabic community are the perpetrators themselves. Men referred to the programme adamantly refuse to take responsibility for their violence and require arduous efforts to convince them to engage. Although this is an issue for all perpetrator programmes, with men from the Arabic community their resistance is reinforced by the level of acceptance of abusive behaviour in the community. Treatment of wives is considered a private matter, in which no one has the right to interfere. Furthermore, seeking help about internal family matters is considered a sign of weakness, that a man is incapable of keeping his family 'in order'. This belief system places particular pressures and expectations on women, resulting in many accepting the abusive behaviour of their husbands as normal. What limited recognition there is of domestic abuse is confined to physical assaults that result in serious physical harm. Financial, emotional and 'light' physical violence are rarely considered abusive. Again, whilst such minimisation is not uncommon, there is a specific and strongly held view among Arabic speaking men that their actions are justified.

These beliefs also result in women often being blamed for the violence they are subjected to by their abuser and the wider community. This is often understood as the outcome of women competing with their husbands, wishing to play a stronger role in the affairs of the family, undermining his authority. This construction means that any intervention which questions violence is seen as supporting women's desire for greater independence.

Culture and Religion

Although not all members of the Arabic speaking community are Muslims, their behaviour and attitudes towards domestic abuse tend to be underpinned by a set of cultural values which include the right of husbands to control their wives. Gender roles in the Arabic community are usually a mixture of religious (Islamic) and traditional cultural values. Arabic speaking men regard their identities and behaviour as men, husbands and fathers as rooted in religious teaching through the Qu'ran.

Whilst I hold the view that Islam does not encourage domestic abuse and that the majority of Muslim men are peaceful and loving husbands and parents, there are interpretations of certain religious texts which cause serious concern and enhance men's resistance to domestic abuse intervention programmes. One such problematic interpretation is that of a verse in the Qur'an, which is seen to give the husband the right to discipline his wife (verse, 4:34).

(Men are the protectors and maintainers of women. because Allah has given the one more (strength)[1] than the other, and because they support them from their means. Therefore the righteous women are devoutly obedient, and guard in (the husband's) absence what Allah would have them guard. As to those women on whose part you fear disloyalty and ill-conduct, admonish them (first), (next) do not share their beds, (and last) beat (tap) them (lightly); but if they return to obedience, seek not against them means (of annoyance): for Allah is Most High, Great (above you all).

This verse outlines the relationship between men and women within the family and provides husbands the right to discipline wives by hitting as a last resort, after other measures are ineffective. It also affirms a very important principle in Islamic gender relations, namely that of the guardianship of men, which invests them with power and control over women. The verse also characterises the notion of the 'ideal wife', who is righteous, devout, and defends her modesty in her husband's absence.

The majority of scholars and Imams[2] I have discussions with adhere to this widely accepted interpretation of this verse, which has for centuries legitimised 'light and lenient' beating of wives. It is popularised by the famous and renowned Muslim scholar Shiekh Qaradawi who has a weekly television programme on the satellite channel Al-Jazeera that is widely followed by Muslims all over the world. There is an emerging dissenting view by Islamic scholars who deplore abusive behaviour. They argue strongly for the abrogation of this verse. However, they remain a minority and are rarely heard.

Although no mosque or Imam would publicly condone domestic violence, this is distinguished from chastisement and appropriate discipline. The outcome is a silence and failure of some to act and publicly denounce domestic abuse. This causes grave concern, given that they will be giving advice to men (and women) who seek their help. This is evident from the number of perpetrators who quote prominent scholars or Imams from their local mosque to justify their abusive behaviour.

As for the principle of guardianship and male dominance, the majority of scholars think the verse expresses the 'natural' order of things. Some will argue that although they do not disagree with the interpretation of the verse they would not encourage men to resort to such measures. To my knowledge no prominent or influential scholar has yet to present an interpretation that clearly prohibits the use of violence and abuse or sends a clear message about the unacceptability of violence and abuse in familial relationships.

---

1   Brackets in original translation Ali, Abdullah Yusuf, 2001. *The Meaning of the Holy Qur'an*: Amana Corporation.

2   A Muslim preacher who leads prayers at the mosque and who has the responsibility of interpreting the Qur'an.

This is of paramount importance to our work, since religious interpretations support men's positions when they defend their abusive behaviour. Some even think they have divine approval, exercising what they see as their duty. Unsurprisingly, such men are resentful and hostile towards any kind of intervention. As an example of the strength of such beliefs, Al-Aman staff face risks to our own personal safety from some elements in the community who see our work to empower women to challenge the abusive behaviour by their husbands as tantamount to breaking up Muslim families.

Overcoming Men's Resistance

This context means that to counter resistance to the programme it has had to be made more sensitive to the cultural and religious context of our clients. This adaption has to strike a balance between respecting cultural and religious sensitivities and maintaining DVIPs principles on the unacceptability of violence and abuse and holding the perpetrators solely responsible for their behaviour. Whilst the overall content and model of work from DVIP is used, with materials including the power and control wheel (see Price this volume) translated into Arabic, some adaptations have been made to accommodate cultural and religious issues. For example, when offering alternatives to abusive behaviour we draw upon elements in religious and cultural traditions which promote equality between men and women. We use the abundance of Prophetic traditions, which prohibit maltreatment of women and children and state clearly that the best men are those best treat their wives and children respectfully. Historically, men were the sole interpreters of the Qur'an allowing them to interpret the verses on the status of women in accordance with their interests. Ignoring, for example, what the Prophet Muhammad said pointing to his wife Aisha: "take half of your religious teachings from her". This clearly shows that women have the right to interpret the Qur'an.

Mobilising the Community

There is a strong view in Arabic communities that domestic abuse is a western concept: resulting from the weak family bonds and the absence of religious teachings. Therefore, Al-Aman has dedicated a lot of effort to raising awareness among community and religious leaders. This is done through holding joint meetings and workshops with the aim of creating trust and supportive working relationships. This also enables us to educate about the role of other agencies including police and social services. We simultaneously raise awareness in the statutory and voluntary sectors about working with the Arab speaking community. We hope to form a community committee in the near future which will regularly discuss domestic abuse, plan and implement strategies aimed at prevention and intervention.

The result of these efforts has been encouraging as there are increasing numbers of community leaders who have begun not just to discuss domestic abuse openly, but also to speak out against it. A small group of men have also emerged who reject any justification, whether cultural or religious, that allows husband to abuse their wives. This helps to create more possibilities for women and men to seek help.

Working with Imams

It is extremely rare for an abused women in the Arabic speaking community to report to the criminal justice system: most remain silent, choosing to bear the violence to which they are subjected out of fear of losing status and/or being castigated by their family and community. Making private pain public is even more difficult where there is little trust in external agencies. When abuse becomes unbearable the most likely route a woman will take is to seek the advice of an Imam. Approaching the Imam, however, can be a dangerous move as their actions may be exposed to their husbands if the Imam views his behaviour as acceptable. It is, therefore, imperative for us to work closely with the Imams, to raise their awareness and try to improve their responses to domestic abuse. To achieve this, we developed a unique training programme for Imams and community workers in mosques: to date 30 have attended, covering 12 mosques and Islamic centres in West London. The content here includes encouragement to use positive messages about equal treatment of women and the upbringing of children. Imams are asked to highlight positive examples from within the religion and cultural traditions that emphasise the importance of good and equitable treatment of women in their sermons, particularly at Friday prayers congregations: their role as active agents promoting family peace and non-violence is stressed. Whilst many attendees have adjusted their position during the training, Imans are often non-residents and come here from abroad for brief assignments. It is crucial, therefore, that the training is an on-going rolling programme.

Conclusion

The experience of Al-Aman suggests that specialist perpetrator programmes for specific BAMER communities are needed. Changing beliefs and practices which have been religiously legitimised for centuries might be slow work, but is achievable. It requires dedication, passion, commitment and hard work. Throughout my work in campaigning for women rights and equality, which spans more than twenty years, I have never faced such a challenging task as working on domestic abuse in the Arabic speaking community. However, I have never been as optimistic or excited about change: grass roots change within the Arabic speaking community in London is happening, new voices are emerging to challenge the established norms and traditions and to promote a form of Islamic understanding that is truly progressive.

Chapter 16

A Fuss About Nothing?: Delivering Services to Black and Minority Ethnic Survivors of Gender Violence – The Role of the Specialist Black and Minority Ethnic Women's Sector

Marai Larasi

Introduction

The United Kingdom (UK) benefits from being one of the few regions in the global north to have an established network of specialist services for black and minority ethnic (BME) women and girls who have experienced gender violence.

The specialist BME women's sector has played an essential part in tackling violence against women and girls (VAWG), while being key actors in the struggle for equality for all women and girls. Yet BME women's organisations are often marginalised at both local and national levels and their stories are often missing from the narratives of the feminist movement. This chapter will explore aspects of the sector's journey from the early days of its development to its current position both within the UK and globally.

It is important to note that it is not possible, in one chapter, to do justice to the collective journeys and experiences of the BME women survivors, activists, academics, workers and supporters that are all part of the rich tapestry that is, and has been, the BME women's sector. This piece seeks to capture some of the essence of the sector's work, alongside its achievements and challenges.

Specialist BME VAWG Services as Sites of Resistance

Over the last four decades, the provision of services to women who have experienced gender violence has been a crucial aspect of the UK feminist landscape. Service providers and their supporters would generally argue that gender equality is not achievable simply through rhetoric or through lobbying and campaigning: that the provision of safe spaces which provide protection and routes to self-determination is a clear demonstration of feminism in action. While as activists we continue to strive for gender equality, violence against women and girls remains a painful, harsh reality and as such, the need for effective and relevant services continues to be essential.

For many BME survivors of gender based violence, an effective service is one in which the response to their experiences of violence is framed not only within an analysis of gender but also of 'race'[1], culture and ethnicity. This position is reinforced by *intersectionality* theorists, such a Kimberlé Crenshaw, who argue that aspects of oppression interact on multiple levels (often simultaneously) and that it is responses to these intersections which generate complexities around social inequality. Intersectionality theory challenges the widely held belief among many feminists that gender is always the primary factor which determines a woman's experience of oppression: for BME women, experiences of oppression occur at the intersections of 'race', class, gender and where relevant other areas such as sexuality and disability. Translated to a service delivery perspective, for many BME survivors, 'race' is relevant, in terms of experience, access and empowerment.

Thinking Specialism

BME specialist services hold extensive experience and expertise in responding to, and working to prevent VAWG. They also benefit from holding a wide range of additional skills and expertise relating to specific BME communities.

Specialist BME VAWG organisations are designed to respond to the needs of BME women who have experienced gender based violence. Such organisations are independently developed, led, and delivered *by* BME women, *for* BME women. They are also framed within an analysis of the impact of gender, 'race' and culture. Holistic support is provided in safe, confidential, non-judgemental spaces, to support women to move forward from violence and assist their journey towards rebuilding their lives.

Specialist organisations provide varying types and levels of services. Most services are frontline, first-tier responses that offer one or more of the following: refuge accommodation; emotional and practical support; counselling; advocacy; specific services for young people; outreach; mental health support; resettlement programmes; support groups; helplines; awareness-raising sessions; prevention work in schools and training. Some frontline organisations such as Southall Black Sisters work locally, while also carrying out extensive campaigning and lobbying work on a national basis.

In addition to the work delivered by frontline organisations, Imkaan provides national second tier specialist support for BME VAWG services, which includes

---

1   The term 'race' is widely contested, as it is often understood to be a biological indicator of difference and is often conflated with ethnicity and culture. In scientific terms 'racial' difference does not exist. What is often described as 'race' is in fact ethnicity. Therefore throughout this chapter 'race' will appear in quotation marks.

strategic advocacy, policy and voice, campaigning and lobbying, training and capacity building.

Valuing Identities: The Birth and Early Years of the Specialist BME Women's VAWG Sector

The 1970s was an important decade for new social movements: rights-based discourses around 'race', gender, disability and sexuality started to emerge in unprecedented ways. During this period many BME feminists had worked and fought alongside white women in the struggle for gender equality, whilst other BME women found it difficult to even identify as feminists, as the (re) presentations of feminism often appeared white and Euro-centric. In addition, the representations of BME women were often distorted and essentialised as exemplified in texts such as Rosa Maria Cutrufelli's *Women of Africa: Roots of Oppression*, in which she states:

> My analysis will start by stating that all African women are politically and economically dependent (Cutrufelli 1983: 13).

Further:

> Nevertheless, either overtly or covertly, prostitution is still the main if not the only source of work for African women (Cutrufelli 1983: 33).

Contestations about these issues were raised by black feminists in the UK as well as by their counterparts in the United States, with theorists such as Chandra Talpade Mohanty (1988) critiquing the work of white Western feminist writers such as Cutrufelli. One highly publicised example was the open letter by black, lesbian, feminist, activist writer, Audre Lorde to white feminist writer Mary Daly, following the publication of Daly's ground-breaking text *Gyn/Ecology* (Daly 1978). Lorde stated:

> I ask that you be aware of how this serves the destructive forces of racism and separation between women—the assumption that the herstory and myth of white women is the legitimate and sole herstory and myth of all women to call for power and background, and that non-white women and our herstories are note-worthy only as decorations, or examples of female victimisation. I ask that you be aware of the effect that this dismissal has upon the community of black women, and how it devalues your own words ... When patriarchy dismisses us, it encourages our murders. When radical lesbian feminist theory dismisses us, it encourages its own demise. This dismissal stands as a real block to communication between us ... Should the next step be war between us, or separation? Assimilation within a sole Western-European herstory is not acceptable (Lorde 1984: 66–71).

In the UK, BME feminists were also highlighting that their concerns about racism were often ignored within feminist dialogues or addressed through a kind of benevolent racism. Pratibha Parmar and Valerie Amos (1984) illustrated exactly this in *Feminist Review*:

> It would be naive of us to suggest in any way that the white women's movement is a monolithic structure or organisation, indeed we recognise that it is a variety of groups with a diversity of interests and perspectives.
>
> However, our concern here is to show that white, mainstream feminist theory, be it from the socialist feminist or radical feminist perspective, does not speak to the experiences of Black women and where it attempts to do so it is often from a racist perspective and reasoning (Parmar and Amos 1984: 6).

Further:

> Few white feminists in Britain and elsewhere have elevated the question of racism to the level of primacy, within their practical political activities or in their intellectual work. The women's movement has unquestioningly been premised on a celebration of 'sisterhood' with its implicit assumption that women qua women have a necessary basis for unity and solidarity; a sentiment reflected in academic feminist writings which is inevitably influenced by the women's movement and incorporates some of its assumptions (Parmar and Amos 1984: 6).

BME women's concern not only with the impact of male domination, but also with legacies of colonialism and the pervasive impact of white supremacist thought, meant that they inevitably often engaged with BME men in the struggle for 'race' equality. Yet within anti-racist activism, the issue of gender equality was often side-lined. Many BME organisations repeatedly failed to address sexism, seeing discourses on gender equality as dividing the black family/community and taking the emphasis away from the more pressing issues of racism. As a result, BME women activists began to organise, establishing groups such as Organisation of Women of Asian and African Descent (OWAAD), AWAZ (Asian Women's Movement) and Brixton Black Women's Group all of which addressed racism and sexism and other inequalities. These groups campaigned and protested around a range of issues, from state sanctioned violation of Asian women at airports to the 'Sus' laws[2] and racism in education.

---

2   The 'Sus Laws' referred to: 'Sus 1' – a section of the Vagrancy Act 1824 under which an accused person could be brought to trial on no other evidence than that of acting suspiciously in the eyes of two police officers. 'Sus 2' was 'embodied' in the Immigration Act 1971 and gave the police the power to arrest anyone who they suspected of being an illegal immigrant. 'Sus 1' was used primarily against African-Caribbean males leading to

It also became necessary for BME feminists to acknowledge that the needs of BME victims and survivors of gender violence were not adequately considered or met within the wider feminist movement or within the 'race' equality movement. For some BME women, this meant working within services such as rape crisis centres and women's refuges. For others, it meant taking on new challenges to raise funds to set up services led and run by BME women. As a result, the period from the late 1970s to the 1990s was marked by the emergence of organisations established to respond to the needs of women from BME communities.

Organisations such as Southall Black Sisters (SBS) developed direct services for women alongside effective and well-documented campaigning and lobbying work (Southall Black Sisters 2003). Projects such as Saheli[3] and Asha[4] were developed for South Asian women, while organisations such as Amadudu[5] which focussed on addressing the needs of all black women were also established. Although most services were focussed on meeting the needs of South Asian women, there were organisations established to meet the needs of African, African Caribbean, Chinese, Jewish, Irish Traveller and Latin American women. In some instances, women used the expertise they developed through their involvement with non-BME services to support the establishment of specialist provision. Other organisations such as Chinese Women's Refuge used strategies such as negotiating with housing associations to use 'short-life' accommodation to house women, while they sought to develop a more permanent site for the service.

BME women experiencing gender violence were thus increasingly able to access support provided by BME women. These organisations created spaces in which it was possible to recognise nuance, shared journeys and cultural contexts. Crucially, BME survivors were not positioned as the 'other'. Indeed, as in the wider VAWG sector, many of the founders were themselves women who had survived gender-based violence: distinctions between worker and 'service user' were less established than currently, meaning the work was marked by a strong sense of collective experience and 'sisterhood'.

However, any narrative describing the developments and challenges of that era must not be over-simplified. Despite some shared ideological perspectives, the BME women's sector did not develop as a unified entity. Organisations emerged at local level, driven by women with varying political positions. Some were primarily concerned with providing support to women from their 'community' but did not see this as connected to a wider feminist project, others were committed to establishing secular spaces, while still other women saw faith and spirituality as important components of BME women's experiences. Disagreements also

---

a disproportionate number of 'Sus' arrests. 'Sus 2' was used primarily against South Asian communities and led to indefinite detainment with no right to trial in an open court.

3   Saheli , refuge and services for South Asian women, established in Manchester in 1976.

4   Asha, refuge and services for South Asian women established in London in 1984.

5   Amadudu, refuge and services for black women, established in Liverpool in 1991.

arose around the politics of sexuality and in particular the status and roles of bisexual women and lesbians in organisations. These contentions were not always addressed or resolved leading to fractures within, as well as disconnections between, organisations.

Questions were also raised about some of the arguments being used to demonstrate the need for specialist services for BME women. Amina Mama, writing in 1989 about black women and domestic violence, notes in the section on specialist refuges:

> ... findings indicate that the arguments made by both black and white women in the movement centre around particular notions of race, some of which this author would refer to as culturalised notions. This means that they hinge on conceptions of cultural difference (language, dress, culinary habits) rather than an understanding of racial inequality. The written policy on separate refuges accepts that they are necessary but only on the ticket of culture ... The problem is that this culturalisation does not fundamentally challenge all the forms of racism that cannot be reduced to 'cultural difference'. This may explain the fact that Asian refuges have been resourced over and above refuges for other black women who are assumed to speak better English and have grown accustomed to English culinary habits (Mama 1989: 292).

Mama goes on to suggest that 'culturalised' understandings and arguments were more acceptable to funders, and that none of the organisations appeared to have been funded on the basis that *racism itself* placed BME women at a disadvantage. She argues that this *"muddled thinking"* which "conflates racism and culture" must be "challenged because it does have political consequences for the anti-racist struggle" (Mama 1989: 292).

This 'muddled thinking', which was indicative of many of the ideas promoted by race relations theorists such as Rex and Tomlinson (1979), and reproduced by some BME activists, had far-reaching consequences for the BME women's sector. Race relations theorists had, and continue to have, a major influence on Britain's approaches to 'race' and racism, with some actively promoting contrasts between what they posit as fixed, South Asian identities, rooted in 'strong cultures' in which languages, traditions and religious perspectives remain intact and fragile Caribbean identities which had experienced 'cultural deprivation'. Translated into the policy/funding context, South Asian women are therefore perceived as more in need of culturally specific services than their Caribbean counterparts who would accept "British culture along with their servitude" (Rex and Tomlinson 1979: 291).

Despite the reservations expressed by researchers such as Mama, BME women's services were largely funded on the basis of assumed cultural needs. That 'black' (used politically to unify African, Caribbean and South Asian peoples), was itself, a contested identity even in the BME women's movement, added to the complexities of an already challenging terrain. What emerged from those early challenges therefore, were services targeted, not at wider populations of black/ BME women, but primarily serving South Asian women.

Adapt or ... Fold

This era of growth and development was also marked by on-going financial uncertainty and insecurity. Over time, smaller grassroots services which had operated as collectives were encouraged/required to adopt hierarchical structures. These were deemed to be more 'professional' and therefore more acceptable to funders. Organisations also found themselves under increasing pressure to formalise as charities in order to receive funding. In other words, 'adapt or fold'. This was part of a wider shift in the ways small grassroots social justice projects were required to operate in order to survive. However, while these changes allowed organisations to apply for much needed resources, it inevitably had an impact on their ethos. Like many other women's organisations, BME women's groups found themselves grappling with structures which appeared to replicate the power imbalances that they were established to question and change. In addition, the focus on delivering services and meeting funder requirements drew many organisations away from their other activist work, which they had previously undertaken in parallel. The radicalism which had been such an essential driver behind the development of services became more and more side-lined as women found their energies taken up by the struggle just to keep services open. As Amrit Wilson (2006) notes:

> Starved of funds and seeking desperately to raise them, many Asian women's refuges became registered charities, since, increasingly this was the only way to raise the sort of money required to run a refuge. However, this brought them under charity law, which required them to keep clear of anything that could be considered political.
>
> By this time, open feminist debate had diminished and collective discussions among residents of refuges were not always prioritised. Although 'educational recovery' had been incorporated into service provision, in many refuges this work was done in one-to one discussions with case workers. Given the restrictions of charity law, only in a minority of refuges were residents actively encouraged to inform themselves about current affairs or involve themselves in any political activity outside the organisation (Wilson 2006: 164–165).

In addition, the translation of an individual and/or collective political passion and commitment to the running of a service was, and remains, an area of challenge for activists of all persuasions. Many of the skills required to support and empower women and challenge the acceptability of violence were not those that were required to demonstrate need or raise money, nor did they fit the requirement to offer services within rigid funding frameworks. Where the skills were missing from the group, women were required to adapt and develop new areas of expertise. Many did so willingly and effectively, while others still speak of this, and subsequent periods, as times of personal and political sacrifice that they still struggle to come to terms with. For many, the new face of organising meant a loss of 'the heart of the work' and they began to feel emotionally and politically redundant.

Sacrifices were made in order to secure the sustainability of individual organisations, but others folded largely due to lack of resources. Where difficulties were defined as being as a result of management committee 'burn-out', for example, these might nevertheless be traced back to a lack of funds to recruit, pay and support workers.

Some BME women's services failed to resolve internal challenges about structure, approach and ethos. For example, one London-based service which closed in the early 1990s was embroiled in differences about how the organisation should be run, while grappling with 'founder syndrome' and concerns about poor practice. In other cases where practice concerns were raised, BME organisations found their autonomy removed by local authorities (as funders) and housing associations (who owned the refuges). Instead of investment in appropriate capacity building work to support organisational sustainability, some services were simply absorbed into generic housing association provision. This resulted in a loss of independence and self-determination and served to further undermine an already economically fragile sector.

Supporting People?

Those organisations that continued to survive, often against the odds, functioned on shoe-string budgets throughout the 1990s. When the Labour government (elected in 1997), as part of its declared war on homelessness, introduced the Supporting People funding programme in the early 2000s, many hoped that their days of struggling for money had ended. The programme was intended to streamline income for organisations providing housing-related support for vulnerable people. Women's refuges for the first time were asked to cost their services with a view to ensuring that they could be adequately recompensed.

It was clear from the outset that the programme would present opportunities and challenges. Through Supporting People, a number of BME organisations were able to stabilise services and even increase their staffing numbers to more appropriate levels. Some were even able to establish new provision and improve on the range of services being offered.

Others became anxious as the housing associations, which owned the buildings they were using, began to indicate an interest in directly running the services or elements of the service. Larger mainstream refuge providers appeared poised to take over smaller services and worry spread as to whether Supporting People would strengthen or destroy the financially fragile BME sector. In the period leading up to the introduction of Supporting People (April 2003), and in the first stages of its implementation, Imkaan in partnership with Women's Aid, England engaged in negotiations with the then Office of the Deputy Prime Minister to establish a principle that BME women's services would not fall by the wayside. Reassurances were given that the programme would not be used to further marginalise or decrease BME women's organisations; and despite major concerns, there was also hope that things would get better for the sector.

On the surface, in 2012, the picture appears to be a mixed one. In reality, since the introduction of the Supporting People programme, little has been done centrally, regionally, or at local level to preserve specialist BME led VAWG services. The successes have been few and far between, with even well-established organisations such as Newham Asian Women's Project or Ashiana Network, Waltham Forest, still having to fight to maintain existing provision and to hold on to gains made over the years. Nine years on, the already small, independent BME sector has shrunk beyond recognition. Fears of de-commissioning, take-overs and service closures have been realised across the country. Successive government policies from *community cohesion* to the new phenomenon of *localism* appear to provide strategies to 'wriggle-out' of funding specialist BME services. For example, the recommendation of the Commission on Integration and Cohesion report published in June 2007 dedicates an annex to the issue of single group funding which it describes as funding "awarded on the basis of a particular identity, such as ethnic, religious or cultural" (Commission on Integration and Cohesion 2007: 161). Single group funding should "be the exception rather than the rule" for funding bodies, and a range of arguments are provided as to why this position was important, including that such provision might: "increase insularity and a sense of separation" (Commission on Integration and Cohesion 2007: 160–161).

In 2008, Southall Black Sisters (SBS) won a landmark victory against Ealing Council, which had sought to withdraw their contract on the basis that the organisation was unlawful under the Race Relations Act because it excluded women in the 'majority community' and was therefore discriminatory and divisive. While this legal challenge was a success for SBS[6], and a major confidence boost for the BME women's VAWG sector, it has not prevented other local authorities from questioning the need for specialist services, or awarding contracts to larger mainstream organisations such as Refuge[7] to deliver "culturally specific services for women and children from minority ethnic groups".[8]

Crucially, Amina Mama's warning about the use of culturalised arguments as the key justification for specialist BME services was well placed. Larger providers and local commissioners alike, have been able to 'tick the box' by offering 'culturally specific' services under a mainstream/non-BME umbrella structure

---

6   http://www.southallblacksisters.org.uk/campaigns/save-sbs-campaign-2008/.

7   Refuge, refuge services for women, established in London in 1971.

8   http://refuge.org.uk/about-us/what-we-do/.

therefore ignoring how such arrangements, in and of themselves, reinforce structural inequality and negate any commitment to BME women's leadership.

New Growth

Despite funding and other challenges, the BME VAWG women's sector has continued to work in creative and innovative ways in order to ensure that women continue to receive services and that VAWG remains on the wider political agenda. Over the last two decades, services have emerged in ways which have altered the landscape, including the way that BME VAWG work is defined and understood. Organisations such as Iranian Kurdish Women's Rights Organisation (IKWRO) and Karma Nirvana have sought to highlight the specific issues of forced marriage and honour based violence using media and other mechanisms to support their campaigning and service delivery. BME women have also continued to organise to challenge specific areas of concern. For example, Daughters of Eve is a non-profit organisation, established by a group of young BME women, which works to protect girls who are at risk of female genital mutilation. Despite being a fledgling organisation, just in the process of establishing itself formally, the women involved have very quickly developed their profile as activists and campaigners, demonstrating the importance of diverse approaches to this work.

(De)Valuing Difference?

The BME women's sector has always sought to work in partnership with other women's organisations with respect to both campaigning and service delivery. Many refuge providers are members of the Women's Aid networks[9] and see themselves as part of a wider women led VAWG sector. At a national strategic level, the work led by SBS on 'no recourse to public funds' has been supported by a number of non-BME sister organisations including Rights of Women. Crucially, the End Violence Against Women (EVAW) coalition[10] has sought to exemplify good practice by ensuring that its board is diverse in representation around social identity with representatives from both SBS and Imkaan holding seats. EVAW is jointly chaired by a black woman and a white woman, both of whom are responsible for chairing the board and each having sub-groups they are responsible for. Dialogue between the staff team and between the joint chairs is regular and meaningful. This way of working provides a useful template on how power may be shared when a wider community of women organise. The EVAW approach has

---

9   There are networks in England, Scotland and Wales each with specialist BME women's group members.

10   www.endviolenceagainstwomen.org.uk.

also facilitated genuine partnership which supports the work of the BME women's sector without attempting to dominate or marginalise member organisations.

Yet such positive experiences of partnership are few and far between. The BME women's VAWG sector faces a range of challenges, linked to complex layers of discrimination in a range of contexts. For example, in the wider women's VAWG sector there is often a failure to accept and understand the need for BME led services for BME women. BME women's VAWG services struggle to create equal, meaningful partnerships with their non-BME counterparts. As a result, grassroots BME services often find themselves competing at local level (for services that they already provide) with larger organisations who are able to market themselves more effectively and who are able to present more acceptable 'value for money' arguments. When BME women's organisations do enter into partnerships or partnership discussions, their attempts to achieve equality within those relationships are often met with affront, resentment and even bullying. For example, one BME provider reported how the organisation was 'forced' by commissioners to enter into consortium discussions with local non-BME providers. It became clear early into the discussion that the other (larger) providers disagreed with the need for BME led, BME specific services and had no interest in preserving the service. This led to the BME provider withdrawing from the discussions, being politically side-lined locally and then having their contract terminated by the local authority.

BME women's organisations are often not integrated within the wider voluntary sector landscape at all levels. They tend to have limited access to local strategic partnerships (and other multi-agency strategic structures) and are rarely represented at regional level. Despite organisations adopting and adapting to the now dominant perspectives on professionalism, structure and effectiveness, they continue to be seen as less credible and less professional. This had led many to wonder if, in order to survive, BME women have 'sold the heart of their work' at the cost of a loss of ethos, but with very little benefit. The situation is likely to be compounded as the landscape becomes more competitive and as new 'players' enter the work. The Ministry of Justice's decision, in 2011, to award a major contract for trafficking services to the Salvation Army despite that organisation's stance on issues such as abortion and LGBT rights, is concerning for all feminist organisations. For the BME women's VAWG sector, the prospect of faith-based organisations operating with anti-feminist values, which may now be able to compete at local level to deliver women's services, is particularly concerning; especially as policy makers often choose to prioritise engagement with 'community leaders' who are generally male and self-appointed. The retention of secular spaces has been an important principle: one which has been campaigned for by organisations such as SBS over a number of years (see Patel and Siddiqui this volume).

Independent BME women led services often find themselves having to justify their existence, not only on obvious political terms but also in relation to the value that they actually offer. At the heart of the specialism, is the recognition of the difference in the individual and collective experiences of BME women, who have experienced marginalisation on the basis of their ethno-cultural identities as well as their gender. Many BME women find their experiences of violence 'othered' within mainstream structures. Their cultural, 'racial' and religious identities are ignored, misunderstood or viewed as burdensome and problematic. It is not surprising then, that in one Imkaan survey (Thiara and Roy 2010), 87 per cent of the BME women participants stated that they preferred to access specialist BME services as opposed to mainstream VAWG provision. BME specialist services provide more than 'cultural literacy' and linguistic support: they are spaces in which BME women's experiences of multiple, intersecting oppressions are recognised and women using the services experience being understood and 'held'. This recognition of so many fundamental aspects of one's self is crucial in facilitating everything from disclosure to effective therapeutic interactions. Yet with a back-drop of social cohesion, scare-mongering about immigration, a global recession, growing Islamaphobia, 'localism' and the 'Big Society', these precious spaces are under more threat than ever.

The women that fought to establish services in the 1980s and 1990s recognised that BME women were being failed in services time and time again. Now in 2012, we would ask, "Has anything changed?" The women using services would probably say, "Not enough!" For all the professionalisation and service development, BME women still do not have a guarantee that they will be able to access services which meet their needs and support their aspirations.

Across the women led VAWG sector, organisations are being forced to grapple with increasing gender neutrality. Domestic violence, which was historically understood as a gendered phenomenon which disproportionately impacts women and their children, has been reframed in many settings as 'domestic abuse' or 'family violence'. The links between domestic violence and other forms of violence against women are being ignored, despite a national VAWG strategy. On the ground, this means that some organisations are being forced, through commissioning processes, to also provide services for men.

Worryingly, many non-BME women's organisations and the women leading those organisations, who warn against gender neutral approaches in a policy and practice context, still fail to make the links between gender neutrality and 'race' neutrality. While they challenge patriarchal structures, they are content to engage in benevolent racism, one which does not recognise the importance of *independent* BME leadership and voice. Many argue that women-led services need to be protected, and that the growing trend of domestic violence services being delivered by registered social landlords and other such providers, has a negative impact on the quality of provision. Yet they are happy to compete against small BME women's organisations to provide local services.

When challenged about this some of the larger women's service providers have referred to the specialist BME workers that they employ, or the culturally-specific services they run, as demonstrating their commitment to dealing with the issues affecting BME women. But a critical perspective on 'race' and power, including within feminist organisations, is either over-simplified or non-existent. The result is that BME women working in non-BME services are often 'foot-soldiers', under-represented in management and governance structures.

New Challenges?

Over the last year, Imkaan members have expressed concerns about how the current economic climate is likely to have a disproportionate effect on the services that they provide. For example, one member reported that in their local area, the other services have experienced 25–30 per cent cuts; however the county council cut their already limited grant by 50 per cent. Another provider has reported 100 per cent cuts to the local grassroots services they provide. Organisations also identified a range of internal challenges including struggles with governance and strategic planning. All of those surveyed cited lack of capacity as a major challenge to their ability to develop and adopt robust systems for planning, generating unrestricted income and engaging in strategic advocacy. At the same time, members have also expressed a lack of confidence around engaging with new agendas and frameworks such as 'localism', the 'Big Society' and the new health and police and crime commissioning structures.

Policy and practice approaches which have emerged over the last five years have tended to emphasise criminal justice outcomes and risk management as opposed to an overall vision of women's empowerment. These developments fail to make the link between gender violence and women's status in society. Whereas, organisations such as Imkaan and SBS argue that a holistic approach is required, which includes work on prevention, as this will address women's immediate concerns while also supporting their longer term independence and self-determination.

The Conservative-Liberal Democrat coalition government has sought to demonstrate its commitment to tackling VAWG. In 2010, the government published its strategy *A Call to End Violence Against Women and Girls* (HM Government 2010). This was followed in 2011 by an action plan which was recently refreshed. Despite the localism agenda, which promotes local services being funded at local level, the government has committed to continue central financial support for multi-agency risk assessment conferences (MARACs), independent domestic violence advisors (IDVAs) and much needed rape crisis services. The funding of rape crisis services has been based, rightfully, on the argument that these services have been underfunded and thus unevenly distributed over many years. Although similar arguments have been made around the need for BME led services, to date, the government has not taken any action to ensure the sustainability of the BME women's VAWG sector. Instead arguments around localism are used by officials, who reiterate that they are unable to direct local authorities to fund specific services. Surely the independent BME led VAWG sector could have been and should be prioritised? This marginalisation and side-lining is at the heart of the challenges faced by the sector.

Moving Forward

This chapter argues that the BME women's VAWG sector has important roles to play as activists and as providers of vital services for BME women. Yet our voices are not always heard and listened to. At times we are dismissed as 'difficult', 'angry', 'banging-on about racism' and 'making a fuss about nothing'. For us, this 'nothing' is our everyday lives and the lives of the women and children who we continue to work with and for. For this 'nothing' we *are* sometimes 'difficult' and 'angry'. We are also committed, passionate, loving women who dare to dream of a just and equal world.

The current socio-political landscape presents new and increasingly complex threats to the BME women's VAWG sector. Our responses need to be as diverse and as creative as ever: we are not a homogenous, same-thinking group, nor should we be. Yet there are lessons to be learnt about the challenges and joys of BME women's organising. There are lessons to be learnt about the many arguments which we used to help us develop services, that have also served to create hierarchies of needs and therefore hierarchies of services, and which are also now being used against us. There are also lessons to be learnt about the need to celebrate achievement while allowing ourselves space to grieve when services are lost. We must recognise and create spaces to nurture and validate the activism of many BME women, who could not, or would not adapt to the new structures and who continue to express political heart-break.

The sector must ensure that it continues to raise standards. While it is necessary to critique external agendas, it is also important that practice is reflective, and that organisations are willing and able to look inwards and change. There is a need to explore new pathways to ensure sustainability, irrespective of the state's agenda. In many ways the battles for resources such as Supporting People funding, have immobilised us. Supporting People became a kind of 'funding opiate' damaging our radicalism and taking us away from the core of who we are as black feminists. We must re-instil our politics into our work. We must ensure that we retain our independence.

Supporters and providers of specialist BME services are not suggesting that BME women should only use BME services, or that mainstream VAWG services should not operate within structures of equality and inclusiveness. Neither is there the suggestion that specialist BME services should be pigeon-holed into providing services around areas of violence that may be more prevalent within some contexts, such as forced marriage, female genital mutilation and 'honour'-based violence. What is contended is the most basic right, the right to *choose*. In this case, the right of a BME woman surviving gender violence to choose where, how and who supports her. For BME feminist activists it is simple; we reserve the right to fight alongside white women for gender equality and the right to fight alongside BME men for 'race' equality, but most importantly we reserve the right to speak for ourselves in all of our struggles and aspirations.

References

Commission on Integration and Cohesion. 2007. *Our Shared Future.* [Online: Commission on integration and Cohesion]. Available at: http://collections. europarchive.org/tna/20080726153624/http://www.integrationandcohesion.org. uk/~/media/assets/www.integrationandcohesion.org.uk/our_shared_future%20pdf. ashx [accessed: 19 April 2012].

Cutrufelli, M.R. 1983. *Women of Africa: Roots of Oppression.* London: Zed Books Ltd.

Daly, M. 1978. *Gyn/Ecology: The Mataethics of Radical Feminism.* Boston: Beacon Press.

HM Government. 2010. Call to End Violence against Women and Girls. [Online: Home Office]. Available at: http://www.homeoffice.gov.uk/publications/ crime/call-end-violence-women-girls/vawg-paper?view=Binary [accessed: 20 April 2012].

Lawrence, E. 1982. Just Plain Common Sense: The Roots of Contemporary Racism in *The Empire Strikes Back: Race and Racism in 70s Britain*, Centre for Contemporary Studies University of Birmingham. Hutchinson & Co. Ltd.

Lorde, A. 1984. An Open Letter to Mary Daly in *Sister Outsider: Essays and Speeches.* California: Crossing Press.

Mama, A. 1989. *The Hidden Struggle: Statutory and voluntary sector responses to violence against black women in the home.* London: London Race and Housing Research Unit.

Mohanty, C.T. (1988) Under Western Eyes: Feminist Scholarship and Colonial Discourses. *Feminist Review,* 30, 61–88.

Parmar, P. and Amos, V. 1984. Challenging Imperial Feminism. *Feminist Review,* 17, 3–19.

Rex, J. and Tomlinson, S. 1979. *Colonial Immigrants in a British City: A class analysis.* London: Routledge & Kegan Paul Ltd.

Southall Black Sisters. 2003. *From Homebreakers to Jailbreakers.* London: Zed Books Ltd.

Thiara, R.K. and Roy, S. 2010. *Vital Statistics: The Experiences of BAMER Women and Children Facing Violence and Abuse.* London: Imkaan.

Wilson, A. 2006. *Dreams, Questions, Struggles: South Asian Women in Britain.* London: Pluto Press.

Index

Note: bold page numbers indicate figures and tables; numbers in brackets preceded by *n* are footnote numbers.